Daniel Defoe

BEYOND BELIEF

The real life of Daniel Defoe

JOHN MARTIN

Published by Accent Press Ltd – 2006
ISBN 1905170564
Copyright © John Martin 2006

Printed and bound in the UK
By CPD (Wales) Ltd, Ebbw Vale

Cover Design by Emma Barnes

For
my daughter
Alice

John Martin has worked for the Express Group of newspapers and as a freelance journalist. He is the author of a number of non-fiction books on management, consumer affairs and politics. He has published two novels:

A Land Without Heroes (2002)
Absolutely Perfect (2003)

John Martin has worked for the Express Group of newspapers and as a freelance journalist. He is the author of a number of non-fiction books on management, consumer affairs and politics. He has published two novels:

A Land Without Heroes (2002)
Absolutely Perfect (2003)

Contents

Preface

UNTIL 1752 ENGLAND USED the Julian calendar whereas Scotland used the Gregorian calendar from 1660. The Gregorian calendar differed in two ways: it was eleven days ahead, and the New Year began on 31 March. In this work I use the Julian calendar but I have assumed the New Year to begin on 1 January.

I follow Furbank and Owens in their ascription of Defoe's works rather than J.R. Moore, which limits the number to 252. However, following work at the University of Houston, I accept that there may be upwards of 80 additional works for which Defoe may have been the writer in whole or in part. To my surprise, in the course of this work I have taken a contrary view to Furbank and Owens on several occasions. I have followed my instincts. Where I have included non-ascribed works, I have given either an explanation in the text or a note setting out my reasons.

This book is a biography. I have not sought to write a literary critique of Defoe's works which would have taken up far more space and time than was available to me and for which I do not consider myself fully qualified. However, this book is fully sourced.

I acknowledge the extensive debt I owe to all Defoe's biographers. I am particularly grateful to Paula Backscheider, for listening to me and looking up her research notes on a matter of significance. Maximillian Novak has accumulated vital particulars of Defoe's life and works, and all biographers are grateful to him. The recent work of both these eminent Defoe scholars has added significantly to the known facts about Defoe. Robert Clark of the University of East Anglia, a distinguished Defoe scholar, did a service by challenging me. Richard Holmes, a great biographer and teacher, helped me in more ways than he realised. Irving Rothman kindly and patiently explained his work on stylometry to me. None of these people are responsible in any way whatsoever for what I have written.

I thank also Rita Harris, who made many original findings in the Essex Record Office; Jeremy Palmer; and my wife Larisa, whose painstaking work at the Public Record Office was crucial to the uncovering of new evidence. Dr Clare Thomlinson read and corrected my typescript to its very great benefit and Dr Susan Forsyth provided an index.

Any researcher of public records owes a debt to vast numbers of unknown clerks who patiently and conscientiously have kept records on matters of public interest over the centuries. They would be amazed at the uses posterity has made of them. The staffs of the Public Record Office, the Corporation of London Metropolitan Archive, the British Library, and the Essex and Borough of Hackney Record Offices were invariably professional and helpful.

Lastly, I am immensely grateful to my publishers. Their enthusiastic support for my endeavours at every stage of this work was immensely reassuring

Abbreviations

BL: British Library

C: Chancery Records, PRO

CRO: Corporation of London Metropolitan Records

CSPD: Calendar of State Papers

H: *The Letters of Daniel Defoe*, (Ed. George Harris Healey, Oxford University Press, 1955).

ERO: Essex Record Office

HRO: London Borough of Hackney Record Office

N&Q: Notes and Queries

PCC: Prerogative Court of Canterbury

PRO: Public Record Office: The National Archives

Illustrations

Introduction

It is something strange, that a man's life should be made a kind of Romance...that the World should be so fond of a formal Chimney-corner Tale, that they had rather a Story should be made merry than true.

The Life and Actions of the Late Jonathan Wild
Daniel Defoe, 1725

DANIEL DEFOE IS THE biographer's nightmare. The author of *Robinson Crusoe, Moll Flanders, Roxana* and many other works, his fictions have sold in vast numbers around the world for nearly three hundred years and have earned him the reputation of the 'father of the English novel'; but notwithstanding their success, very little is known about Defoe and much that has been written about him is mistaken. This is not to denigrate the many fine biographies that have been written but to state the obvious. In the words of a recent biographer, 'the man and his mind have not yet become clear to us'. Defoe remains to this day a biographical puzzle and an obscure and mysterious fellow.[1]

Peter Earle, who knew a great deal about Defoe's life and times, wrote that an adequate biography of Defoe would never be possible because of the obscurity and subterfuge with which he enclosed his life and the lack of documentary evidence. By evidence, he meant the stuff of biography: reminiscences, correspondence, the trace of him in the records and memories of others, the very particulars of a life lived.[2]

William Minto suggested that Defoe sought obscurity in his personal life for very good reasons and that he, 'was a very great storyteller in more ways than one. We can hardly believe a word he says about himself without independent confirmation' and that, 'he [Defoe] was a great liar, perhaps the greatest'.[3]

It cannot be said that Defoe as an author occupies a place in the imagination and loyalties of his readers. Arguably, Defoe's greatest work is *Robinson Crusoe* written nearly three hundred years ago. Both Alexander Pope and Virginia Woolf, writing in different times, have reasoned that it was difficult to think of anyone as having written *Robinson Crusoe* and that it was just there and always had been. In saying this they tell us something profound about the book: that it occupies our mind as a fable and an archetype of what is involved in facing up to life's dangers and difficulties.

In giving us Robinson Crusoe's story, Defoe offers the hope that the fears and dangers individuals experience can be overcome even when they are alone, isolated and cast away. Biographers have revealed that Defoe, like Crusoe, was often an isolated and suffering figure and when in the Preface to

Robinson Crusoe he writes, 'Here is invincible patience recommended under the worst of misery, and indefatigable application and undaunted resolution under the greatest and most discouraging circumstances,' it is hard not to conclude that he is writing about himself and that the book is autobiographical in some respects. Defoe suggests as much in replying to critics by saying that he was portraying his own life allegorically.

Defoe wrote *Robinson Crusoe* in 1719 when it is generally believed he was fifty-nine years of age and it established his reputation as a writer. *Robinson Crusoe* was Defoe's first and most popular book. It was immediately acclaimed, although it has had its critics, and reprinted many times in Defoe's lifetime. The story has universal appeal and its readership has spread across the world. It endures in the popular imagination of its readers but particularly among children.[4] In days when most people owned few books, *Robinson Crusoe* was to be found on the shelf alongside the Bible, some Shakespeare, and John Bunyan's *Pilgrims Progress* and, much later, with Hardy and something by Dickens. Today it is under siege by Harry Potter and computer games but it resists their advance – it persists.

Why does *Robinson Crusoe* have such universal appeal? Manuel Schonhorn offers a partial answer. He wrote that anyone familiar with the typology of *Robinson Crusoe* could predict its ending from its beginning. It told the story of the younger son setting out in life to prove himself.[5] Crusoe could only find himself by disobeying his parents. Young readers sense this as a revolutionary message for they know that they too will to have to rebel and wonder at the consequences of doing so.

Robinson Crusoe has been singled out for acclaim by literary critics, with the assertion that it is arguably 'the most significant landmark in the history of the early English novel'. It seems obvious that the book must have a greater significance than Schonhorn has suggested. Other explanations, although fascinating, have failed to satisfy. It is easy to agree with literary critics that the book must have been concerned with the religious, economic and political issues of the times in which it was created but the ordinary reader knows that it 'transcends the particular issues which inform it'.

All the ideological and cultural issues identified as influencing the book have a significance of a kind. For some critics the book has been seen as a fictional manifesto of a new mercantilist culture of the late seventeenth and early eighteenth centuries. Others understand it best as a form of spiritual autobiography, 'a kind of secular version of Bunyan's Grace Abounding'. For certain Marxist critics, it is an archetype of homo economicus and an early form of colonialism.

The children in and among us perceive the story as both escapism and a hazardous adventure. Dangerous journeys into foreign places (which Defoe always envisaged as a seaway to glory and riches) are common in children's books. In my childhood, *Robinson Crusoe* was coupled in the imagination with the enjoyment of reading such adventure stories as *Swallows and Amazons*, *Treasure Island*, *King Solomon's Mines*, *Lord Jim* and, later, *Heart of Darkness*.

Great adventure stories offer more than pleasure. Even when I hid my copy of *Robinson Crusoe* beneath the pillow and read it after lights-out in the fear of cannibals and the creak of footsteps on the stairs, I knew what I could not conceptualise: that I was reading a real person's story in the form of a moral fable. I was being offered not only an opportunity to get near to Crusoe's self-communing exile, his delusions, dreams and nightmares in the comparative safety of his stockade and his cave but also to his author, Daniel Defoe. It was a wonder to me then, and it still is, that Defoe could make his quest for the meaning of his life, for him a spiritual and temporal journey, in such a peculiar and singular manner.

To find Defoe and to answer for myself the question of what were the sources of his fears and the resilience with which he confronted them, I set out to discover all I could about him. I found that he had led a dangerous and exciting life with many severe crises. All these crises were accompanied by terrible fears, impetuosity of action, a certain knowledge that he was in the right and a strong desire to have the last word.

The number of questions increased. Why the repetition of these awful moments? What was Defoe seeking to achieve? And why, at the many testing moments of his life, was he so alone, isolated without friends and besieged by so many enemies?

The Introduction to my copy of *Robinson Crusoe* told me that Defoe had written the book in 1719 and that, in a late burst of literary activity, he published in 1722 *A Journal of the Plague Year, Moll Flanders, Colonel Jack, Captain Singleton, Due Preparations for the Plague* and, later, other literary works. When I read these works, I experienced much of the excitement and fear that I encountered with *Robinson Crusoe*.

It seemed that the unifying theme in these various works was Defoe himself and that all these writings must be, in some sense, 'autobiographical'. For the most part they are written in the first person and in the past tense. This form of narrative is the modern way and, compared to what had gone before, Defoe had increased the possibilities of resolving his conflicts although he remained hard pressed to do so.

Are these books really fictions? Defoe never called his works novels and insisted that they were not works of fiction.[6] He writes in the Preface to *Robinson Crusoe*, in the guise of the Editor, that 'The Editor believes the thing to be a just history of fact; neither is there any appearance of fiction.' I accepted that Defoe was never shipwrecked on a desert island but I knew him to be there and that, beyond the truism that an author is always present in his books, he had given his readers 'autobiography' skilfully presented as fact. Defoe gives the readers of *Robinson Crusoe* a wealth of circumstantial objects and events to convince them of the reality of Robinson's experience on the island, but it becomes apparent to the reader that the recounting of this island experience contains recollections and emotions of overwhelming importance to the author as he looked back.

I was bound to accept that there would be acute difficulties in finding Defoe in his fiction, for there are considerable problems in making decisions on what to include and what to ignore. It was apparent from the outset that it could not be assumed that what Defoe seemed to be telling his readers was literally true. I decided to apply the simple test that when it was possible to confirm a fictional statement by a provable particular of his life it could be taken into account.

I concluded from an exhaustive reading of Defoe's writing that there was a sense in which he wished his readers to discover him. Perhaps he was driven by egotism or natural self-pride. I needed to crack what I dubbed The Defoe Code. The application of the Code to his fiction is explained in this text. It led me to the most stunning, exciting – and ultimately disturbing – revelations about Defoe's life which, in my opinion, change fundamentally all published understanding of him as a writer and a man, and for ever.

I discovered also an extensive and powerful use of signifiers in Defoe's writing: that is the use of words and phrases that have a hidden meaning for some or all of his readers, other than a literal understanding, which is obscure to the modern reader. Interpreting the signifiers has had an electrifying effect on the meaning of the text.

There was a further difficulty, and one not considered by Peter Earle. Over two hundred and fifty years a huge volume of works was attributed to Defoe, most of which were not signed or admitted to be his in his lifetime. These included an abundance of works of fiction, pamphlets, articles and poems. There has been a reaction to these so-called ascriptions. It is generally accepted that over half of them are not credible. Ascription confusions, when taken together with the paucity of provable information about Defoe, have led to very different biographical accounts. During Defoe's life, and since then, there has been controversy about his character. Most biographers are divided between hagiographers, who deny the significance of duplicity and dishonesty and who have invented romances as a substitute for reality, and debunkers who can see no virtue in him.

It would be a foolish biographer who denied that Defoe often lied or dissembled. But the task of revising romantic, iconic and child-like accounts of a subject presents the biographer with problems. A common reaction to the revelation of lies is that readers think less well of the 'hero', the subject of the biography itself. The question is asked as to why the biographer has chosen to write about such an unreliable character. Weakly, it might be responded, we do not always choose our 'heroes', they select us, and despite our better judgement. However, such a response will not do. A biographer is expected to persuade his reader of the worthiness of his subject while proceeding with circumspection, and a good biographer is expected to grapple with contradictions of character and event and to do his best to reveal the 'truth', so far as it can be ascertained. After all, the reader might say, 'truth is stranger than fiction' and more interesting. What is more, I believe that 'truth' is something owed to the subject as well as to one's self.

There is a very simple reason why biographers of Defoe persist with what appears to many to be a hopeless quest: Defoe is one of the first writers widely accepted as being a progenitor of the modern novel and is, therefore, grappling in his writing with a nascent sense of his individuality in a world we recognise as our own. He was among the first authors to break away from stories based on legend or myth of Greek and Roman origin and to give his readers characters, plot, and something which amounts to 'realism'. Admittedly his characters are often shadowy, unconvincing and unlikeable, but they represent distinguishable individuality and they engage the reader. They are characters that can be recognised and identified with and their human endeavours represent something of us.

The issue of 'realism' in the novel, a genre that is fictional, is a subject of enduring literary controversy. The sense of the worth of an individual life and the importance of human society is dependent on a belief in reason. Among the elements of realism must be a concern with the lives of ordinary people facing dilemmas which are recognisable to the reader and with a relationship to what has gone before and to the events which unfold. Historically, this sense of individuality and individual destiny was only possible from the beginning of the eighteenth century. Philosophically, it is associated with a departure from the classical belief that there were universal truths to be apprehended from the physical world and their replacement by truths based on human perceptions and the evidence of our senses. This departure places human personality and imagination at the heart of the pursuit of knowledge.

By the eighteenth century, the drift of people from the countryside and the development of trade and commerce with its specialisation of function had undermined the cohesion of community and cast men adrift to their own devices. Crusoe's world, although strange, is the contemporary world. It is our world in its earliest form, with the places in which we live, love, struggle and, ultimately, fail.

Defoe's sense of identity is troubled, and troubling, because his imagination is focussed on two very different 'realities'. On one hand, the foundation of his ideas is to be found in the seventeenth century, where life and beliefs are accountable to God in an endless queue for a place in heaven, while, on the other, in his writing can be seen the effects of the cynical marketplace of an embryonic eighteenth-century capitalism with its materialistic struggle for riches and survival.

Yet still I hesitated. In attempting to reveal the 'truth' I risked creating a portrait of Defoe which would repel. Victoria Glendinning writes that the question biographical writers are most frequently asked about a particular subject is, 'Do you like him?' She suggests that what the questioner usually means is: 'If I read your book will I meet someone whom I like?' [7] Biographers often start out with enthusiasm for their subjects and finish liking them less. Yet those researchers whose affinity with their subject remains unshaken after long acquaintance may have lost all objectivity and usefulness to their readers. A subject becomes the biographer's friend but also his enemy; without friendship a difficult task cannot be attempted but without distrust there would be no 'truth'.

There is no general answer to Victoria Glendinning's question. In relation to Defoe, it can be said that those who like a 'who dunnit' should not hesitate to read on. The serious-minded can be sure that in Defoe they are in the presence of a man of singular intelligence writing in the revisionist tradition. Some readers will always think of Defoe as a great and compelling man whatever others might say of him although, as they get to know him better, their liking may turn to a grudging respect and their judgement to sympathy. In the end, all judgements are personal.

Then, as in any worthwhile biographical task, in unravelling Defoe and his times the reader can learn something more of himself and the age in which he lives which, surely, is justification enough for the time spent reading about him. For those who can abstract themselves from tumultuous times and dreadful choices, concern with the meaning of Defoe's life can be justified in Defoe's own words 'Tis evident … that the history of men's lives may be many ways made useful and instructive to those who read them.'

Background

DANIEL DEFOE LIVED DURING a critical period of English history. His birth, around 1661, was early in the restored monarchy of Charles II. His father, Charles I, had been cruelly put to death in 1649 following a bloody Civil War over the issue of how England was to be governed. An attempt to govern England as a puritan republic had ended in failure. A majority of people who had joined, or acquiesced, in a republic came to accept that the restoration of the monarchy was the best way to re-unite a divided country. They were willing to come together with the supporters of the Stuarts to heal the bitter divisions of the Civil War. This majority wanted the country to be governed as a parliamentary democracy; they wanted a protestant king willing to share sovereignty with parliament. The English nation has never changed its mind.

To those living through the twenty-eight years of the restored Stuart dynasty and later, under William III (1688–1702) and Queen Anne (1702–1714), it never seemed certain that the compromises of the Restoration were safe. Stuart pretenders across the Channel were aided by Roman Catholic France, the mightiest military power in Europe, whose mercantile and political interests were best served by a servile England. France had to be denied, but so did the Dutch, Britain's natural political and religious ally but commercial rival. It seemed to an entire nation that England was continually at war, waging battles on land as well as at sea. These wars sapped the energies and the economic resources of an entire nation and created a huge national debt. British people developed the attitudes to the European continent that are recognisable in politics today. Britain became willing to act against any European power seeking continental supremacy because both British political independence and overseas trading would be threatened.

The Restoration placed the Church of England at the centre of the British constitution with the monarch at its head. Parliament, administration and justice were in the monarch's name. The nation's fragile consensus was threatened from the right by High Anglicans and Roman Catholics (many of whom favoured a Jacobite restoration following James II's departure from England in December 1687), and from the left by religious dissenters, some of whom remained revolutionary in their intentions and sympathies. These dissident communities were small and vociferous, restless for their full religious and political rights, which were denied them by the majority in fear of regicide and renewed fratricide: fears which never materialised and in the end were recognised as groundless. The Restoration settlement remained intact and the Test Act, 1673, which required those in official positions to swear an oath of loyalty to the Crown, remained until 1828 as a widely accepted assurance against rebellion.

Daniel Defoe's family was positioned in the dissident minority, some ten per cent of the capital's adult population. By the end of Defoe's life in 1731, this minority was weakened and ideologically undermined; most men had come to accept the compromises needed to preserve the unity of the realm.

The Restoration maintained parliamentary democracy and with the passage of time parliament began to be more representative. Unlike its continental neighbour France, it became accepted that parliamentary democracy could not be overthrown. In France, the revolutions of 1789–92, 1830, 1848 and 1870 drew upon a variety of constitutional traditions of absolute monarchy, republicanism and dictatorship. In Britain, progress was evolutionary through parliament.

Britain continued to develop as a multi-cultural society while protesting that it did not wish it. Defoe's family were second or third generation Huguenot immigrants who had fled as religious refugees from Catholic France and from Flanders. After the Edict of Nantes in 1685, it is estimated that over 50,000 Huguenot immigrants came to Britain; an equivalent social impact to over 600,000 people today. Public attitudes to these 'new Britons' were contradictory, just as they are today whenever and wherever British people are confronted and obliged to live together in harmony with 'strangers'.

Britain's population, trade and industry expanded greatly during Daniel Defoe's lifetime. The population continued to move from the countryside to the city, and family life became fragmented and difficult, although the majority of people lived on and from the land. Scientifically and industrially there were huge advances. The Royal Society was founded. There were fortunes to be made in trade and on the primitive exchanges that financed both economic growth and ruinous wars. The City of London became the indispensable provider of capital to both commerce and the Crown. Even the poorest in society could, with determination, be educated and change their family's fortune.

It was a time of vast inequalities: between men and women, rich and poor, capital and labour. Society was split by economic and social class. In the towns some twenty per cent of people lived on the streets. Crime was rife and justice existed only for the privileged and the corrupt. It was a time for the cunning and the strong and it was unwise or unfortunate to be weak, a woman, poor or ill. Despite these difficulties, the universal individual rights to self-expression and the freedom to live a personal life removed from the dogma of church or state, concepts which were already rooted, came to be accepted more widely in Defoe's lifetime.

While the church thought otherwise, the majority of the population ceased to believe in angels or devils or in predestination or inevitability in human fortune. Men could shape their own fate, bring about changes for good or ill, and make something of their own lives. In this they were on their own. Sometimes they were in the right and sometimes not. Defoe was no different from anyone else.

Prologue

When his Enemies had him in their hands, they did not know what to do with him.

Walter Wilson

IT IS AN IRONY of human life that at the pinnacle of worldly success men are most in danger of a fall, and that those who cheer you on the way up are equally apt to revile you on your way down.

The world in which Daniel Defoe struggled to rise was an age of spectacle as well as ideology, of new wealth and high fashion, as well as tumult, brutality and drunkenness. People rejoiced in avarice while the statute book groaned under the weight of new offences. Some men enjoyed the excitement and rewards of crime and corruption while others sank into misery and poverty. There was much talk from pulpits of morality and virtue and much sinfulness to report.

Nowhere were these fears and pleasures experienced more than in the Great Wen of London. Each day saw the enrichment and fall of many; there were fortunes to be made on the high seas and landed estates to be lost. Men rejoiced at their own good fortune and turned the downfall of others into public spectacle at the direction of the courts. Life could be nasty and short but it was a joy to be healthy and alive.

The 29th day of July 1703 dawned fine and dry in London. In Cornhill, close to the Royal Exchange, men from the Sheriff's Office worked happily enough to finish their construction of a pillory into which some poor wretch was to be put to stand for three hours. Hinged wooden boards were articulated to form holes through which the malfeasant's head and wrists were to be inserted.

Once these boards were locked together and attached to a pole, the head and wrists could not be withdrawn. Thus trapped, the victim could not defend himself against missiles – stones, rotten vegetables, excrement or anything else to hand.

To be held still, grasped in an unnatural position, placed great physical stress on wrists, arms and neck. There was a real risk of blinding or permanent maiming. Sometimes the mob got behind the board, stripped the miscreant of his clothes, and beat him black and blue, breaking his ribs. It was thought by the crowd, relieved that it was not its turn, to be an occasion of great fun.

Where there are crowds there is money to be made. The hawkers plied their trade. You could buy rotten eggs for the pleasure of a shy.

The crimes of these miscreants were usually of a petty nature, such as street theft, perjury, burglaries and sodomy, but sometimes they were of greater significance to the state and society and the victim more notable. This was such an occasion.

The workmen made good progress in putting up the centrepiece; they had done it all before and would do so again. They worked silently at first, for the work was a serious matter and it was important for the job to be done properly, but when warmed by the rising sun they broke into conversation:
'Who are we doing this for, then?'
'A geezer called Daniel Foes. I think that's what he's called, for he has a lot of names.'
'And who's Foes when he's at home?'
'A bust businessman. He had premises in Freeman's Yard. You know Freeman's Yard, three hundred yards to the left. The fool had a coach and horses, servants, everything. Got a lot of money from his wife's dowry, borrowed, and blew it all. Kept on his premises, borrowed more, lost it again. You know the kind of thing.'
'A lot of people looking for him then.'
'They won't have far to go today.'
They laughed.
'Is all this for debt then?'
'No, course not. He fancies himself, this Foes, as a writer. He published a pamphlet insulting Queen Anne. Said he didn't mean it, but course he did. She decided to get him for it.'
'That stupid bitch… '
'Shut up, you idiot, you never know who's listening at a jamboree like this.'
'Isn't there more to it than that?'
'Yes, but what we don't know we can't speak about. If you get my meaning.'

The streets were busy now. The rattle and creak of fine carriages and the snorts of horses on their way to the marble halls of Westminster was a regular pattern of sound on the cobbled roads. Carriage curtains twitched and wigged heads and painted faces loomed out of the dark as if in a theatre circle.

City gentlemen, the contrivers and drivers of the new wealth, in all their finery, picked their wary way on foot to their desks, counters and coffee bars, pausing awhile to observe the excitement before passing on to the serious tasks of making money.

The everyday cries of hawkers, stallholders and traders were at their usual level of cacophony. On the steps of the Exchange, beggars prayed for the immortal souls of passers-by, and women with sores, and children in bundles of rags, consumed their usual portions of gin.

A crowd had gathered. The worthy among them clung together for their own safety, keeping their purses tight against themselves. The windows opposite were full of the faces of the curious.

Friends of Foes, or so it was claimed, distributed leaflets on which was written a poem by him entitled *A Hymn to the Pillory*. It must have been a good poem for it caused much mirth. Villainy and offence, it declaimed, lay with a cowardly and tyrannical government and not with Foes.

The smells of London were everywhere: perfume and sweat, spices, roasting coffee and rotten waste. They wafted on the breeze from numerous side streets, awash with liquid sewerage. Men complained of the smell of newly creosoted wood which they said, to great guffaws of laughter, would finish off the villain before the fun could begin.

The sun shone. The sky was blue. In short, everything was normal.

Around mid-morning the prisoner arrived from Newgate. He was not a pretty sight and even less so when strapped into the pillory. When the Earl of Nottingham, the new Principal Secretary of State, had issued a warrant for Defoe's arrest, and had caused posters to be displayed, he had added a description:

He is a middle sized man of about forty years old, of a brown complexion and dark-brown hair but wears a wig, a hooked nose, a sharp chin, grey eyes, and a large mole near his mouth, was born in London, and for many years was a hose factor in Freeman's Yard in Cornhill, and now is the owner of the brick and pantile works near Tilbury.

When Defoe's acquaintance, and former school contemporary, John Dunton, knew that Defoe was on the run, he advised him to give himself up, for his hooked nose, large chin and mole would make him immediately recognisable.

It is said that on Defoe's arrival the crowd cheered him heartily, friends formed a ring around him to protect him from missiles, and then pelted him with flowers. When at the end of his ordeal he stepped to the ground, he was acclaimed by his supporters.

London newspapers, noting the event on the subsequent day, took a cooler view of the happenings. *Heraclitus Ridens* reported, with an eye on the significance of the event, that among those present were 'worthy citizens, knights and aldermen... city friends... and the Dissenting tribe'. However, they described Defoe as being surrounded by 'scum'. Others thought they detected 'party' money behind the scrum and the hawking of Defoe's works.[8]

Whether the events described happened in this way is disputable. Anecdotal evidence tends to embellish and support myth. Defoe was not the only dissenter to stand in a pillory. Twenty-eight years earlier, Benjamin Harris, a journalist, published material offensive to Lord Chief Justice Scroggs in July 1675 and in December of that year was sentenced to stand in the pillory. Anecdotal reports tell of his friends arriving: 'he and his party hollowed and whooped, and would permit nothing to be thrown at him'.[9]

Defoe stood in the pillory for two more days. It is not known whether there were friends to help him. All that is known is that it rained.

For the next six months, Defoe languished in Newgate prison, broken and disconsolate for lack of the money to provide for the sureties needed for his release. His business was ruined, he became bankrupt once again, and his large family became homeless.

This could have been the end of Defoe's reputation, for to his contemporaries he would always be known as a scoundrel and a rogue. It is true that people did restore themselves from the humiliation of the pillory. To the foreigner of the time, it was always amazing that the English, seemingly, were able to recover from the most degrading of public humiliations. Defoe did recover, although the way in which he achieved his renaissance lacks any credible explanation.

If Defoe had died in the pillory in 1703, it is unlikely that posterity would have recognised him by anything more than an historical footnote. He was to live for another twenty-eight years. On his death in 1731 newspapers took note of the passing of a polemical political journalist of poor moral character and prodigious output. They remembered his bankruptcies and imprisonments and, in an age which valued partisanship, his ability to write on both sides of any issue and on all the greatest controversies of the day.

That is to say something, but not very much. Those who came later might have thought it of little consequence. But then something very peculiar happened. Like Topsy, Defoe's reputation grew and grew. Later in the century, he was recognised as the author of *A Tour Through the Whole Island of Great Britain* which was seen not only as a travel book but also as an engrossing social description of the country as it was in the 1720s. Subsequently, when it was fashionable, he was dubbed an economic radical and linked with Cobden and Bright. G.M. Trevelyan named an historical era after Defoe when he entitled part of his English social history, The Age of Defoe.

Defoe's rise became exponential. Victorians claimed him for a supporting role in the Whig version of history, as a revisionist writer on the right side. In the twentieth century academics recast his work as moral and religious philosophy, to be mentioned in the same breath as Locke, Hobbes and Bunyan. Defoe was presented as a victim of religious and political persecution and, in the extreme, as a progenitor of the American Constitution and of rights for women.

This enhancement of Defoe's reputation was supported by the ascription of many works to his name, almost half of which are not now thought to be his. It became an academic joke that in the case of any difficulty with an eighteenth century work the safe option was to ascribe it to Daniel Defoe. It might have been questioned more thoroughly how any one person could write so prolifically. Is it credible that Defoe could contradict himself by writing on both or many sides of any issue? Was Defoe utterly without principle or consistency of thought?

*   *   *

The Sheriff's workmen had remained to the end, for as impresarios they had, so to speak, to wrap it all up. It had proved to be extremely enjoyable. A good day had been had by all. As they packed up and made their way to their favourite tavern, the conversation continued:

'Go on, tell me, for I know that you know. How did this fellow Foes get into such a terrible scrape?'

'Well, OK. It happened like this…'

The tavern in Exeter Street, off the Strand, was smoky and smelly, cramped and over-crowded, but it had everything that a working man might be thought to need. There were homely wenches where they should be, in the kitchen; dotted around straw-covered wooden floors were brass spittoons, and there was the very best of company. The Sheriff's men were well known here and took their fair share of good-natured banter from the lawyers who had flooded out of the courts and their chambers. After a bit of elbow work, they lodged themselves in a high-stalled snug and Edward, who was the elder statesman of the two, as evidenced by an ample stomach, grave demeanour and greying locks, continued where they had left off. Warmed by the hot ale he allowed himself a diversion:

'I've seen Foes before, you know. Twice, actually. First time in Lill's, in flowing robes, long wig freshly curled and the largest sapphire ring you ever did see, and fully displayed on a crooked finger.'[10]

He paused for full effect.

'And then in Rotherhithe, just like you and me and down among the jolly Jack tars. There's a contrast for you.'

Will leaned forward. He had, thought Edward, an annoying habit of imitating a small dog, with fair hair flopping over his forehead, nose forward and mouth gaping. Panting, he begged:

'Tell me about it.'

'Well, that's another story when I'm sure of my facts. But I'll tell you this. I felt sure… I could swear it… he was a Molly.'[11]

He went on:

'This Foes is too clever by half. And that's how he makes his mistakes.'

Edward shook his head slowly from side to side to indicate that he, Edward, could not possibly have made such a mistake given that the wisdom and power of the authorities, of which he was an essential part, was unlimited. Edward picked up his narrative:

'Last December he published a pamphlet, 'cept no one knew it was his until we got hold of the printer. He wrote it as if he was some sort of High Anglican. It ranted on that now the throne was in the hands of Queen Anne, a true friend of the Church of England, it was time to put the dissenters in their place and if a simple law were passed condemning any person at a

15

conventicle to be banished and the preacher hanged, there would be no more talk of disunion. The time had come, he said.'

'More work for us,' said Will, before recovering weakly. 'Bit extreme isn't it? Surely, they're harmless enough, aren't they? Why did he do it?'

'Why did he do it? Who knows really? What he said in his own defence was that these views of the Anglican High Flyers were so daft that everyone who read the pamphlet would know that he was playing games, for no sane person could share them. Of course, she is not in favour of any such thing. But, everyone was deceived by it: Anglicans said, 'hear, hear' and the dissenters wailed in a great state of alarm, fearing for their lives and limbs. 'Course, when they thought about it everyone knew they had been tricked, and they were very, very angry. Not least the Queen!'

Edward's voice rose a full octave.

'She thought, and so did her ministers, that Foes was trying to unhinge her new administration by raising the people against her. Rebellion again! Sedition and libel! She thought that a 'party' was being raised against her and Foes was its mouthpiece. Maybe she was right. Maybe there was. Anyway, that's what Foes did.'

Edward had slowed down. The pomposity slipped away. He drank deeply and looked thoughtful before he spoke again.

'I'll tell you this, though. He was the concern of some very mighty people. My cousin Robert Wey works at the prison and twice he took Foes off to Whitehall to see Nottingham. He tells me Foes was very quiet about it. Robert asked Foes what Nottingham wanted to talk about. He said Nottingham wanted to pump him dry about his connections and what he had discussed with them.' Edward laughed. 'He mumbled something about political stuff, the Partition treaties and continuation of the war. You know the kind of thing. Anyway, Robert could not reckon it.'

Edward looked confounded himself and drank some more. Then right out of the blue, he said:

'Look Will, I know you like a little titillation, shall we say, and you can keep a secret can't you? Let me see you nod your head.'

Will nodded obediently.

'Well, I've got this.'

He pulled a crumpled piece of paper from his pocket.

'This is Foes. Foes the bard. Not the original, you understand, but a copy. When we arrested Foes he had this in his papers. Foes' very own lampoon.'

He passed the piece of paper over to a goggled-eyed Will. It read:

The Knighting of Sir David Hamilton
The Queen's Physician
The Queen rose up, the Doctor kneeled
And lifting up the Royal leg,
With gout and dropsie swel'd full big,
Over his head she raised it high,
As sword is brandisht in the skie,
Rise up, Sir David, says the Queen,
The first Cunt knight that e'er was seen.

Will whistled and then coughed – a long and careful cough. Good Lord, he wondered. What sort of man is this? He asked nervously, 'Did she… did the Queen get to see this?'
'Who knows? Perhaps Nottingham lacked the spunk. But if he did… curtains for Foes! Don't you think?'
Edward drew his hand slowly and emphatically across his throat.

EARLY LIFE

1661/2 to 1683

Chapter 1

Beginnings

The end, I say of everything is in the beginning, and you must look to the end, or you will never begin right.

Review, VIII, 514 (for 614)
Daniel Defoe

AROUND 8PM ON 27 JULY 1662, in fading light, the curate of St Mary the Virgin in Chadwell, Essex, was summoned from his modest dwelling near the church. It had been a hot and tiresome day and he could have done without a call of any kind but a priest's duties required him to be available at any time of day or night and he knew he must not complain. A tall and rather handsome man was standing by the lych gate. His clothing, a dusty jerkin and cloth trousers, leather riding boots and a wide brimmed hat, suggested he had been riding hard and that the journey had been a long one.

In his arms the visitor carried a baby wrapped in a silk shawl. Politely, he apologised for the inconvenience of the time, but he had little of that to spare, for he was passing through on the London road and the day was closing in. He requested a baptism and registration for the child he was carrying.

Stilling his protests, for the priest was as conscious as anyone of the necessity to bring this little soul into the protection of God's grace, he agreed. No parental names were proffered.

'What shall we call him?' enquired the priest.

'Daniel,' replied the visitor. 'Yes, Daniel, I think, for it is a family name and we are certainly saving him from the lion's den.'

And the priest recorded the baptism as 'Daniel son of a stranger.'[12]

Biographers of Daniel Defoe have assumed that he was born into a devout puritan and dissenting family which offered him a stable upbringing. It has been written that he was educated in a dissenting academy, which trained him for the ministry and that he then embarked on an adventurous career which, while mysterious, secretive and contradictory, created a man who, in the words of a recent biographer, 'some historians feel worthy of being thought of as the hero of his age'. On these foundations a mighty edifice has been created.

There is substance in what has been written about Defoe but, as his own words remind us, the early life of a subject tends to shape the adult and, unless that early life is understood, it is unlikely that the adult can be truly appreciated. For the biographer of Defoe, there is no alternative to starting

21

the search where least is known: at the very beginning. The mysterious baptism record described imaginatively above, inconclusive though it is, is in all probability part of this beginning. Daniel Defoe was the illegitimate son of unknown parents who was brought, by events that are unknown, into the care of James Foe, a London butcher, tallow chandler and merchant. Biographers have combed parish records across London and the southern counties for details of his birth but nothing other than the Chadwell St Mary the Virgin baptism record has been found. If this record relates to Defoe then it was a strange beginning to a remarkable life and a clue to the question of what sort of man he might have been.

It is not strange that there is confusion about his birth. Until 1837, when the registration of births became compulsory, the parentage of many people and their dates and places of birth were often difficult to ascertain. Defoe does not help his biographers either, there is no mention in any of his writing of where he was born and when. He does not write about the names of his parents or, with certainty, the gender, number and dates of birth of his siblings. But although the start of Defoe's life has been obscured it can be surmised. By far the most probable explanation behind the many doubts about his parentage is that at least one of his putative parents, James and Alice Foe, was not his biological parent.

What is least probable is what is most commonly believed: that Daniel Defoe was born in 1660/1 in Cripplegate, London and brought up there by his parents, James and Alice Foe, in a small nuclear family of firm Presbyterian and dissenting beliefs. Biographers have come to assume that this is so, not because there is conclusive evidence of it but because there is no sustainable alternative. It is necessary to consider it in detail here in order to reject it, at least in the form in which it is advanced.

The link of Daniel Defoe to James and Alice Foe has rested on flimsy evidence. As a result of the research carried out for this book, Daniel's family relationships can be clarified. James Foe was married at least three or four times and children were brought into the marriage by at least three women. It is generally accepted that James and Alice Foe had two daughters, Mary and Elizabeth, and that their births were registered with the designation 'Not baptised' (which is rare), in the Parish Church of St Giles, Cripplegate, London where they lived, on 13 November 1657 and 19 June 1659. Some time around 1668, Alice died or left home.

There were two other children living in James Foe's household. As hinted at in *Colonel Jack*, where three brothers share the same Christian name, and in *Robinson Crusoe*, where Crusoe had an elder brother who served in the army, Daniel Defoe had a real elder brother. He too was called Daniel and became a cavalry officer in the British army. This previously unknown Daniel Defoe was a Captain Lieutenant in Captain Desbordes' Regiment of Dragoons raised in Portugal in 1706. In the entire army commission lists from 1661–1714 his name is the only Foe/Defoe to be found.[13]

In *Colonel Jack*, Defoe writes of his nurse 'It happened that her own son (for she had a little boy of her own, about one year older than I) was called John [Jack] too, and about two years after she took another son of shame, as I called it above, to keep as she did me, and his name was John too.' Thus, if the nurse's own son was ignored, there were two 'sons of shame', with the same name, whom she had taken in. These two brothers were Daniel Defoe the author and his elder brother of the same Christian name.

In addition to these two brothers there was at least one other child, of unknown gender, within the Foe family. This child was living with James Foe and Elizabeth, his wife at this time, in 1691/2,[14] but by 1695/6 the child had disappeared.[15] Also living with James Foe in 1695/6 was a servant called John Seal and a female servant called Dinah. It is possible that this person, John, was the model for Captain Jack, the third and younger brother in *Colonel Jack*.

The only other Foe family to be found in London in 1695/6 was headed by William Foe. He is described as a bachelor of at least twenty-five years[16] and was living with a widower, and Susannah Foe, who is described as a maid. In this context a maid was a female carer not otherwise categorised within the household. This Susannah Foe is of interest because late in Daniel Defoe's life when Mrs Brooke, a creditor, was pursuing him, she named Defoe's wife as Susannah. In *Colonel Jack* it is Will who leads the young Colonel Jack into serious gang crime. It is highly likely that all these Foes are related. There are not many of them. There were no Foes at all to be found living in London in 1638.[17]

The child living with James Foe in 1691/2 might have died, or as Bob, in *Captain Singleton,* it might have been abducted, or as the younger brother in *Robinson Crusoe*, it might simply have disappeared, or yet again, as with Captain Jack in *Colonel Jack*, it might have merely vanished from the scene.

The probability is, therefore, that James Foe had two daughters, Elizabeth and Mary by Alice and one other child, of unknown name, by Elizabeth, and that the two Daniels were brought under his guardianship, or within his family, by other women to whom he might or might not have been 'married', and if not siblings, then William and Susannah Foe were cousins.

To round off this explanation it is worth noting that the Jacques Foe shown as living in French's Court in 1673, at the same time as James Foe, might have been a French relative of some kind.[18] When the fictional Colonel Jack returns to London he pretends to be Colonel Jacque and speaks French. Jacques Foe might have been the model for Colonel Jack, and one of the Foe boys might be his son.[19]

While not entirely conclusive, this account makes redundant the attempts to establish the reason for Defoe's birth not being recorded in St Giles' church register in Cripplegate. It is not in the register because he was not born in Cripplegate and Alice Foe was not his mother.

*   *   *

Thomas Wright, a Victorian biographer, believed that a branch of the Foe family lived in Colchester, Essex. However, what he believed to be the only surviving record of them doing so in Chadwell St Mary turns out to be false.[20] If the baptism discovered in the same parish is Daniel Defoe's, as I argue it is, his birth would most likely have been in 1661/2. Defoe's original tombstone records his death in 1731 as being in his seventieth year, which is consistent with a birth in 1661/1662. There is plenty of evidence that Daniel Defoe had family in Essex, both from his books and from written records. Moll Flanders comes from the area and on two occasions Defoe attempted to build country estates in the Colchester area.

While a conception outside marriage could be righted by a subsequent marriage of the couple and was acceptable to the Church of England and most Presbyterians, illegitimacy was considered a sin. However, for anyone believing in child baptism, it would have been important to perform a ceremony as soon as possible. The extended Foe family were Presbyterians and one of them might well have wanted to save the soul of the young Daniel by an early baptism, even if he were illegitimate, or against the opposition of a parent.

Assuming that the biographer can draw upon Daniel Defoe's fictional writings for autobiographical content, it can be argued that the circumstantial evidence of his own disquiet about the nature of his birth and early childhood is strong. The reader will find much in Defoe's writing to suggest an uncertain multiple parent background, additional siblings, and a boarding-out to those who took money and apparently cared very little for him. Responsibility for Daniel's welfare seems to have been passed from one person to another.

For example, in *Colonel Jack*, the young Colonel Jack, seeking pity, claims that he did not know his parents. All he knew was that his father was a gentleman and wished him to be one too. The nurse tells him 'I have known colonels come to be lords and generals, though they were b---- ds at first, and therefore you shall be called Colonel.'[21]

In the language of the time, Colonel Jack's nurse, the woman deputed by his father to look after him, was a child-taker. Defoe often writes of them. In the Preface to *Moll Flanders*, Defoe describes Moll's governess as running through in the course of a few years 'all the eminent degrees of a Gentlewoman, a Whore, and a bawd; a Midwife, and Midwife keeper as they are called, a Pawn-broker, a Child-taker, a Receiver of Thieves, and of Thieves purchase'.[22] By 'Child-taker' was meant a foster mother paid by the parish to look after deserted children, some of whom were allowed to die in order to save the cost of their upkeep.

The issues of legitimacy and acceptance were life-long problems for Defoe: issues of religion and method of worship, of the monarchy, actual and putative, and of political practice and philosophy. He certainly supposed that, as illustrated by the Pentateuch, he was self-selected as a member of a chosen tribe for the next life. Some would argue that the persecution of dissenters and their families and friends in the reign of Charles II was a sufficient cause of Defoe's bitter sense of exclusion for being and feeling 'illegitimate', but it may be that the early childhood feelings were of personal exclusion and abandonment and that religious alignment as a dissenter was an effect and not a cause.

These fictional childhood memories of isolation, loss and abandonment cannot, of course, be taken literally; early memories are always fragmented, half-hidden and fantastical. Of course, great care must also be taken about the interpretation of Defoe's fictional statements but, as I have begun to demonstrate, they are likely to have affinity with his recorded life.

What Defoe tells his readers are never literal accounts because he is using literary conventions: the existing conventions of spiritual autobiography, best known and illustrated by John Bunyan, and tricks and devices of his own making in the telling of tales of embryonic poverty to riches, from lost to found, which in the next century were to be borrowed and adapted by Charles Dickens in *Oliver Twist* and *Great Expectations*.

Daniel Defoe was willing to deceive his contemporaries about the circumstances of his birth in alluding to a date in 1660/1. Almost all Defoe's writing makes contemporary political statements.[23] In *Robinson Crusoe*, for example, the span of time of Crusoe's stay on his island of twenty-eight years coincides with the period between the restoration of the monarchy in 1660 and the Glorious Revolution of 1688. In using this period of time, Defoe is making a political point as a dissenter: the Restoration had cast him out and denied him his religious and political rights, and the Glorious Revolution brought him to the promised land.

What is interesting about autobiographical accounts of early life in Defoe's writing is that they all convey the emotions of being cast out and abandoned; a 'casting out' first by his unknown mother and then by the Foe family. Defoe would have felt this rejection as a punishment by God for earthly transgressions.

In the seventeenth and early eighteenth centuries moral writers, of whom Defoe is one, used arithmetical techniques to relate to the 'fitness of things'. In particular, rewards and punishments reflected a need for justice and the belief that they should be meted out in proportion to a scale.[24] Most commentators point out that Crusoe's disobedience to the wishes of his 'father' would be considered a punishable sin by Presbyterians, and a serious offence for a son. But is not twenty-eight years a disproportionate period of time?

Defoe's silence about his beginnings can be taken as an indication of his rejection by others. His behaviour was condemned throughout his life, both by those who did not care for him, and by others who cared a great deal. Silence seems to have been Defoe's reaction to this disapproval.

Defoe's response to rejection would not in itself have resulted in the creation of *Robinson Crusoe*. There must surely be more to it than that. If a reader knew nothing of Defoe as the author of *Robinson Crusoe*, he might assume that the adult experiences of its creator as described in the book must have had an origin in earlier childhood happenings and that the adult Crusoe was most likely revisiting earlier childhood traumatic experiences.

Not everything about Daniel Defoe's beginnings is unknown and it is understandable that biographers have latched on to the particulars they can find. The 'adoption' of Daniel by the Foe family, especially if there was a loss of other children, is entirely possible. It is incontestable also that James Foe had an influence on the writer because for some time at least he was in loco parentis and, therefore, for good or ill he was part of Daniel's life.

James Foe was born in 1630 in Etton, Northamptonshire, the third son of a farmer named Daniel Foe. The name Foe is of Huguenot origin and Daniel's forebears may have been protestant refugees fleeing religious persecution in France or Belgium. In *Roxana* the father is a wealthy Huguenot. Foe is one family name among numerous Huguenot names in the Colchester area of Essex. It is rare now in Northampton, but there have been border changes over the years between the adjacent counties. The evidence suggests, therefore, that Daniel was a second or third generation Huguenot immigrant.[25]

James Foe's father left the farm to his elder son, also called Daniel, but the farm and the family line seem to have disappeared soon after. It is most likely that farming became uneconomic for the family and the farm simply disappeared as part of a general drift from the land. James followed his elder brother Henry to London some time during the 1640s. Henry became a saddler and James became apprenticed to Henry Levitt, a merchant member of the Butchers' Company.

James Foe married in the 1650s a woman called Alice, most probably in the late 1650s, and the tax rolls show them as living in Cripplegate in the City of London.[26] No record of their marriage has been discovered, nor of James's other marriages. The failure to discover marriage records, or a burial record for Alice, is not surprising. In the confusion of the Civil War, the system of voluntary registrations operating through parish churches broke down; registrations were haphazard and difficult to trace, particularly among nonconformists whose meeting places frequently lapsed into desuetude.

The London of James Foe's time experienced the high drama of the English Civil War. A king was executed and a Roundhead administration raised its money and recruited for its armies with the enthusiastic support of City merchants. There is no evidence one way or the other to suggest that James Foe was greatly affected by any of these events. It is assumed sometimes, and mistakenly, that great happenings become the centrepiece of the lives of ordinary people when in reality they swirl about them as they go about the everyday tasks of earning a living and feeding their families.

However, there is a curious fact to explain. James's apprenticeship lasted ten years which, while not extraordinary, was longer than the minimum of seven years stipulated by the Butchers' Company.[27] There are several possible explanations: it may be that the price for this apprenticeship could not be afforded, James might have been needed to work on the family farm or to look after relatives, or, like his 'son' Daniel, he might have thought it prudent to flee from the City and the grasp of creditors.

It is, of course, possible that James Foe might have been politically involved and kept quiet about it. If on the parliamentary side, he may have found himself vulnerable in a factional power struggle, or, more dramatically, perhaps he was on the wrong side and was careful to keep quiet about an involvement. It is conjectured that in the 1660s he became part of the religious nonconformist minority and it seems that he was a man of piety, but if the adage is that 'the apple does not fall far from the tree', then the father might have shared with his 'son' the desire to be silent about his past. In this past there would have been time for an earlier marriage and children.

Nothing is known of the Foe family in Etton in Daniel Defoe's lifetime. However, it is known that following the death of the elder Daniel Foe in 1631, Daniel's paternal grandmother Rose twice remarried and her daughter, Jane Foe, an aunt of Daniel Defoe, may well have been the Jane Foe that Daniel stood bail for in 1686 when she was arrested for attending an illegal dissenting religious meeting.

A number of biographers have suggested that Rose was Defoe's model for the Quaker wife in *Roxana*. She is portrayed sympathetically by Defoe and from this it is argued that as Quaker women are rarely to be found in early eighteenth-century novels, Defoe would have needed a model. However, as this story reveals, Daniel found a congenial, real life, Quaker woman.

In his *A Tour Through the Whole Island of Great Britain*, Defoe writes sympathetically about many places known to him but there is no mention of the place where James Foe was brought up, and there is no evidence elsewhere in his writings of any personal identification with the locality.

Defoe created speculation in suggesting that he had a grandfather who had a huntsman and a pack of hounds named after the generals of the Civil War[28] and that he was distantly related to Sir Walter Raleigh through a family link with the De Beaus. This background would have some of the swagger of the cavalier about it but, try as they might, biographers have been unable to verify the allusions. It is possible that this mention is a Defoe joke, for he was undoubtedly vainglorious and such a name would have increased his social standing.

If true, this grandfather could not have been on James Foe's side of the family because his father died in 1631 before the start of the Civil War.

However, if Defoe was illegitimate a connection to an aristocratic lineage is possible.

Biographers further suggest that when Daniel changed his name to Defoe around 1694, and paid his fees for a coat of arms, he was somehow claiming his mother's heritage. As Daniel's elder brother used the name Defoe, written as one word, there might have been Defoes within the wider Foe family.

In his will, James's father Daniel left a small sum to the church at Etton, which suggests a religious commitment to the Church of England. There are no surviving records of him fulfilling any role in the governance of the church, which might be an indication that his social position was that of yeoman farmer.[29]

As a busy merchant, James Foe would often have been absent from home. Although a member of the Butchers' Company he seems to have been a general merchant. In Defoe's *Compleat English Tradesman* a merchant is defined as a trader conducting business overseas. Such a merchant at this time would have traded with France, Spain, Portugal and the Low Countries. Defoe's elder brother joined his regiment in Portugal which suggests the possibility of a family connection there.

Consequently, James Foe would have been absent from home on many occasions and for long periods of time. When 'widowed' for the first time, he would have sought other female partners and there may have been more of these than of wives; with numerous children to look after, he really had no choice but to find female carers and it would have been surprising if he had not. In the City of London in the 1660s there were far more women than men, few jobs for women, and a high child mortality rate. It would not have been difficult for James to find willing female partners.

Married partners in Daniel Defoe's fiction, more often than not, enter into their liaisons in precarious ways, in private arrangements, and careless of the existence of other spouses. If James was lucky, he might have enjoyed new and loving relationships, but it seems more likely that his domestic relationships fell short of romantic ideals.

The evidence suggests that James Foe was moderately successful in business. Within the Butchers' Company he achieved positions of responsibility without ever scaling the heights. Materially, as would be normal, his fortunes waxed and then, when he grew older, waned. He started in rented accommodation in Swan Lane and then moved to a substantial property in French's Court, a far more prestigious address, before falling back to where he started and, finally, he moved to rented rooms at the Bell Inn, Broad Street.

James Foe appears to have been trusted. He was named as executor in a number of wills, which suggests that he was respected in his business dealings and in his wider community. The only direct evidence of James Foe is a letter he wrote in 1705 giving a job reference to a servant applying for a position in a clergyman's family and who, at one time, had been in his own employ. The letter is written in good plain English with the usual and conventional pieties, from which it can be deduced that James Foe had been given, or had acquired, literary competence. Descriptions of James Foe in the documents that survive are invariably about his function as a merchant and only on one occasion is he described as a gentleman.[30]

In contrast to the known particulars about Defoe's putative parents and siblings, his journalism and fiction are a rich source of information on family relationships in general.

The nearest Defoe gets to a description of a father who might be his own is in describing Robinson Crusoe's father. Defoe writes, 'My father, a wise and grave man, gave me serious and excellent counsel.' He refused to consent to his son going to sea. Crusoe consulted his mother at 'a time when I thought her a little pleasanter than ordinary'. (This suggests that she was not ordinarily very pleasant.)

In his fictions, Defoe refers to brothers not sisters. In *Captain Singleton*, Bob, the central narrator of the story, was abducted from his parents and raised by two others: first, by a beggar woman, and then by a gypsy who looked after him well for six years (a period during which Alice Foe might have been responsible for him) until her death. She had confessed that she was not his real mother. After her death he became the responsibility of a parish. He acquired a master and called him 'father' although he, the master, had children of his own. Defoe writes:[31]

My good gypsy mother, for some of her worthy actions no doubt, happened in process of time to be hanged and as this fell out something too soon for me to be perfected in the strolling trade, the parish where I was left took some care of me.

If Defoe's real mother had been a Quaker she might well have been itinerant, in the sense of time spent in travelling to meetings (time away that was grudgingly acknowledged by Daniel). A worthy act might then have been one prompted by religious convictions for which she lost her life. This is pure speculation, however, for many past searches have not found Alice Foe among the names of known Quaker martyrs.

In Defoe's fiction multiple marriages and liaisons are the rule. In *Moll Flanders* there are five marriages, one of which is, unknowingly, to a brother and in *Colonel Jack* there are four. Not counting her Prince, Roxana has three husbands.

In Daniel Defoe's fiction wives and mothers cannot be relied upon; they become whores or abandon their husbands for others more to their fancy. Invariably there are numerous children, most of whom are readily or callously cast aside at the convenience of the adult protagonists.

In contrast to the emerging evidence of James Foe's disjunctive multiple marriages, Defoe's biographers have assumed that his parents had a conjugal or 'companionate' marriage in keeping with social trends of the time and bound by the religious practice of Presbyterians, to whom family life was important.

It is far from clear that the social changes biographers refer to were so certain and uniform as they imagine. The evidence is conflicting. Habakkuk has suggested a reversion to marriages of economic convenience in the latter part of the seventeenth century, whereas Lawrence Stone argues for a continuous evolution to modern marriage.[32] The base evidence is confused by the absence of any statistical approach. A consequence of the voluntary recording of marriages was that many marriages could be private and unrecorded. It is simply not possible to be dogmatic about the incidence of marriages, their legality, or the extent to which they were 'companionate'.

At the turn of the century there appears to have been a population imbalance with a surplus of unmarried women and a reluctance among men to marry. Domestic help and sex, without the tie of marriage, was freely available. Puritans tended to favour marriage ties but, no doubt as ever, practice was often not in line with theory or personal family beliefs.

The evidence of James Foe's domestic arrangements which I have presented shows multiple parental relationships. Some of these arrangements would have been within legal marriage and some not. It is possible that there were other 'marriages' and children apart from those I have identified. There would have been acute family difficulties in coping with the children known about and some, including Daniel, might conceivably have been put out to board or found themselves in the care of the parish.

If it is accepted that Daniel Defoe was part of this extended and hard-pressed family, and if their likely circumstances are taken into account, it is possible to begin to explain the complexities of Defoe's character and behaviour, much else that is obscure, and the nature of the choices open to the young Defoe at various stages of his life.

The biographer needs to be cautious. Whatever side he comes down on, there is conjecture. A son aspiring to something better than his parents is common to every age. It is usual for children to fantasise about their origins. Children often imagine that their 'true' parentage is other and better, [33] and when children come into an understanding that their parents are not perfect their imagination becomes engaged in the task of freeing themselves from them. Freud stresses the versatility and many-sidedness of the fantasy which enables the child to meet every requirement of its emotional life. He suggests connections between fantasy and 'historical intrigues': the dramas of history, the bravery of kings and great warriors, the tears of great queens and their motives of 'greed, wickedness and folly'.

There were a great many of these dramas in Daniel Defoe's life and writings. An aspiration to embrace worldly wealth, to be a gentleman, was an achievable ambition in his time and from where he started in life. It could have been fashioned by a belief that his present family position, although worthy in some respects, was not his 'true' inheritance. As Defoe fashioned a self-image that was fantastical, he seems to have reached back into the past to embellish, restore and smooth out fragments of memory, and to obscure, exaggerate, or hide all those things which would detract from or diminish his reputation.

To describe a man as a Presbyterian and, as such, committed to a disciplined and devout family life is not to say that he is a good father or role model for a son. When James Foe and Daniel were at home together, James might have thought it necessary to compensate for lost parenting time by being the stern father, and in his absence his proxies (over-pressed female carers) may have striven to discipline boys outside their control. Occasional admonitions from adults may have fitted uneasily with the freedom of young boys to roam the streets.

It would have been best for young children when confronted with moral strictures to keep their own peace and to bear moralising in silence, but if there were words, and surely the young Daniel would have developed a great supply, it would have been necessary to develop verbal tools of duplicity and easy and facile acceptances.

It can be imagined that there would be punishments: the copious copying out of relevant passages of the Bible, and banishment to a bedroom from which the only escape would be out of the window and across a rooftop to a neighbouring lane. Through an open window, Daniel would have heard the shouts of street vendors and the rattle of carriages: signals of excitement and danger which became irresistible to him.

Conflicts of this kind may have been responsible for the dualities in Daniel Defoe's values and behaviour, his writings, and his attitudes to women, dichotomies by which ideals are contrasted with prosaic and sometimes dishonest alternatives.

These dispositional dualities of the young Defoe (the functions of his character and personality) fed into the wider cultural phenomena of puritanism. It is undeniable that the puritanical values and disciplines of his time released a considerable positive energy which created wealth, but it is irrefutable also that they led to parochialism and the self-preserving retreat of dissent.

For all these reasons of ambiguity about family status, individual character, split identity and intellectual and moral uncertainties, it is generally a mistake in interpreting the adult Defoe to accept a statement of the ideal as being his true, consistent, belief much less a fail-proof guide to his actions. Neither is it advisable to think of Defoe's work as occupying rooted and rounded philosophies and ideals (although there may have been some), for invariably it will be discovered that any view, no matter how vehemently expressed, is only provisional. When circumstances change it is necessary for Defoe to argue the opposite. Such assertions as these do not deny Defoe a quota of sincerity but they do place the reader on eternal watch.

It has been the fashion, for literary reasons, to eschew any serious attempt to gain a psychological understanding of the 'real' Daniel Defoe and to create an alternative person: the 'veritable writing machine' of modern scholarship. Enquirers are fobbed off. They have been asked to accept that an analysis of Defoe's copious and contradictory writings, no matter how flimsy their attribution, and taken at their face value, will reveal the only Daniel Defoe that exists. The reader is asked to accept that the 'dynamic intersection between events, ideas, and writing that has come down to us' is the only Defoe that can be known.

What can be asserted at the beginning of Daniel Defoe's story, beyond serious challenge, is that a complex personality, an overwhelming ego, a life driven by fear, desperation and resilience in the most extreme of circumstances is not the outcome of a stable family life. Thankfully for posterity, it is not at all likely that Daniel Defoe had one.

Chapter 2

Childhood

It is as if, like his own [fictional] heroes and heroines, he saw life from the point of view of a homeless orphan. It is as if people were what his own Will Atkins calls 'Aliens to bring Home'.

Virginia Ogden Birdsall
Defoe's Perpetual Seekers

IN 1871, WHEN DEFOE'S coffin was dug up to erect a monument to him, it was noticed with astonishment that he had a very large chin. In portraits of Defoe there is no hint of this, although satirical attacks on him sometimes mentioned it. It is common for young children to make fun of physical abnormalities and numerous sayings come to mind: a lantern jaw, a chinless wonder, leading with your chin, and so on. Defoe must have experienced bullying references to his appearance.

The runt of a pack must display great energy and resolve to survive. Defoe describes himself in *Colonel Jack*: 'I passed among my comrades for a bold, resolute boy and one that durst fight anything. But I had a different opinion of myself, and therefore shunned fighting as much as I could…I had a natural talent of talking, and could say as much to the purpose as most people…[and] many times brought myself off with my tongue.'

Appearance was important to Colonel Jack and as soon as he had money he bought clothes to pass himself off as something of a gentleman, which was to be important to Daniel Defoe all his life. A large chin would have caused people to hesitate in dealings with him; there would be thoughts that 'things were not quite right'. But by display he could make people see him differently and with greater respect. He was often laughed at for his long and unfashionable wigs but these may have been an attempt to disguise his unusual facial features.

The adult Defoe experienced the fear of many crises which may have had their origins and causes in his childhood. Being thought risible or untrustworthy was a difficulty but was not the stuff of nightmares, of a fleeing from unknown shapes, shadows and noises. The adult Defoe often felt himself to be engulfed. On many occasions he desperately sought secure and safe places, refuges in which he could cower and pray for a relief which rarely came.

Try as he might, there was no relief or comfort in the power of speech in which Defoe took pride. He would have been told by the adults in his life that daytime fears and terrors of the night were of his own making. He was sinful. God punished the sinful and there was no hiding place. All Daniel could do was to run away from the adults who told him these things and, when that was not possible, he had to face whatever couldn't be avoided.

Daniel would always remember the nightmares of the Great Plague. He would have remembered neighbours finding a swollen corpse in the lane outside their tenement building. The voices of agitated adults could be heard within their dwelling. Hastily, there was a packing of household essentials. Uncle Henry came with provisions, lent them a horse, and waved them goodbye. A saddler, he joked that if they were to fall off and come to grief it would be from the finest of saddles. Grown-ups cried. There was a long journey with bunking down in open fields under night skies, and an arrival with hugs, sobs and much relief.

It is not a common view of Defoe's childhood that it created nightmares sufficient for a whole lifetime. Dottin writes that Defoe's childhood was a happy one.[34] This must be far from the truth, for when allowance is made for an uncertain family life and the political and religious context in which his family sought to better itself, his childhood must have contained great difficulties.[35]

Daniel's nightmares arose partly from where he started in life. The high drama of his earliest days was lived out within one square mile of central London. Although he was to leave it, and on occasions for long periods of time, he always returned to London and the finalities of his life were ordered there.

Daniel expresses his feelings about the capital at the beginning of *A Tour Through the Whole Island of Great Britain*. He writes, 'I began my travels, where I purpose to end them, viz. at the city of London.'

In the *Tour* Daniel is overwhelmed by the spread of buildings and people in the capital and his inability to describe the problems confronting the metropolis. The difficulties seemed insurmountable. How was this population to be fed? How was the excrement and detritus to be removed? How were the bodies to be disposed of?

In the struggle for human survival it was important to take what was needed when the opportunity arose. But others were at that game. The streets were dangerous and exciting. The parish of St Giles, where his immediate family home was situated in Swan Lane, was part of a maze of narrow alleyways which intertwined with the broader thoroughfares of the City. It was a dangerous and diseased place in which to live. When some eighty years later the author Henry Fielding, acting as a London magistrate, sought to enforce the law in London, it was in Cripplegate that the citizenry offered the least cooperation to his constables in their task of detecting thieves and villains and making arrests. Here, John Sheppard the extraordinary burglar and escapologist was arrested and placed in the St Giles' Round House, from which he was to escape.

Early in Defoe's life his family was confronted with religious persecution and the need to hide when public control over religious dissent was tightened. In August 1662, under the Act of Uniformity, Presbyterian pastors were ejected from their places of worship. The effects of dissent were severe. Under the Clarendon Code a failure to take an oath deprived dissenters of public office and places of education. It is known that Dr Samuel Annesley, the Defoes' family pastor at St Giles, Cripplegate, steadfastly ignored the constraints and was fined for breaches of them on many occasions.

It was a time when worship took place wherever it could be arranged, often in houses with lookouts, and there would be hurried departures through stairways and passages to the rear. Informers would spy for a reward. It was best to remain silent about what was important; secrecy and subterfuge were desirable. People who compromised their convictions and returned to the Church of England could mitigate these religious fears, but then they feared punishment by God.

It was best to be meek and docile when confronted with the threat of arrest, but not everyone could be. In 1662 it was from their Meeting House in Swan Lane that the Fifth Monarchists rose up in 'the name of Jesus' to oppose the restored monarchy. They were bloodily put down, so 'confirming for any who doubted it that religious conformity would be enforced'.[36] Later, the Crown relaxed the enforcement of its powers to persecute but the powers themselves remained.

It was feared that the return of religious persecution could take the form of a foreign invasion that might result in Roman Catholicism. The consequences of such an invasion for dissenters like the Foes would have been horrific. This type of external threat could arrive quickly. In rapid succession came the Great Plague of 1665 and the Great Fire of London in 1666 which reached out to the the area where the Foe family lived, and then the Dutch navy sailed up the Thames to bombard English ships at anchor.

Daniel tells us little directly about his early memories, feelings and family relationships, but he is not silent about the Great Plague, for he wrote about it at length. The plague had been predicted. People had been warned to be godly but they behaved badly and had not learnt the error of their ways. In *Due Preparations for the Plague*, punishment is predicted for wrongdoers. The mother tells her son that, 'a plague might reduce the nation to a state of barbarity ... all will be filled with horror and desolation, everyone mourning for himself ... and a messenger sent from God to scourge us from our crying sins'. [37]

The greatest danger to Daniel, however, could have been from his own family. What happened in his childhood may well have made him the extraordinary person posterity knows him to be. Something traumatic may have happened to Daniel but the nature of it must remain conjectural.

On the face of it, all should have been well. James Foe was a devout Presbyterian. As such he would have believed the 'mother's' prediction of the plague. James would have believed it to be his duty to punish children for their wrongdoing, as he would have been punished. There is no reason to suspect that James Foe did not believe in the importance of family life, but by modern standards his understanding of what good family life was would have contained a punishing set of practices and values.

In a devout Presbyterian household there would have been family prayers twice a day, in the morning and evening, at which even children had to account for themselves and their sins, and then bear the punishment for their wrongdoing. On Sundays, when the Foes made their way secretly to a Meeting House for prayers, they went together as a family.

The Foes lived in crowded, cramped and very smelly premises, even though James was a reasonably prosperous merchant and could afford to pay for servants. In these crowded premises a well-schooled teacher might have been brought to the house to instruct the children. At that time, children would learn to read by studying the Bible and to write by copying it out. When they were punished, which may have been frequently, they copied out more pages. They were taught a little geography, history and the physical sciences. Later, if they were lucky, and male, they would receive some formal schooling.

It would have been an immense relief to escape from the house to play with other children, but then they would be called indoors for family evening prayers. When those had been said, it would have been off to bed while outside in the street life went on without you.

A family such as the Foes would have enjoyed three concentric support networks: the extended family and neighbours; the religious community, organised as a personal and social support agency; and the self-governing agencies of the City of London, which were open to the livery members of the Guilds. James Foe was a member of the Butchers' Guild.

Of the extended Foe family, little is known until the 1670s. Among the relatives not already mentioned was James's bachelor brother, Henry, who lived comfortably in nearby Barrs Street. In 1673 there was a bachelor, Thomas Foe, living in Bishopsgate and Defoe's aunt Jane lived in the City where her husband had a business. There may also have been other family members. When Robinson Crusoe was in London seeking money to enable him to go to sea, he raised £40 from his relatives, which suggests there were a number of them.

Religious dissenters, many of them merchants and traders, amounted to some ten per cent of the population of the City of London. They traded with each other and, with a self-confidence bred from success, supported each other. Daniel would have encountered many of James Foe's business friends and acquaintances. The Foes may have been acquainted with the powerful traders and merchants of the City of London. These men had provided monarchs and administrations with the money needed to sustain their power. In doing so, they had earned a measure of independence from the government, and indeed in important respects the Guilds were self-governing. Members had the right to vote in parliamentary elections. They had funded the republican side in the Civil War and, despite efforts by the Stuarts to bring them to heel, they never came over to the royalist cause. Without the financial support of the City, no foreign war could be waged successfully and civil administration would grind to a halt. It was a proud thing to be a Citizen of London.

Industry and commerce were booming, overseas trade expanding and fortunes could be made any day of the week; the Stuarts had brought back colour, fashion, riches and personal scandal to the capital, and breathed new life into the arts. Technology and scientific enquiry flourished as never before, so why could not a clever lad like Daniel Defoe be assured that he would enjoy a prosperous and happy future?

All was not well. It might have been said that, 'Something is rotten in the state of Denmark.' Defoe's world was grossly unjust. Great wealth existed cheek by jowl with dreadful poverty; the social class system was rigid and restrictive, despite some movement among the classes. The poor could witness the rich at play in all their proud array of perfume and powder, bewigged and gartered, but they could not join them. While the prosperous merchant could buy his way to privilege, position and a vote in national affairs, it was always a passage for the few; while for women, powerless and disfranchised, there was hardly ever a chance of advancement unless through a good marriage.

Within families all was not well. Imbalances of power existed: from master to mistress or servant, and in the absence of the master, between female carers and children; between elder sons, who were privileged and would inherit, and younger siblings; and between brother and sister. Social historians argue that as one goes back in time the existence of abuse is greater and at the turn of the eighteenth century as much as eighty per cent of families would have experienced serious abuse.

Claire Tomalin has written of the attempts of Samuel Pepys to seduce his wife's female servants and his indignation when his rights to do so were challenged. Recent studies show, however, that the female head of a household was and is the principal source of abuse within the family, especially in the absence of the 'master' and when she herself feels abused.

To suggest, therefore, that there is much in Daniel Defoe's life as it is known, and in his writing, which suggests he was the victim of sexual abuse from the guardians responsible for his care, is not a wild conjecture: it is more likely than not to have been the case.

*   *   *

In 1665 it was Uncle Henry who helped the Foe family flee from London during the Great Plague. Defoe was four years old. He did not return, except for trips during school holidays, until ten years later when a decision about his future was required. Uncle Henry is the narrator of *A Journal of the Plague Year*. Henry was a saddler living where HF, the fictional narrator, lived. HF refers to his elder brother and his family, with their house and storehouse in Swan Alley, where it is known James Foe and his family lived.

HF narrates that his elder brother had moved out of town to relatives in the countryside and this is where Frank Bastian produces evidence of finding Daniel Defoe. HF says:

'I was surprised that when I came near my brothers house which was in a Place they call Swan Alley, I met three or four women with high-crowned hats on their heads ... as I came to the gate I saw two more hats come out of the yard ... when I looked towards the warehouse there were six or seven more ... fitting themselves with hats as unconcerned and quiet as if they had been at a hatters shop buying for their money.'[38]

This account does not have the feel of invention. Neither do HF's reports of incidents in and around Swan Alley, which read like real stories told by neighbours to those returning. HF's anecdotes, such as the housewife washing herself with vinegar to ward off the plague, and shopkeepers washing small coins in vinegar before they would be accepted, might have been fictionalised, but they are just the type of recollections that might be expected from a small boy.

In the years following the Great Plague, Defoe was educated in Dorking, Surrey. In Surrey, Daniel went to school reluctantly and perhaps not at all when he could avoid it. The Reverend James Fisher was the diligent and parsimonious teacher who ran this boarding school for boys. He was an elderly Independent minister who had been ejected from his living at the Rectory of Fetcham, to the north, in 1662.

It hurt and surprised James Fisher to be outside the broad skirts of Anglicanism. To himself, he defended his intellectual right to disagree with the church on points of doctrine, but it dismayed him that others had thought it necessary to punish him for them. When Cromwell had permitted it, his form of independence had been tolerated within the church, but under the Restoration there was no room for independent dissent. In some ways he was more Anglican than the Anglicans and while in his teaching he stressed the close study of the Bible, he rarely departed from the truths he had lived by over a long life.

James Fisher was educated at Emmanuel College, Cambridge where he would have experienced a puritan ethos. It is known that he was a sophisticated and intelligent man. He bequeathed Latin and Greek primers and copious lecture and teaching notes.[39] His form of Calvinism, with its belief in predestination and Election for Salvation as one of a chosen few, may well have been a legacy of the puritanism he imbibed at Emmanuel. He may have passed these strong views on to his pupils.

The doctrine of predestination, as James Fisher taught it, became a life-long influence on Defoe.[40] In times of distress, Defoe never doubted that he would overcome his difficulties. God, through his providence, would punish but never abandon him.

James Fisher's students would have been sons of independent traders and merchants. His conscience demanded that he should do what he could for all the students in his charge. He instructed them in the basics of reading and writing. The Bible provided the basic texts in Latin and Greek. He also taught them history and geography and, for cultural reasons, some French.

Sometime in the late 1660s or early 1670s, James Fisher can be imagined compiling school reports. He had reached 'F' for Foe, which came before 'M' for Marsh, whose family had housed the young Daniel and who may have recommended Daniel to Mr Fisher. His problem was not what remarks to include but the many observations he might make which prudence suggested he should exclude.

Fairness required that he should acknowledge Daniel Defoe as a boy of exceptional intelligence, quick to absorb knowledge, with an enthusiasm for learning, and a rare ability to express himself orally and in writing. On the face of it, Daniel was well conducted and polite, but the appearance of civility belied wilfulness, obedience disguised wantonness, and compliance hid a strong propensity for waywardness. This was not a boy to be trusted unless your desire for his obedience coincided with his firm conviction that it was in his interest to obey.

It can be imagined that worse observations might have been added. His attendance was irregular and unpredictable. Daniel had absented himself without notice or permission and had been known to abscond not only from school but also from home. Sometimes he had boarded at the school but it had caused disciplinary difficulties with other boys: he had been a bad influence. On occasions, the Marsh family had given him up to others for respite, and on others, he had been withdrawn when fees were not paid.

And yet, Daniel had been persisted with, and others championed his cause, for he was a most extraordinarily clever and articulate boy. Mr Fisher paused. And wicked, he thought. But then he decided not to write the words down.

Daniel spent many years in Surrey.[41] Bastian maintains that, following the flight from the Great Plague, he stayed there with members of the Marsh family, to whom Alice Foe may have been related, and attended James Fisher's school until he was sixteen years of age, and only then did he attend the Morton Academy for Dissenters in London.[42] Defoe does not write about the Great Fire or of the efforts of the City to rebuild, and the cost of it to Londoners. James Foe's taxes would have risen sharply and he would have grumbled at it.

It is common to make great play of the importance in Defoe's development of his higher education at Charles Morton's Academy for Dissenters. No doubt, if Defoe had attended the Academy for any significant period of time, or at all, it would have been of significance in his development. However, if he lodged and was educated in Surrey for up to ten years, his experiences there must have been of great importance also.

Biographers are fond of quoting Defoe to the effect that as a child he copied out the Pentateuch (the first five books of the Old Testament) at home for fear that it might be taken from his family as part of the religious persecution from which they suffered. It is far more likely that Defoe did the copying in Surrey as a punishment for wrong-doing, or as a normal part of an education which used copying out the Bible for religious education and for practising writing, and that no religious persecution was involved.

There are only two important differences between a protestant bible, such as the 'Geneva' Pentateuch, and the authorised King James version. First, the 'Geneva' version might contain homilies and guidance to readers, as do evangelical versions of the Bible today, and secondly, it includes the Apocrypha, beloved of Roman Catholics and incongruously maintained by the protestants of Defoe's time. It was not likely that dissenters would 'go to the stake' for either.

Today, a journey to London from Dorking is lightly taken, but not in 1670. Such a journey in Daniel Defoe's time would have required a horse and, perhaps, a carriage, which if not his own would have to be paid for. While, no doubt, Defoe would have returned to the Foe household in Cripplegate from time to time, a boarding-out in Dorking would have appeared to him as banishment. Allegiance and loyalty to the accommodating household might well have been lacking.

Daniel may have been banished for his own good: fresh air, better accommodation and access to a basic education at an affordable cost. He may have been got rid of, however, because he was a nuisance or not wanted. In any event, Daniel knew he had to make his own way in life. It was never possible for him to succeed in following James Foe. Defoe's illegitimacy made it improbable that he could inherit James Foe's estate, and even if illegitimacy were not an issue, his father's estate would go to his elder brother.

Throughout Defoe's lifetime there was always a mother figure in the Foe household who could have argued the case for a child inheriting: but not his mother, and not him. Daniel was on his own and would have felt his plight keenly. He would have felt excluded, cast away, and with a need to make his own living.

What did boarding-out in Surrey do to the character of the young Defoe? It may well have contributed to, if not created, the violent behaviour of which there is some evidence. Bastian suggests that accounts of boorish and violent behaviour in Dorking, in Defoe's *A Tour Through The Whole Island of Great Britain*, are of Daniel's own actions as a boy. It is further suggested that the making of explosions mentioned there was a lifetime obsession for Daniel and that these 'Dorking incidents' are used elsewhere in his fictions.[43]

Others are more sceptical. Novak maintains that these accounts, although they use the first person 'we' in describing the London boys who did these deeds, are not conclusive evidence of Defoe's involvement in violence or of his youthful behaviour in general.[44]

However, there is anecdotal evidence of violence in Daniel's make-up and in his writings. Bastian[45] suggests that when Daniel Defoe was twenty years old and in France, it is certain that he fought a duel and it is probable that he killed a man. There is good evidence from his *Review* that he repented a duel,[46] but Bastian's principal fictional source, *The Memoirs of Majr. Alexander Ramkins*, is no longer attributed to Defoe.[47] We know that Defoe carried a sword and there are anecdotal accounts of him demonstrating his willingness to use it when threatened. There are also duels elsewhere in his fiction.[48] Notably, there is a rumour of his supposed duel with the publisher Nathaniel Mist.[49]

If his family rejected Daniel, can it be conjectured that this created his life-long restlessness? Like Defoe himself, his fictional characters, Captain Bob in *Captain Singleton* and Colonel Jack, are people on the move. Their childhood fate was to live day to day, from one carer to another, home to home, parish to parish, until they were on their own. They had lives of ill repute while maintaining a mask of respectability. In the end, they were fugitives from the law.

Daniel tells readers that he was in other places in his childhood, within easy reach of London, where the associations were to be life-long: Harwich and Ipswich, when he was eight years of age: perhaps Colchester and Tilbury. In Harwich, at some time during the Dutch war,[50] he claims to have seen, '100 sail of men of war and their attendants, and between three and four hundred sail of colliers in the harbour'. Maybe he was moved from household to household and place to place at the convenience of adults. If he was obnoxious he might have outworn his welcome too often for his own comfort.

At some time it must have become rooted in young Daniel's mind that the ultimate escape and refuge was to be at sea. At some time in his young life he came to regard the sea as a passage to riches, but it also came to be an image of the testing of God's purpose, in the fear and destruction of an Atlantic storm.

In the *Journal of the Plague Year* the great sailing ships are berthed upstream, away from the infection. They cannot trade, for their entry into foreign ports is blocked for fear of the disease. HF watches them as Defoe must have done at other times when wishing to trade or to evade his pressing creditors, and finding that he could do little for lack of resources.

However, there are other explanations for Daniel's attraction to the sea and to ships. What did going to sea as a sailor really mean to the young Daniel? Robinson Crusoe tells his readers, 'It was my great misfortune that I did not ship in all these adventures I did not ship myself as a sailor.' He could have worked himself up from an ordinary sailor to a master, but as he needed to retain the appearance of a gentleman he bought himself into a venture at sea. In *Captain Singleton* there was no prospect of starting in a position of equality. Bob fell in with a master. Daniel writes, 'I would have called him father, but he would not allow it, for he had children of his own.'

There are sexual connotations to this. Bob/Daniel was in the care of a man who did not wish to be a father to him but a 'master' and Bob wanted to become a 'master' himself. Bob went to sea as an ordinary seaman but he never lost his gentility. Although the ship's crew was debauched, Bob remained untouched. In the end he was to become a master. Jack in *Colonel Jack*, was a young rascal but the bystanders could see that he was a gentleman. Jack was shipped overseas as a slave to Virginia, but he is not to be pitied, for soon he is enslaving others.

At some time during puberty Defoe realised that he was homosexual. Later in this biography his adult homosexuality is proved beyond doubt, but it was a sexual orientation he discovered in his youth. The eighteenth century gave the term a different meaning to our own times. Sexuality was romanticised. A man could assert his power over others by sexual acts, whether they were women or men. Early in Daniel Defoe's life this behaviour was accepted but unlawful.

In the Foe family ran a tendency for men to remain bachelors and to place themselves in places and occupations where casual same-sex might well have been the norm. These men would often have been in situations where they could demand sex or pay for it. Other bodies could have been sought in shared beds in wayside inns and bought and sold in the streets. Daniel came to accept his sexual orientation and to express it.

Homosexuals starting out in life from a middle class social position, a social standing that Robinson Crusoe was advised to secure for himself, needed to consider what occupations might be taken up. How could he be true to his sexual orientation and evade the punishment of the law? He could become a priest, preferably a Roman Catholic priest, but as a dissenter that was a big leap. He could become a soldier, as his elder brother before him, but then soldiering was very dangerous. He could go to sea. There were lots of ways of doing this. A ship could be bought for the purposes of a merchant adventure. If such adventurers were willing to take risks they might become rich. Then they could buy a 'protection' or a peerage. The law could not reach them if they did. What these young men could not do very easily, whatever others might say, was to stay on the middle ground. The advice Robinson Crusoe was given by his father was impossible to accept: there was no 'protection' on the middle ground.

In reading the character of Daniel Defoe there are always conflicts between suppositions which, at their most compelling, are not based on fact. This is true for Daniel whichever way the biographer turns. It is difficult not to conclude that the young Daniel must have had a difficult upbringing. However, it must be accepted that a simple reading from his fiction could be misleading.

That said, the evidence in his writing of a disturbed family background is compelling. It has been argued that there are stages in adult treatment of children through the ages: infanticide, abduction and direction being the earliest. In London at the close of the seventeenth century all these primitive stages were on display. Early in the morning, when the mist had cleared from the Thames and the tide had ebbed, the bodies of drowned and unwanted babies could be discovered washed onto the mudbanks. When a child was unwanted it might be put into the care of the parish and given to a carer. Research suggests that fewer than one in four of these children survived their infancy.

This lack of care for the young haunts Daniel's fictions. In *Captain Singleton* the central character, Bob, whose story is told from infancy to young manhood, is abducted when very young. Daniel writes, 'My good gypsy mother, for some of her worthy actions no doubt, happened in the process of time to be hanged ... I went to a parish school, and the minister of the parish used to talk to me to be a good boy.' Bob led a wandering life without roots in family life. Defoe writes:

'I believe I was frequently removed from one town to another, perhaps as the parishes disputed my supposed mother's last settlement. Whether I was so shifted by passes, or otherwise, I know not.'[51]

In *Colonel Jack,* the callousness is no different. Defoe writes:

'my nurse [acting for the Parish] told me my Mother was a Gentlewoman, that my father was a Man of Quality [... my Nurse] had a good piece of Money given her to take me off his Hands ... My Father gave more [to ensure that he] be put to school'.[52]

And then he was enticed away to sea.

Education is rudimentary in Defoe's fictions. In *Captain Singleton,* Bob had a country education. He acquired a master, learnt some Latin and then began to steal. Defoe writes, 'I was diligent indeed, but I was very far from honest which, by the way was their very great mistake.'[53]

Lack of care for the young usually results in their criminal delinquency. In *Colonel Jack,* Defoe writes:

43

'I got some reputation, for a mighty civil honest Boy; for if I was sent on an Errand, I always did it punctually and carefully, and made haste again; and I was trusted with any thing, I never touch'd it to diminish it, but made it a Point of Honour to be punctual to whatever was committed to me, tho' I was as Errant a Thief as any one of them in all other Cases.' [54]

In *Captain Singleton,* by piracy and merchant activity, chicanery, gallantry and comradeship, Bob twice made a fortune and on the first occasion lost it. The reader is in little doubt that he will quickly lose it again.

For those not willing to concede Daniel a troubled childhood, it is arguable that there might be a simpler explanation for any problems he may have had with his home life: the severity of a Presbyterian upbringing at that time. A young rebellious boy might have hated religious ritual and sought excitement and danger in roaming the streets to the distraction of responsible parents. In the alleyways there were the dangers of abduction, as in *Captain Singleton;* of thievery, as in *Colonel Jack,* and of violence and death, as in *Moll Flanders.*

However, it is now known that Defoe's childhood was in the main not spent on the streets of London but in leafy Surrey lanes. If he was not back in London before the age of sixteen, his sexual orientation would in all probability have been determined by then.

Although Daniel's childhood must have contained daunting experiences it must also have included much that was reassuring. It would have become apparent to him that he was cleverer than other people. His education might well have been of variable quality but he had found the keys to go on informing himself about his world. He must have discovered and improved his natural ability to explain himself verbally and in writing. There was another side to his verbal dexterity: he became able to deceive and manipulate those around him. Daniel developed the power of observation; there were secrets to discover and things to hide. A life on the move had its excitements and fed a sense of adventure. It produced self-confidence and resilience.

If it is likely that these writings are 'autobiographical' then it is also likely that the memory of the incidents in them is distorted and not to be considered as the literal truth. Defoe's narrative suggests the effects of trauma and the recollection of events from his childhood. Leigh Gilmore has shown the distorting effects of trauma on memory and recall and its reinforcing nature. [55] Traumatic experiences repeat themselves. The mind is compelled to revisit psychic wounds. Each visit reinforces the trauma. It is unchallengeable that Defoe experienced deep trauma in his adult life, for example, frequent arrest and imprisonment, as this book will discuss. Bastian, also, draws attention to traumatic repetitions in Defoe's writing. Defoe gives his readers two other versions of the famous scene when Moll Flanders robs a small child of a necklace but resists the temptation to kill her.

It can be added that nightmares, daydreams, fantasies and fictions can be seen as compromises which in more or less distorted fashion express both our desires and defences against them. Lesser has suggested that in fiction, 'Our desires are chiefly satisfied by subject matter, our defences by form.'[56]

Revisits to traumatic sites by Defoe are accompanied by a degree of masochism. Backscheider has traced thirteen times when Defoe spent time in prison. A puritan conscience may have demanded that sin or waywardness be punished and that without it there could be no redemption. It is possible to conclude that Defoe could have avoided some of these imprisonments: on some occasions he appears to have sought them out and gained relief by shutting himself away.

It is sometimes conjectured that the rational, reasoning factor of the mind is lost when trauma is revisited. Behaviour becomes unpredictable and extreme. A loss of control occurs in all Defoe's crises; there is a pattern to his distress and a seeming inevitability. Control over irrationalities can be gained by success, worldliness, money and status which, even if temporary, will act as antidotes to psychic wounds, and the greater the need, the greater the ambition. Fame and the recognition of authority are exciting and can be romanced, invented and acted out, but like all imagined worlds they are not places of abode.

Adler has shown that feelings of inferiority or shame can be compensated for by their opposites, superiority and self-praise; few could accuse the adult Defoe of lacking a sense of superiority.

In Defoe's writing the reader is confronted with a confusing dichotomy between an 'ideal' world, which is justified in rational terms, and which has a religious and moral dimension, and the dark, anarchic irrationalities of the world that his fictional characters inhabit. This contradiction is present in all human experience, but in Defoe's work the contrast is stark. For him the contradiction is multi-dimensional: he appears to have created new selves to cope with severe traumatic experiences in his childhood. When pain and ignominy became too much to endure, Defoe dissociated his self and departed to other places and other selves.

The structure of control and management of the process is complex and unstable. It appears that the adult Defoe could function in what would seem to others to be a thorough-going, purposeful and integrated way (and with great determination) by having many subsystems which, it appears, operated independent of a controlling self. Like an actor he was capable of performing contrasting roles with equal conviction; but, unlike one, he lived out these roles in everyday life. Thus his self-identity was, in some sense, an illusion. The characters of his sub-systems had as much, or greater, reality as the outward appearance he gave to the world; and he invented their daily discourse in his writing to the bafflement of those seeking to explain their numerous contradictions.

In modern jargon Daniel Defoe might be described as schizoid. If as a young man he had been subjected to psychiatric examination, it might have been predicted that at some time in his life he might experience severe psychiatric problems and mental breakdown.

Defoe's complex psychology is a consequence of a taxing childhood. I have hinted at some of the possibilities. I recognise that my suggestions and conjectures will be controversial, but they explain the facts of Defoe's life. As Defoe's story unfolds in these pages, the reader will come to understand that the conventional pieties used by biographers to explain Defoe's life are highly misleading.

What I am arguing for is the recognition that Defoe's childhood contained pain, squalor and ignominy and that when it became too much he 'left it behind' and tried to dissociate himself from it by departing to another place. All his life he did this, to the confusion of friend and foe. This assertion is not a psychological absurdity, rather it demonstrates the extent to which the human mind can adapt in order to survive.

The reader of Defoe's fiction is moved by compassion for the pathetic fates of his characters. The reader senses that many of them have uncertain futures; they wander on to the stage of life and then – as we come to care about them – vanish without any explanation whatsoever. Readers want them to survive, as Robinson Crusoe survives, to conquer their fears and difficulties and to triumph in the end, for they, the readers, in their own way, may have suffered like the characters – but then they are disappointed, for Defoe's characters, their purpose served, have disappeared.

Chapter 3

Growing Up

E're Science was, or Learning had a Name,
Dilated Memory recorded Fame:
'Twas long before Forgetfulness was born.

Daniel Defoe, 1691

GOOD TAVERNS WERE RARE in Chadwell St Mary, Essex in 1678 but they thought it worthwhile to celebrate, this young lad Daniel Defoe and the older man who accompanied him. It was not every day of the week that a boy of sixteen bought a long lease on a valuable piece of land, albeit fit only for the grazing of sheep and the growing of a little corn. It appeared from their conversation that he planned to lease the land for something more than the mortgage payment and that if all went well he would have a regular income from the transaction. Despite their way of speech, which carried a London accent, they were not inhibited in the ale they drank, which was understandable, given the occasion.[57]

The young Defoe must have had adult allies in life. Uncle Henry may well have been one. Henry died in 1675 after a long and painful illness. So far as is known, Henry was a bachelor. He left his estate to his brother James Foe. Its value is unknown. Henry Foe, knowing he was dying, may have made some provision for his nephew: perhaps money for his education and land in Tilbury and elsewhere.

If so, the event must have been immensely reassuring and exciting for Daniel because it would have transformed his prospects. Daniel would have been around the age at which a decision needed to be made about whether he entered into trade, like his father, or trained for a profession. In *Robinson Crusoe* the father wanted his son to train for the law.

What actually happened to Daniel, as with Crusoe, was that no decision was taken at that point. It is said that Daniel started a course of formal education at Charles Morton's Academy for Dissenters in Stoke Newington around this time and that he was destined to become a minister by completing a divinity course. The evidence for this is to be found in Daniel's own words, in particular his defence of these colleges when they were attacked by Samuel Wesley as a hotbed of republicanism and for the addiction of its students to immoral, salacious and non-Christian literature. However, when the continued existence of these colleges was threatened by the Schism Act in 1713, Defoe thought it a matter of little consequence. He did not send his sons to one.

For the biographer there are dangers in accepting Defoe at his word. Throughout his life he re-invented himself: he was a specialist in re-writing curriculum vitae. The biographer eagerly explains that dissenters were excluded from Oxford and Cambridge because they were unwilling to profess their commitment to the Anglican Church and had to resort to establishing their own colleges of further education: colleges with high standards of teaching which were open to new ideas. All of which is true. Thus, the existence of these colleges comes to exemplify religious persecution and its consequences. And Defoe, when he became a controversial journalist after 1704, was anxious to defend himself against allegations that he was ill-read and poorly educated and talked up his own education.

If it is assumed that Daniel's central characters are real life figures the evidence, such as it is, suggests that the young Daniel sought a more exciting life than that of a divinity student. In *Colonel Jack* the 'three Jacks' and cousin Will were on the streets in their teens. When the four of them had been active for some time and were getting into more serious crime, Defoe writes that, 'Will was about twenty and as for me /Daniel, I was now about eighteen.' Soon after Colonel Jack/Daniel claims that for twenty-six years he was engaged in trade and commerce every bit as immoral in its practices as activity on the streets. In terms of Daniel Defoe's life, this would take him to 1704/5 when it could be claimed that he was off the street and fully engaged in political journalism.

Accounts in other Defoe fictions place the young Daniel as seeking to trade in the period 1676 to 1684 by investing in merchant ventures involving trips abroad. Bastian has traced mentions of locations abroad in Defoe's fiction which suggest a detailed knowledge of places in France, Portugal, Spain and Italy. Backscheider thinks that he may have taken up an apprenticeship with a relative in London.

Defoe does not assist the biographer in any way because he is silent about what he was doing in his youth, even in his fiction. He did not wish readers to know about his activities, except in passing, in this period. Nothing that he might have written would have profited him later.

It is difficult for the literary-minded to accept that he did not have a demanding exposure to an institute of further education. In his writings can be traced an acquaintanceship with the Classics, the work of contemporary philosophers and scientists, and an appetite for information about the scientific, technological and industrial discoveries and processes of his time. How could Defoe have developed the conceptual frameworks needed to comprehend his world without a formal and high quality education?

The probability is that all these conjectures are correct in some way and that he may have ventured into the various fields suggested to him, including higher education, but that he settled for none of them.

Whether Daniel Defoe truly valued a period of full-time education, or whether he was swept up emotionally in matters more important to him at the time, is a matter for conjecture, as the poem quoted above (composed for

John Dunton's *The Athenian*) appears to show. However, the excitement of starting formal education might have been the occasion for Daniel to begin to formulate a religious and political philosophy of his own. There must have been a juncture somewhere between childhood and adulthood when the young Daniel realised that every action had a consequence, not only in the abstract, or even as something witnessed in the street, but for him personally.

In a sense, Daniel had relied on providence, and the feeling that God had chosen him, for his security. But there came a moment when he realised that God was not entirely to be relied upon in a world where the strong and the greedy grabbed what they could regardless of whether they really needed it, while the weak and the deprived were punished for their sins by hunger, disease and the gallows.

For Colonel Jack/Daniel, pursuing a life of crime as a young villain, the epiphany came with the realisation that theft was a capital crime and that his brother and his friend were about to be killed by an avenging society. The realisation that crime was wrong did not turn Jack away from wrongdoing, although sympathy for the wronged led him to occasional repentance and retribution. Jack was able to displace himself from the scene of the crime but not the crime itself. The camera panned on, he was there and he benefited, but was he really the perpetrator? It would be better to live a virtuous life, to be at ease before the Lord. And then the reader hears the last cries: it was 'necessary', all men are entitled to live, and then there were the rewards of crime. Be reasonable in your judgement; everyone, rich or poor, was at it and in truth there was no real difference between the robber in the street and the market speculator. Perhaps some were worthy and virtuous men despite their delinquency, and was not he entitled, as any other, to the riches of the earth, to worldly recognition?

Alas, it was necessary for Daniel to be a sinner in this life. But then, as he writes, he would be penitent and call to mind things past and 'as Job says, to abhor [himself] in dust and ashes'.

All this does not amount to a moral philosophy. To sin, man must first be willing to abandon virtue. To Daniel, virtue was best surrendered by a philosophy of non-resistance. Faith must be retained, which it was believed would save men in the end, and then men might glide almost imperceptibly into sin, offering the minimum of resistance. Lord save me from sin, but not yet! In a noble or righteous cause, and there was no end to righteous causes, there was believed to be no sin committed at all. For the rich and powerful some sins could be avoided but there was no virtue in it, and for the powerful there were no petty crimes at all.

The question of God's forgiveness remained, however. It would be best to take no chances. Daniel writes, 'in collecting the various changes and turns of my affairs, I saw clearer than ever I had done before how an invisible over-ruling Power, a hand influenced from above, governs all our actions of every kind, limits all our designs, and orders the events of everything relating to us'.

All the young men of Charles Morton's academy at Newington Green believed themselves to be sinners. Most, but not all, were dissenters who were habituated to a daily struggle. They beseeched God to help them in heartfelt prayers twice a day. They truly repented. Many wished to become ordained ministers and dedicated themselves to biblical studies and moral philosophy.

Some teaching timetables of Charles Morton's academy have survived so it is possible to form some notion of what was taught. Lessons were conducted in English rather than Latin and a wide range of subjects were read: geography, history and politics as well as science. Novak quotes Edward Calamy who said of Morton, 'He had indeed a Peculiar Talent, of winning Youth to a love of Vertue and Learning, both by his Pleasant Conversation, and by a familiar Way he had of making difficult Subjects easily Intelligible.'

Morton encouraged rhetoric and debate both as teaching methods and in the belief that it was in the contrasting of opposites that truth could be revealed. In this he seems to have anticipated the Hegelian dialectic with all its virtues and limitations. In Morton's approach an emphasis was placed on plain English and coherent argument, virtues which we find in Defoe at his best.[58]

Charles Morton was the only principal and teacher at his academy and when he was absent, which may have been frequently, older pupils took lessons. Thus the academy had all of Charles Morton's virtues and limitations and, while he was no doubt learned in much, it is difficult to conclude that he was master of everything.

This loose teaching regime must have permitted and tolerated absence. The whole of London, with all its temptations and excitements, was on the doorstep. These young men must have spilled out on to the streets of London to add their voices and presence to the disturbances of the time.

Morton was subject to religious persecution and in the end had to flee both his academy and the country to avoid it. (He fled to America where he became Vice-President of Harvard College.) It is widely assumed that persecution is always unjustified, which in important ways it is, but the fragile compromises of the Restoration were no proof against teaching and practice that was revolutionary in intent.

At their best the dissenting academies offered sound instruction and encouraged a spirit of enquiry. Lord Harley, who entered such an academy as a dissenter, left it as an Anglican while remaining a puritan. He was then able to fulfil the family expectations of a role as a parliamentary man and practice politics at the highest level of State, to the benefit of the commonweal. At their worst, the academies bred intolerance, self-righteousness and social turbulence.

If Daniel attended the Academy it seems likely that the virtues of wide-reaching inquiries into the meaning of things, and the inculcation of the spirit of enquiry fostered by Morton, encouraged his obsessive life-long interest in the mechanics of an emerging mercantile and manufacturing society, and in the processes by which men, in advancing their own material interests, in becoming gentlemen, could advance a wider social good which would in its turn legitimise the activity.

The Morton Academy trained pupils for a divine ordination within the dissenting community. If Daniel attended the Academy for the purpose of becoming a dissenting minister, it is clear that he failed. Perhaps it was a matter of whether he had a vocation, or it may have been his conduct in general that caused him to fail. By some process, it was determined that he was not to continue on that course. Given that he went on to preach and earn money from a ministration of sorts, it might have not been a decision of his, but of his elders.[59] Defoe's own words tend to support rejection by others. He writes that he was, 'first set-apart for, and then…set-apart from the Honour of that Sacred Employ'.[60]

Samuel Wesley, in attacking Morton's conduct at his Academy, criticised him for a revolutionary bias in favour of a republic in his teaching of political science. It is thought that in a pamphlet entitled 'Eutaxia', not now extant, Morton argued in favour of a Commonwealth. Wesley criticised the dissenting academies in general for fomenting anti-monarchical views. What Morton may have been guilty of is encouraging thought on forms of government, which might, in a loosely organised institution, have led to students expressing themselves freely on the political issues of the day. For Samuel Wesley it could not be the purpose of a college of divinity to add to the political and religious tumult of the times. Wesley believed that such thoughts, and the activities they prompted, endangered freedom of religious expression itself.

Wesley, in attacking licentiousness at the Morton Academy, criticised the practice of students reading and circulating sexually explicit and pornographic poems by Rochester and others, and of lampoons in imitation of them. This is a charge which seems valid, for it is known that Defoe became a fervent admirer of Rochester at this time and sought to imitate his writing.

To be at a dissenting academy was, for most students, a statement of their identity or, more precisely, their parents': not only that one belonged to London's mercantile and trading community with a daily interest in the making of money, but that one was distinguished and justified by one's works, and had a commitment to being useful. Greek and Latin, although taught, were to be regarded as languages of a dead past and of contemporary classes of men who lived idle lives on their estates and whose daily conversation was designed to dazzle and deceive.

Liberty is an intoxicant. It was difficult to persuade those whose families enjoyed the freedoms of the City of London to govern themselves free from the tyranny and governance of kings, to limit their personal liberty to dissent from established views on religion or personal behaviour.

The grandfathers, fathers and uncles of these pupils had served in armies raised by men like them for the very same causes of political, religious and economic freedom. At the last, they had been willing to condone regicide and the beheading of a monarch. They had founded a republic and were surprised and saddened by its loss. Neither the republic nor the compromises of the Restoration had given them any absolute guarantee of the freedoms they sought.

These young men believed that it fell to them and to their generation to secure these freedoms. If these tasks could be achieved without bloodshed, so be it, but if not, they would be gained by the sword. Those who stood to be replaced by revolutionary change were not supplicants for mercy; they recognised their enemies and were willing to strike the first blows that their power, seemingly, gave them liberty to do.

The dissenters felt themselves as being the vanguard of a movement that would sweep away an unwelcome regime. It is a hallmark of revolutionary movements that those on its radical wing regard themselves in such a light, and this is where Defoe positioned himself.

It did not make him a republican. The evidence is that he was always in favour of a monarchy so long as this guaranteed a protestant succession that was responsive to its citizens and accountable to parliament. Daniel traced monarchical legitimacy back to the Tudor stand against the Papacy and foreign powers that sought the cover of a Roman Catholic allegiance to threaten the liberties and commercial interest of the realm.

These views, or more particularly the willingness to uphold them on the streets of London, had consequences. In Daniel's lifetime he was vulnerable to the charge that the logic of his arguments was to surrender to the mobs on the street and that, in claiming to speak for 'the people', he threatened the very legitimacy he claimed for his assertions.

It is the nature of the radical left that it claims a monopoly of an ideological truth. For Daniel this ideology was rooted in the Old Testament he imbibed from a Presbyterian upbringing. In modern times in Great Britain the cry of 'No surrender' has been limited to the streets of Northern Ireland. In England, in Daniel's adult life, this cry did not lose its potency until after the defeat of the Pretender in 1715 and the confirmation of the Hanoverian succession.

Daniel's positioning of himself as a spokesman of the dissenting minority was no doubt genuine. It might also be true to suggest, however, that it gave him several advantages he was anxious to exploit. Dissenters were numerous in the urban financial and commercial centres of British life, in particular in the City of London. In the serious business of making money, which was so important to Daniel, dissenters recognised bonds to each other. They met in coffee bars and religious meeting places and in the markets and exchanges of a new and expanding economy. There was a communal bond that linked them across social boundaries, as with the Jewish communities which preceded them, and the Masonic lodges which were to open up shared privileges later

Throughout his life Daniel was to exploit his religious links with the dissenting community but its potency diminished in his lifetime. What did not diminish was Daniel's passion for the accumulation of wealth and the establishment of himself as a gentleman and a celebrity with a secure place at the tables of the mighty. It was this overwhelming desire, allied to an overweaning self-confidence and a complex sexuality, that was to bring him down.

In fractured and feverish times when the impulse to change beats upon fragile social structures, it was rare to find a young man with an unalloyed set of values. While Daniel might have read Locke at the Morton Academy, for he professed an acquaintance with his 'systems', there would have been much that he loved and wished to emulate in a Court where the principals professed a belief in Hobbesian philosophy.

Thomas Hobbes was for a time a tutor to Charles II during his exile in France. Hobbes maintained that all human life was driven by fear towards pleasure or mere self-preservation and that the sole purpose of society was the securing of wealth, security and glory. Where mankind was left in a state of nature, Hobbes maintained there would be a 'war of all against all' which would lead to the aggrandisement of a strong leader. Hobbes argued that only the present existed in nature. Things past existed in the memory only; things to come did not exist at all.

Hobbes's advocacy of living for the present must have been appealing to the young revolutionaries at the Morton Academy. The thought that man could and should be governed by senses, desires and passions, and that there might be no supernatural punishment or reward, might have been abjured in theory but acted upon in practice.

Defoe was influenced also by Dryden and found in his work an acceptable endorsement of a form of psychological hedonism. Dryden wrote:

Happy the man, and happy he alone,
He who could call the day his own.
He who can secure within can say
'Tomorrow do thy worst, for I have lived today.'
Be fair, or foul, or rain or shine,
The joys I have possessed in spite of fate are mine.

Daniel was a romantic who passed through the world disguised by the mask of puritanism. Romanticism was not an outlook possessed only by Cavaliers: Cromwell had his troops of horse as well as the romanticised Prince Rupert. Daniel had a lifelong interest in piracy and a love of horse racing. He spent hundreds of hours riding horses. He imitated and admired the Court grandees and fops, including the Duke of Monmouth, who displayed themselves at the Newmarket races. Moreover, in his fiction, his portrayal in *Roxana* of a high-class courtesan showed his fascination with worldly display.

Whatever the childhood causes of Daniel's fears, it seems probable that if 'he was too clever by half' and obnoxious at the Morton Academy, he would have suffered for it grievously by some form of bullying. Throughout his adult life Daniel complained of threats to his life and physical safety. Many would have objected, to paraphrase the words of Disraeli to Gladstone, that they did not mind Daniel always producing a card from up his sleeve, but they did object to his belief that God had put it there. If he over-dressed while a student, as he did as an adult; if he was thought a fop, or something more provocative, he would have been mocked for it then as he was in his adult life.

His intelligence would have saved him from disaster; he would have sold something of it to others when papers or discourse were required of them. Words would have saved him. He would have honed his words and sharpened his mastery of rhetoric in rehearsal for what awaited him. He would have read and retained more than the average pupil. It is possible to read in Defoe's writings on education a belief that knowledge was in some sense a fixed quantity that you could acquire by diligence. All his life he endeavoured to fill the void, to know more, and more quickly, than others. Under threat he would have hoarded what he knew and oscillated between being centre stage and sulking in silence in the wings.

It is not known where he lived during these formative years when he was at the Morton Academy and who looked after him. It does not seem likely that he would have stayed at home, for he would have been subject to a governance he hated and female attention that was unwanted. If he boarded-out it would be a continuance of the practice he was used to in Surrey but with the added advantage to him of a licence to absent himself when he chose. He might have boarded with fellow students whose parents were known by his father. Daniel might have found advantage in lodging with children whose fathers were richer and more powerful than (or simply different from) his own.

The streets of London were paved with more than gold. Daniel's life was lived mainly on these streets and within a square mile of his father's starting point in Swan Lane. In these streets it seemed that all human life in its rich diversity could be found. Along its mighty waterway sailing ships from every part of the world could be seen and in the taverns of the Square Mile could be found their boarders: sailors from strange countries, with remarkable cargoes and tales to tell. Fortunes were won and lost in a storm and gambled away in mercantile adventures his father could not imagine, let alone practice. It must have gone to his head. What more could a master of fiction desire?

THE WHOLE WORLD
AT HIS FEET

1684 to 1692

Chapter 4

On The Loose

Presbyterians design nothing less than the ruin of the monarchy and our family ... For if His Majesty does not entirely submit to them and become less than a Duke of Venice, rebellion must follow.

James, Duke of York, 1679

THEY GATHERED IN THE Green Ribbon Club, where Shaftesbury and Buckingham had organised two parliamentary elections between 1679 and 1681, and in taverns throughout the City of London where dissenters were numerous. These elections had resulted in emphatic House of Commons majorities for the newly designated Whigs and frustration for isolated Tory minorities. Power, it seemed, had shifted but not, as it turned out, quite as had been imagined. At the Devil's Tavern kept by a Cromwellian veteran, it was said that the landlord was dubbed 'Scatter 'em' for his barroom prayer, 'Scatter 'em good Lord, scatter 'em'. The continuation of the rebellion was in the air but fear of the license and anarchy of the 'good old cause' was as strong as ever.

Undoubtedly, the times and the streets were dangerous. At the height of his powers it was said that Shaftesbury commanded ten thousand 'brisk Protestant boys', an impressive and fearful London mob. The leaders of the mob swaggered about the town with pistol and sword while the apprentices and working folk armed themselves with the fearful 'Protestant flail', a short lead-weighted cosh which, while it was small enough to be hidden in one's breeches, was a devastating weapon in a street brawl.

In the 1670s, it was the parliamentary conviction, despite the presence in the Commons of placemen and hirelings, that the king reigned by permission of parliament and that the monarch of the day must fully respect the rights of protestant succession to the throne. The Stuarts never accepted either proposition. Continuous conflict and a search for tactical advantage were the daily reality in Whitehall.

Civil conflict could not be contained in marbled corridors. In the streets of the capital a tide of action and reaction flowed across religious and political fault lines. It was not only dissenters who believed that Stuart monarchs retained their position by an alliance with Roman Catholics. It was true, and widely believed, that it was in the interest of Roman Catholic France, Europe's strongest military power, to seek to uphold Stuart absolutism. When parliament denied the Crown its supplies it was French subsidies and secret treaties that maintained royal pretensions.

Religious dissenters, some ten per cent of the capital's adult population, were the unfortunate victims of this feverish and desperate political struggle. In October 1678, the discovery of the body of Sir Edmund Godfrey, a London magistrate, had seemed to confirm accusations made by Titus Oates and Ezrel Tonge of a plot to murder Charles II, to result in a consequent massacre of protestants and an invasion of Ireland by France. Every day, for some months, the streets of London were awash with rumours and a hunger for news.

In 1680 the focus was on the exclusion of James, King Charles's brother, a Roman Catholic and heir to the throne, from the succession. The many compromises offered from the Crown were scornfully rejected. The opposition power was misused: Members were expelled from the Commons, 'delinquents' arrested throughout the country and judges impeached; militias and mobs ruled the streets. Feiling writes, 'An atmosphere of cruel panic – of plots, meal-tubs, Jesuits, and murder – brought back the worst days of 1641, and to breathe a word for the Crown was to brand oneself as a Papist.' Indeed, a Tory member exclaimed, 'tis purgatory to stand it'.[61]

Among those who gathered at the Green Ribbon Club, and in taverns and coffee bars throughout London, was Daniel Defoe. Daniel was one of the students, tradesmen and commoners whose task was to roam the streets of the City in search of Papists and to punish them with any weapon to hand. Defoe believed in the rumours of plots. He tells readers that he:

'frequently walked with [a Protestant flail] about me, and tho I never set up for a Hero yet when armed with this Scourge for a Papist, I remember I fear'd nothing…the very apprehension of it soon put an end to the Murthers and Assassinations, that then began to be practised in the streets'.

There is an obliquity and absurdity in Daniel's account. It is difficult to avoid seeing the young Defoe in the heart of a street gang feeding itself with the frenzy of rumour and seeking 'Papists' to assault. In today's Britain, we have seen similar activity on the streets of Belfast and similar claims and counter-claims played out with violence and mayhem.

While the allegation that there was a Popish plot was far-fetched, the fears of a Roman Catholic succession were real, and while Daniel's vivid and fertile imagination could have invented anything, religious persecution was not imaginary. Like the menace of the plague, persecution was a hidden menace that could strike the godly with devastating effect at any time.

At the beginning of the 1680s, the number of arrests and prosecutions for offences under the raft of legal discrimination from which dissenters suffered rose sharply as Anglican spies reported on illegal meetings and conventicles. It is estimated that up to 8,000 people were imprisoned for failure to pay fines on trumped-up charges and many good men, some of whom were known to Daniel, perished as a consequence of incarceration in primitive prisons.

One did not need to possess the imagination of Defoe to mourn them, nor his anger and righteous indignation, to wish to retaliate. Thousands awoke each day in the City of London to the possibility that today the authorities might strike at them, that this day might be their day of reckoning. And who would suffer first? As in all tyrannies, the first to go down would be the innocent, the godly and the good.

While all this was happening, the details of the period of Daniel Defoe's life between 1678 and 1680 (when in all probability he left the Morton Academy), and December 1683, when the license for his marriage was issued at St Bottolph's, Aldgate, in London, are largely unknown.

The young man loosed upon the world must in his own special way have been formidable. There is no portrait or description of him at this age but with the benefit of hindsight we might imagine a serious-minded person of average height and looks with an air of determination and possessed by a sense of rising self-confidence. He was hardly handsome, for he possessed a hooked nose and a large jaw, but he was purposeful. One might imagine him walking briskly, defying passers-by to ignore him. His very presence would have asserted a claim: I am as good as any man and, indeed, better.

The young Daniel would have been fluent in his speech which, while formal when required of him, would revert to the coarser language of the street. He wrote well in the plain style of the tradesman, but was experimenting as he read more widely. He had an untried certainty of self-definition arising from his dissenting background and membership of a Presbyterian elite. He wished to prosper and become a gentleman, although he scorned and reviled those who inherited the status.

Daniel must have approached the life that stretched before and around him as did Robinson Crusoe when surveying his island: he dreamt of foreign adventures and fighting for a glory greater than himself and of serving a mighty master for the common good and his own glorification. He was vainglorious and often well dressed, at least within his means, perhaps overly so, being bejewelled on some days.

He was opinionated and obstinate, although he borrowed most of what he declaimed, and formidable in any argument, with a penchant for claiming the last word.

Daniel would have had few friends, and those he possessed became so because they were swept along with the cohesion of a shared religious, political or financial passion, and then friends only so long as the passion lasted. He would have started to make enemies but it is unlikely that they were yet of great importance. Alone in his world, he would have claimed kinship and sought to use family ties for his advantage. He may have been admired but it is not likely that he was liked much, for he would have seemed jejune, on the make and unreliable.

Daniel often lost his temper and was bitter about those whose social position possessed the status and wealth he desired. When barbs or jibes were challenged by him, or criticisms tested, he would sometimes become violent. Ultimately, it is unlikely that he would have proved to be a reliable colleague or friend. He sulked and took refuge in solitariness and silence.

His singularity and intellectualism would have been immediately recognisable and, when given the opportunity of connection, the well-placed might have marked him out as a potential hand-maiden, while regarding him as a possible menace. In either of these two conjectures they would not have been wrong. For a time, they would have underestimated the young Daniel Defoe's ability to contribute to the revisionist cause in a turbulent age when anything that moved or was acted upon was subject to change and confusion. Many who sought to serve in some capacity would have been amongst those who observed him most closely and some would have thought him to be a potential ally.

Not everyone who noticed him would have wished to take a relationship any further. Few would have shared his religiosity and some who did would have been puzzled by his zeal and readiness to preach.

As a young man he must have been sexually active but he does not write directly of it. His intensity and interests in the unconventional, deprived and depraved would have made him disturbing and attractive to both men and women. He shared a common masculine attitude with men of position: a belief in entitlement and the right to assert their sexual needs on women by the exercise of power and money. Such claims were perhaps most easily forced upon servants, widows and the poor. In *Moll Flanders* and *Roxana*, Defoe explores these relationships.

This common attitude was combined with values arising from Defoe's puritanical religiosity which cast women, from the moment of temptation in the Garden of Eden, as the source of evil in the world and responsible both for sexual misdeeds and their social effects. Sexual relations with women were conceived of as perfunctory and compulsive acts for the satisfaction of male libidos and the raising of children: they were the fulfilment of necessary functions.

Daniel's own sexual practices included homosexual acts. Homosexual activity in his time was widespread, not only among a debauched aristocracy and a Court given over to joys of the flesh, but in masculine societies, clubs, coffee houses, aboard ships and on military campaigns. In his fiction Defoe alludes to these practices but does not write directly of them and, with certain exceptions, which Daniel admired, neither did other writers. In the 1680s homosexual practices were crimes, but there were few prosecutions and little or no homophobic rhetoric. In the 1690s and beyond, public opinion turned decisively against homosexuals and it became dangerous to be one.

Daniel's attitudes to women, marriage and children – apart from his conduct books which are a poor guide to his actual feelings – are peculiar and commonly misunderstood. In his writing women are seen as objects of exchange. There is a 'dryness' in his characterisation of women, and when the opportunities arise for expressions of passion and love he leaves his readers short. In seeming to argue a feminist case, Daniel never argues from a feminist position; he would prefer women to be more like him. He seems to regard women as 'substitute men' and he admires in them attributes and values that he wished for himself.

It is likely that between 1678 and 1680 Daniel made some sort of profit from trading and dealing and had travelled to Spain, Portugal, Italy, France and Germany; perhaps on his father's account and, where he could, on his own. He would have recorded his experiences and spoken of them with confidence and credibility.

By whatever means he would have sought to make some serious money, but then he may have lost it just as quickly through risky investment or speculation. He decided that although he did not like the prospect of marriage, he must obtain a wife, for it seemed that a substantial dowry was the only way to obtain the capital he needed to build a significant business.

Daniel married Mary Tuffley, the daughter of John Tuffley, a cooper, property owner and trader, of substantial means. The large dowry he obtained was used to build a business as a hosier in Freeman's Yard, but it might also have been used, even at this very early stage of his business life, to pay off debts.

How he managed to contract his marriage is a source of speculation. It is possible that he might have been introduced to the Tuffley family through his father. The source of information about the dowry of £3,700 (over £300,000 today) is Defoe himself, but he does not tell us about the jointure he had to set aside for the financial support of his wife should he die before her. Dowries were rising towards the end of the century, but so were jointures.[62] If Samuel Tuffley was good for the £3,700, was it probable that the young Daniel would be good for the jointure? In the event, he was not.

James and Daniel Foe's generations were not overly sentimental. Fathers anxious to marry off their daughters in a marriage market balanced in favour of men were apt to advertise their availability in the popular news-sheets of the time, as were men seeking fortunes. There must have been room for intermediaries who might make a quick profit on a successful transaction. Was the young Daniel Defoe one of them? Was he making some easy money while seeking his main chance?

At this stage Daniel had not chosen between directions which are considered now to be career options. He was a 'jack of all trades'. He preached in the dissenting cause, wrote and traded in anything within his reach which seemed to offer high rewards, and dabbled in political and religious activities at a time when to do so could imperil himself, his family and his friends.

In 1680, Daniel would have known something of the death from syphilis of John Wilmot, the Second Earl of Rochester. Rochester was a notable attendee at the Court of King Charles. He was a notorious rake, who did not discriminate between men and women, and a poet of considerable talent. His reputation as a rake and writer of obscene and sexually explicit verse fixed him in the public imagination.

Daniel was an admirer of Rochester. He copied his verse and wrote lampoons in his style. An admiration for Rochester did not necessarily single out Daniel as unique or extraordinary, for even the punctilious and prudent Lord Harley, who was certainly a puritan, was an admirer of Rochester. Henry Fielding in Shamela, his parody of Richardson's Pamela, has Mr B. accusing his heroine of reading Rochester's poems with enjoyment (the accusation being that she was no different from a man in seeking sexual titillation from them). In a manuscript held in the Huntingdon Library, in which Defoe records sermons of John Collins, are poems by him which, at least in the judgement of Novak, owe as much to Rochester as to Dryden.[63]

Daniel defended Rochester in public. In about 1721 he was believed to have written:

> Dorset and Rochester and those superior poets, who, as they conceived lewdly, so they wrote in plain English, and took no care to cover up the worst of their thoughts in clean linen; which scandalous custom has assisted to bury the best performances of that age, because blended with profaneness and indecency. They are not fit to be read by people whose religion and modesty have not quite forsaken them; and, which, had those grosser parts been left out, would justly have passed for the most polite poetry that the world ever saw.

This opinion would seem to miss the point: without their grosser elements much of their poetic output would amount to nothing at all.

In 1680 the nation was fascinated by Rochester for another reason. On his deathbed, when suffering from syphilis, he was said to have made a confession of his wicked ways and sought God's forgiveness. The evidence of this confession came from the Rev. Gilbert Burnet, 'a fashionable and ambitious confessor' who, like Rochester, was something of a nuisance at Court but without his entertainment value.

At this time, Burnet was thirty-six years of age and Chaplain to the Privy Council. It was said that he had warned Charles II against the evils of a dissolute life and that he told him that in another life he might be burned alive for his follies. The king's view was that while he lived Burnet would not dare to say anything, and when he was dead it would not matter what he said. When Charles II was dying, Burnet was deprived of his chaplaincy for preaching an anti-Catholic sermon and fled the country. He returned under William III and became the Bishop of Salisbury.[64]

On Rochester's death in July 1680, Burnet published an account of Rochester's confidences which became a phenomenal success. His pamphlet tapped into a large and well-established literature of conversion: of personal accounts of men on their deathbeds, regretting their evil deeds and crying to God for mercy.

As part of this literary genre there was a considerable market from the seventeenth century onwards for 'true confessions'. Among these were the confessions of prisoners at Newgate awaiting their deaths. The procurement of these confessions was in the hands of the Ordinaries of Newgate who were usually priests of the Church of England appointed to minister to the souls of the condemned, and who supplemented their modest income by inducing prisoners to confess. They then sold these confessions for profit to those with an interest in popularising them.

There was a limitless market on the streets of London for cheap pamphlets telling of these criminal confessions. Anecdotally, it is said that on more than one occasion, 'to his lasting regret', Defoe wrote and had published such confessions. If this is so, among these unknown pamphlets (which were almost certainly written anonymously) were the first recorded writings of Daniel Defoe. The suggestion here is that either Daniel served for a time as the Ordinary at Newgate, perhaps in 'emergencies', or that he bought rights to publish from one of them. It is difficult to accept the first of these alternatives because, of course, he was not an ordained priest of the Church of England; on the other hand, a 'Scarlet Pimpernel' may appear in many guises.

Why was he ashamed? An obvious cause would be that as a puritan he would have been ashamed of writing lurid and sensational 'biographical' accounts for profit. Perhaps if his authorship had been discovered, others would have been ashamed of him. If he had financed the publications he might have lost money or spent it before the printer was paid. His behaviour might have been immoral, in the light of puritan values. An Ordinary might have married prisoners when unqualified to do so. A woman prisoner could not be executed if pregnant and, of course, to avoid or put off execution she might become pregnant while a prisoner.

Following Burnet's publication of Rochester's confessions, sinners of another sort rushed Rochester's work into print and later in 1680 there appeared a collection of Rochester's poems entitled, *Poems on Severall Occasions by the Rt. Hon. The Earl of Rochester*. The Rochester family denied their authenticity and offered a reward for the identity of the miscreant. It was never collected.[65]

If Defoe wrote such pamphlets at this time (and it is probable that he wrote or contributed to such works later in his life) he might have made and lost considerable sums from doing so. It could have been money well spent, for at this time he would have been making a start in journalism and also in the arts of fiction and biography.

Rochester's confessions would have been of interest to Daniel for other reasons. There was competition for Rochester's soul (not least with the Devil, for his mother thought that her son was subject to the influence of the Devil through his friends). Burnet had sought to achieve a conversion which Rochester resisted. Rochester found refuge in a form of deism, to which Daniel would have been sympathetic. Burnet gave Rochester an Old Testament prophecy of the truth of the crucifixion and asked him to dwell on it. Parsons, his mother's chaplain, gave Rochester a reading of the 53rd chapter of Isaiah. Neither proselytiser seems to have succeeded. Parsons records that Rochester felt an 'inward force upon him' which enlightened his mind. Parsons concluded that Rochester had not become convinced of the truths of Christianity by reason. The truth of any confession made by Rochester is problematic. Rochester was slipping into insanity and was 'in no fit state to be convinced of anything'.

Without wishing to simplify the nature of Daniel Defoe's religious convictions at this time or later in his life, there was in him something more than the Lutheran belief in justification by faith and something less than the bold claim of Predestination or the heresy of Antinionism. Daniel seemed to believe that he was accompanied in life by a good spirit which afforded him a certainty of judgement in all the trying situations in which he found himself. In this conviction he seems to have had affinity with Rochester's dying conviction: that the Holy Spirit could and did come to him.

Others might think that a personal conviction that they had been chosen by God to be rather annoying, especially when it seemed to them that a virtuous life was not being led. For Defoe and, in the end, Rochester, however, a belief in the power of the Holy Spirit was a shield and a sword. It led Daniel to the practice of gospel preaching even though he was not ordained. Exactly when he started to preach is not known, but that he did so at intervals throughout his life is certain. It is claimed that he set up a dissenting place of worship in Tooting with Joshua Oldfield in the 1680s, or that he supported one by preaching there. There is local evidence in church histories and the use of street names which support these claims.[66]

In terms of Daniel's own religious beliefs, something has been made of him attending and recording the sermons which John Collins preached in London in 1681.[67] Novak makes the point that Collins's texts, 'involved advice to those who would go out to preach the gospel, and led to the idea of appealing to a sinner's sense of peace and contentment'. Collins believed that God desired to save sinners and had entered into a contract with all true believers to save those who lapsed into sin. It must have struck Daniel that sin did not condemn him. Collins believed (and it might be surmised that Daniel followed him in this) that if a sinner continued to have faith and belief in God, and if his religious observances were 'right', he would experience the power of the Holy Spirit in union with God and salvation would be his. This sort of belief is not far from asserting a claim that the Kingdom of Heaven remained a certain destination, even for the sinner, if there was faith.

It is wrong to imagine that Daniel's youth would have been taken up by mighty affairs of state and of religious controversy. It was far more likely that he was busy with the tasks that his upbringing and inclinations led him to believe were important aspirations in life: the serious business of making money, achieving respectability and becoming a gentleman.

Daniel's marriage to Mary Tuffley was a first step to achieving social as well as financial aspirations. Arguably, in contracting his marriage in an Anglican church, Daniel was making a serious social, financial and religious statement in apparent conflict with his views as a dissenter. Until the Marriage Act of 1753, a couple's freely given promise to marry constituted a valid and legal marriage, but to acquire the rights to inheritance and a dowry required the marriage to be solemnised in church.

Daniel Defoe was seeking to acquire these rights. He hoped that he was marrying for and into money (the Tuffley family had succeeded in achieving a modest fortune by trade and shrewd investment in property), and not just for the dowry, although this was a substantial amount to him. Daniel was highly knowledgeable about dowries and the legal implications of marriage and wrote about then in the *Review* as well as in his fictions.[68]

Daniel tells us nothing about his obligations under the dowry agreement. The rise in dowries was associated with increases in jointures. Habakkuk has argued that this jointure increased from a multiple of three to ten in the eighteenth century and that the rise was linked to changes in the laws of inheritance in favour of the first born son. He maintains that the father became a life tenant on his estate with administrative rights upon the birth of a son but with no influence beyond death. These changes, he reasons, were in response to human desires to aggregate family wealth, particularly in land. The cultural result was an increased male acquisitiveness, the growth of personal wealth and the creation of the dynamic required by a capitalist society.

In Daniel's fiction the possession of dowries works out badly for women. The banker in *Moll Flanders* loses hers, while Roxana refuses the Dutch merchant's offer of marriage because she does not wish to lose her dowry. It would seem that the dowry Daniel received for Mary was akin to a gambler's first throws of the dice; there would be a quick fix, some random gains, the jointure arrangements would have been raided, lost and then replaced by credit and loans. In the end it might have been irredeemably wasted, to his shame and to that of the two families, in breach of a family contract.

Habakkuk argues that the trends he describes were responsible for a decline in 'companionate' marriages towards the end of the seventeenth century. For these reasons, if no others, it was not likely that Daniel Defoe and Mary Tuffley married for love, in the sense in which most contemporary writers with a concept of romantic marriage would wish it to be described. Of course, it had the potential to be a good marriage, but that was for the future.

Daniel bought himself respectability. He established a business in Freeman's Yard in the heart of the City, paid off his debts, and speedily incurred new obligations. He employed five servants and bought a horse and carriage emblazoned with a coat of arms (to which he had no legal claim), and Mary Tuffley was established in family accommodation above the business.

It was a high point. Defoe had not yet arrived but, like Dick Whittington, he stood at the golden gate. It cannot be said that he was untrammelled, for already he was in some respects shop-soiled, but neither the shortcomings nor the damage were irredeemable. He had worked his way to a position where his ambitions for himself must have seemed achievable. At this moment everything was before him.

Chapter 5

Romance And Realism

I told him [the Czar of Muscovy] that all the lands in my Kingdom were my own ... I had not one person disaffected in my government or to my person ... they [his subjects] would all fight for me ... that never tyrant was so universally beloved, and yet so horribly feared, by his subjects.

The Farther Adventures of Robinson Crusoe
Daniel Defoe, 1719

IT WAS THE THIRD week of June 1685. The City clubs, coffee bars and taverns were alive with news of the armed landing in Lyme Regis, Dorset, of the Duke of Monmouth, the illegitimate and protestant son of Charles II. The invasion had been some time in coming but was no surprise when it did.

Monmouth was once a favourite with Charles II, who gave his son discreet recognition at Court. Monmouth was an exuberant, athletic and fun-loving womaniser who spent his life in a dissolute manner; he was more associated in the public consciousness with riding his own horse at Newmarket, and for jousting in the flesh-pots of the capital, than for acting in matters of state.

Monmouth was a protestant. This would have been of no consequence had Charles been able to provide an heir to the throne. When it became clear that Charles could not, however, people thought of Monmouth, for they realised that Charles's brother James would succeed him. No one doubted that James would return England to a Roman Catholic allegiance. As this threat to a liberal protestant England grew, Monmouth became ambitious and permitted himself to be used as the tool of others determined to thwart Roman Catholic absolutism.

When it became obvious to Charles that Monmouth was not truly repentant of his implication in the Rye House Plot (which if successful would have led to Charles's murder on the way back to the capital from Newmarket races), he removed his son's royal protection. The net closing around him, Monmouth thought it prudent to decamp to Brussels where he was joined by his mistress, Lady Henrietta Wentworth.

Back in London confederates and envoys plotted on his behalf. Arms and a ship were bought and Monmouth's chances were debated throughout the capital. Royal spies logged every move. Honest and God-fearing men confronted the choice between involvement in a rebellion and betrayal of the 'good old cause'. Most, with a heavy heart, made the judgement that an invasion by Monmouth could only lead to failure and their own ruin or death, if they should support it.

Daniel was undecided about the action he should take. His heart and his purse told him to participate. A proud descendant of protestant religious refugees, his family had not made the sacrifice of leaving their own country to succumb once more to a Roman Catholic monarch. It was not what they had expected, for, under the Tudor monarchs, Henry VIII and Elizabeth I, the protestant reformation in England had seemed secure.

As important to Daniel, however, were the prospects of royal reward and the recognition of public office. If he moved decisively to support Monmouth from the outset of his invasion from Holland, and if Monmouth were to be successful, why should he not be preferred by him? Yet, if he joined in and the rebellion was to fail, the consequences were too horrible to contemplate.

They had arranged to proceed in the dead of night. Horses had been moved to the east of the City where there was least chance of detection by the guard mounted at the bridges and highways. Daniel led a packhorse from Freeman's Yard at three in the morning, a trading licence to leave the city having been granted to him. He wore a sword but that was normal, for it was dangerous for merchants who travelled alone on the highways and byways, even in normal times. He would have to rely on others for a pistol.

Although they waited, in the end only three of them passed over an unmanned bridge into open country. Once safely away, they pitched a tent and caught up with missed sleep. Early in the morning their presence was spotted by an agitated local farmer and hastily they moved on across tangled tracks, keeping clear of highways and habitation.

They reconnoitred the first town they came upon, for their food would not last long. Special Constables were guarding the entry points; at best they would be turned away as unwelcome strangers, at worst they would be taken. Finding a small wood they pitched camp by a brook, a welcome source of fresh water.

They were seen there also and in the middle of the night they were challenged by Special Constables riding out from the nearest town. They had taken the precaution of hiding their weapons elsewhere in the wood and, for the moment, their story was accepted. They were advised to go back, however, for others might not take the same view.

There was no further sleep that night as they discussed whether to go on with all the hazards of adventure or take the prudent, if cowardly, decision to retreat. There was no agreement between them, and no certainty for any man.

Daniel left his borrowed pistol where he had hidden it and took the open road back. Late on the third day he rode into Freeman's Yard, to the relief of those who depended on him. Of course, most men would have thought him to have been prudent but Daniel sought his bed with a profound melancholy. When it had come to it, he had lacked the courage required of a hero.

My account is fictional and disputatious. It cannot be proved but, without falling into Defoean casuistry, I believe it to be accurate on the balance of probabilities. Arguably, Daniel wrote about the experience. In the *Journal of the Plague Year*, three men sought to leave the City:

> The watch placed upon Bow Bridge would have questioned them... Crossing the road into a narrow way turns out of the hither end of the town... avoided any enquiry there. The constables everywhere were on their guard... because of a report that was nearly raised... that the poor people in London were up in arms and had raised a tumult... Here they were examined... To forward this fraud they obtained [from] the constable at Old Ford a certificate of them passing through Essex... directed to the next Constable.

When they hove to for the night in a barn, they were accosted and one of them was 'challenged like soldiers upon a guard'. The travellers found themselves unexpectedly inconvenienced because the horse that carried their baggage was obliged to keep to the road while others could go across the fields. The constables remained 'obstinate'. They were denied entry to towns and had to camp in the forests. In the end they had to give up and go back to the city.[69]

This tale of Defoe's is often used by biographers in a literary sense and given various meanings. It is tempting to quote it here, for I argue that contrary to the widely accepted view, it is most unlikely that Daniel Defoe participated in the Monmouth Rebellion. The most that can be claimed is that he seriously considered doing so. Daniel may have tried to leave London, but if so his attempt was an ignominious failure.

There is evidence that Daniel was forced back into the city, or never left it, in his impressive recall of criminal proceedings against a person called Dangerfield whose trial began on 30 May 1685, twelve days before Monmouth landed. The trial concluded with a sentencing on 24 July after the Rebellion had ended in failure.[70]

A question to be posed by those who argue that Daniel Defoe did take part in the rebellion is why should a young man with a wife, children and a business to take care of, join a rebellion with so little prospect of success?

A romantic might do so, and Daniel Defoe was one, but then he lived in an age of reason when individuals were expected to behave rationally. The romantic tradition presented a world where an individual could blaze his way by the sword and alter his status and social position by the force of glorious deeds. Daniel certainly dreamt of doing this as a young man. He believed in heroic deeds. In a volume recounting heroic deeds of the past, entitled *Meditations*, which it is thought the young Defoe presented to Mary Tuffley as part of his courtship in 1683, he gives an insight into his imagination at that time. He associated himself with warriors and accepted them as role models.[71] These images stayed with him throughout his life. Defoe wrote the words quoted at the head of this chapter when around sixty years of age, but he had started out in life as an adherent to them and to the historical concept of a warrior-king, that is how, after five successive reigns over most of a half century, he ended it.

In Robinson Crusoe's island kingdom, Crusoe's rhetoric is of absolutism and the submission of the subject. Daniel Defoe does not speak the language of the social contract. For Crusoe, an understanding between monarch and subject follows an anterior condition that presupposes they have entered into a mutual compact, whether tacit or explicit. It is an understanding upheld by force of arms, with 'a naked Sword by my Side, two Pistols in my belt, and a Gun upon each Shoulder'.

Beliefs of this kind provide an insight into Defoe's character and his ideas. They are mythological in origin. Novak summarises the subject matter of *Meditations*. He writes:

Of the 140 separate apophthegms or anecdotes, the greatest number concern Alexander … with Julius Caesar and Augustus having three each. The Great Schanderberg, the Albanian hero who fought so bravely against the Turks appears in several stories and fifteen concern soldiers … forty involve death and execution … and many … involving religious themes have their share of violence in them.

Daniel had presented himself to Mary as a romantic hero rooted in religious purpose, in epic and certainty, who conquered the iniquitous by force in a turbulent and dangerous world. By contrast, the tendency in recent critical exposition of Defoe is to modernise him by relation to a Whig version of history, to the rights of man, parliamentarianism and republicanism, but the truth about his deepest emotions must lie in his seventeenth-century roots. Only an understanding of this can explain the thoughts expressed in *Meditations*.

A truly modern man can take God out of his heaven and seek his own material advantage. To protect worldly gains made by the power of the sword or gun was a troublesome matter. On his island Robinson Crusoe sought to colonise and dominate his new world. Crusoe/Daniel does not share a modern preoccupation with the dangers of executive power, but resistance to it was to become the dominant constitutional issue for the English parliaments of his time. Throughout his life Daniel was a vigorous defender of monarchical control when in the hands of a righteous monarch (one he approved of) and became agitated when it was challenged.

A sane man will not be wholly in the grip of romantic myths and symbols and will draw back from the brink of acting out his romanticism, whereas an unbalanced man motivated by biblical certainty may not. With Daniel Defoe, no one can be quite sure where he stood on the delicate balance between the two. This drama was played out in Daniel's early life.

Unless Daniel's belated admission of participating in the Monmouth Rebellion is believed, there is an historical difficulty about how his dream of glory was acted out. Most recent biographers, against the balance of probability, continue to believe in the myth of his participation in the rebellion. It is worth considering the claim in detail in order to dismiss it.

Defoe's claim of participation was made in elliptical form in 1715, thirty years after the event.[72] Earlier biographers were sceptical. Chadwick, writing in 1859, said, 'but when Defoe affirms that he was there as a fighter, what must I say? ... he must have been thoroughly watched by the government and marked out for destruction. Defoe was not there, though he says he was'.[73] Later, Chadwick states, in his own quixotic manner, his reason for this belief: the lack of any observation whatsoever that he was. 'If L'Estrange, Ned Ward, Tom Browne or Oldmixon, had at that time affirmed that Foe, the hosier, was a Captain or a General in Monmouth's force, I should have rejoiced to record the fact.'[74]

Minto writes that 'he boasted of this when it became safe to do so'.[75] Minto, in common with others, thought that the fact that other graduates of the Charles Morton Academy had participated in the rebellion was circumstantial support for Defoe's involvement. Sutherland is more judicious. In 1937 he wrote that 'he may have been gambling on Monmouth's success ... riding about in the west country [on business] and curiosity ... induced him to ride with the rebels. It is probable that he remained on the fringe. If he had fought ... he would have told us so'.[76] In 1955 Charles Moore expressed his view with more certainty. Defoe had said goodbye to his wife and had 'rode westwards through the by-lanes ... avoiding the pickets who guarded the main roads'.

In 1980 McDonald Wigfield seemed to put the matter beyond doubt when he discovered the name of Daniel Defoe among a list of those who were 'engaged in the late rebellion and to be inserted in the general pardon'.[77] This was a fact never mentioned by Defoe.

In reality, to make good an assertion of Defoe's participation in the Monmouth Rebellion there are four matters to consider: first, whether it would have been possible for him to leave London undetected to join the rebellion, secondly, whether it would have been possible to participate without anyone noticing and telling others or confessing it, thirdly, whether he could have escaped detention after the rebellion had collapsed, and lastly, to explain a royal pardon which went unpublicised for the next forty-six years.

The government in London had been aware of the possible invasion for some months and had taken effective action to prevent dissenters in the capital from joining it. London had been seen as an important recruiting ground for the rebellion but, in the event, probably no more than four hundred had joined it. Dissenters had been picked out as potential rebels, their homes were systematically searched and arms and horses confiscated. Once the landing was known, soldiers were used to block off all the entries and exits to the capital. Special magistrates were appointed and over two hundred dissenters were arrested and held in custody. While it would have been possible to leave the capital it must be considered unlikely and even if it had been contrived the chances of apprehension were high.

Any supposition that Defoe was travelling westward with former schoolmates from the Morton academy is clearly wrong. McDonald Wigfield[78] has been able to list over 1,500 rebels who were within the royal pardon, including Defoe and three former students of the Morton academy (Battiscombe, Jenkyns and Hewlett), who are described by Defoe as 'western martyrs' in a 1712 pamphlet.[79] Battiscombe and Hewlett came over from Holland with Monmouth. Jenkyns rode out from London but was arrested on suspicion in Ilchester and released by some of Monmouth's soldiers. If he had been accompanied by Defoe the whole world would have known of it. John Shower, another Morton academy student, came from Holland, and was pardoned. None mentioned Defoe.[80]

The supposition that Defoe could have participated in the rebellion without anyone knowing about it or reporting him afterwards is absurd. There was an intense pressure on participants to confess, with the assurance of a lighter sentence. Confessions were extorted and rewards were given to informers. Confronted with this implausibility most biographers have assumed that in some way Defoe was on the fringe of events and did not 'bear arms for the Duke of Monmouth' as he claimed. This assumption is not credible: if he had been involved in any way he would have been named by someone.

The hunt for the fleeing rebels was relentless and most were picked up while escaping to the nearest port, relative, or at home. Each parish was instructed to 'go to every house, and produce lists of men absent and arms discovered or taken'. Money could be made from the transportation of the rebels and there was a known price on their heads. Backscheider writes, 'That Defoe had remained uncaptured was simply amazing: at best a one in fifteen chance.'[81]

King James issued a General Pardon in March 1686.[82] The pardon excepted 'all Fugitives and persons fled from our Justice of or into parts beyond the Seas or out of this Our Realm who shall not return and render themselves to Our Chief Justice before the 29 September next ensuing'. If Defoe had participated in the rebellion and had fled abroad this would have accounted for a wish to be included specifically within the royal pardon. However, we know that he was on tax rolls and petty jury lists and gave bail to two people during the years 1685/1686 and 1687 and this reasoning would seem not to apply.[83]

The fact that he was added to a list put before magistrates for inclusion within the pardon is not concrete evidence of participation in the rebellion.[84]

The preparation of additional names in lists was notoriously unreliable and corrupt: people could pay to gain inclusion and at any time there was a going rate. Defoe could have got himself on to a list for a payment of £50.

Defoe leaves a clue as to what might have happened in *Colonel Jack*. Colonel Jack's wife planned to obtain a pardon for him when he was in exile abroad for treasonable activities. 'She would write to a particular Friend in London, who she could depend upon to try to get a Pardon ... within the expense of two, or three, or four hundred pounds ... he should have Bills payable by such and such a person on Delivery of the Warrant for the thing.'[85] The stress here is upon the untrustworthiness of the correspondent and the request that nothing should be done unless the pardon was certain, that his involvement in the rebellion was not known, and that a pardon was only precautionary. In the event, Colonel Jack did not need the pardon.

In 1715 Daniel had an urgent need to restore his standing with the new Whig administration. He needed to become a boy scout with the right 'badges of honour'. This need to diminish the hostility of friends and foes must have been uppermost in his mind. However, it is probably true that Daniel would have been inclined to join the rebellion, for at the time every dissenter knew two things about Charles's brother James: that his marriage was childless, and that as time passed it was likely that he would die without an heir, and that as an avowed Roman Catholic he felt spiritually committed to return England to the Roman Catholic Church.

And there is no doubt that the Duke of Monmouth was a role model for Daniel. In 1702 there were three possibilities for the succession: Edward, son of James II, and a Roman Catholic monarchy; an Hanoverian heir, in the line of the Electress Sophia after whom, so it was said, Daniel named his daughter Sophia, and which turned out to be Anne and, with her, national devotion to the Anglican Church; and the Earl of Dalkeith, Monmouth's protestant son. In *The Succession to the Crown of England*, Daniel asks why the claims of the son of the Duke of Monmouth are not at least given impartial consideration.[86] In the 1680s Defoe could not predict the succession but, in all probability, he knew already that he preferred Monmouth.

It was only in 1715 when the Hanoverian line had been confirmed that Daniel Defoe felt able to mention a role in the Monmouth Rebellion. In doing so, he made no mention of the royal pardon. He might have been ashamed of it, not because of the inclusion as such but because he had invented his participation, or that he had done nothing on an issue of importance to him when many among his friends and fellow dissenters were killed in battle or executed. It is time to face up to the probabilities. As Chadwick wrote, 'Defoe was not there, though he says he was.'

Notwithstanding the temptations to a biographer of accepting Daniel's account, I believe he made up the story of his participation. If so, what does it tell us? Of course, he was tempted to join the rebellion for the reasons argued here. Even though he decided not to participate, he must have wanted it to succeed for he would have thought the cause to be noble and righteous. However, reason and observation would have led him to doubt the prospects of a triumph for the Duke, and cowardice may have played its part.

The failure of the rebellion was a setback for the dissenters who had been the dominant force in it. While Defoe turned his attention to adventure and business it must have seemed obvious to him that to succeed in life required position and place. He had faced the first test of his determination to succeed and had failed, but his analysis of his situation in life was surely right. As he had defined himself by his family's dissent, he would be handicapped in the struggle for preferment without a protestant monarch.

Daniel only had to wait three years for the accession of William and Mary for the realisation of his dream of a protestant monarch. While no actor could fulfil the role of Daniel's warrior king, William III came very close to it. A protestant, he had fought against France and his armed foray into England, at the request of the leading Whig politicians of the day, was an invasion which, to the dissenter at least, had saved protestant England from a steady but inexorable slide into absolutism and papacy under James II.

It was a political change that occurred without the firing of a single shot. While James hesitated, William camped out in open country. When James fled, William advanced towards London; when he reached Reading, and it was clear that there would be no armed opposition to his advance, Daniel rode out to join a gathering throng.

It was truly a bloodless revolution. Gradually, in the confusion of these historic events, it became clear to the English what had been done in their name. The people, through parliament, had asserted their right to depose a king, whether or not it was maintained that he ruled by divine right. Feiling points out that the English need not have been so surprised. He writes that:

> Between 1327 and 1688, for nine sovereigns who reigned continuously and died in their beds... there were the forced exile of three kings, the public execution of a fourth, and the foul murder of another four. [87]

Unbeknown to most, the constitutional position had evolved to the point where parliament was willing to devolve administrative and executive power to a monarch, while retaining the right to hold him to account. It was a balance that would only achieve effective and stable government if the two worked closely and amicably together. It had become part of this balance that the monarch should sustain the vitality of the protestant religion.

It was in the interest of the European Roman Catholic powers, in particular France under Louis XIV, to destabilise any such balance between the English monarch and parliament. Throughout William's reign there was constant warfare. Against the backdrop of the English, Scots and Irish in constant civil conflict (religious, political and economic), England engaged in bitter armed struggle on land and sea. On William's arrival, Holland was at war with France. Parliament was in no position to deny William, whose involvement in England was always part of his strategic battle against France, and England engaged itself in a nine year conflict until the peace of Rhyswick in 1697.

Unable any longer to bribe a royal mistress, the French concentrated on buying the House of Commons. In retaliation, the king and the Court bought its own placemen and resisted the attempts of both Houses of Parliament to limit royal preferment. William used his executive powers to promote what the public understood to be 'his foreign wars' with a resulting rise in national debt and higher taxes.

Now was the moment for Defoe to enter public life but he still had to find a way of doing so.

Chapter 6

Making It

Farther within the land… we saw no idle hands here but every man busy on the main affair of that is to say, getting money.

A Tour Through the Whole Island of Great Britain
Daniel Defoe, 1724–26

THROUGHOUT HIS ADULT LIFE Daniel Defoe was obsessed with the business of making money. While the causes of his behaviour were complex, it is never safe to assume that they are known unless the question is first asked how he earned his income or in what investments and speculations he was involved. This caveat applies to all Defoe's activities. He wrote for profit; he speculated for financial advantage; he cheated to gain materially and to hold on to his gains; he exploited his family and friends for narrow pecuniary advantage; he sold his soul for patronage, and he traded on religiosity long past the point at which he abandoned his dissenting beliefs. While these judgements may seem harsh, they resolve a great many conundrums about Daniel and what happened to him.

The aspiration to be a success consumed the whole of Daniel's long life. Over this lifetime, it is possible to identify numerous occupations and business activities in which he was involved: merchant adventurer, marine insurer, entrepreneur, financial speculator, horse dealer, property developer, brick manufacturer, hose-factor, timber wholesaler, journalist, and propagandist and government spy. This list is not exhaustive.

Starting out is never easy for a man without capital or powerful connections. That he was fully aware of the problems of trading with too little capital can be seen from his own writings, for he wrote movingly about it in his *Compleat English Tradesman*.[88]

By the date of his marriage in 1684, he was established in premises in Freeman's Yard and trading as a hose factor. His wife's family provided him with the capital to expand the business. He was to deny emphatically that he was a retailer of women's stockings, and it does appear that he was a wholesaler of them. Hosiery was highly popular at this time and the import of the latest continental hose was in fashion. This trade was not confined to stockings. In modern terms, Daniel was trading in haberdashery: hats and nightcaps, socks, gloves and ribbons.

As a factor he travelled extensively to distributors and retailers throughout the country. He set in motion a behaviour which became habitual, absenting himself from home and travelling by horse and carriage to places which were novel and diverting to him. He made it his practice to make contact with dissenting communities throughout the country and to gain information about their worries and concerns. In time it made him well-informed about all kinds of people, work-places and situations that were to inform the work that gave him fame in his lifetime, and for which, and for a long while after his death, he was best remembered: his *A Tour Through the Whole Island of Great Britain*.

Daniel began to form a constituency for which he felt qualified to write and agitate. These early writings are not known, they are not extant and, with one exception, not mentioned by Daniel. In *An Appeal to Honour and Justice*, written in 1715, Daniel mentions the exception. He writes:

The first Time I had the misfortune to differ with my Freinds (on the Whig side), was about the Year 1683 when the Turks were besieging Vienna and the Whigs in England, generally speaking, were for the Turks taking it; which I having read the History of the Cruelty and perfidious Dealings of the Turks in their Wars, and how they had rooted out the Name of the Christian Religion in above three score and Ten Kingdoms, could by no more agree with: and then tho' then but a young Man, and a younger author, I opposed it, and wrote against it; which was taken very unkindly indeed.

At this time the English dissenters were among the most enthusiastic supporters of the Turks because they believed that the Hungarian forces who fought alongside them were attempting to create a protestant revolt against the Roman Catholic Austrian monarchy.

It is most unlikely that these stated reasons for Daniel's disagreement are true. *An Appeal to Honour and Justice* is essentially an apologia in which Defoe seeks to justify his past behaviour. It is helpful to his argument that it is written retrospectively. Daniel gives the siege of Vienna as an example of the Whigs not always being right and disagreement with them as not always being disloyal, but the reader knows that the Turks did not succeed in the siege of Vienna and that, this being the case, the debate had no practical consequence.

Daniel's described his writing of thirty-two years earlier (it is not known whether this was a tract or poem), which was hardly likely to be recalled, and it was safe for him to assume a statesman-like posture and establish the independence of his thought from any constituency. It is possible that Daniel made up the entire story and that there was no such writing. If there was writing of some kind it might have followed a subsequent and well-worn practice of Defoe's to write contrary to a tide (and anonymously) in order to invite a greater controversy and increased sales and profit.

The probability was that he was writing mostly poetry at this time, and in common with the fate of most of human expression, his writings have vanished without trace. He was honing his craft as a writer, largely unsuccessfully (but occasionally making money), and anonymously for fear of identification with the ideas expressed. It is not known what he might have been writing about the siege of Vienna. While fame may come suddenly to some, it is not common. Daniel worked hard to gain publicity. Sometimes he would have money and at other times he would not.

At this time there were literary societies which gathered in coffee bars where writers were tolerated or even encouraged. Here, discussions embraced literary fashions and happenings which would have been fascinating to the aspiring writer. Daniel would have encountered difficulties in these gatherings, from which he would never be free. The literary world was small and largely concentrated in London, although a provincial market was developing. Literature was confined mostly to an Anglo-Catholic audience of men who, like the authors, were products of Oxford and Cambridge. The subject matter was refined for the sensibilities of a narrow reading public[89] and Daniel was always an outsider in this world. The fierceness with which he defended his education as a dissenter and the antipathy he expresses for dead languages and gentlemanly pretensions arise from the tensions of seeking an audience as an outsider. This being surmised, it is likely that Daniel paid printers to publish him; their street sense in refusing him so often would have taught him something important about the needs of a reading public.

The marriage dowry he received would have heralded a false dawn and given a moment of ease in which he felt himself to be the gentlemen-trader he is so scathing about in *Moll Flanders*. There he writes, in self-parody, that Moll, 'was not averse to a Tradesman...that was something of a Gentleman...that should look as if he was set on his sword, when his sword was put on to him, and carried his Trade in his Countenance...Well, at last I found this amphibious Creature this Land-water -thing called a Gentle-man Tradesman'. As Daniel wrote those words in 1724 he was looking back on events of forty years ago. He must have shared a sense of absurdity with his readers, for he carried a sword while dealing in women's hosiery. At the time he would not have wished it otherwise, for he was determined to transcend the one to become worthy of the other.

This was not the route followed by James Foe. He seems to have pursued trading activity steadily throughout a long working life. In business, steadiness, reliability and dedication to known activities always offers success of a kind, but the rewards can be modest. Defoe had eschewed such a route. He desired a world which offered great rewards for risky and glamorous activities and he determined to have a part of it, whatever the risks. A path to fame and fortune was not ridiculous for him to imagine. As with Dick Whittington before him, great fortunes could be made in a man's lifetime; he really believed that a man like him could become the Lord Mayor of London and join the great of the realm.

As part of this strategy, Daniel needed to acquire the rights of a livery man. James Foe's respectability in becoming a livery man as a member of the Butchers' Company enabled Defoe in January 1688 to claim a right of patrimony and become one as well. The fact that he was entitled to membership by reason of birth would not have worried him. It was convenient. He would have been able to apply for membership as a gentleman defined as being a person claiming the title, with a supposed capital of over £6,000 and an income of more than £60 a year. Daniel qualified on each of these counts. In the 1680s Defoe's name starts to appear on parish lists as a person with responsibilities who could be depended upon by his community. In all this, Daniel was following the example of James Foe, but at this point in the narrative their paths diverge.

For Daniel Defoe there was always more to life than steady application to commerce: there was the romance of trading on the high seas and the excitements of the disturbance of trade routes by England's foreign enemies. There was also the challenge to God's providence, for violent weather might result in the devastating consequence of the loss of both ship and cargo. Daniel seems to have suffered such losses when ships in which he had an interest were captured by the French or damaged and sunk in great storms.

At first, as in *Robinson Crusoe*, Daniel would have bought into the venture of someone else's ship which meant that he would not have been the owner or part owner of it but paid the owner to carry his merchandise. He would sometimes have travelled with his cargoes to places in Britain and on the continent. In ports of call he would have picked up goods for passage back to Britain.

Daniel traded widely. It seems from his fiction that he had a detailed knowledge of ports in many European countries. He may have traded further afield, for he shows knowledge of the West Indies, Madagascar and Maryland in America. The further the voyage, the greater the length and hazard of the enterprise.

Gradually, he would have built a network of factors and trading partners in various ports and territories. He would have made arrangements to collect cargoes for shipping from foreign ports, and payments would be due to these factors and to the ships' masters.

It does not appear that Defoe specialised in any way. There are surviving records from 1690 of a cargo for which he was attempting to recover the duty. 'It consisted of six pipes of beer, six pipes of port, four hogs heads and two barrels of tobacco, one barrel of tobacco pipes, two trunks of hose and stuffs, a hundred and twenty gallons of English spirits and a hundred pounds of Spanish stuff.'[90]

This trade was risky. The selection of trading partners required good judgements about both character and financial viability; the trade itself was, in the end, based on trust. The most profit was earned by owners of ships. Daniel bought an interest in a ship named Desire. Surviving records of this ship suggest that it was unreliable and unseaworthy for much of the time.

Daniel would have learned from City sources that marine insurance offered the prospect of both profit and loss. A gambler, he would have ignored the risks and pursued the gains.

Speculation, gambling and poor business judgement were the causes of Daniel's trading difficulties, but the central problem was the man himself. Daniel was simply too unstable and restless a person to succeed in the taking of speculative risks in a variety of business ventures. Indeed, he wrote about a businessman such as himself:

> when he finds himself grown rich, to have his head full of grand designs, and new undertakings. He finds his cash flow in upon him, and perhaps he is fuller of money than his trade calls for; and as he scarce knows how to employ more stock in it than he does, his ears are the sooner open to any project or proposal that offers itself; and I must add, that this is the most critical time with him in all his life.

In all these pursuits it must have seemed obvious that business connections formed his best chance of success. The dissenting community offered entry to a society of fellow spirits which, while it may not have taken him far (for economic self-interest, as ever, governed individual decisions), it would have opened doors.

In the bars, taverns and coffee shops of London there was fellowship of another kind. There was a social and political mix there. A clever fellow could get a hearing from his superiors and an ingenious one with imagination could gain knowledge of the latest speculations and earn the opportunity to participate in them.

At some time it is possible that Daniel became a mason. It would have been difficult for him to become one because of the social exclusiveness of Masonic lodges, but the printers and City men around him achieved membership, and Daniel would have found a way in. Membership would have been useful to him because masonry opened up a wealth of personal contacts across social boundaries, ranging from the royal family and the aristocracy to the scions of industry and commerce.

Backscheider has suggested that later in his life, around 1706–7, Defoe was able to acquire access to the Scottish aristocracy during the negotiations for the Union of Scotland and England, when he was in the pay of the English government, because he was a mason.

Masonic lodges were highly secretive about their membership and proceedings (there are no extant membership lists) and it is difficult to prove whether any individual was a member. However, it seems probable that sometime before 1703 Defoe became one.

More controversially, Defoe could have been using his sexuality to gain advantage. Defoe's sexual activity is hardly likely to be logged anywhere; it is only later in his life that his homosexuality can be spoken about with certainty. But a man is not likely suddenly, late in life, to find himself with a sexual orientation not experienced in his youth.

In the 1690s it became more dangerous for a man to be openly homosexual. It appears that the Glorious Revolution of 1688 ushered in a cultural change. The revolution was in a sense a defeat for the French. The anonymous author of *A Satyr against the French* wrote, 'All Europe to their fashions bends the knee, In that they've gained the universal monarchy.' France was alleged to be 'the source of tyranny, anarchy, and luxury, despotic Lords and effeminising delicacies, frogs, fricasseed and coxcomb-pies'.[91]

The Stuart Court was considered to have been under French influence and now it was time for a change. Relations between men could be homosocial, and even homoerotic, but homosexual practices were to become incompatible with a more masculine political culture. Outward display was to become frowned upon as effeminate and contrary to the spirit of a mercantilist and trading age.

Instigated by the crown-sponsored Society for the Reformation of Manners, prosecutions of homosexual practices (and executions of men committing them) doubled after 1688. Homosexual practices were seen as inherently associated with effeminacy, and effeminacy was seen as a danger to the state. The tyranny of the state was to catch the poor and unsuspecting. For a time, high social position and social class would guarantee immunity and 'protection' could be bought.[92] For some, life went on as usual.

All his life Daniel was curious about the changing world around him. His intellectual output at this time must have been prodigious. There was no better place than London to view the scientific and industrial discoveries being made. Daniel's nature would have meant that he was constantly engaged with this process of change.

A problem for the biographer at this stage of Defoe's life is to explain his family relationships. It would have been impossible for him to have spent much time at home with Mary Tuffley. It seems probable that even in the 1680s he preferred to spend his time away from her and that he had a second home in the country. Very little is known about what his wife thought of this or how she spent her time.

According to biographers, and on very little evidence, Mary and Daniel produced eight children, of whom two died young. The dates of birth of these eight children claimed as Mary Tuffley's are uncertain, for only Sophia's birth was recorded, but it is probable that in the four-year period to 1689 Mary had two children. By 1689 one child, also called Mary, had either died, or had been put out to care with the parish, or taken into the care of someone else. In that year Mary was pregnant with another child. In the period 1690 to 1713, when it is generally accepted that the couple hardly spoke to each other and lived apart, it has been supposed that Mary had seven children, of whom six survived. To achieve this, Mary would have had to give birth to the last child when she was over forty years of age.

What biographers have not considered is that some of these children were not the outcome of the marriage between Daniel and Mary Tuffley. Mary seems to have been a forthright woman with a temper. Earlier biographers have suggested that she was something of a shrew, or perhaps rather unstable. Given Daniel's conduct towards her, however, this is perhaps not surprising.

Indeed, what might he be up to? Among the many biblical quotations which Daniel was prone to use, one was from Proverbs 'Be all things to all men'. Like many biblical sayings it is capable of multiple meanings. However, in the context of preferment, of finding and holding your place, the saying is normally construed as meaning a willingness to do all that might be demanded of you by any man for the favour you sought. When a man hungered for favour and his rightful place in the sun, just what might he be prepared to seek and offer?

The reader might wonder where the Daniel Defoe he knows about is to be found in this story of business and personal recklessness. It seems impossible to imagine him not writing but, if he was, nothing has survived from this period which can be claimed as his without controversy. Was he not in his late twenties and early thirties campaigning for political revision and change? Is not there a Defoe seeking the removal of social disadvantage and religious discrimination? Was he not the victim of religious persecution?

The answer to all these questions is, not really. The Defoe of the 1680s possessed many advantages of education, wit and place. In 1688 the protestant succession had been secured by the accession to the throne of William and Mary. With this accession came freedom to worship. It is true that privileges were granted only to those who accepted the authority of the Anglican Church, and that public office was dependant upon this acceptance, but in time it might reasonably be expected that these restrictions would be lifted.

Defoe was to emerge as a champion of religious and political equality in a revisionist tradition, but not at this stage of his life, and he was never the modern Whig portayed in many of the texts written about him. And when he did come to notice as a political propagandist, his message was mixed and not entirely his own.

In 1684, when Daniel married Mary Tuffley, what was needed was to secure, for the mass of the people of England, a level playing field. The Glorious Revolution did not finally settled all matters of concern to the nation but in reality it replaced the Stuart dynasty with a stable and unchallengeable protestant succession. It was to take another quarter of a century, however, before this was secure. For most of those who sought to participate in society during this period, it was not certain that the political changes they favoured had been, or would be, brought about. It remained necessary for those who took part in the political struggles of the time to be cunning in order to stay alive while taking part in a dangerous political game.

TRIUMPH AND DISASTER

1693 to 1703

Chapter 7

Bankruptcy

I might instance here the miserable, anxious, perplexed life, which the poor tradesman lives under before he Breaks ... how harrass'd and tormented for money ... how many, little, mean, and even wicked things will even the most religious tradesman stoop to ... as his very soul would abhor at another time: and for which he goes, perhaps, with a wounded conscience all his life after?

The Compleat English Tradesman
Daniel Defoe, 1727

SIR JOHN POWELL, A London magistrate, was no respecter of persons. On 29 October 1692 he was presented with a straightforward petition by Walter Ridley, a haberdasher, and three other traders, Cornelius Shadwell, Jerome Whichcote and Nicholas Barrett. These traders were owed money by Daniel Defoe; they had given him time to pay but Defoe had made promises of payment that were never honoured. It was necessary to call in the debts and commit this fellow to the Fleet prison until they were paid and this is what Sir John Powell did.

Daniel had been on the slippery slope for some time, losing money in multifarious ventures, hopelessly and desperately extending his credit and resorting to whatever stratagem was to hand, regardless of its honesty.

Daniel made some kind of an arrangement, or paid some kind of bribe, to get out of prison. It was not difficult. Of 1,651 prisoners charged and sent to the Fleet from 28 April to 1 December 1696, 'only three hundred prisoners had been discharged by regular procedure', and the others escaped by bribery.[93]

However, there was no escape for Daniel from his troubles. Desperately, he tried to save himself and by October 1692 he succeeded in persuading 140 creditors to whom he owed £17,000 to agree to a composition of 15 shillings in the pound, but four creditors with debts amounting to £200 refused. Accruing so large a number of desperate creditors might be thought to be disaster enough, but they were not the whole of it. Defoe omitted all the creditors he thought he could avoid. In November, two creditors, one of whom was owed the considerable sum of £700, lost patience and on their suit Daniel was committed to the King's Bench prison and then on to the Mint. He was there some time before he was able to obtain his release.

A ray of hope was to be found in the passage through the Commons of the Merchant Insurers Bill but then the bill was defeated in the House of Lords on 9 March 1694. Defoe's name was among nineteen on that bill, and a late entry. If the bill had been passed Defoe would have obtained relief on some of his debts if two thirds of his creditors had agreed.

It remains uncertain to what extent Daniel had incurred mercantile insurance debts and when: it is possible that he may have incurred them after his bankruptcy. Daniel tells his readers that he was present at the consideration of the bill by parliament. It must have been cruel for him to witness his hopes go down as fast as the ships which created the losses in the first place.

The disgrace of a bankruptcy requires explanation and many reasons have been forthcoming for Defoe's. It has proved difficult to make a sound case for extenuating circumstances. The times have been pleaded in mitigation, for the City of London was full of all kinds of merchants growing rich at a faster pace than would have been possible for their forebears. It must have seemed to them all that it was possible to become a gentleman with servants, carriages and expectations. The financial world of stock jobbing, bills of exchange, private banks, lotteries and speculative projects was upon them in a raw and unregulated fashion. Why should not the young Daniel become one of them? He was intelligent and quick with a good head for figures, interested and well-informed, diligent and unceasingly energetic and up to date about every new service venture or development.

Daniel's admirable qualities were to be shown not to be enough. Sutherland puts this generously. He writes, 'Defoe was now ready to make his fortune. That he did not do so was due to bad luck and partly to the defects of his character.'[94] Sutherland discovered that between 1688 and 1692 Defoe was the subject of eight claims in Chancery suits. Some were settled against him while others dragged on until the plaintiffs either died or gave up.

Sutherland, having studied these claims, was left with the impression of Defoe's duplicity and dishonesty. Perhaps most damning was a suit against him by his aunt-in-law Joan Tuffley when she failed to recover an investment in civet cats bred for their perfume. Joan Tuffley alleged 'manifest fraud' and during the case she stated that Defoe was a 'gay deceiver'. It must have been a hard blow for Joan Tuffley and have been felt as ingratitude, for she had been helpful in his acquisition of land in Tilbury.

Some biographers have rushed to defend Defoe against charges of bad faith and dishonesty, pleading the difficulties of under-capitalisation of his business affairs and bad luck. They point out that in *The Compleat English Tradesmen*, as quoted at the head of this chapter, he 'apologises' for his shortcomings, claiming that they were implicit in the conduct of trade.

The reader of the quotation understands that Daniel Defoe had experienced distress over these matters. However, Defoe is not contrite or apologetic. He places the narrative voice 'outside himself' to prescribe the ideal while practising the perfidious. The reader notices the 'perhaps' and the final question mark. What, he might wonder, is the question?

Peter Earle has written that Defoe's problems arose from factors outside his control on the high seas, and losses in the risky business of marine insurance. However, the Chancery claims were concerned with widespread general trading requiring a variety of skills. Hence the possibility of Daniel's ill-judgement must be considered.

With access to more material than Sutherland, Paula Backscheider is more damning of Defoe's character and behaviour. She writes that the greatest causes of his bankruptcy were his inattention to detail and his speculations:

> In the 1690s his conduct was reprehensible. He cheated his friends and relatives, took advantage [of those] who kept extending his credit to give him time to recover and borrowed money he could not repay in order to delay court actions or to invest in yet another enterprise… The story is the familiar one of over-expansion, unwise speculation, divided attention, and unsuccessful efforts to recover, with a touch of vanity, deceit and overconfidence. The enormous contradiction of five servants and a debt of £17,000, the attack on Defoe's self-image, the years of financial struggle, and financial collapse changed Defoe *for ever* from a prominent joiner of respected groups to a solitary with secrets, and from tradesman to a writer.[95]

The arguments in mitigation have not yet been exhausted. It has been argued that Defoe's difficulties were caused by the failure of a speculative project. In October 1691 he bought ten shares costing £200 in a company formed to exploit a patent for a diving machine invented by Joseph Williams. The lure was the possible discovery of riches from the wrecks of ships lost at sea. Defoe had a life-long attraction to the possibilities of rescuing valuables from wrecks. Fictionally, this is represented in *Robinson Crusoe*'s efforts to swim out to his shipwrecked vessel and the use he made of its contents. Daniel lost his £200 when the company failed.

This loss was insignificant in relation to his outstanding debts and not the cause of them. However, in insolvency the precipitating factor may be trivial in itself, often the action of a small but persistent creditor whose tolerance is exhausted, or a creditor who is determined to punish a recalcitrant even though to do so would lose him his money. A tiny rent in a sail when the wind is up may bring it down and capsize the ship.

Successful business practice requires mental stability, a willingness to concentrate on rational objectives, and constant and unremitting attention to detail. Defoe did not possess any of these characteristics. Any description of his business activities suggests restlessness and a failure to concentrate on the business opportunities to hand. Even in a long life, the sheer length of the list of Daniel's economic and commercial activities and the diversity of the occupations they represent would suggest a man not settled in his business intentions. What excited Daniel was the prospect of the aggregation of wealth and the position in society that it would buy him.

It can be argued in Daniel's defence that the culture in which he lived was acquisitive and, in a sense, formed by the prospects of acquiring wealth and changing personal status in society. Such an assertion raises more doubts than it solves. A conclusion that Daniel's greed was excessive is inescapable. The questions multiply. Was his avarice and desire for the riches of the world a product of too little love, attention and material sustenance as a child? Did Daniel suffer from a form of childhood anal retention against which he was defenceless and which in his adult life took the form of aggrandisement? Was he doomed to seek possessions and to retain them even when their utility to him was doubtful?

Whatever Daniel's other values and activities, it is true that throughout his life he was ceaselessly and restlessly preoccupied with the making of money. Unfortunately for him and for others, however, he was rarely willing to give any one activity the devoted attention and discipline needed to make a success of it. He was a jack of all trades and, until his journalism and his writing of fiction, the master of none.

The surest route to success for an intelligent man such as Defoe was to apply himself to a City career in which he made himself useful to others. He needed connections and to make himself indispensable to persons of place and influence. This is what he attempted and, to some extent, he succeeded in doing. Such a strategy requires patience, reliability and trustworthiness. Daniel was deficient in all these qualities. Even lacking these qualities of good character, Daniel would have succeeded if he had been accomplished enough. But in business, as in so many activities, accomplishment is the product of assiduous daily practice.

As for writing, until the lifting of the licensing laws in 1695, with their draconian policing of publishers and printers, it was difficult for a rebellious or impulsive writer to find an audience. Daniel wrote but it is not likely that by writing he could make a steady living. If he kept his identity hidden, even from the printer, there were opportunities to make an occasional profit, as described in an earlier chapter, but then it would not have been known that the writer was Daniel Defoe and later, when he might have told us he was the author of this or that pamphlet or poem, he is silent.

Finally it has been argued that Defoe became bankrupt because he devoted too much time to politics and writing. To fill the vacuum in what is known of Daniels activities in the 1680s and 1690s, and to round their characterisation of Defoe, it has been tempting to earlier biographers to ascribe anonymous works to him. Many of these early ascriptions are now thought not to be Defoe's at all and, while it is probable that he was writing, perhaps the activity was not as great as is often supposed. George Chalmers, an early biographer, writing in 1790 states that Defoe 'did not become a bankrupt because he had taken to writing; he became an author because he had failed in business'.[96]

Even today the consequences of bankruptcy in England remain severe and the act carries a moral stigma. However, now a bankruptcy puts an end to the financial troubles of the bankrupt in that all his debtors are bound by a Court Order. The bankrupt need not have the consent of any of his creditors and, providing the terms of the bankruptcy are honoured by the defaulter, he will in time be free of all remaining obligations upon its termination date. However, it remains true that a debtor in modern England can find himself in prison for a debt if he places himself in contempt of a Court Order.

In earlier times debt was regarded far more harshly and in many places as a capital crime; in England, some bankrupts were executed for their debts late into the eighteenth century. At the time of Defoe's first bankruptcy, any creditor could prevent a general composition with creditors and the consequence for the debtor was incarceration in prison where there was a constant fear of mutilation or death. Bribery of the gaolers was one means of escape, buying off the creditors who had caused the prison sentence another.

Once free, prisoners remained subject to the pursuit of their creditors. Other people, possibly enemies, could buy debts, pursue them in the courts and get people put out of their way. While in prison, people could not earn a living and the creditors got nothing. The creditors had a financial interest in dealing with debtors but for serious offences and for emotional reasons some preferred revenge to part payment.

Twelve years later when Daniel had secured release from prison after his ordeal in the pillory, he was again bankrupted. In a sense the two bankruptcies were linked: the unsuccessful resolution of the first had led to the second crisis. In the 1705/6 session of Parliament, after Daniel's second bankruptcy, a bill entitled A Bill to Prevent Frauds Committed by Bankrupts was passed and a commission in bankruptcy established. The Act enabled a bankrupt to achieve a situation, subject to the investigation of the commission, where creditors could be bound to accept a bankruptcy, even when some objected, and where the bankrupt could keep up to five per cent of his assets. The Act departed from past attitudes in that it benefited the creditor as well as the debtor and enabled the honest bankrupt to make a quick and complete settlement with creditors.

Daniel criticised the bill in the *Review* [97] and wrote about it to Lord Robert Harley where he stated that he had been advised not to seek advantage from the new act as his creditors would all come at him. Then, between 18 and 22 July a notice in the London Gazette announced that Defoe's bankruptcy was being investigated by the commission and that he had been ordered to attend a meeting. Daniel avoided attending by going to Scotland, but he could not do so for long. The commission had considerable powers of initiative: it could act on the evidence of others, it could seize records and books of account, oblige witnesses to attend and answer questions and make a wide variety of orders.

Some biographers assume that the London Gazette advertisement was placed on Daniel's initiative but it could just as well have been on that of the commission acting on its own or on the prompting of others. Certainly there were many creditors who believed that Daniel was hiding assets and they would not have been shy in coming forward.

It is not difficult to imagine the scene. In early August the committee ordered to deal with the affairs of Mr Daniel Defoe considered the evidence for the third time. Before removing himself to Scotland he had provided the committee with a long statement of outstanding debts, some supporting accounts, other information and a plea. From information given to the committee from other persons, the members had decided the information was incomplete. Daniel was asked to provide additional information and to address specific issues. He responded and was brought before them.

The officials were precise men charged with specific responsibilities under an Act of Parliament. They were not to be easily satisfied by generalities or rhetoric. While they did not possess judicial powers they felt themselves bound to act as if they did. Confronting them was a well-dressed, if shabby, man of average height and build, with a wig too long for the fashion and fatigued with travel and worry. He was not a handsome man, for he possessed a jutting chin and a disfigurement of his face, but undeniably he had presence. Despite his fatigue, he displayed a frenetic energy. He fidgeted with his papers, and interrupted members in full flow, responded to precise questions with a flood of words, and gave answers which prompted more questions. All in all it was quite a performance.

These officials were not to be denied, for they knew what they wanted and had the forensic skills to find it out, but they were men of the world with other duties to perform. They did not have infinite time. In the end they gave up. Nothing could be resolved one way or another, in favour or against. Daniel had earned himself a hard-won draw which he could claim as a victory. Some would deny such a claim, for there was just the thought, perhaps no more than a rumour, that the chairman had been bribed!

Daniel claimed the commission's findings as a famous victory against formidable enemies. He wrote to Lord Harley stating that he had gained 'at last a Compleat Victory Over the most Furious Subtill and Malitious Opposition That has been Seen in all The Instances of the Bankrupts Act' (H 124). He claimed that he had received financial relief under the Act, but the relief he spoke of was emotional. Daniel's denied creditors continued to hunt him down for the rest of his life. He was never safe from a knock on the door.

The unanswered question for all those biographers who seek to interpret the evidence of Daniel Defoe's bankruptcies to persuade readers of a good character for Daniel, one arising from a sound and stable family life, a strict

Presbyterian upbringing and schooling, a possible calling for the ministry, and with the secure basis of a rich dowry, is how does his business activity turn out so badly? No doubt there was ill-fortune, and the hazards of war must have been a factor, but there is evidence of wilfulness, immoral business dealings and recklessness. There is far more present in his behaviour than the amorality needed for the conduct of a successful business, and nothing of the conscientious puritan.

Defoe's bankruptcy did not finish his business career, although his name was blackened in the City of London, but the easy days of persuading people that his word was 'as good as his bond' were over.[98]

Chapter 8

Marriage And Family

He used me very handsomely and with good manners upon all occasions, even to the last, only spent all I had, and left me to rob the creditors for something to subsist on.

Moll Flanders
Daniel Defoe, 1722

DANIEL COULD HAVE BEEN accosted in the street in Cripplegate, London, by Nathanial Sammen, a weaver and follower, some time in 1695. Daniel had been a lodger of Nathaniel's for some time, and on numerous occasions Nathaniel had offered refuge to Daniel: when he had been thrown out by his family, when he was avoiding creditors, or when he was on the run from the law. Nathaniel had supported Daniel because he believed him to be a great man. He was deeply attached to him. Daniel was often in funds and had been generous to him and his family on many occasions but, for Nathaniel, his loyalty was never a matter of money.

Daniel's generosity had extended to his wife Elizabeth and they had become a threesome. It was not a surprise to Nathaniel that his wife had become pregnant by Daniel, for it had happened before, but it did require discussion. There would be expenses and new arrangements and understandings. Nathaniel did not mind it, but others might. He did not want the news spread, for whatever Daniel got up to on his journeys, this was Spittalfields, London, and there was the issue of Daniel's public standing to consider. Daniel had not denied responsibility for the child. He said he would do the right thing, as he had done before, and Nathaniel did not doubt it.

This time, Daniel decided there was a need to distance himself from gossip by setting up a separate establishment where he and Elizabeth could bring up their children. The Marriage Assessments records in the City of London Metropolitan Archives show that in 1695/6 Daniel Foe was living in London on the left side of Moor Fields in the Parish of St Botolph's, Bishopsgate, with his wife Elizabeth, their children Daniel and Sarah, and one servant, Hannah How.[99]

It might be argued that this statement provided by the couple to the surveyor of taxes is untrue but there is supporting evidence that the Sarah referred to was a child of Elizabeth Sammen and baptised as her child by Nathaniel Sammen in April 1697.[100] The entry in the Parish register is peculiar. Upon a first reading it could not be found. A second search found it out of sequence between two other entries, as if it had been placed there after the event.

It would not surprise the reader of Daniel's fictions that he and the Sammens had something of a ménage à trois. In *Moll Flanders, Colonel Jack* and *Roxana* there are similar arrangements, some explicitly stated and others implied. But the nature of these relationships is surprising. They are considered at length later in Daniel's story.

In real life Daniel's marital relationships were complex. He acquired three 'wives' by whom he had eight surviving children. From around 1694 he always had two 'family' households to maintain and sometimes three. These households were real: wives and children looked to Daniel for financial and emotional support; he looked to them for refuge and acceptable domesticity (that he could leave and return to as he pleased). He needed them for a veneer of respectability: as a cover for other necessary identities which included an active homosexuality.

These marriages and the children they created are set out in a chart at the end of this book, together with Daniel's principal same-sex relationships. It can be seen from the chart that Daniel maintained these relationships for long periods of time and that his need of them was life-long. Almost certainly these dependencies were the result of a recognition of the need to sustain the children they produced, but also the need to conceal beneath a veil of domesticity the troublesome nature of his sexuality.

Daniel's relationships with the Sammens gave him 'family' cover in the City of London. It was needed only when his bankruptcy finally burst asunder his legal marriage with Mary Tuffley. The marital arrangements he created with Mary Norton provided 'family' refuge in Tilbury. It was important for Daniel to keep these 'family' worlds separate and the knowledge of them protected. He was never wholly successful with the necessary subterfuges, for rumours of them dogged his every step, but it has been difficult for posterity to prove their existence.

Mary Tuffley was Daniel's only legal wife and remained so until Daniel's death in 1731. His marriages to Elizabeth Sammen and Mary Norton were by private treaty. They were something more than mistresses who had produced children and are called marriages here because the people involved believed they were: the adults accepted responsibilities for each other, and were committed to looking after the children of their union. While such marriages lacked legality, they were for most circumstances accepted as valid unions. Their principal drawback was that they conveyed no automatic inheritance rights for widows and children. Those difficulties were to complicate Daniel's last days and led to him making complex arrangements for his children and dying intestate.

Nevertheless, it is puzzling. Why would Nathaniel Sammen apparently accept a situation where his wife would live with Daniel and Sarah and yet be willing for the child to be baptised as his?

The explanation lies in the close friendship of the two men and their mutual definition of it; they were willing to share the same woman and the resulting children.

The relationship between Nathaniel and Daniel lasted a long time. They knew each other through common residence in Cripplegate. Nathaniel stood by Daniel throughout the difficulties leading to his arrest and his punishment in the pillory. When on 20 May 1703 Daniel was arrested on a warrant alleging seditious libel, he was at Nathaniel's home. It had been a place of refuge for Daniel over many years. Later, in September 1704, Nathaniel was arrested for involvement in distributing Daniel's pamphlet, *Legion's Memorial*. He did nothing to incriminate Daniel in its authorship and distribution, and for his loyalty was sent to languish in Newgate Prison.

Following his imprisonment, Nathaniel had been forced to work as a journeyman and in a real sense he was a ruined man. Rumours about Nathaniel and Daniel were rife throughout their lifetime. When in 1706 Daniel was in Scotland, an anonymous pamphlet appeared which attacked him. It was provocative in stating, 'One thing Daniel, I want to know that, is whether you keep up your Beau habit, your long wig, with Tossels at the end of it, your Iron-bound hat, and your blew Cloak? As also whether you have left your old Wont, of holding out your little finger to show your Diamond Ring.' This description is full of sexual innuendo which would have been recognisable to readers of the pamphlet: it is a description of an effeminate man, or Mollie, or both. The author then goes on to accuse Daniel of an affair with Sammen's wife and of having a child by her, and alleged that Nathaniel's association with Daniel had ruined him entirely.[101]

Previous commentators have remarked upon these rumours. Among the most recent, Maximillian Novak wrote, 'The rumours concerning an illegitimate child were persistent, and they should not be swept under the carpet in the manner practised by all previous biographers without some consideration of the nature of his [Daniel's] sexuality.' However, in his biographical works Novak did just that: he buried the issue of Daniel's sexuality.

The Daniel junior shown in the Marriage Assessment, 1695/6 is Daniel Defoe's elder son, previously assumed to be a product of his marriage to Mary Tuffley. Among the considerable body of supporting evidence for the younger Daniel's illegitimacy is the record to be found in Dudley Ryder's diary.[102] Ryder speaks of meeting a young Defoe, a fellow pupil at the Inner Temple. This Defoe described himself as Daniel senior's heir apparent. Ryder believed that this boy, therefore, must be Daniel junior and was surprised that he turned out to be Benjamin. But unknown to Ryder, Benjamin Defoe was entered at the Inner Temple on 29 August 1715, as the 'son and heir apparent of Daniel Defoe of Stoke Newington'. It is generally supposed that Daniel junior was older than Benjamin. This being so, Daniel junior would not have been his father's heir only if he were illegitimate.

Similarly, at the end of this story, when a Mary Brooke was seeking to gain letters of administration and power to seize assets from Daniel's 'legitimate children' she did not name Daniel. She was given leave by the court to extend the hearing to a further date so that she could find Benjamin, Daniel's legitimate heir.[103]

Most recent biographers have assumed that the Defoe-Tuffley marriage was a happy one. It can be seen now that it was disastrous. From the beginning it could hardly have been worse, with infidelity on both sides. Since it is easy to blame Daniel, it is worth considering whether there is blame to be placed on the other side too.

Daniel received a large dowry and this might have been because Mary was not very marriageable. It was not only Daniel who suggested that Mary might have been mentally unstable. Once freed of the control of the Tuffley family, Mary may have found the strains of marriage to a difficult man too much for her. However, it was convenient for both Daniel and Mary to continue with the marriage.

There were many defining moments in the marriage and one of these was Daniel's bankruptcy in 1692. It is easy to imagine the family consequences. In 1693 when the news of Daniel's bankruptcy could no longer be kept a secret, there would have been a family gathering initiated by his brother-in-law, Samuel Tuffley, and attended by James Foe. The understandings they were to reach then would last their lifetimes. Finally, it became obvious that the family was going to break up; they were not surprised, for there had already been difficulties to contend with.

Daniel may have described these difficulties in his account of Colonel Jack's first marriage.[104] Daniel writes, 'We soon found a house proper for our dwelling [but soon] she resolved to seem nothing but what she really was...perfectly loose [and] she kept company that I did not like.' He thought that she was spending too much money and 'She took fire at that and flew out in a passion, and, after a great many bitter words, told me in short that she saw no occasion to alter her conduct.' It was 'Daniel' that broke things off. He writes, 'I began the separation first, and refused her my bed.' She had a son but it did not reconcile them. He left home but 'kept a couple of agents to spy on her'. Sure enough, another son was born but not one fathered by Daniel/Colonel Jack.

If this is an account of Daniel and Mary's early years together, it cannot be taken literally. It might be more reasonable to suppose, from all that is known, that the truth was the opposite to the account. If a gender reversal is used, it would be Daniel that did the over-spending, was often absent, and keeping bad company (which might include sex with men). The first child born out of wedlock could have been Daniel and nothing is known of the second. This child might have died (a child called Mary did die) or the father might have taken responsibility for it.

There was much Tuffley family indignation at the social and religious disgrace of the bankruptcy and the dishonouring of family financial agreements, but there was an over-riding need for practical arrangements to be put in place. Even as the family gathered there would have been an agent near-by watching the house for Daniel and a bailiff on call.

It was decided that Joan Tuffley, Daniel's aunt-in-law, was to accommodate Mary's children and Daniel his own. It might be supposed that the Tuffleys would have decided on certain house-rules: that, for example, Daniel was not to visit the house unannounced or in daytime and perhaps, if he did so, he was to enter and leave by the back entrance to avoid the nuisance of creditors and bailiffs. Almost certainly, they would have discussed how these children were to be supported financially. Both families were determined to make Daniel pay for his misdeeds.

Harsh words would have been spoken but they would not have been the last words on this subject. In his lifetime, Daniel was in severe money difficulties on many occasions and spent much of his life contriving to avoid creditors or the law. The unrelenting pursuit of his creditors, the public allegations and opprobrium, and the continual threat of the bailiffs, must have outraged Mary. The subterfuge of getting money to her in someone else's home must have dispirited her, while the public disgrace of his imprisonments would have been shameful. It is likely that her life would have been extremely difficult. Defoe wrote in *Serious Reflections,* 'His wife could not bear it…went first away from him; and afterwards away from herself turning melancholy and distracted.'

Thomas Wright suggests that this period of matrimonial rupture lasted for twenty-nine years, the period of Robinson's stay upon his island. This statement may seem at first to be nonsensical but Daniel himself gives credence to a long family rupture. Writing on the 23 August 1706, Defoe says he had been in retreat for fourteen years (from his first bankruptcy to his stay in Scotland) with 'jeopardy, broils, and most of his time spent in banishment from his family'.[105] From the Act of Union with Scotland in 1707 (the passing of which was his reason for being in Scotland) and the date at which he returned to England, there is no evidence of Daniel living with Mary Tuffley until 1714. And then, as I shall suggest, the occupation of the house in Stoke Newington was not as Daniel has presented it.

It was a difficult period for most men and women to dissolve marriages. If it had been easier, Daniel's marriage to Mary Tuffley would not have lasted long. As it happened, it survived forty-seven years. It is argued by many biographers that there was love and respect in the relationship. The protagonists for this point of view point out that upon Defoe's arrest and subsequent trial for seditious libel in 1703, Mary Tuffley interceded on his behalf at a meeting with the Earl of Nottingham.

The source of this information is Daniel himself. He went on to complain that Nottingham sought unsuccessfully to seduce his wife. Daniel is one of the world's greatest liars and the reader must always look to his motive in making statements. A complaint about the seduction of the weak by the strong, and the humiliation of one man by another in claiming a privilege over his wife, was common at the time. Daniel was seeking to show Lord Harley, the recipient of this information, that Nottingham's motive in issuing an arrest warrant was to humiliate him (and others who held his view) and to influence Harley in his favour and against Nottingham.

The understandable reactions of the Tuffley family to Daniel's bankruptcy would seem to have angered Daniel. When Daniel writes in *Serious Reflections* that his family rupture was caused by 'the unsuitable conversation of some of his nearest relations', he may have been referring to the Tuffleys. It was to be expected that their criticism of the breech of Daniel's obligations to Mary would be extreme, but Daniel was never to accept their protestations. He is adamant on the point in *Serious Reflections*. He says, 'not all the tears and entreaties of his friends, no, not of his wife and children could prevail with him to break his silence'. His words read as if it was the bad behaviour of his family which caused the breach with Mary; that it was their ill humour which was the occasion of it because they treated him with provoking language, which put him into indecent passions and urged him to give rash replies.

In reality, the Tuffleys were fed up with Daniel and his behaviour, having been lumbered with a family which they needed to sustain and support. Daniel expresses their feelings in fiction. In *Roxana*, her husband's family is sternly resistant to taking on the care of her children when he absconds and, in desperation, she arranged to abandon them on the family's doorstep.[106]

All this is not to say that Daniel Defoe did not regret his alienation from his first family and his hopes for it, for surely he did. In *A Journal of the Plague Year*, in a passage of great warmth and feeling, Daniel writes of a poor waterman who sits outside his house where there is infection but who provides for his family within:

'Why,' says he, 'if they may be said to live, for my wife and one of my children are visited, but I do not come at them'. And with that word I saw the tears run very plentifully down his face: and so did mine too, I assure you [...] 'I do not abandon them from want [...]' I had happened on a man that was no hypocrite, but a serious, religious, good man [...] in such a condition as he was in, he should be able to say his family did not want. The waterman says, 'I seldom come on shore here, and I came only to call on my wife and hear how my family do, and give them a little money.' I turned a little away from the man [...] for, indeed, I could no more refrain from tears than he had a family to bind him to attendance, which I had not.[107]

Might this not be Daniel, displacing his real self to a fictional character, speaking of all those years of absence from his first wife and family? Might he have been writing here about a place where Mary Tuffley's family had given them a permanent home while he resorted to alternative shelters? Might he not be writing of his efforts to support them? Is this not his grief, at least in that moment of recollection, at rupture from them? But, perhaps, they were no more than crocodile tears.

There is also Daniel's marriage to Mary Norton, and his other illegitimate children, to be accounted for, subjects so long glossed over by biographers. One of the purposes of this biography is to unravel these matters. The extent to which these arrangements of Daniel's were known to Mary Tuffley and her children is unknown, but if they knew of them, and they must gradually have come to know everything, the awareness must have been painful.

The earliest source of stories about these other arrangements starts with contemporary gossip, and not only about Elizabeth Sammen. In about 1721, a hack writer, Benjamin Norton Defoe, who worked for various newspapers, made his sorry appearance. Sutherland writes that, '[a]ccording to Pope, who got his information from Richard Savage, this Benjamin Defoe was a bastard son of Defoe's... Daniel Defoe's son of love by a lady who vended oysters'.[108] Sutherland argued that the evidence was inconclusive while admitting the circumstances to be suspicious. Defoe's biographers, earlier and later, have indignantly (or imperiously) ignored the evidence that he was indeed Daniel's son.

In the early eighteenth century it was unusual, as Sutherland points out, to find a boy with two Christian names, especially as the middle name is a surname, and the common sense conclusion is that this addition is the recognition of a mother. There is a contemporary record which shows that Benjamin Norton referred to himself as Mr Norton. Daniel's second and legitimate son was called Benjamin. The question posed by previous biographers is whether there were two Defoe Benjamins.

The answer to this question is that 'they' cannot really be the same person. There are a variety of records identifying who the legitimate Benjamin is: the registration of his entry into Edinburgh University in 1709, his wedding to Hannah Coates in Norwich in 1718, the birth of his son, also called Benjamin, in 1719, two years before the appearance of Benjamin Norton, the registration information at the Temple in 1715, his naming in Mrs Brooke's application for power of administration over Daniel's estate in 1732, and a place for him in Mary Tuffley's will in 1732. There is never an occasion in these records when use is made of the middle name of Norton.

Mary Brooke, when seeking administration of Daniel's estate in 1732, told the court that Benjamin could not be found, that he had not been seen for five or six years and that he was either dead or gone overseas. It was not likely that he was dead, for otherwise his mother would not have left him a sum of money for him to buy a ring in her memory.

Mrs Brooke was well-advised and serious in her searches. If the 'two' Benjamins were one and the same man, she would have had no difficulty in locating him in the form of the London journalist Benjamin Norton. If the legitimate Benjamin had disappeared around the years 1725–7, seven to nine years after his marriage, he can hardly have been the Benjamin Norton whose wife had had nineteen children of whom only three survived in the same period.

Daniel was a great coiner of allusions. Sutherland points out that 'Benjamin' in Hebrew means 'Child of Sorrow' which is suggestive but not conclusive of anything. For Sutherland, what is conclusive is the unreliability of anything said by Richard Savage and the fact that Defoe denied rumours about his sexuality. About Richard Savage it might be said that Sutherland has a point, especially on the subject of illegitimacy, but even liars such as Savage may on occasions tell the truth.

There is a basic flaw in Sutherland's reading of Defoe's character. A man who professes to be purer than most, and is not, invites retaliation, and retaliation invites protestation. When Defoe writes, 'But if I must act the Pharisee a little, I must begin thus; God, I thank thee, I am not a drunkard, or a swearer, or a whoremaster, or a busie-body, or idle, or revengeful, etc., and I challenge all the world to prove the contrary', we know he is on safe ground because he is not accused of any of these vices. When he claims that his relations with women are beyond question and that '[h]e frankly defies the world to bring fair proof of his being guilty that way',[109] it might be answered that even if it were assumed that the evidence could be gathered, men might differ on what they considered to be fair proof. It might be said of Sutherland's judgement that if there was nothing in the rumours about Benjamin Norton's parentage, it would have been in Defoe's interest to deny them specifically. He was never to do so.

James Sutherland is a distinguished biographer and it can be said that if he had in his possession the evidence that has been gathered now about Daniel Defoe, he would have reached a different judgement. There can be little doubt that Daniel Defoe had a variety of domestic and sexual relations with men and women.

If then there are two Benjamin Defoes, who is Benjamin Norton Defoe? He is the illegitimate son of Daniel Defoe and Mary Simmons, whose maternal surname was Norton, and he was born on or about 1695 in Coggeshall, Essex, some five miles from Colchester.

A marriage of Richard Simmons to Mary Norton is included in the records of the Colchester Quaker Meeting held on 17 January 1675, as follows:

Richard Simmons son of John & Elizabeth Simmonds of Chesterford to Mary Norton daughter of Samuel & Mary Norton of Coxall' (Coggeshall).[110]

Another Richard Simmons was a son of this union, and a carpenter. When Richard Simmons junior died in 1741 he left a croft of freehold land in Fordham, which he had bought some years earlier with a mortgage, and his executor was charged with the selling of it and distributing the estate among his three children who included a daughter Mary. This Mary called herself Mary Norton. This land is adjacent to the land Daniel leased from the Corporation of Colchester in 1722.

When Daniel could not pay the first annual rent for his land, a Mary Norton lent him £200 pounds as a mortgage to enable him to do so. The indenture was created at the home of Edmund Raynham, a former alderman and town clerk who had just been appointed Lord Mayor. The indenture was signed by Mary Norton and witnessed by Edmund Raynham and William Coe, on production of the money. On the 27 November 1727 this mortgage was redeemed by Daniel and Mary Norton signed to release him from further obligations.[111]

A link between Daniel Defoe and Richard Simmonds, carpenter, is found in the papers of John Ward, the farm manager appointed by Daniel to manage his interests in the land. A sum of £7 12 shillings is included in a schedule provided by Ward in his Chancery claim against Daniel, which shows that Ward paid Richard Simmons, carp. on behalf of Daniel Defoe.[112]

It is possible, although unlikely, that the Mary Norton who mothered Benjamin Norton is the Mary Norton who married Richard Simmons in 1675. This Mary seems to have lived to old age, because her probable date of death was in 1747. It is more likely that Daniel Defoe's Mary Norton is her daughter who would have been born in the 1670s and who was approaching twenty years of age in the mid-1690s and was unmarried. In Daniel's fictions[113] there is support for the case of this being the younger Mary, and I conclude that it is her.

All the principals in this story and their immediate friends and acquaintances are Quakers. The knowledge that Defoe was associated with a Quaker community of interests explains his fascination for Quakers in his writings. There is no way of knowing the precise age of Benjamin Norton. As he was born illegitimately to a Quaker mother, it is not likely that his birth would be registered anywhere. As he became known as a young journalist in London in the early 1720s it is likely that he was born in the 1690s.

The Quaker communities of which the Nortons and the Simmons were a part included oyster merchants and dredgers, and it is entirely possible that Mary Norton sold oysters. So, when Pope writes that, according to Richard Savage, Benjamin Norton Defoe was the bastard son of Daniel's 'by a lady who vended oysters' he was, for once, telling the truth.

It is not entirely true that no biographer has given any consideration to Daniel's other women or to the importance of his life in Colchester and the surrounding area. What has been known for a long time is that Daniel bought marshland at Tilbury Fort in Essex in the 1670s and 1680s, with mortgages in the names of Marescoe, Stamper and Ghisleyn, and that the land included a brickworks and the use of a wharf and house.

The leases for 70 acres of land were excluded from his bankruptcy settlement in 1692 and Daniel succeeded in resisting the efforts of the mortgagees to recover their advances, first by slowing them down and then by winning the Chancery case they brought against him in 1699. He achieved this by arguing that what is called the equity of redemption applied. Under this principle the mortgagees could not succeed until the debt with its accumulated interest reached the actual value of the property. Defoe argued successfully that rents paid to the mortgagees should be taken into account.[114]

Writing to Harley, Defoe stated that the brickworks at Tilbury, 'began to pay me very well... I began to live, Took a Good House, bought me a Coach and horses a Second Time'.[115] It was not an establishment that Mary Tuffley and her children enjoyed. According to gossip, and amplified during a court action against Daniel for overcharging on beer he sold to his factory workers from a hostelry he had established in Tilbury, he had set up home with another woman. As we know now, the other woman was Mary Norton.

What can be seen emerging in this discussion about Daniel's 'family life' is a pattern of behaviour. Daniel never chose to be long without a family support system. When his first family disintegrated Daniel re-created it elsewhere. Daniel was constantly on the move but his allegiance to Essex was unshakeable. Between 1694 and his death in 1731, he was almost always in possession of land in the Colchester area: he traded, farmed and operated businesses there, and he had domestic arrangements there which included his 'wife' and children.

There was never any question of Mary Tuffley joining Daniel in these other parts of his world, but he was rarely on his own. Daniel had created 'substitute families'. When on the run and taking refuge, he needed shelter and food, but also the challenge and comfort of sexual relationships and their affirmation of his manhood. In business, he seemed willing to use his sexuality to seal a bargain. As he was rejected in one place, he found another. In an age when sealing the marriage bond could be informal and not easily checked, he entered into domestic understandings that amounted to marriage bonds, whatever else they were called in public.

The marriage with Mary Tuffley may have been a disaster from the very beginning, but perhaps it contained hopes and dreams which did not easily fade away. It is said that in a close or long union the deceived partner is always aware at some level of the misconduct of the other. It may be that Mary 'knew' of these other arrangements and tolerated them as and when they were created. But at some point she ceased to care and decided to make her own way because she was seeking to defend the welfare of her children. Mary may have come to hate Daniel for his sexuality and bad character, but she may have admired him for his intelligence, industry and worldly success.

There might be many reasons for being able to write that when Lord Harley, the puritan, was relying on both Swift and Defoe for propaganda, that Swift, the Anglican, went in by the front door and Defoe, the dissenter, by the back.[116] The vituperation and malevolence of Daniel's enemies can be explained by many factors, but one was their knowledge of his use of sexual relationships with men. Daniel's appearance and his foppishness were not mere affectation and the desire to be thought a gentleman, but the outward sign of promiscuous activity. For a time, at some level of awareness, Mary would have been loyal to Daniel, despite all the reasons she had to despise him and the constant pain and provocation he brought to her life, because she knew that he could not help his behaviour. He might well have wanted to be a good husband and father yet have been unable to fulfil those roles.

By this stage in Daniel's story, the time of his bankruptcy, Mary would have known the nature of Daniel's sexuality and have had a sense of what it might become. At the very beginning his behaviour might have been seen as relatively harmless to her. The nearest approximation to a gay sub-culture was to be found in the backrooms of taverns and coffee bars, where there were male brothels and young boys to hire. Cross-dressing was common and seen both as an expression of high spirits and a declaration of personal freedom by both men and women.

Arguably, what was inherited from an earlier age was a form of homoeroticism which was usually not physically expressed. It was common for men to write to one another in terms of deep and sentimental affection. When a man was ambitious, as Daniel was, it was common to ingratiate himself with the powerful in homoerotic terms, and the possession of power was often accompanied by the pleasure of receiving such approaches.

But there was a point in time, which might have been very early in the marriage, when Mary seems to have decided that she was not going to share her bed with a husband who had just shared his with another man – perhaps, any other man, and a culmination of activities in a tavern which carried the risk of catching an incurable and nasty sexual disease.

Chapter 9

Recovery

The God that gave me brains will give me bread.
An Elegy on the Author of the True Born Englishman
Daniel Defoe, 1704

GOD GAVE DANIEL DEFOE more than brains. He gave him a steely resolution, inexhaustible energy and an eye for opportunity. In his many setbacks and vicissitudes Daniel Defoe showed great resilience: although cast down and dispirited he always bounced back to show new spirit and enterprise. In some respects, however, it can be seen that he never recovered from his bankruptcy in 1692.

Following the bankruptcy, Daniel's first inclination was to conduct his affairs as normally as possible. It was to be business as usual. His hosiery business in Freeman's Yard continued but the work was conducted by his assistant. While Daniel could not front the business, because of pressure from creditors, there must have been some financial understanding between the two men which enabled him to keep going. Perhaps Daniel traded the use of the accommodation above the shop, now vacated by Mary and the children, while preserving a bed for himself. Whatever the terms of the arrangement, it made funds available to Daniel.

When the next trace of Daniel is found, it is in the organisation of private lotteries from an address a few doors down from his premises in Freeman's Yard, which suggests that they remained for a while at the centre of his activities. These lotteries were in the interest of Thomas Neale, a groom-porter in charge of gambling in the anteroom of the royal palace. He had a licence to conduct them. Neale had the reputation of being something of a gambler himself. In 1692–3 he was involved in over thirty-seven projects from which he made a profit. He spent his money in pursuit of influence and gain.

Daniel Defoe was named as a 'Manager's Trustee' of these lotteries and would have taken money from them. Thomas Neale was also named as a Trustee. There is little doubt that these private lotteries were corrupt and the public tired of them in the end. All offices of this kind and even, or especially, state appointments were accepted as conferring a licence to print money. However, although illegal profits could be made, it was regarded as poor form to overdo it. Even the great Samuel Pepys got into trouble for corrupt practices. His most recent biographer, Claire Tomalin, does not deny that he took the usual quota of pickings.

Lotteries as a form of gambling were disapproved of by nonconformists of all shades. Even to this day a solid body of religious opinion frowns upon all forms of gambling. Daniel would not have wanted to be prominently associated with gambling and, to the extent that he wished at this time to retain the confidence of his nonconforming followers, he may have wished to move on as soon as possible.

Thomas Neale had an inside track to the happenings at William III's Court. How he came to achieve it is not known but for the next seven years, until he over-reached himself, he possessed, in a royal license, a permission to 'print money', but, to make it, he needed the active collaboration of the determined, conscientious and unscrupulous.

As an outsider William was dependent on the use of his royal prerogative to influence public affairs and to get things done. As the nation was drawn into foreign wars, the power of the executive expanded and opposition to the Crown grew with it. As royal policy became to be opposed by parliament there was an executive need to circumvent it. The rewards for collaboration with the Crown grew to fantastic extremes. A major national war effort always brings the very worst of society to the light of day and for some years under William there were rich pickings for the unscrupulous.

Daniel became one of Thomas Neale's 'bag men'. He had the qualities to succeed in the role. The evidence from his fictions discussed later suggests that Daniel and Thomas Neale had a long-standing sexual relationship. Daniel would have taken advantage of the relationship to be moved 'onwards and upwards'.

Neale introduced Daniel to Dalby Thomas, a fellow lottery Trustee. In 1695 Dalby became one of three commissioners to devise and supervise the collection of the duty on glass. Dalby Thomas gave Daniel the job of accountant to the commissioners at a salary of £100 per annum, rising to £150.

The commission had been created to raise money for William's wars and became unpopular as the public resistance to these wars grew. This was Daniel's first state appointment and he was not to mention it until 1715, twenty years later.[117] A great deal of public money would have passed through his hands and he would have had a share of it.

Defoe had good reason to stay quiet about this appointment until the issue of the 1673 Test Act was less controversial. The Act required all those taking up an official post, civil or military, to swear an oath of allegiance to the monarch and to submit a Sacrament Certificate showing that they had taken Holy Communion in an Anglican church on at least three recent occasions. There was no exception for Daniel Defoe. Daniel's many biographers have been slow to appreciate that the position he occupied as accountant to the commission was an office under the Crown and that Daniel was required to conform to the requirements of the Test Act.

In 1695 parliament heard from King William of a plot to assassinate him planned from Paris. There was an overwhelming parliamentary majority for the actions William thought necessary to deal with the conspiracy. On 27 January 1696 William ordered all those holders of offices under the Crown to renew their oath of allegiance. A period of time to the end of May was given to conform. Daniel swore his oath in April 1696 and his name is recorded in the Chancery record for the month ending 29 April 1696.[118]

There are gaps in the Chancery and Exchequer records for Sacrament Certificates in the period 1695–1700 and it is not possible to trace Daniel's. It is possible that he may have deposited a certificate in a Quarter Sessions convenient to him. If so, some diligent researcher may find it.

However, as is common, Daniel wrote about the experience. In the *Tour*, Daniel writes about the emotions felt by a dissenter taking the sacrament in an Anglican church:

I remember that going with some friends to show them this magnificent Palace…[the Royal Chapel at Windsor]…when the Dissenters were a little uneasy at being obliged to kneel at the Sacrament one of my friends… who was a Dissenter… fixed his eyes on the alter-piece… he whispered… how can your people persecute us for refusing to kneel at the Sacrament… that was not the place for him and I to dispute it… we did [later], but brought it to no conclusion, so tis useless to mention it any more.

Arguably, the dissenter in the church is Daniel, and his friend, the narrator, is his conscience. The Royal Chapel is the symbol of a royal appointment but it is not likely that Daniel took communion there.[119] The true occasion can be imagined: St Jacobi's Parish Church served a rural community and its parishioners came by cart, horse and on foot three times on a Sunday from many a mile away. Nevertheless, it was a close-knit congregation where neighbours knew and cared for each other. Strangers were rare and commented upon. In October 1694 the congregation were curious about a stranger muffled in a cape too thick and warm for the clement autumn weather and a wide-brimmed hat which hid his face and expression. Reverently, he joined the queue for communion and when done he moved away. When all was finished, he was to be found cloistered with the vicar who seemed to know of his purpose and obliged him.

This common misunderstanding of the nature of Daniel's appointment as accountant to the Glass Commissioners is compounded by another startling discovery in research for this book. It is assumed that when the tax on glass was abolished in December 1699 the work of the Commission ended and the staff was dismissed. However, my research shows that it did not wind up its affairs until 1712, nearly thirteen years later. The commissioners and their staff, which included Daniel Defoe, went on receiving salaries throughout this period. This information is to be found in the final accounting statement of the commission, dated 16 July 1712, which was prepared by Daniel Defoe on behalf of the commissioners.[120]

In the opening preamble to these accounts it is explained that the offices were held 'until such time as they were determined' and that they (the officers) were empowered to collect the tax and 'the issuing, expending and laying out of the same [funds] to paying the salaries to the said Commissioners [and] the Officers, Clerks and other employees under them in the managing and collecting the duties or for the Incident Charges of their Office… and for the accounting of all hereafter'.

In these accounts it is specifically stated that Daniel received his salary in 1700 and 1701. In 1704 and 1710 special warrants were issued for the payment of arrears of salaries and expenses. No doubt these monies were to plug holes in the revenues collected from the late payers of duties caused by the commissioners and officers paying themselves ahead of any counterbalancing sums. In 1712 Daniel received specific remuneration for the preparation of the accounts but the amount is not stated.

It is amazing that the commissioners were permitted to spend nearly thirteen years collecting overdue taxes and winding up their affairs. During this time they were paid generous salaries out of public funds and enjoyed the benefit, no doubt, of additional revenue from corrupt practices.

It is of great interest and significance also that these tawdry accounts were signed off and the commissioners' affairs brought to an end by the signature of Harley, both in his name and as the Earl of Oxford. There is evidence that the relationship between Robert Harley and Daniel cooled in 1712. If it had not, would the commission have rolled on for a further two years until the new Whig administration brought it to an end?

In his lifetime, Defoe campaigned strenuously against dissenters seeking public office and obeying the Test Act and against the practice of occasional conformity, whereby dissenters could hold offices in corporations so long as they took communion in an Anglican church from time to time. In his public arguments, Daniel stated his belief that the act debased the communion service and tempted men to equivocate on what they really believed for private gain. Daniel claimed to know more about occasional conformity than any man in Britain: he may well have been right. His pamphlet arguments, often presented anonymously, were logical, consistent and compelling and, in their personal attacks on named individuals, extremely unpleasant.

A man might reasonably object to the Test Act. However, it stood the test of time as an assurance to the public that servants of the Crown would not use their positions to assist rebellion against lawful authority. At the very least, it can be seen that Daniel's relentless attacks on individuals taking the Test were not principled. Why did he make these attacks? Perhaps there was a kind of rage at the disappointment of being overlooked for elected office. In reality, there was no possibility, after his bankruptcy in 1692, for Daniel to achieve public office in the City of London, for his reputation was ruined. Later, despite all Daniel's requests and manoeuvrings there was no hope of a position under the Crown elsewhere, despite his occasional statements to the contrary.

Daniel knew he was talented. He believed himself to be more knowledgeable and more energetic than the dignitaries he saw preferred, but he was distrusted and actively disliked. Perversely, throughout Daniel's journalistic career he was most venomous in attacking those individuals who occupied positions that he coveted or careers he would have liked to emulate.

Unlike other biographers, who have denied or ignored the nature of Daniel Defoe's occupation of a corrupt public office, I have faced up to it and to the conclusions which must be drawn from it. In this account of his life I have largely ignored the stream of Defoe pamphlets on the Test Act and on occasional conformity. Harsh judgement though it might be, in the light of his occupation of a corrupt office under the Crown for over fifteen years, his crusade against others performing just such offices was little more than hypocrisy, jealousy and cant.

In 1696, Dalby Thomas was instrumental in helping Daniel in another venture from which he made money. On his 70 acres of land at Tilbury and with money from his profits from administrating the duty on glass, Daniel built a factory for the manufacture of bricks. In 1696 the factory was supplying bricks for Greenwich Hospital and became the chief source of supply for roof pantiles in London and elsewhere. Although the Tilbury marshes are isolated and inhospitable, Daniel spent a great deal of time there.

It has been argued that at this time, for political and journalistic services rendered, Daniel received money from William III. Daniel Defoe would like readers to believe that he was close to the monarch, for whom he set up some kind of intelligence network. There were connections to the Court, of whom Thomas Neale was one, but it is doubtful whether they amounted to the relationship suggested by Daniel and some biographers.

There could be no truth in the thought that in some way Daniel had a special or friendly relationship with William, for the social distance between them would have precluded it. Quite apart from the determining factor of class and position, William was an austere and withdrawn figure, often absent abroad and surrounded by his Dutch advisors. For Daniel, William was something of a remote father figure, to be admired at a distance, much as it seemed the young Robinson Crusoe related to his father.

It has been supposed that Daniel was a member of the Royal Regiment chosen to be 'the guards for their majesties' persons' and thus in a special position at Court. The evidence for this is Oldmixon's description of a military pageant organised in honour of William and Mary on 29 October 1689, in which Daniel took part. However, Daniel was there because he was a liveryman, a position to which he was entitled through his father's 'guild membership'.

Thirty years later in one of Gildon's satires, the author imagines Defoe's fright at the thought of serving abroad in the Royal Regiment. It is not likely that Gildon knew one way or another whether Defoe was part of the regiment. If conjectural, it was probably based on hearsay: that Defoe had boasted of a membership to those who knew no different. The Royal Regiment was full of City of London grandees and to them, after the disgrace of bankruptcy, Defoe was strictly persona non grata.

What is far more likely is that Daniel contrived to be of use to the king through Thomas Neale. Once established in Tilbury, Daniel was able to pick up his trading activity. He would have been able to provide sweeteners to those merchants and factors he needed to use and seek out new trading partners. It was likely that with a more stable trading base he was able to restore trading relationships. This trade enabled him to continue his travels to various parts of England and to report back on political happenings and opinion.

This gathering of evidence of opinion might well have been useful to the king's advisors as an antidote or correction to the City of London and parliament. If so, Daniel may have been paid sums of money for this work through Thomas Neale. When Daniel writes later of setting up an 'intelligence service' he was over-cooking his role. What he was doing was receiving money for occasional reports.

In his own mind Daniel might have gone back into the City, where he had business to conduct, as a kind of royal emissary. In reality he had no protection at all and his every movement brought him closer to jeopardy. In the City of London, Daniel's name was mud. It was widely and rightly believed that Daniel had not declared all his assets and it is likely that his debts were such that had he declared them all he would have been overwhelmed. By avoiding declaration Daniel made himself the prey of others for a very long time but at least he could get on with his life.

Daniel seems to have decided that the way out of his difficulties was to take even greater risks with the hope of great rewards, for it would only be by speculations that he could make the money needed to pay off his debts or, alternatively, to achieve the social position in life from which he could face down his creditors. Daniel needed to be seen as successful and a gentleman of means. He persuaded himself that this was the way to earn the confidence of others and to convince them that he was a man to do business with. How else could he be expected to pay off his debts?

Despite the bravado, the effects of his bankruptcy must have devastated Defoe and in Backscheider's words it had changed Defoe for ever from 'a prominent joiner of respected groups to a solitary with secrets, and from a tradesman to a writer'.[121] The changes were forced upon him.

The social and religious consequences of his bankruptcy have been underestimated. It would have been common practice for a Presbyterian church to expel a member for his bankruptcy (an event which would be shameful). Studies of nonconformist church records have revealed that even into the twentieth century nonconformist churches were expelling members for their financial problems.[122]

It is not known for certain whether Daniel was thrown out of his church but it is highly likely that he was. When Daniel tells his readers that he was fearful of going to church because his creditors might find him there, his words are best interpreted as meaning that he was no longer welcome to the congregation. No nonconformist church of this time would have permitted such a disgrace to go unpunished.

An expulsion would have marked the first stretch line with the dissenting communities so necessary for Defoe's sense of identity. It may have made him an itinerant. It was possible for him to visit a church but not as a member. He was cast outside and vilified for being there.

The Tuffley family were devout dissenters who held strong views on bankruptcy and would have been among the first to condemn the bankrupt. James Foe must have held similar views. James must have passed through some very difficult times in his City career as a merchant but, as far as is known, he would have been proud of his achievements. If he were a devout dissenter, as has been suggested, he would have been horrified by his son's bankruptcy and imprisonment, although as a trader himself he might well have understood the events that had led to it. Novak has suggested that James Foe would have been proud of his son; it is far more likely that he disowned him.

The reactions of Daniel's families and friends were severe and exaggerated but understandable. The strength of Daniel's reaction to them was extreme. In Tilbury he was well away from them all. His financial support of Mary Tuffley and her children was sporadic and inadequate, but for the time being he did not care about it and put them all out of his mind. In London he would stay with Elizabeth Sammen and sometimes with the Sammen family, depending on his resources at the time. Daniel was raised in an extended, dysfunctional and dislocated family and it would appear that as an adult he had created one of his own.

None of this is to suggest that Defoe did not care about his children or their fate. Although Defoe's desire to better himself, and his restlessness, carried him away from them, and while other sensual appetites may have diverted him, there is evidence of a father's concern for his children's welfare and education.

His children by Mary Tuffley owed it to the Tuffley family that they had a permanent home, while Daniel set up establishments elsewhere. It would have been resented by the Tuffleys, as they became aware of them. Perhaps for some of the time he was treated as a leper and kept at arm's length, despite his wish to have news of the children and to provide for them. A really bad man would have turned away and abandoned his family altogether

109

but, as Daniel suggests to us, 'he was no hypocrite, but a serious, religious, man' committed to the welfare of his family. There is evidence which bears him out.

Nevertheless, it was infuriating to many of Daniel's contemporaries that both these judgements of Daniel might be true, for they preferred to think ill of him without mitigation. The moral majority was not willing to go along with Daniel's own judgement of himself; that his upbringing had made him a serious and religious man but, being weak and as sinful as other men, he had succumbed to temptation. Daniel believed that providing he showed some repentance for what he had done, which in his better moments, he determined he would, God would forgive him. In the end, God's providence would work in his favour.

After a few years, Daniel must have felt much happier. He was out of harm's way in Tilbury. The Glass Commission gave him a steady income without demanding much from him. In Tilbury he could continue trading. His brick works were making money. He had secured an office under the Crown and made powerful friends. He was a big man in Tilbury and was beginning to live the life he had aspired to. In London, if he were careful, he could be near any new political, religious, industrial or scientific development. He put money into property, speculated when he could, and exchanged gossip in the coffee bars, clubs and taverns. He was on the alert for any advantage or threat.

In London his children were being cared for by Mary Tuffley and her family and by Elizabeth Sammen. Benjamin Norton, his son by Mary Norton, was with him and Mary in Tilbury. On occasions his Tilbury ménage came to London when Daniel needed to be there, and his Sammen ménage encamped to Tilbury when Elizabeth Sammen needed relief. Daniel became a practised conjuror of place and time. These families and children had to be supported financially on a regular basis. Part of the answer to the question as to why Daniel was obsessed with the need to earn money is that his wives and children needed a steady flow of it.

The evidence in his fiction is that the marital arrangement with Mary Norton was happy and successful. She was a simple girl, semi-literate, as her writing shows, with a love of children. Her Quaker background may have made her mild and honest, straightforward and calm. She loved children and they loved her. Daniel did not want more children but Mary did. Without Mary being wilful or cunning in any way, they may have come about perfectly normally as the result of an undemanding intimacy.

Daniel had sailed into calmer waters and easier times. On a quiet day, when looking over the Tilbury estuary where trading ships made their way to London or Harwich, Daniel's mood may have been bitter-sweet. It could not have been possible to look back without deep melancholy. However, Daniel had a sense of the mutability of human existence. As he looked across the steely-grey waters to those great ships on the horizon, he knew that his bankruptcy had changed some things for the worse and *for ever* but that he had come through.

MAKE ME
AN OFFER

1704 to 1714

Chapter 10

A Rush Of Blood

Queen Anne was ... a narrow- minded, bigoted woman; the tool of ambitious priests, who wished to protect or increase ecclesiastical power ... and wealth at the expense ... of the community. She showed herself the true daughter of James II. With her the church was always falling (and aspirants gathering places by following) 'the cry of the church is in danger'

William Chadwick

IF WILLIAM III HAD proved to be an exception to the rule and had turned out to be immortal, no one would have been happier than Daniel Defoe.

William had been unable to abolish the Test Act, for prudence demanded that he needed the support of Anglicans and the country Tories as well as Whigs and dissenters, but under his tutelage, at least at the beginning of his reign, passions subsided. Anyway, Daniel was willing to cheat. He took public office, kept quiet about it, and concentrated on the task of becoming seriously rich.

Daniel's writing came to public notice with the publication of *An Essay on Projects* in 1697. It was part of his design to enrich himself by involvement in public projects.[123] The Essay is a collection of proposals, all of which were already in the public domain, in the form of projects for bettering society. These projects include Banks, Highways, a Pension Office, Bankruptcy, Academies (in particular an Academy for the improvement of the English language, and an Academy for Women), and the welfare of seamen.

The Essay is dedicated to Dalby Thomas and produced for him. Dalby Thomas was Daniel's mentor at the Glass Commission and the person ultimately responsible for obtaining his appointment. He served on many governmental committees and commissions charged with public welfare and the raising of money for William's wars. Lotteries and other public projects were seen as ways to raise money. Dalby Thomas was on the Board of Greenwich Hospital and was probably responsible for Daniel getting an order to supply pantiles for the hospital. They were produced at his factory in Tilbury.

Dalby Thomas's public prominence, and the career of another associate, Thomas Neale, Daniel's friend and a Member of Parliament with influence at the Court, took a nasty turn when they were arrested in 1699 and charged with embezzling funds from a lottery. Neale was expelled from the House of Commons and died in December. Thomas used the influence of powerful friends to secure his release, but then was charged again for bribery in relation to a distilling bill under consideration by the House of Commons.

Daniel's *Essay* had something of the modern political 'think tank' about it. It disseminated ideas already in circulation and which might catch on in the form of a project. If they did, and as Daniel requests of Dalby, he would like to join in.

The mistake that is usually made in commenting upon the *Essay* is to assume that the ideas mooted are Daniel's. In fact they constitute Daniel's judgement of what projects might catch on and which would capture the energies of his sponsor, and, no doubt, he favoured those projects from which he could benefit.

The projects that Daniel seemed to favour were mostly dirigiste: that is they depended upon central government initiatives to bring them about and both the capital expenditure and revenue running costs would need to be raised from the taxpayer. These projects have never been greatly favoured in England down to our present time, and those that we remember, such as the Millennium Dome, are derided.

The triennial elections from 1695 to 1701 all produced more country party Tories who were opposed to the war with France, for which they and their constituents were paying. When the Treaty of Rhyswick in September 1697 brought about a welcome peace, these country members led a movement to disband the army, and 'to turn swords into ploughshares'. The Junto Whigs, Halifax, Somers and Orford sought a consensus to keep the army that William said was needed to maintain a European peace. There was a need to influence public opinion and Somers, the Lord Chancellor, orchestrated the campaign.

Daniel joined in this debate when he published in December 1698 a pamphlet entitled *A Brief Reply to the History of Standing Armies in England*.[124] The background to the timing of this work is that it was public knowledge that Louis XIV of France was determined to rebuild his army to take advantage of the situation which would follow the anticipated death of Charles II of Spain. William III was determined to resist the French and maintain English preparedness for war. Parliament strongly opposed the maintenance of a Standing Army in peacetime and a parliamentary resolution was passed reducing the army to eight thousand, so long as they were 'of his Majesty's natural born subjects'. This resolution sought the disbandment of William's trusty Dutch guards.

The pamphlet is closely argued and persuasive and seeks to persuade doubters that an effective army raised and sustained by Parliament was not inconsistent with the maintenance of a free parliament under a protestant monarch, and that the alternatives of a militia and the recruitment of foreign troops would not be effective and their advocacy would send the wrong message to England's enemies.

Daniel's motives for writing the pamphlet were mixed. No doubt he believed his arguments but they ran in the same direction as his financial and family interests. He was writing in support of William III, from whom he was hoping for patronage and preferment, and for his brother, threatened by the loss of his commission if his regiment were to be disbanded.[125]

In writing this pamphlet, Daniel had entered public life in support of William III who in all probability rewarded him with cash payments. William fought not only the French but also a parliamentary tide which had turned against him and which sought to limit his use of arbitrary power. A parliamentary committee sought to investigate the generous grants of public money given by William to his friends, and the punishment of his enemies by the policy of forfeiture of estates in Ireland. When the committee reported, it urged the rescinding of some grants and rewards. William was forced to give way.

It was only one year earlier that the Peace of Rhyswick had brought the war with France to an end. Its closure, and the attribution of it to William III, was enthusiastically greeted in London. However, William's popularity did not last and the election of 1698 confirmed the demand for a peace bonus and ushered in a period of parliamentary instability.

For the first time in his life, Daniel was active as a propagandist at the highest level in the production of extant works of genuine public interest, written in a persuasive and recognisable style. In the period 1698–1703 there are nineteen works that are ascribed without doubt to Daniel on a narrow range of subjects, partly political, which feed into the major parliamentary and diplomatic matters of debate at this time.

As I have argued earlier, Daniel was in touch with royal officials and it is probably true that he saw it as a profitable course of action to propagate the Court's point of view. Sometimes this may have been on his own initiative but on other occasions he may have been paid to propagate a particular line under the 'editorial direction' of others. The language and casuistical skills deployed, however, were always his own.

Daniel had most of the right credentials for this work: he was a dissenter and hence a foe of the Roman Catholics and High Anglicans agitating for changes which would have advanced them. He would have claimed in private conversation to have been a 'participant' in the Monmouth Rebellion, and was a fervent supporter of the Glorious Revolution, and, after his *Essay on Projects* was published in 1697, he was seen as a proven writer on matters of public policy. Apart from the making of much needed money, he must have felt that he could make himself useful and achieve the patronage and place that was so important to him.

Daniel was not alone in pushing at the gate for it follows from de-attribution that there must have been other writers of anonymous propaganda deploying a similar style to Daniel and on like subjects. In the ruck it is difficult to isolate Daniel's distinctive views. Schonhorn writes, 'The determination of Defoe's political stance during the years he was engaged as a government pamphleteer for William III is problematic because of his extensive resort to personae, aliases, and satiric voices, and the vexing problem of attribution.'[126]

The task of identifying Daniel's views is made even more difficult because of the persistent tendency of those who write about him to interpret history in Whig terms. It is common to see the period 1698–1702 as a triumph for a Whig struggle to complete the achievement of the Glorious Revolution and thus to place Defoe among the modernising radicals. In reality, the main political division of the time was between the 'country party' and the Court. From 1695 there was a majority for a 'country faction', mainly landed Tories, which inch by inch sought to chip away at a royal prerogative which William was determined both to protect and enlarge.

In becoming an increasingly agitated propagandist for William, at a time when authority was drifting away from his monarch, Daniel alienated all those potential and natural allies who sought to limit the royal prerogative, enlarge parliamentary control of the political agenda, limit the national debt and lower taxes.

The struggle for parliamentary supremacy had been bitterly fought throughout Daniel's adult life. The Stuarts had attempted to frustrate these claims. The University of Oxford was the first to sound the trumpet against the Crown. In July 1683 the university selected a long list of propositions[127] from the writings of their opponents and condemned them as 'false seditious and impious …and destructive of all government in Church and State'. They went on to assert that all civil authority was derived originally from the people: that there was a mutual contract, tacit or express, between the prince and his subjects, and that 'if he perform not his duty they are discharged from theirs'. The university maintained that the sovereignty of England was in three estates – King, Lords and Commons, and the king had but a co-ordinate power and could rightly be overruled by the other two. Moreover, they asserted that it was possession and strength that gave the right to govern, and success in a cause or enterprise proclaimed it to be lawful and just.

The accession to the throne of William and Mary in 1688 was an endorsement of the university's position, but the arguments of the university, for limits to the exercise of the royal prerogative, remained just as valid during their reign. As William, under the pressure of unceasing warfare against France for advantage on the continent, sought to enlarge his prerogative at the expense of parliament, public sentiment was against him.

Political debate at the time was lively, personal and full of invective to an extent which in modern times would be regarded as illegal on the grounds of libel or anti-racism. Journalists felt no compunction in bloodthirsty attacks on public figures or each other. There was an abiding danger that the worm of government would turn and react savagely under the Sedition Act, as Daniel would discover, but, amazingly, journalists rarely drew back from savage personal attacks. While Lord Somers, if he were careful, could organise, plot and propagandise without fear of sedition proceedings (but not of impeachment) this was not true of Daniel: for even when writing anonymously, his identity as an author could be unmasked by a determined administration.

One such journalistic enemy of Daniel's, who claimed the most impeccable of revolutionary credentials, was John Tutchin. Towards the end of 1699 Tutchin joined in the attack on William and his entourage in a vicious verse-attack entitled *The Foreigners*. The verse related how the 'Israelites' (English) had freed themselves from a tyrant and replaced him by a Prince from 'Gibeon' (the United Provinces), but had been mad enough to allow into the country with him a 'boorish brood', born from bogs and 'natures excrement' to pry upon the land. What had the 'Israelites' to do with such vermin as 'Bentir' (William's favourite Hans William Bentinck), who not only devoured whole provinces in 'Israel' but also presumed to divide the possessions of the unfortunate 'Hiram' (King of Spain)? What had they to do with such as 'Keppech' (another of William's favourites, Arnold van Keppel, Earl of Albemarle), who mounted to high position 'by the usual course/Of whoring, pimping, or a crime that's worse [that is, sodomy]?'

Tutchin's was a shrewd attack on William and the 'Court faction' and had the merit of being largely true. When the details of the secret Partition Treaties dividing up the King of Spain's possessions upon his death, made without the consent or knowledge of parliament, became public 'heads were to roll', and the knowledge of indefensible patronage, favouritism, corruption and sodomy at the very highest levels of the Court scandalised Anglicans and dissenters alike.

Tutchin's attack upon the Court was popular and struck home, but it was not his verse that was to echo through time, but Daniel's reply. In his apologia, *An Appeal to Honour and Justice* (1715), Daniel sought to describe his feelings when reading this attack upon William. He describes the verse as 'a vile abhorred pamphlet...in which the author...fell upon the King himself, and then upon the Dutch nation: and after having reproached his Majesty with crimes that his worst enemy could not think of without horror he sums up all in the odious name of Foreigner'.

Most of Daniel's instantaneous and angry reaction is cant because the essence of Tutchin's attack was true and Daniel knew that it was because he participated as a supporter of the Court, at the edge. But the central theme of the poem Daniel wrote in response stings and sings throughout time: that is, it was nonsense to ascribe the sins of English society to the foreigners in your midst, and that to be addicted to this nonsense was to enslave yourself to an arrant absurdity which bit at the citizen's own recognition of identity. Daniel's reply, *The True Born Englishman*, published in 1701, is profound, simple, and recognised by most English people throughout time to be true: that to scratch an Englishman is to find an immigrant.

For most writers, and in particular poets, it would be a dream to carry down through time a single work, a well-turned phrase, or even a single line. In the beginning, when he started to write, Daniel wished to be a poet. He cannot be fairly described as the equal of the great poets of his time, for he is too loose, too clumsy, crude and plain, but *The True Born Englishman* and the *Hymn to the Pillory* which followed it are memorable and they have passed down to posterity. Their fame was a signal of two things: Daniel's ability to tune in to the most singular and particular of attributes, and his involvement in the spirit of the times.

Daniel is not complimentary about his countrymen, for they are accused of the sin of ingratitude, of 'An ugly, surly sullen, selfish spirit,/Who Satan's worst perfections does inherit'. And he thinks even less of other nationalities, for the Spanish are too proud, Italians too lustful and the Germans are but drunkards. For the English, a mixture of all that is bad, there is no room for boastfulness or false conceit or disparagement of others.

The True Born Englishman is a poem with many memorable lines and succeeds in conveying passion, humour and rage. Daniel uses a compelling rhythm and movement based on repetition. But if the reader feels the better for the reading of the poem, he is also more confused: for Defoe conveys something of the very same splintering of national and personal identity which enables one to disparage a neighbour while feeling no better oneself. It was a difficulty for him and a legacy for us.

The True Born Englishman was an immediate success and popular. So much so that in other publications Daniel described himself as the author of it. It went to his head. He felt that he was no longer a bystander but could with equanimity be a participant without danger to himself. Alas, he was wrong.

Defoe's political pamphleteering in the period 1697–1703 is largely confined to a single subject: the war of the Spanish Succession. There were many variants: the maintenance of a standing army, the return of a parliament of right-thinking gentlemen who need not be of the landed interest, and the desirability of settling the claims to the throne of Spain by negotiation and compromise without a war with France. Even when, on the death of James II, Louis recognised his thirteen-year-old son Edward as Pretender to the English throne, Daniel, at least in his public writings, was willing to turn the other cheek so as to maintain a focus on the Spanish issue.

This issue was one of extreme difficulty for the English nation. The controversy was in a sense a rehearsal of what was to come: the resistance to a Napoleonic Europe at the end of the century and resistance to German domination in two twentieth-century wars, and in our own days, opposition to foreign expeditions as part of a war on terrorism. The arguments are always the same. England could never permit foreign powers to dominate the continent, to disrupt its trade and commerce, and at a time of their choosing to invade its island.

In these continental matters, Daniel can be seen to be serving his royal master on subjects within a legitimate area of public debate. Emotionally it was easy for him to do so, for his own identity was that of a foreign entity, a Huguenot protestant, as well as an English merchant, an eighteenth-century national equivalent of a British muslim today.

It is significant that in this fusillade of words Defoe has nothing to say about the Act of Settlement of 12 June 1701 which succeeded in settling the succession in favour of Anne while limiting the royal prerogative in ways which William must have found humiliating. The Act of Settlement is rightly seen as cementing the supremacy of parliament and establishing legally that a monarch ruled only so long as he recognised it. The Act has been seen as a triumph for the revisionist movement and an achievement of the Whigs, to whom Defoe was loosely aligned at the time, but in reality, as Feiling argues, it represented the constant constitutional programme of the 'country party' since the Revolution of 1689.

As Daniel did not write anything, at least which is extant, on the Act, we can but suppose his thoughts. He would have approved of the Act's legal definition of the powers of individual members of the Privy Council, that no pardon should bar an impeachment, a clause forbidding placemen to be members, and measures to protect the independence and security of tenure of judges.

On the other hand, Daniel's allegiance to his own paymaster, William, would have caused him difficulty: no future sovereign after this Act could rush England into war as William had done in 1689, or could leave England for months in time of peace, or employ foreigners in the Privy Council.

The Act caused Daniel to do a most remarkable thing. In the Act of Succession it was stipulated that Sophia, the Electress Dowager of Hanover and her family were to succeed to the throne if neither Princess Anne nor William had any more children. In the event, William turned against Sophia and she did not succeed, but at the time it seemed that she would.

Daniel decided that he would record, not baptise, the birth of a child and name a new daughter Sophia. He did this at St John's parish church in Hackney. The record reads '1701 Dec.24. Sophia dau. of Daniel de Foe by Mary his wife'. It is my belief that this child was by his third 'wife' Mary Norton who might well have called herself Mary de Foe. He had not been living with Mary Tuffley for nine years, but he was co-habiting with the second Mary in Tilbury. By merely recording Sophia's name, Daniel avoided the need for mother and child to be present. As a Quaker, Mary Norton would not have baptised her child in an Anglican church, but then Mary Tuffley never baptised any of her children in one either, to the best of anyone's knowledge. She was buried under the name of Defows.

So why did Daniel do it? It is a question posed time and again by his biographers about many aspects of Defoe's life. If Sophia was to succeed William, Daniel had the notion that he would be able to say that he was one of the first to recognise her significance; there could be no more loyal profession of allegiance to this new majesty than naming your own daughter after her. It was an act of fealty!

From 1697 to 1702 Daniel wrote four times attacking occasional conformity, a legal avoidance by which a man could gain public office by occasionally taking communion in an Anglican church. He did so in the most logical and biting terms and by naming defaulters, upbraiding them for a 'new sort of religion that looked two ways'. His arguments were consistent, logical, personal, unpleasant and unrelenting.

The desire for a place within a national church, for 'comprehension', had been an unfulfilled Cromwellian aspiration and the schism of 1661–62 had been deeply regretted by Presbyterians even when they followed their ministers into dissent. Occasional conformity could be seen as a healing medicine although Daniel was probably right in his belief that it encouraged movement back to the Anglican Church.

In practice you make few converts by insulting people and maligning their characters. In the long run it was not legislation alone that changed men's civil rights and dignities but a toleration of differences, a lowering of tension to the point at which discriminatory laws could be changed or allowed to pass into desuetude without discontent. Men learnt to live by the civilisation of double standards.

As has been argued earlier, Daniel himself had benefited from 'occasional conformity' in that he had sworn an oath of allegiance to the Crown and attended communion at an Anglican church in order to take up and maintain his appointment as accountant to the Glass Commissioners.

To be fair to Daniel, he made a distinction between an office holder, who had to take an Anglican communion to keep or be chosen to do an official job, and a person performing a political office, such as a mayoralty, when the office holder already had an occupation. However, this is a distinction without a difference for the principle is the same. And, if we are to be strictly balanced, it can be added that Daniel was running a brick factory and obtaining money through journalism, which were his occupations at the time of his taking of an oath and attending Anglican communions.

At this time, Daniel's agitation on occasional conformity might have been caused by frustration at exclusion from City offices. It would be understandable if failure in business, expulsion from membership of a church and potent challenges to tenets of religious belief had caused some loss of self-belief and had undermined his sense of personal identity.[128]

*   *   *

On 2 December 1697 a man acting quickly, in fear of detection and public arrest, and with some agitation, posted a copy of Daniel's pamphlet, *An Enquiry into the Occasional Conformity of Dissenters, in Cases of Preferment*, on the door of St Paul's Cathedral. On this day, Sir Humphrey Edwin, a well-known dissenter and Lord Mayor of London, was to attend a thanksgiving service in the Cathedral. The *Post Man* reported it as a 'foolish pasquil, reflecting on the Lord Mayor' posted on the door. Did Daniel post his own pamphlet, so invoking the practice of Martin Luther and asserting the rights of protestants to dissent from established church practices? It was a histrionic gesture, of which Daniel was capable. Anecdotally, it was accepted that Daniel did post the pamphlet.

What is undoubtedly true is that in the period 1700–3 Daniel was not a mere man of past memories and words but of action. He supposed, albeit wrongly, that parliament would not act to defend his monarch and through him the protestant cause and that he, Daniel Defoe, must take action.

It was a highly dangerous and foolish conclusion to reach and the actions which arose from it succeeded in alienating friend and foe alike. In this period Daniel repeatedly lost all rational control of himself, to the dismay of others and to the detriment of family, friends and himself. In November 1700 Sir Thomas Abney had attended a service at St Paul's followed by attendance at his usual Meeting House at which John How was the preacher. Daniel reissued his 1697 pamphlet specifically addressed to How. He asked a question: 'If the Service of their Country be so dear to them, pray why should they not chuse to expose their bodies and their estates for that Service rather than their souls?' How fought back, confident that he was speaking for the majority of dissenters, and an acrimonious exchange took place.

Such a debate merely enraged proponents and opposers alike and fuelled the animosity that led, through a Commons committee, to a move to abolish occasional conformity. The Bill died a natural death with the death of William III. Logically, Daniel should have supported such a bill but when it was re-introduced in 1702 under Queen Anne he opposed it on the ground that it was part of a fearful tightening of the screw against dissenters.

It is not known with certainty what role Daniel took in the preparation of a petition to parliament by the Kentish Petitioners urging preparation for war against France. However, in September 1701 in a pamphlet which included the text of the petition in which the Petitioners urged the dissolution of the House of Commons because it did not act to protect them against a French invasion, he makes a vigorous defence of the Petitioners. Almost certainly the petition was part of the Whig agitation against the government orchestrated by Lord Somers, and it is probable that Daniel had been in touch with Somers. The House reacted vigorously to this challenge to their authority and after a five hour debate arrested the five men of Kent who had presented the petition.

Their treatment provoked Daniel to the authorship of a far more revolutionary attempt to influence the Commons to act against its will. In *Legion's Memorial* he listed fifteen grievances against the present House of Commons and demanded in the name of all the people of England that 'all just national debts be discharged, all persons illegally imprisoned be released or bailed, John How be made to retract his aspersions on the king, vigorous resistance be given to the growing power of France, and the thanks of the House be offered to the Kentish Petitioners'. It ends, 'Our name is Legion, and we are many.'[129]

Daniel professed to be acting for the people of England and he writes, 'but if you continue to neglect it [the petition], you may expect to be treated according to the Resentments of an injur'd Nation; for Englishmen are no more to be Slaves to Parliaments, than to a King'.

While these sentiments are in line with the views expressed by Oxford University that 'all civil authority came from the people', Daniel goes further: his is a threat to overturn parliament by the power of the mob. He might state that the French had bought individual Members but William had done like-wise. Parliament believed that in the ultimate reckoning a parliament man was thought likely to exercise his vote according to the national interest. Parliament was not to be set aside on an issue of judgement by a threat from the street.

There is controversy about the method of delivery to the Commons on 14 May 1701 of this troublesome manifesto. The current inclination is to believe Daniel when he wrote that he marched into the House of Commons guarded with about sixteen gentlemen of quality but there is earlier anecdotal evidence that Daniel presented this petition in a highly novel manner.

The presence of sixteen gentlemen would not have prevented Daniel's arrest if the contents of the petition were known. In aligning himself with numerous men of quality, Daniel is repeating a common technique of his in asking the reader to assume that he was acting for numerous others and assuming an important leadership role when in fact he was acting alone.

Oldmixon writes that Daniel asserted the manifesto in a letter addressed to Harley, the Speaker of the Commons. If so, although there is no evidence, it might be that Harley was willing to present the petition in his own interest but misjudged the mood of the House.

An older anecdote quoted by George Chalmers is more intriguing. He suggests that Daniel, disguised as a woman, presented it to Harley as he entered the House. This older tradition suggests to the reader that Daniel might have been the sort of person who would dress up as a woman. Daniel's sexuality made this possible for him.[130]

Legion's Memorial advances the doctrine in the most clear and unavoidable polemic that parliament existed by the consent of the people and that if this position of trust was abused by default and bad faith, or by neglect, the authority of parliament could be first challenged and then overthrown. In this Daniel was restating the constitutional argument of Oxford University. But the pamphlet reads as the defeated demand of the Levellers of the English Civil War and exposed Daniel to the charge, which he denied, that he was one.

In practice, Daniel was demanding that the duty of parliament was the defence of its protestant religion, of William its protector, and of the realm which made these things possible. It was a stinging attack expressed and delivered in such a way as to confound and repel its audience – parliament, the Anglican bishops, the Tory placemen and country members – and to stir them into retreat. From the moment that those who had been attacked by the pamphlet recognised that Daniel stood behind it, they marked him out for revenge.

The political debate changed in March 1702 when William III died as a result of falling off a horse in Windsor Park. The accession of Anne led to a dramatic change in political and religious fortunes. The so-called Junto Whigs, Somers, Halifax and Orford were swept from office. In came Rochester, the queen's uncle, Godolphin at the Treasury and Nottingham, a narrow-minded Anglican, as Principal Secretary of State. In the offices of state and the corridors of Westminster Palace new, and not so new, elites worked to create a parliamentary composition which would give a Tory majority; to perpetuate themselves, and to restore the fortunes of Queen Anne's beloved Church of England. The panoply of hated Dutch advisors and their hangers-on left the country.

In pulpits at university chapels and up and down the country, preachers denounced in ringing tones recusants, rebels and dissenters; now was a time for the revenge of the righteous. Among them and leading the pack was Reverend Henry Sacheverill who had published a sermon which attacked dissenters in forthright terms.

It is said that no one not alive at the time could fully recognise the fears and anguish of dissenters. In the United Kingdom, it is known that this is not true, for those who lived through the troubles of Northern Ireland in the last thirty years of the twentieth century know that brand of religious bigotry only too well.

It was all too much for Daniel. How he felt, is best deciphered from Robinson Crusoe's discovery of 'the Shore Spread with Bones', for the High Flyers of the Anglican Church threatening to bang on Daniel's door (or so he imagined it) were for Robinson the native savages invading the peace of his island. Robinson finds bones on a shore and a boat far out at sea but approaching the island. He writes:

I looked up with the utmost affection of my soul ... gave God thanks... I was ...distinguished from such dreadful creatures... I continued pensive and sad [then] I thought nothing but how I might destroy some of these monsters ... I contrived to dig a hole under the place where they made their fire and put some five or six pound of gunpowder [there] ... I loaded muskets [at the place where they might land] ... [and then, much later] I saw that God [had granted me] the protection of His Providence.[131]

In real life Daniel was not pacific. His heart was full of rage and despair gripped him. Just as he was poised to become a person of distinction, in serving a royal master and the true protestant cause, his hopes were confounded, to the joy of his enemies. He just had to do something about it.

In December 1702 an anonymous pamphlet was published in London. It was a satire written in the voice of a Henry Sacheverill, and titled *The Shortest Way with The Dissenters: or Proposals for the Establishment of the Church of England*. The author stated that for nearly fourteen years God had suffered the purest and most flourishing church in the world to be humiliated by its enemies but that now the throne was occupied by a true friend to the Church of England (Queen Anne) the day of deliverance was at hand. It continued by urging an end to a tolerance which punished recusancy by a mere fine, for it was a crime to separate from the true church. If a simple law was passed condemning any person at a conventicle to be banished and the preacher hanged there would be no more talk of disunion. 'With popery on the one hand, and schismatics on the other, how has the Church been crucified between two thieves [...] Now let us Crucifie the Thieves.'

Extreme Anglicans, including Dr. Sacheverill, greeted the pamphlet with enthusiasm while dissenters received it with dismay as a prediction of the fate that awaited them. It took but a few days for the public to realise that it had been duped. No one was pleased: Anglicans thought it a vile abuse, dissenters that it had placed honest men at risk. The queen, identified as the prime mover of extremist measures, was outraged; new placemen and the queen's new advisors were suspicious of what they understood as 'party moves' to de-stabilise the new administration, and the government's political opponents ran for cover.

Daniel's attack in *The Shortest Way* was not upon an externalised form, such as an Act of Parliament. It read as a personal attack upon Queen Anne and her compliance to advisors. With the death of William, all Daniel's hopes of patronage and fortune had been lost. Now he was threatened by something much, much worse.

Nottingham issued a warrant for Daniel's arrest. Daniel went into hiding with the hope that the whole affair would blow over. Bastian suggests that Daniel fled to Scotland, a former retreat outside the jurisdiction of the English courts. If he had stayed there he would have been safe. It appears, however, that that he had to return to London to deal with a persistent and dangerous creditor. If so, he misjudged the balance of risk, for he was arrested at Nathaniel Sammen's home on information leaked to the authorities.

There began a complicated game of shadow boxing. Nottingham caused Daniel to be taken from Newgate Prison to his rooms at the Palace of Whitehall where he questioned him at considerable length. Nottingham was convinced that there was a 'party' for whom Daniel was acting. It was an opportunity to do a deal. If Daniel told all he knew of the matters he had been involved in over the past two years, and if this amounted to something worthwhile, he might escape punishment.

Daniel was released from prison on bail set so high that it might be supposed that Nottingham's suspicions were well-founded and that behind those who stood as surety for him were others of mightier means. Daniel wrote a letter of explanation of his pamphlet to the queen and obtained an audience with her. She was not impressed. Daniel asserted later that his long-suffering wife Mary obtained an audience with Nottingham to plead his case but, as I have written elsewhere, he made up this story.

Then, with patience running low, Daniel was indicted for seditious libel in June 1703 at the Old Bailey, in a trial presided over by the Lord Mayor of London, Sir Samuel Dashwood. Included among the judges were Sir Edward Ward, Sir John Fleet, Sir Edward Clark and Sir Thomas Abney, all of whom had reason to resent Daniel. Otherwise, it might have been supposed that there would be sympathy there for a member of the Foe family which had achieved respectability in the City, but Daniel had long since made too many enemies, alienated too many friends, and even his fellow dissenters, by his bankruptcy and the waspishness and unpredictability of his behaviour.

Whatever the technical and legal arguments, and there were some, in reality there was no hope whatsoever of a fair trial. It was a done deal. Daniel recognised this in pleading guilty. This course of action opened up the possibility of leniency. Daniel was sentenced to a fine of 200 marks, to stand in the pillory on three separate occasions for the duration of an hour, and to find sureties for good behaviour for a period of seven years. It could have been worse but it was a heavy blow.

On the face of it, there is no rational explanation for so crass and ill-judged an intervention in the affairs of State at so inflammable a moment as the publication of *The Shortest Way*. It was a crucial misjudgement arising from personal vanity. In the first place it was plain wrong to assume that the immunity from legal prosecution that Daniel enjoyed while writing in defence and support of William and his administration could somehow be extended to him when he was attacking an administration he opposed, for even powerful political associates lacked such an immunity.

Then there is a related error, a failure on Daniel's part to understand that an attack upon a royal official, or in Queen Anne's case, Anglican bishops and priests, was treated in law as an attack on the royal personage appointing them. Daniel's explanation that he was attacking the extremes of Anglicanism did not run, for Anne herself was part of the extreme.

There were intellectual errors and confusions. There is an issue of Daniel's perspective. *The Shortest Way* was an ingenious and convincing satire in an age of satire. Daniel genuinely believed that it was through satire that the 'truth' could be revealed. Moreover, he believed that there was such a 'truth' and that he had in *The Shortest Way* revealed it. This was his defence. What had he done? His defence of himself was that he had revealed (proven, really) the proposition he had addressed. Earlier, I have commented that Daniel tended to assume that the 'truth' was a quantifiable entity and could be proved if the mind was addressed to it. Not for him the proposition that not every problem has a solution or that when an intellectual position was arrived at it should be treated as a provisional outcome.

In 1705 in replying to a particularly nasty attack on him by Lord Haversham, Daniel suggested that he might more likely have ended in the peerage than in the pillory had William III continued to live. In defending himself from Haversham, Daniel makes a claim for himself. He writes, 'I was ever True to one Principle, I never betrayed my Master or my Friend; I always Espoused the cause of Truth and Liberty, was ever on one side and that cause was ever right; I have Liv'd to be ruined for it, and I have Liv'd to see it Triumph over Tyranny.' Brave words, indeed. But even when allowance is made for the occasion and the rhetoric, the informed reader, as is demonstrated in this text, knows this defence to be simplistic and wrong.

It is possible to argue that in *The Shortest Way* Daniel was making a serious attempt to deflect the new administration from a change of policy and to persuade Queen Anne to shift her general position closer to the Whigs by ridiculing extremist advisors. If so, it was a serious intellectual endeavour which miscarried because of the fever of the time. There is strong circumstantial evidence of Daniel's involvement with influential Whigs at this time but, in all probability, in the publication of the pamphlet Daniel was acting alone.

Daniel suggests his involvement with 'a party' in *Hymn to the Pillory*. The poem was circulated by his friends at the pillory. In it he asserts that he was being punished for not betraying his friends. Daniel's principal defence in this poem is that he was the victim of the state's punishment of authorship and that the pillory was the machinery by which it punished 'fancy'. It is easy to agree with Daniel, for by any modern standard his punishment was barbarous and unjustifiable. And, of course, it is true, as Daniel argues, that if 'justice' was extended to the rich and powerful the numbers would be too great for the state to handle. But then, Daniel's allying himself with the dissenting victims of the past is less convincing; his offence was not that of the protestant martyrs who went before him.

If modern standards of behaviour and legality are applied to Daniel's case, it can be argued that his highly personal attacks on others would be treated as libels and he would have been challenged in the courts by those defamed. Admittedly, Daniel lived at a time of vicious personal attacks by journalists, but even by contemporary standards he was not slow in coming forward.

In delivering the poem to the mob surrounding the pillory, Daniel bravely challenged them. Did they, he asks, really know what was happening? Well, perhaps they did not, but then, perhaps they did. Those who knew what the Sheriff's men found when they rifled through his personal documents, the letters and lampoons, might well have thought, 'God almighty, he was really asking for it!'

If so, why such serious misjudgements by Daniel?[132] There was a kind of conceit here. Daniel saw his action as a last throw of the dice, a vain attempt to retain influence as the ground shifted beneath him. Was it more than a misjudgement? Was it a breaking point? Perhaps Daniel could not bear the stress any longer. Recklessly, he plunged on. Action was the only way he could escape from unbearable tension and fear. The making of these terrible mistakes could not be avoided.

Chapter 11

Beyond The City

... the road to Farnham is very remarkable... From this hill is a prospect either way...This hill reaches from Guilford town's end to within a mile and half of Farnham...and at the top stands the gallows, which is so placed that the towns people...may sit at their shop doors, and see the criminals executed.

A Tour Through the Whole Island of Great Britain
Daniel Defoe, 1724–27

AS DANIEL DEFOE SLIPPED out of Newgate prison, probably unannounced, early in the morning of 8 November 1703, he would have glanced over his shoulder lest a creditor had got news of his release. As with Robinson Crusoe, a protective place was both a restraint and a refuge from assault by enemies, a hidden place to be welcomed, feared and, ultimately, from which one would find release. If a friend had supplied a horse, he would have used it, but more likely he walked to the Sammens' house. There he would have holed up for a few days before taking a coach or a horse to Tilbury.

Daniel had spent six months in prison after his ordeal in the pillory. His brother-in-law Robert Davies had tried to help him out at the Tilbury pantile factory but his efforts had not saved it; perhaps it had been in difficulty before his troubles and was already doomed. Daniel claimed that he had lost some £3,000 during his imprisonment and that this sum had bankrupted him once again, but there is no way of knowing whether that was true. If true, numerous new creditors would have been added to the old. These creditors would have sought him out. Subterfuge and government protection were needed to avoid them.

He must have gone to Tilbury in a state of trepidation in order to put his affairs there at rest. In *Roxana* Defoe writes of the husband winding up his affairs as a necessary preliminary to flight and disappearance:

Early the next Morning he gets out of Bed, goes to a Window which looked out towards the Stables, and sounds his French Horn, as he called it; which was his usual Signal to call his Men to go out. But he had no intention of doing so. 'It ... was ...at five a-Clock ... I heard him and his two Men go out and shut the Yard-Gates after them...I never saw my Husband more... I never heard from him, or of him ... or either of his two Servants... no more than if the ground had open'd and swallowed them all up, and nobody had known it; except as hereafter.'[133]

The emotion expressed in this passage, and the stratagems implied, must have been felt by Daniel many times in his life. There was always an emotional cost for precipitating a failure, however he might shrug it off. He would have had feelings of despair at the closure of his premises at Freeman's Yard following his bankruptcy in 1692 and now, once more, at the loss of his Tilbury establishment.

Daniel had been rescued from prison by a powerful friend, Lord Harley, a member of the government and the Speaker of the House of Commons. Harley sought to gain Daniel as a propagandist in his cause. Daniel wrote about it and his rescuer in *An Appeal to Honour and Justice*, 'a Message was brought me [in prison] from a person of Honour, who, till that time, I never had the least acquaintance with, or knowledge of... by word of mouth thus: Pray ask that Gentleman, what I can do for him?' Daniel replied in Biblical terms. Four months later, Harley having nudged the Earl of Nottingham to one side and then out of the government entirely, represented his case to the queen, who gave Mary Tuffley a thousand pounds and Harley paid a further £1,000 to Daniel to take care of his immediate creditors.

Daniel's account is not strictly accurate. It is important to get the record straight because Daniel Defoe's relationship with Robert Harley is crucial to the understanding the next ten years of his life. Around 1698 Daniel met Robert Harley and the two embarked on a complicated homosexual relationship which was expressed in many forms as their circumstances altered over a period of sixteen years.

In 1698 Daniel wrote to William Patterson asking Patterson to bring him to the attention of Harley. This letter was written five years before Daniel's punishment in the pillory and before the Kentish Petition and *Legion's Memorial*. Patterson probably did arrange a meeting. The next public record of them cooperating together comes from a pamphlet entitled the Welsh Monster, which was written anonymously in 1708. The writer accused Harley of collaborating with Daniel to write *Legion's Memorial* in 1701 to the public knowledge of leading Whigs and in a concerted political campaign with them. This writer suggests that the two of them were conducting a homosexual relationship and that Robert Harley was a sodomite.[134] If any of this is true, it is not likely that Harley was entirely innocent of the stratagems that put Daniel into prison and the pillory. Once Daniel was imprisoned, Harley waited for the right moment to get him out.

If these conclusions go too far and too quickly, there are several interesting and unanswered questions. Did the two men meet in 1698 and begin a relationship? If so, why did Daniel feel obliged to lie about it in 1715? Did Daniel really present Harley with *Legion's Memorial* dressed in the disguise of a washerwoman outside the House of Commons? And what does such a lark on a deadly serious matter tell about the nature of their friendship? Arguably, this method of delivery might have been the only sure way to get the pamphlet to Harley as the Speaker of the House at the right moment and without implicating either Harley or Daniel. Implicating Harley in what?

The evidence suggests that Daniel sought to replace William III with an alternative 'father figure' and chose Robert Harley as his patron and 'protector'. In this, Daniel chose well. Robert Harley had impeccable credentials coming from a family of good standing and a devout puritan background. Early in his parliamentary career he was a supporter of the Revolution and its principles and in the early Stuart parliaments he was Whiggish. He made himself a master of the constitution and became a 'party manager' with acute skills. In William III's parliaments he supported impeachment in the secret Partition Treaties, which was enough to get him elected as Speaker of the House of Commons. He held the office of the Principal Secretary of State from time to time for almost ten years, shifting skilfully with every change in party fortunes. Coming from the centre-left, as do many parliamentary leaders, he was able to carry the consciences of the left while retaining the votes of the Tory right with whom he shared his instincts. But in the end no one believed him, for as was said of the Duke of Wellington, 'He had sat so long on the fence that the iron had bitten deep into his soul.'

Robert Harley was a genial soul who loved the arts and artists, conversation, good food and fine wines. He created for himself a wonderful library which is now an adornment of the British Library. He retained the friendship of a wide variety of friends over a long and controversial career because of his good nature. He was invariably a better judge of men and events than his enemies. These qualities infuriated the hard-working mediocrities who waited for their turn to climb the greasy pole.

There are ostensible reasons for Robert Harley's interest in Daniel Defoe which are widely used by biographers. Harley had an interest in creating a system of intelligence of the kind that Daniel had sought to provide for William III, and which he had created in some form in the 1690s. Harley was to become a manipulator of the press. Through a team of talented writers, Harley sought to influence the opinions of a male audience which was increasingly enfranchised and whose votes he needed in successive triennial elections.

Harley would have had little doubt about Daniel's competence as a polemicist but there must have been questions about his trustworthiness. Harley had to decide whether Defoe could be controlled or whether his punishment at the pillory had embittered him too much to enable him to be used by any government. Whatever one might think about the merits of *The Shortest Way*, there was no denying its power to reach and disturb. Had it not brought upon Daniel the anger and attention of the queen and the presence during his imprisonment of two powerful ministers?

Harley waited while his political enemies weakened and until it was clear to him that he had the political leverage to be able to make use of Daniel.

132

Daniel became impatient for instructions. On 16 May 1704 he wrote to Harley, stating, 'I impatiently Wait to receive your Ordrs' (H 7). When it pleased Harley, he replied, but his response is not extant. A pattern was established in their relationship. The surviving letters from Daniel to Harley are numerous but his replies are scarce. Later, Daniel was to complain that his letters were never answered, but in 1704 they must have elicited some response, for what Daniel did was to arrange, with Harley's financial support, the establishment of his news-sheet, the *Review*. For nine years, the *Review* was to be Daniel's mouthpiece and a medium through which Harley sought to influence the electorate.

A surviving letter from Daniel to Harley sets out in detail what Daniel would like Harley to do to become a supreme leader ruling through an inner cabinet and winning the enthusiastic support of the country (H 14). After all, if one was to replace the sceptre with the sword there was little point in using half measures.

Harley endeavoured to conceal his correspondence with Daniel. Until the autumn of 1706, and then some times later, Daniel signs his letters with a symbol, or on occasions with the initials of a pseudonym, 'Alexander Goldsmith'. On their receipt Harley often, but not always, tore off the bottom of the final page to remove the signature. Sometimes letters from Harley to Daniel were addressed for his collection at a coffee bar (H 7 & 8 and footnotes).

It was some months later, in the autumn of 1704, and again in 1705, that Daniel set out on his journeys throughout England to establish a network of contacts drawn mainly from a dissenting background. These contacts became a source of intelligence and information on local affairs and on the principal political issues of the day and a means of distributing the *Review*. These visits and Daniel's comments appear in Healey's collection of Harley's correspondence. They show the identity of some of the people who received Daniel and others who sought to embarrass and pull him down.

Daniel's mind and resolve were not weakened by the pillory and imprisonment, but he was a changed man. Realistically, what had gone was the hope of high office, yet he retained it as a possibility. What existed of his dissenting beliefs would have virtually disappeared, although dissenters remained as his audience. He went on performing for them but he recognised that it was his addiction to dissent, among other causes, that had led him to the pillory. In the end, and whatever the support he had received from some individuals, his friends and supporters had been unable to save him from public ignominy.

From this point Daniel felt that although he was of the dissenting brethren he was no longer part of them. In modern terms, he had lost the membership of a club and many of the loyalties associated with membership. The price had been too high. He still attended the games, but only when he chose to do so. They remained his team and he was hugely proud of them and wanted them to win, but there was no fever in or because of it.

For many the ignominy and physical stress of the pillory and imprisonment would have been overwhelming, but not for Daniel. He believed, as was common in his times, that victory (in this instance the survival of great trials) was evidence of the righteousness of one's cause. God's providence and grace had been demonstrated in his favour once again.

While Daniel believed that God had saved him, it was preferable to help oneself. What was required was 'protection'. When coming from a humble birth, a powerful protector was needed. Out of the darkness of Newgate came the great light of Harley, a public figure and member of the administration, who was to be 'the Foundation of all [Daniel's] further Concern in publick Affairs'.

Daniel tells his readers that Harley was from this point (1704 until Harley's fall in 1714) a patron such as William III had been. Daniel suggested to his readers that a righteous patron should be given allegiance and loyalty. In this respect Daniel had the need for an idealised father figure. He accepted authority, gave dogged devotion and, when the tasks were defined for him, performed to the best of his considerable abilities. Actually, however, he was rebellious, wayward and impulsive. He did his own thing and while the withdrawal or suspension of payment could draw him back to his duties, it did not prevent him straying for excitement or reward.

There was far more to his relationship with Harley than fealty. Harley was extravagantly generous and indulgent to Daniel, way beyond any reasonable measure of value. Daniel had bought protection on a large scale and immunity from prosecution so long as he served his master. What did he pay for it?

The terms of Daniel's sentence in 1703 included a provision that he should not publish any more works. The breach of this condition could throw him back to prison. Others believed it could too and they were anxious to achieve it. There were serious challenges to Daniel on his travels when enemies sought to get him arrested. Daniel sought a pass which identified him as acting on government business and, reluctantly, Harley gave one to him (H 37). On his travels in 1705, Daniel was accompanied by young men. They were not heralded by Daniel but just appeared and disappeared without any explanation, to be replaced by others; sometimes their expenses were paid for by Harley.

Confident of the protection of his patron, Daniel wrote prolifically. Some of these writings had nothing to do with the administration but others were paid for by Harley and Daniel accounted for his actions to him. The first weekly number of the *Review* appeared on 17 February 1703. It was to be Daniel's mouthpiece for over ten years. At first it was published once a week, but it became a twice weekly publication with a *Little Review* appearing at the weekends and a special advice section, the *Scandalous Club*, was published separately.

Whether Daniel would have chosen to dabble in the new market for political journalism without Harley's money (which he always denied he was receiving) is open to question. It was not much money compared with the other sums given to him by Harley, probably no more than £200 per year, and from this had to be deducted the printing and distribution costs but it was enough. Daniel had somehow to continue to pay the most persistent of his creditors and he had families to support. The *Review's* direct revenue came from various sources: it retailed at a penny per copy, it took advertisements, and from time to time there was money for Daniel writing in support of the mighty or in favour of particular legislation.

The *Scandalous Club* became a separate publication in September 1704. In this way Daniel could gossip about personalities and deal with personal problems, separate from the serious issues of the day. The *Scandalous Club* became a sort of 'agony aunt' and the first of its kind.

At the outset the *Review*, unlike its competitors, was not a newspaper or mere news-sheet, but a journal of opinion on the political matters of the day. It appeared under a strange title:

A REVIEW
OF THE
Affairs of FRANCE
AND OF ALL
EUROPE,
As Influenc'd by that NATION,
BEING
Historical Observations, on the Publick Transactions of the
WORLD; Purg'd from the Errors and Partiality of
News-Writers, and Petty-Statesmen of all Sides.
WITH AN
Entertaining Part in every Sheet,
BEING
ADVICE from the Scandal. CLUB,
To the Curious Enquirers: in Answer to Letters sent them
For that Purpose.

The *Review* announced that it had the objective of providing an impartial account of the affairs of France based on an understanding of its history and culture. Initially, the *Scandalous Club* existed to provide a means of attacking the criticisms and accounts of other journals and newspapers and to rebut their criticisms.

From the beginning the *Review* showed a considerable understanding of the history and affairs of France and sought to diminish fears of French military strength and its dominant role in European affairs. So much so, that Godolphin, who was committed to pressing the war with France to a satisfactory conclusion, wrote to Harley asking for the reasons for Defoe's editorial line.

Concentration on France might have been no more than Daniel executing Harley's positioning of himself closer to the feelings of country Tories who were opposed to the war on the grounds of its necessity and expense. His enemies supposed he was being paid through the French Embassy in London for taking a pro-French line. But whatever it was, it came to an end with Marlborough's victory at Blenheim, which was greeted with enthusiasm in the *Review* and in Daniel's *Hymn to Victory*.[135]

From the outset the *Review* sought to take a high intellectual and an impartial stand. It was a position that his rivals and enemies were not willing to cede nor one that they felt obliged to acknowledge. They scorned it on a variety of grounds: Daniel's supposed limited education, his unprincipled character, which they maintained was common knowledge, and his poor grammar and Latin. It was a pretension of the time that a gentleman's discourse should include Latin. Daniel's Latin was elementary and he could be caught out in error, and when he placed his prose in the context of a classical world, he rendered himself risible to those whose scholarship had included ancient Greek and Roman studies.

However comic or pretentious Daniel was made to appear, he had several overwhelming advantages over his rivals: his efforts to succeed despite a difficult life made him quick-witted in his reactions. He anticipated problems in advance and adapted his writing to the possibilities of criticism. Furthermore, where his opponents were talented and accomplished, Daniel opposed them with the prose of a wayward genius.

Almost from the start Defoe was willing to write for his competitors. James Sutherland has speculated that when Tutchin was in trouble Daniel wrote some issues of his *Observators*, and Furbank and Owens argue for Defoe's involvement in *Master Mercury* in 1704. For a modern freelance journalist, plying for hire is usual (although consistency is still a professional necessity) but in Daniel's partisan times it was seen as unprincipled and an apostasy. Anecdotally, it was said of Defoe at the time that as he wrote his regular column or pamphlet, he had on the other side of his desk their written refutations.

The ability to articulate many sides of the same question can be seen as an attractive intellectual quality stimulated by the teaching of rhetoric and the encouragement of debate. In Daniel, however, there are psychological and behavioural reasons for him not sticking to any particular viewpoint. His propensity to trim his sails made almost any change of direction possible and was infuriating to many of his readers. There is fear in this, for trimming was accompanied by an awareness that the desire and necessity to provoke would result in a threatening reaction. Daniel released himself from this personal dilemma through the use of satire and personation. In *The Shortest Way* Daniel's use of satire had already led to personal disaster but setbacks did not result in him abandoning it. The reader of the *Review* would have observed Daniel developing a number of voices for himself and for Mr Review. Through the *Scandalous Club* he articulates other voices: sounds of the real and imagined lives of his readers who write to him about their problems.

In the *Review*, Daniel often approaches a subject from an unexpected or paradoxical angle which invites thought but which does not always convince. Some readers found this practice annoying and felt that it trivialised their beliefs and values.

The *Review* would have been entertaining for all those readers who loved paradox and satire. Daniel was producing a news-sheet that, for the first time, displayed human foibles and dilemmas in a regular journalistic format. Daniel's readers must have been vastly amused by the problems of their fellow readers and perhaps better informed about the solutions to their problems.

Imprisonment, release, notoriety and protection unleashed in Daniel a flood of words. Over the next two years, and excluding the *Review*, Daniel wrote and published over three hundred thousand words. Even after allowance is made for works which can no longer be ascribed to him with any confidence, his energy was astounding. This output included two important works which were not overtly political and which presaged fictional works to come. It is thought probable that in 1704 he wrote about the great storm which had hit the country in November 1703, and in 1705 he wrote a curious work, *The Consolidator*. The first work displays Defoe's art of spinning fiction and drama from fact, the second work, something of his curious state of mind at the time.

The weather in 1703, even for long-suffering Britons, was awful. Heavy rain and strong winds had battered the British Isles for most of the year. From pulpits up and down the country clergymen warned their parishioners that this weather was caused by the prosecution of unwarranted wars and a turning away from God. For Defoe, storms and winds were acts of God visited upon an unworthy flock: 'Part of the Works of God by Nature'. By observation, however, it was apparent that the British Isles had more than its fair share of them. Did this mean that Britons were more sinful and wayward than the citizens of other countries? Probably not, thought Daniel, but others thought so, and their beliefs and superstitions could be played upon. Preachers used the opportunity to denounce sin from their pulpits and, caught up in the excitement of the moment, Daniel knew there was money to be made in describing the great event.

Daniel appears to have started work on writing about the storm soon after its occurrence in November 1703. He may have been responsible for even earlier works on the storm, the satirical *Layman's Sermon*, for example, and the poetic *Essay on the Late Storm* which appeared alongside *The Storm* in the summer of 1704. It is said that Daniel Defoe placed advertisements in both the *Daily Courant* and the *London Gazette* in which he requested that first-hand observations of the storm be sent to him via one of his regular publishers near Stationers Hall on Ludgate Hill. The wording of the advertisement is identical to an earlier advertisement in the Athenian.

These claims for Daniel's authorship are fraught with the problems of ascription that beset Defoe scholars. Furbank and Owens think it no more than probable the he wrote *The Storm*, and the evidence for his authorship of the other two works is no more than circumstantial. Daniel is not mentioned by name in any advertisement seeking experiences of the storm and it is not at all clear whether the accounts he used were his correspondents' or his own inventions. A great deal of material entered into the public domain and Daniel and many other writers scrambled for the use of it. Daniel was accused by his competitors of plagiarism and the use of unacknowledged sources, and his attempts to incorporate within his narrative a scientific explanation of the causes of the high winds was subject to scorn for its lack of learning.

All this was par for the course in the emerging journalism of the time. What Daniel might have said in his defence, but could not, was that what distinguished his account from those of others was the power of his imagination. Daniel, among others, claimed that the accounts he was giving were strictly factual and that he would give no other, but even a casual reading of *The Storm* shows that they were not and, reluctantly, Defoe admits as much in the text.

Today we can see the work for what it was: high quality journalism which engaged with the storm and its effects on those who suffered it. It was spoilt only by Daniel's need to share the pretentiousness of the times. The careful and punctilious among his readers would have been offended by it, but the rest of the reading public must have loved it. With the benefit of hindsight, *The Storm*, if in any way it is ascribed to Daniel, can be seen as the harbinger of his fiction. The writing was non-political; he created character and a multitude of voices, incident, and atmosphere; and he invented wherever it was necessary for the engagement of imagination.

The Consolidator was written and published by Daniel in 1705. A political satire, it is what might be expected of him at this time. Daniel used satire to attack parliamentary proceedings, which would tack a ban on occasional conformity to a finance bill in November 1704. In this fantasy the Chinese succeeded in landing on the moon to find the happenings there not only to be strange but very like those in England. The theme of lunar fantasy, and the related invention of the 'mad man', was to be used later by Daniel in the

Review. One version of Mr Review was that he dealt in the plain truth and those who disagreed were either living in a fantasy world of their own or were mad.

In addition to what is described here, Daniel was busy with other writing in 1705–6. He was desperate to make money and writing was a means of doing so. It was becoming respectable to be a professional writer and the activity could be combined with other and more serious activities. It was possible at this time to bridge different worlds: statesmen wrote pamphlets; the poor could become rich through trade; riches could buy land estates, titles, public office or a place in parliament; and talent or genius could gain social advancement.

These ambitions were not Daniel's alone and those who mocked him for his pretensions may have harboured similar desires themselves. Even the disgrace of the pillory could be presented as a victory for principle; Daniel could be cast as a martyr in a long line of martyrs who could, according to religious and political beliefs, be admired. Daniel could maintain that he had betrayed neither the good cause nor the mighty men who had engaged his pen for political reasons. Within the government, whose patronage Daniel sought, he was seen as competent: as a man who could reach a voting public with effective prose and who was capable of confounding and exposing political opponents.

The triennial elections had ushered in an atmosphere of constant electioneering from 1695. Factions struggled to obtain tactical advantage. Daniel had come to occupy a place that has always existed in partisan politics: he was a man who could find out what was happening and what was being plotted by political enemies. To do this he had to assume a role for which he was ideally prepared: the role of the double agent, a man needed by both sides who, even as they were being reported on, needed the contact in order to play their necessary but dangerous game of double bluff. Such a man is never loved. Those people who were less successful than Daniel at 'double bluff', or unsuited for it and less talented, cried foul in the abusive language of the time. They were right to do so from their own points of view. Daniel's genius in fulfilling the role would have persuaded him to continue to believe that much of the world he sought as a young man was still within his reach.

Daniel knew that in a socially hierarchical world he was above the Grub Street hacks and superior in talent to his nearest journalistic rivals. What was needed now, if his dreams were to be realised, was to raise his act. He set out to do it. From around 1695 he changed his name from Foe to De Foe. In 1702 he purchased a coat of arms[136] (first used on the cover of *True Collections* in 1703) which, it was said, he displayed on the side of a coach. So far as it can be ascertained, Daniel's right to bear these arms of ancient and distinguished lineage was not substantiated in any way that is recoverable to the enquirer.

To establish his reputation as a political philosopher, he published a poem in heroic couplets in twelve volumes entitled *Jure Divino*. In this poem he attempted to set out the basis of his political thought. To add gravitas, he provided a flattering portrait of himself on the cover, depicted by a fashionable painter, John Tavernier. Even as he dressed up for his portrait he complained to Harley about his difficulties in maintaining a fashionable appearance and stated that he thought of himself as becoming shabby.

Subscriptions to *Jure Divino* were first sought in an advertisement in the *Review* in September 1705 at a price of half a crown but when it finally appeared in July 1706 the price had raised to fifteen shillings, at which it left room for a pirated edition at five shillings. In the poem Daniel argues that God had permitted man to be lord of himself and that his first duty was self-love. He argues against political tyranny and asserts that those who do not fight it are fools with no proper respect for the liberty God has given them, or their own property. He argues further that the rights of government are always secondary to those of property, and that liberty is to be found in the possession of property and in respect for the rights of property holders. Tyranny can appear in many forms and many societies suffered from it. Undue respect for custom, 'the Bastard of Antiquity', assists the tyrant who takes advantage of old allegiances to make his subjects swear oaths which, when examined, are shown to be irrational. The divine right theory of monarchy is likened to popish image-worship and ridiculed, as is the fallacy of the hereditary right to rule. This argument enables Defoe to praise the English constitution, King William and the reign of Queen Anne.

Jure Divino is a poem of more than three hundred pages in length and it may have been started as early as 1701. Taken together with *The Succession to the Crown of England Considered* (1701), *Legion's Memorial* (1701) and the *Original Power of the Collective Body of the People of England* (1702), it may be considered as a statement of Defoe's political position in relation to the constitutional settlement ground out in England between the 1688 accession of William and Mary and the Hanoverian succession of 1715.

In the *Original Power of the Collective Body of the People of England*, Daniel contests the doctrine of the sovereignty of parliament, monarch and Houses of Lords and Commons acting together, on the grounds of the 'original power' of the people of England to govern themselves. In this he is, knowingly or otherwise, following Locke's Second Treatise and asserting a social contract between the people and the rulers of the time. If the governors the people have deputed to act for them betray their power, the people have the right to overthrow them even if they have to seek the assistance of a foreign army in order to do so.

Daniel's assertion begs two important questions: Who are the people? And who is to decide on what amounts to a betrayal? For Daniel, as expressed in *Jure Divino*, the original rights are not embodied in all people but in male freeholders alone, the other inhabitants of the country being regarded as 'Sojourners', who were to be subject to 'such Laws as the Freeholders impose upon them'.

William Payne has shown from an examination of those participating that the electorate in the triennial elections amounted to ten per cent of the male population. This being so, the electorate was broadly in line with Daniel's definition of the people. Why then should not the electorate be the judge of the policies to be pursued by parliament? And should not a general parliamentary election be the chosen method for changing policies if the people disapproved of them? Of course, the franchise and the conduct of the elections were corrupt by modern standards, and to be fair to Daniel's arguments he spoke out about reform, but that is not to say that imperfect general elections were ineffective in bringing parliaments to account and in limiting the exercise of power by governments.

While Daniel could protect himself against the charge that he was a Leveller by limiting his definition to male property holders, he was wide open to the allegation of encouraging mob rule. The logic of *Legion's Memorial* and Daniel's support for the Kentish Petitioners was that parliament should bow to the demands of petitioners acting in the name of 'all the good people of England', whose name was Legion and who were many. It is a feature of a mob, or of those who are Legion, that many of its company would fail to meet Defoe's definition of the people who were entitled to bring rulers to account.

A constant irritation to High Church spokesmen was the exaggeration by dissenters of their numbers and hence the importance of their grievances. Charles Leslie, the principle propagandist of the High Church, took on the dissenters in an uncompromising way in a pamphlet entitled *New Association* in 1702 in which he argued that what the dissenters sought was to rekindle rebellion and that 'if they were now as Considerable as they would make themselves: then Government is in the greater Danger, and have the more Reason to Begin with them, to take power out of their hands in Time... they must have All or None'.

It is easy to demonstrate that in the period 1701–5 Daniel's constitutional arguments were inconsistent and troubling to the public peace, but it is difficult to demonstrate the reasons for their contradictions. For example, in *Legion's Memorial*, one of the main complaints is the slowness of the government to give 'vigorous resistance to the growing power of France'; but in *The Present State of Jacobitism Considered* (1701), *Reasons Against a War with France* (1701), and in the *Review* in 1705, Daniel argued the contrary, that the danger of France was over-stated. When, in 1702, at the instigation of King William, a committee of the House of Commons began to consider the problem of the protestant succession, Daniel seemed not to consider the matter with any seriousness, for in *The Succession to the Crown of England, Considered* (1701), as has been argued here in an earlier chapter, Daniel bizarrely advocated the claims of the Earl of Dalkeith, Monmouth's son, as the only candidate that would suit the Scots. The conclusion of the committee's deliberations led to the Act of Settlement in 1702 which, with hindsight, can be seen as securing the protestant succession. Daniel greeted this building block of the post-1688 settlement with total silence.

It is difficult not to conclude that Daniel's opinions were where his purse was: that he is urging the cases of those who paid him. In the earlier period his commitment is to King William, for whom he wrote for money and whom he admired as a man, a statesman and a fellow Presbyterian. King William was hurt by the Act of Settlement in that it limited his powers and enhanced those of parliament. Thus Daniel could not welcome publicly the securing of the protestant succession, in which he undoubtedly believed. In the latter period, and in the early days of the *Review*, Daniel was in thrall to Harley, his paymaster: as that master of political tacking changed direction, so did Daniel.

None of this needs occasion surprise or indignation unless one wishes Daniel to be cast in the role of supporting revolutionary principles, values and their practical application; principles which did not exist then in the form in which they are now cast.[137]

Chapter 12

Scotland

Keeping still due north... the country appeared so fresh, so flourishing... I found that side of the island much pleasanter than mine.

Robinson Crusoe
Daniel Defoe, 1719

SCOTLAND OCCUPIED A PLACE in Daniel Defoe's imagination. At times when he felt most persecuted and alone he thought of Scotland. When the opportunity arose to go there in some paid official role, albeit as no more than one government agent among others, he took it with relish for what it was, an alternative space free of the reach of his creditors and political and journalistic enemies. Given a breathing space, he felt that in Scotland he could start again in business, and given goodwill from Harley and Godolphin, and their continued power and influence, he might well succeed in obtaining the public office, wealth and prestige denied to him in England.

Daniel devotes significant space to Scotland in his *A Tour Through The Whole Island of Great Britain*. The recollections and descriptions of places in Scotland found there, as with the rest of the book, are probably spread over Daniel's lifetime. His first visit may have been as early as 1689[138] and he may have fled there on several occasions when seeking to escape arrest.

In 1706 Harley, having launched Daniel as a propagandist by financing the *Review*, came under pressure from him to be fully employed in the government's service. To Daniel, the key to active participation in the political life of the country was to be employed in some way or other by the mighty and then to become indispensable to them.

There is some evidence that Daniel sought a mission in France where the great decisions about peace and war were to be made and where the Jacobite Court harboured a Catholic king in waiting. The possibility of supping with the devil must have been exciting to Daniel.

Of more immediate importance and impelling interest to Harley and the government was the possibility of union with Scotland. Union was an old subject of controversy kept alive in Scotland by the potential economic advantages for the country and the financial interests of corrupt ruling Scottish families. In England the calculations were different, there was the political advantage of unifying the Crown to keep out foreign powers, and thus to maintain the peace, and also the achievement of a parliamentary majority for the administration of the day by packing the English parliament with newly ennobled Scottish representatives.

In 1706, when it seemed that the time was ripe, Queen Anne was in favour of the union because it protected the Hanoverian succession. Harley's interest in achieving union wavered as his need to secure a parliamentary majority changed. If Scottish votes were not needed he cared nothing for a union as common sense suggested that it would be expensive for English taxpayers. So it has proved to be to the present time.

Backscheider shows[139] that when four Scottish commissioners were appointed in 1706 to conduct discussions with the English government, Daniel was quick to make contact with them when they came to London. Daniel must have attempted to ingratiate himself with these commissioners by displaying his knowledge about industry and trade and by showing that as a Presbyterian he was one of them. For their part, they must have been assessing whether Daniel would be helpful to their interests.

Daniel was being presented with the opportunity to be a fully-fledged agent, which was a role he was to perform throughout his journalistic career. Daniel was well equipped for the role, for he was reasonably well informed about Scottish affairs and fertile in his notions about industry and trade development projects. To Harley, Daniel could argue that being trusted by a Scottish audience meant he could offer the Scots an alternative interpretation of the political position and tactics of the English negotiators.

The character required to operate as a double agent in Scotland was rare and elusive: it was necessary to be thought to honour the trust of passionately divided interests. It is not likely that Daniel was wholly convincing in the role because he was apt to boast of it to others, but the situation showed him at his best. He was energetic, well-informed and alive to the main chance.

There is evidence that Daniel made a good impression on the Scottish commissioners. Backscheider quotes correspondence from Sir John Clerk to his father in July, praising Daniel and informing him that Daniel was writing in the cause of union and would be coming to Scotland.[140]

Daniel was skilful in suggesting ways in which the union would open up opportunities for trade, and ingenious in his suggestions for Scottish projects which would become profitable in an enlarged market. The feedback to Harley from the Scots must have been positive. Harley hesitated. Was Daniel really needed? If so, would any need of the government outweigh the complications of employing him?

Personal feelings may have complicated and delayed the appointment. Daniel formed an attachment to one of the Scottish commissioners, the young, handsome and talented Sir John Clerk, who was known as 'a pretty young man'. John Clerk, if judged by his correspondence, was besotted with Daniel. These two had common interests: for five years Clerk had travelled in Europe and was well informed about foreign affairs, and they shared a sexuality common to the Scottish nobility.

Clerk's memoirs describe his efforts to avoid the advances of predatory women on his European travels. He was happier and more absorbed in the men he encountered. His memoirs are complimentary on Daniel's role in the negotiations of the union and his *History of the Union*.[141]

Marriages were important among the Scottish aristocracy for dynastic reasons: to cement political alliances and to replenish family fortunes through dowries. Finding marriageable women was a problem for John Clerk for he had dynastic and family considerations to take into account. John Clerk married for the second time in February 1709. The birth of a child in December coincided with Daniel's severance of his links with Scotland.[142]

In September 1706 as the Scottish Parliament assembled in Edinburgh for the crucial session to consider the union bill, and with public opinion running strongly against the union, Harley took the plunge and appointed Daniel. Harley agreed to pay him out of his own purse. He was to be parsimonious and started as he wished to continue by giving Daniel the small sum of £25 to cover his expenses for the ten-day trip north.

The writings of Daniel's that John Clerk referred to in his letter to his father were two pamphlets published in May 1706, entitled *An Essay at Removing National Prejudices against a Union with Scotland*, Parts 1 and 2. In the first of these pamphlets Daniel set out the advantages of the union to the English: no more threat of internal war, safety from any foreign foe and a consequential increase in trade for both countries. In the second, his argument was less direct. He explained to a sceptical English audience that Scotland must be spared punitive taxation as a price for union, and that the growth of Scottish trade would not be at the expense of the English who would remain the centre of an Empire which would benefit from more people to exploit the potential of England's American possessions.

In Scotland he would have to bend his arguments to the hostile Scottish majority against union. Daniel travelled to Scotland in October 1706. His exact brief is unknown and his method of payment, as in his work with Harley in 1705, was obscure. While at first he was paid out of Harley's pocket, later he was paid out of government funds, which is what Daniel desired (and what he needed) if he were to represent himself to Scots 'in the know' that he was acting for the English government.

He entered an Edinburgh in tumult and uproar. It was a dangerous and frightening place and no time to be an Englishman claiming to speak for the English government. The city was full of an alliance of Scots opposed to the union: Jacobites and Roman Catholics found common cause with the Church of Scotland: seamen, crofters and an assorted rabble combined in raucous and violent opposition in the streets. Outsiders, out of curiosity, had come to stay with their relatives, while peddlers and hawkers plied their trade in and off the one mile of what is now Princes Street.

When the parliament met in the autumn the grand people of Scotland assembled in the Parliament House. The authorities were alarmed by the exotically-clad Highlanders who had appeared unannounced from the hills armed to the teeth with swords, pistols, daggers and staffs. The authorities had left nothing to chance. In the City were large numbers of Scottish grenadiers, and the Queen's Commissioner, Lord Queensbury, was accompanied by a squadron of the Royal Horse Guards.

There were over three hundred parliamentarians assembled in Parliament House representing the burghs, shires and the first estate of barons, viscounts and earls. Parliament was deeply divided and there was never more than a tiny majority for the union. However, the opposition was divided and sectarian: the religious sectaries, both Catholic and Episcopalian, opposed the Hanoverians in favour of the Pretender, but the concerns of the Church of Scotland were very different. The Scottish church sought to achieve protection as the established church and to maintain its method of governance.

What the parliament was to consider was a bill for providing the union. Thus, the form favoured the determined minority in favour of the bill, almost whatever it contained, and the task of this minority was to buy off the sectarian opposition in the committee stage of the bill at the lowest cost.

Those favouring the bill for their own narrow advantage, because they had been bribed by the English or could not afford to be left out, were never in a majority. What drove the bill was the widespread awareness of the parlous state of the Scottish economy that forced the poor into joblessness and poverty and the mighty to dispose of their estates. The mob might complain that Scotland was 'selling its liberty for a mess of pottage' but the day to day reality was that it was necessary for the poor to find shelter and food, and that required English money.

Daniel wrote:

Like true Souldiers, tho in a Bad Cause, they [the opponents to the bill] fought Their Ground by Inches. From Article to Article, they disputed every Word, every Clause, Casting Difficulties and Doubts in the way of every Argument, Twisting And Turning every Question, and continually Starting Objections to gain Time; And, if possible, to throw some Insurmountable, Obstacle in the way.

When an attempt was made by opponents of the bill to achieve the right to consult their communities, it was clear that the remorseless progress of union was unstoppable. Good-natured chanting against the bill outside the parliament building turned to anger and violence: the mob threw garbage and stones at the supporters of the bill when they left the parliament. A serious attack was mounted on the coach and horses of the Queen's Commissioner, Queensberry, and death threats were made by post to supporters of union. On 23 October a serious riot took place and government forces took control of key points in the City. Writing to Harley, Daniel used such words as an 'Insurrection is not Unlikely' and complained that his life was in danger.

A note of caution must be sounded. Many accounts of the proceedings of parliament rely on Daniel's published work on *The History of the Union*.[143] Following the advice of William Minto, the reader needs to be cautious:

Daniel writes for effect and for the purpose of portraying himself in the most favourable of lights and, of course, he is a writer with a most vivid imagination. This is how he wrote about his most dangerous moment:

He [had been] watched by the mob: had his chamber windows broken by stones [and] but, by the prudence of his friends, and God's providence, he escaped.

Similarly, Daniel's role in Scotland in his support for the bill, and his disavowing of the opponents of it, is often told in his own words. In the *Appeal* Daniel writes of an audience with Queen Anne in which she says to him, 'that she had such satisfaction in his former services, that she had again appointed him for another affair, which was something nice, but the treasurer [Godolphin] would tell him the rest'.[144] This is pure make-believe. There was no such audience or royal approval, as any reasonably well-informed reader would have realised. So when Daniel tells us of the important part he played in the Scottish parliamentary process of the bill, it is wise to be cautious.

Daniel tells us that he attended committees of the parliament, for whom he had made several calculations on trade and taxes and that he had refuted the writings of Webster and Hodges against the union. His memos were probably limited to providing his friends with the material they needed for committee discussions, but what was true was that Daniel entered effectively into the public debate as the leading and most prolific polemicist for the union.

Daniel followed his first two essays on *Removing National Prejudices, against a Union with England* with three more. In the third essay he sought to re-assure the Church of Scotland and again urged that increased trade would continue to bring prosperity to Edinburgh even though its constitutional role was diminished.

In the fourth, he engaged with a number of constitutional and economic arguments advanced by James Hodges and others. In this essay, Daniel asserted that the proposed arrangement for a 'draw back' of duty paid on foreign salt, and payment of the equivalent would benefit Scotland by £300,000 a year. In this Daniel was correct. England's contribution to Scotland since 1707 has consistently benefited Scotland. So persuasive was this argument that many English supporters of the union might well have hesitated.

In the fifth and last of the essay series, Daniel dealt with the various points raised in objection to his previous writings. In a closely argued tract, Daniel provided many examples of how the union would benefit the Scottish economy.

The essays were not the only contribution Daniel made to the war of words, for at least six other tracts have been attributed to him over the period. Taken together they amount to a substantial contribution to the debate and reinforced Daniel's public reputation as one of the outstanding pamphleteers of his time.

Noteworthy among these writings, although not for its poetic merits, was *Caledonia*, a poem written in honour of the Scottish nation. On the verso page was printed an extract from the minutes of the Scottish Privy Council, giving Daniel the exclusive rights to publish it. The poem is dedicated to the Duke of Queensbury and was printed by Anderson, the eighteenth-century equivalent in Scotland of Her Majesty's Stationery Office. To Daniel, this was an imprimatur of his role in the whole Scottish affair and his attempt to place himself socially.

How useful was Daniel in bringing about the union? His usefulness to the English government is difficult to measure. Although many of Defoe's letters to Harley have survived, very few of his replies are extant. Daniel was to complain that he did not receive instructions. No doubt that was deliberate on Harley's part. Daniel's letters would have been useful to Harley, and to Godolphin, for he was a shrewd and knowledgeable writer quick to understand crucial issues as they arose, but their underlying emotion would have required Harley to evolve a way of reading Daniel so as to extract what he needed to know. He would have made allowances for the emotion, and, of course, he had other sources of information for comparison.

If the judgement of history and of historians is to be consulted, the answer to the question of how useful Daniel was to securing Union is negative: he was not instrumental. Daniel's *History*, published in 1709 and printed by Anderson, has sunk into oblivion and historians have been dismissive of his contribution. W. J. Riley, writing in 1978, was forthright in his judgement. He wrote that, '[h]e was a government agent, employed specifically to support the union in any way he could…on the evidence of his writings, Defoe had as little idea as anyone else of the probable effects of union. It is possible that he did not greatly care either one way or the other'.[145] This judgement is harsh. Daniel was part of the sound and fury which was a necessary part of the debate over the union. No doubt the historian who stands apart from the melée, and with the passage of time, will discount the noise and favour a statement of the underlying causes of such a far-reaching constitutional change, but, at the time, Daniel's part was thought to be central to the debate.

For the biographer, success or triumph is best measured by Daniel's objectives in going to Edinburgh. There were three objectives. The first of these was to perform his services to the satisfaction of his employers. Arising from this, there was the second and over-riding aim of obtaining a lucrative public office. Thirdly, Daniel was on the make. Free from the pressure of his creditors who dogged his every step in England, and favoured by his new Scottish connections, which were unsullied by his English reputation, he could make useful money.

Daniel was quick to portray himself as a victim of religious persecution for beliefs he shared with the majority of Scots. What he could offer his new

Scottish friends and allies was his knowledge of trade and commerce. His mind teemed with the various projects he could summon up. Many of these must have been figments of his imagination but for the moment they would have impressed his newly-found Scottish acquaintances.

There was no doubt that Daniel was successful in gaining access to many powerful men in Scotland who were key players in Scottish politics. The friendship of Sir John Clerk was helpful, for he was a protégé of the Duke of Queensbury who represented William III as High Commissioner to the Scottish Parliament in 1700 and who became a powerful man in Scottish and English politics after the union.

It is possible, although difficult to prove, that membership of the Masons provided a link for Daniel. If he was a Mason, as I think he was, he may well have become associated with some powerful connections through exclusive Masonic lodges.

In April 1707 Daniel joined the Edinburgh Society for the Reformation of Manners and later the Society for the Propagation of Christian Knowledge. The societies were active in discouraging swearing, heavy drinking and lewdness and its members were active in patrolling the streets, encouraging informants and initiating prosecutions for sodomy. In 1707 there was a spate of prosecutions for sodomy across England and Scotland. The various societies initiated in total over one hundred prosecutions. One method of protection adopted by homosexuals was to join local societies as cover for their activities.

In 1702, in a pamphlet entitled *Reformation of Manners*, Daniel had made a satirical attack on the work of these societies. But in Edinburgh Daniel needed extra protection and to take a different line on reform. Harley was not close to hand and Daniel was unfamiliar with the Scottish legal system and the justices. If Daniel had been arrested and detained in prison, publicity would have been unavoidable.

While Harley had been mean in his payments to Daniel since October 1706, he did make him a payment of £100 in February 1707 when union had been achieved, so signalling his satisfaction. Daniel would have felt that he could take pride in a job well done. However, the approval of Harley and Godolphin did not did not lead to public office. Daniel solicited Harley, Godolphin and others for an appointment throughout his stay in Edinburgh. He favoured a position in customs and excise or a surveyor of a major port where the cash flow was greatest, or, if not those, something else of that kind. But the corridors and the mail were full of Scots soliciting office. Promises had been made to the great and mighty and their servants in order to obtain the union and the promissory notes were due. Simply, it did not seem appropriate or prudent for the English government to reward an Englishman of dubious reputation with a Scottish public office.

As for making money, there was hope for Daniel. He entered into a number of business ventures. The scope and substance of these are not known and Daniel's account of them is not always to be taken seriously, but, over the next few years, he involved himself in a number of investments and projects. These included the manufacture of linen, the wholesaling of wine, the selling of horses, and publishing in Edinburgh and elsewhere. When Harley remained in the political ascendancy, Daniel made special reports for which he was paid and he sought to be useful to Harley in a number of other ways. He was always paid.

In all this activity Daniel felt that he was back in the 1680s and 1690s without the encumbrance of bankruptcy. He replicated the behaviour of this earlier period. He cultivated acquaintances and friendships by visiting his new found friends at their homes and drinking with them in clubs and bars, and he sought out the prosperous and influential.

Daniel never settled in Scotland. It was never his country. During the period 1707–12 he was active in Scottish ventures. When not there he employed an agent, John Russell, and their correspondence survives.[146] Daniel continued to work for administrations of different persuasions, for which he was paid, and he employed others to do work for which he had neither the time nor connections. But gradually his involvement in Scotland diminished and his businesses went the way of his English enterprises of the 1690s: they were starved of the working capital and the detailed attention required to make them flourish. Daniel visited Scotland for the last time in 1712.

There are many unanswered questions. Not least is how Daniel found the working capital to invest in new business enterprises. At the time he was mocked from England where his true financial position was known. However, he must have achieved some business momentum by using London connections when he was hot in Scotland. He used these connections to perform services for his Scottish acquaintances: special pleading, and the arrangement of audiences with those in power in England, and 'consultancy advice' on business matters, for which he was paid good money. This advice was subject to diminishing returns with the passage of time. Perhaps he rode on the coat-tails of Scottish merchants and traders, encouraging them to back commercial ventures. It is simply unknown.

What is also unknown is how Daniel managed to carry out his activities in Scotland while remaining very active in London. During his stay in Scotland in October 1706 to February 1707, Daniel continued to publish the *Review*, which was appearing twice a week, with the *Little Review* once weekly. The *Review* prided itself on being topical. Was it physically possible for Daniel to do it all: despatch copy to London, a communication which at its fastest would take many days, check proofs with the printer, and oversee distribution? All this while, when he was playing an important role in Scotland, he was also active in pamphleteering in London, where he continued to be engaged in several disputations.

Daniel's friends assert that it was possible because of Daniel's energy and known output; his enemies argued that it was impossible and goaded Daniel for pretending that he did it all. In this instance, some credence must be given to Daniel's enemies. Publishing was an incestuous business in London: there were not many printers and they tended to know what was going on and who was writing and publishing. They would have been aware of the individuals helping Daniel.

The question is of great importance in Defoe ascriptions. It is likely that throughout his lifetime Daniel used his reputation to trade-off the work of other writers: to edit, re-write, re-present and place the work of others. By 1705/6 he had established a reputation as a propagandist based on an output over at least ten years. This reputation was based on contemporary knowledge of his works. It seems likely that he traded on his reputation to edit the work of others.

In his earlier writing Daniel must have been terrified of falling foul of the censorship created by the Licensing Act. This being so, he thought it prudent to cause confusion over the ownership of his publications. It became a life-long habit. He identified and used a number of stratagems for creating confusion and mayhem which annoy and puzzle his readers today.

ALL THINGS
TO ALL MEN

1715 to 1718

Chapter 13

A Way With Words

Such is the power of words, that mankind is able to act as much evil by their tongues as by hands; the ideas that are formed in the mind from what we hear are most piercing and permanent.

Serious Reflections of Robinson Crusoe
Daniel Defoe, 1720

IN DECEMBER 1706, WHILE Daniel was in Scotland, James Foe died. Daniel did not return to London for the funeral, for which James had set aside the sum of £20. James had made his will in March 1706 and biographers have been unable to understand it.

The laws and conventions of inheritance at the time assume that in the absence of exclusion clauses the elder son inherits. Daniel did not inherit anything but was appointed an executor.[147] Scrupulously, James Foe lists certain debts that he wishes to be paid and names his granddaughters to named mothers (his daughters) as receiving small sums. To his grandson Benjamin is bequeathed a gold watch 'in the possession of his mother'. James leaves his grandson, Daniel junior, £100, and the balance of the estate he bequeaths to Daniel junior's five sisters to be divided equally between them by his father. Daniel and his wife (unnamed) were to use this money for the subsistence of these children, and it would be lawful for them to make use of these funds for these purposes.

The will is puzzling. Why did James Foe not leave his estate to either Daniel or to his elder brother, known as Daniel Defoe, who was alive at the date of the will? The elder brother was a bachelor and a soldier serving abroad. This Daniel was not a biological son and, probably, not in touch with his father. The Daniel Foe named in the will as executor was not his biological son either, and James was not inclined to give him any money. On the other hand, at this time extended families gave priority to relationships, not biology: James accepted his responsibilities and Daniel was a son to him. Mary Tuffley, as Daniel's wife and mother of the children, is not named.

Who are the five sisters of Daniel Defoe junior? Writing recently, neither Backscheider nor Novak can account for them. Novak believes them to be Hannah, Henrietta, Maria, Sarah and Sophia, and excludes Martha. But as has been shown here, it is certain that Sarah is the child of Daniel and Elizabeth Sammen and, it has been argued, Sophia is a daughter by Mary Norton. Backscheider believes that Martha died some time after the will but before James's death and she argues for her inclusion, but she excludes Sarah.[148] The five sisters are Hannah, Henrietta, Maria, and, as been shown here, Sophia and Sarah. Only Daniel and 'his wife' can provide for all these children because he is the father to them all and he alone has access to them all.

And how is the gift of £100 to Daniel junior to be explained? Well, Daniel junior was illegitimate, and Benjamin was Daniel's legitimate heir, so it was Daniel junior who needed financial encouragement. It may be that Daniel junior was a nice boy and people liked him.

Daniel boasted of many exploits which existed only in his imagination but his activities in Scotland in a winning cause were more genuinely something to talk about in his favourite London coffee bars, societies and literary circles. There must have been a fund of good stories for him to tell. It was a time of journalistic opportunities for him. They were the reward not only for pamphleteering services in the cause of the union but also for all his writing in diverse causes since 1695.

Later, in 1720, when Daniel's journalistic activities aroused bitter controversy, he argued for journalism to be considered as a profession, much as that of a solicitor, doctor or merchant. Members of these professions were paid for their services, so why not writers? This statement might be regarded as an ideal; the reality was very different. The reality has always been different. Today, when press behaviour is to some extent managed and the market place diverse, in any opinion poll the activities in least public regard, occupying the bottom two places, are journalism and politics.

Journalists in the 1700s were vitriolic critics of their competitors. No one was as bitterly criticised as Daniel. He was denounced in the most vehement of terms as a 'Mercenary Prostitute' and a 'foul mouthed Mongrel', as practising sedition, as possessing a 'Machiavellian Head' and as 'loving mischief in his heart'. While Daniel gave as good as he got, the extreme abuse he received requires explanation.

In the 1700s journalists laboured under huge disadvantages and dangers.[149] There was no long-established party system: the Whigs and Tories were factions, and parliamentary divisions and alliances were temporary, fluid and fragile. Politicians sought personal alliances around the issues of the day which were subject to constant review. The system of triennial elections from 1695 complicated both politics and journalism because parliamentary majorities were subject to the continuous appraisal and approval of a volatile electorate. To be caught out as a journalist on the 'wrong side' could be very punishing: fines, imprisonment, the pillory and ruin.

Politicians sought influence with their electorates in a savage propaganda battle by buying the press and financing pamphlets. Pamphlet propaganda sought to consolidate opinion in known readership constituencies by demonising other persuasions and opinions, their duration, together with those of newspapers and periodicals, were mostly very short.

It can be argued that writers were experiencing a new dispensation: a breakdown of absolutism and intellectual dogma throughout Europe made it possible for certain individuals, by virtue of their social standing, to express political opinions and influence policy. In the City of London freemen had long ago created autonomous rights in relation to the Crown's prerogative, the tyranny of administrations, and the court system. Flimsy though these rights were, freemen of the City, which included Daniel, felt themselves to be politically empowered. A political consciousness was gradually created where the citizens of London felt that they had a right to participate in affairs of state and to discuss them in coffee bars and clubs and with their neighbours.

However, the gatekeepers to power and patronage, the high officers of the state, remained in place and writers were their paid hirelings in the battle for power. These men were in their place at the behest of the monarch of the day. An attack upon them was an attack upon the monarch herself, for they were her servants. Such attacks could prove fatal.

Writers incurring the wrath of ruling administrations were subject to punishment for treasonable and seditious activities. It was true that the apparatus of censorship of the written word had become less onerous. William's parliament had ended the monopoly of the Stationers' Company, the licensing system which had regulated public printing had been allowed to lapse, and it had become much more difficult to execute printers for seditious printing. However, as Daniel had found to his cost in 1702, it was still possible to catch the bold under the guise of seditious libel and juries remained packed against the victims.

It was not surprising that writers adopted a variety of stratagems for avoiding identification: non-ascription, aliases and satirical voices, and that they adopted narrative techniques which disguised their involvement, such as letters to the press. A common device of Daniel's when he could not avoid identification was to state that a work had been started and largely completed at a much earlier date, with the implication that it could not have arisen from a contemporary event or debate. It was a widely held view that he wrote many letters 'from the public'.

It was impossible for Daniel to deny that an article or leader in the *Review* was other than his, however it was possible for him to deny that he was the author of most that he wrote for other newspapers, even when his authorship was obvious in the trade he practised.

Daniel had a wide variety of stratagems for denying authorship when explanations were demanded, for example, that he had done no more than make some suggestions at the bequest of a printer, or that 'he' had not delivered the copy when a messenger of his had left it for him at a back entrance. These sleights of hand would infuriate the layman but might be of crucial importance in a legal challenge, and few were more experienced and better trained to know it than Daniel.

Journalism was the activity for which an immediate posterity remembered Daniel. It had been created and had been transformed within his living memory. In 1640, on the eve of the English Civil War, some two hundred publications were printed in England every year. The number had grown slowly since the reign of Henry VIII when only eighty were printed and when the reading of the Bible was limited to men. The abolition of the Star Chamber and other royal instruments of social and political censorship led to an explosive growth in publications. Every political crisis swelled the paper tide until the number reached three thousand a year in the 1680s. At this time writings included traditional bawdy and lurid ballads, poetry, pamphlets, newspapers and periodicals. Daniel wrote in all of these many mediums.

London, as the capital city, was the place to be if you were a writer. In London, by the 1670s, some 50 to 60 per cent of the population could read. Elsewhere, and in particular in rural areas, illiteracy was widespread, but even in the smallest village there was someone who could read, and who would do so for others, and there were always opportunities to learn to read and write. Communication remained mainly oral but the transition to print was relentless and even in the most remote of hamlets there was point in distributing a pamphlet, for there was always someone to read it to his neighbours.

The explanation for the purity of purpose and values the press claimed lies with the ideological traditions it inherited. During the Civil War ideological communities were created through the written word and independent of geographical proximity: Levellers and Ranters created a common interest by distributing literature. Similarly, and more immediately applicable to Daniel's story, Quakers defined themselves by the use of print. Literature was prepared, discussed and distributed at weekly meetings and Quakers took to the road to distribute their literature to their folk elsewhere. Women's voices were heard.

Within these communities, suffering was emblematic of an intellectual conflict in a righteous cause. When Daniel is writing to Harley in terms which might be labelled as self-pity, and which describe his suffering, he is appealing to a puritan tradition which Harley shared.[150]

At first, to be heard as a writer one needed to relate to such a community, civil or religious, and later to a political faction or 'party'. To carry conviction a writer needed to belong and his attachment must be absolute and intensely emotional. Commitment was to a 'true path' which, being true, would triumph in the face of much opposition, for the devil was at work through doubters. Divergence from the 'truth' was felt as treachery, treason and heresy.

At the outset Daniel had dissent and dissenters as his audience. In London in the 1680s some ten per cent of adults were thought to be

Baptisms 1662

Daniel son of a strange baptised July 17
Sarah daughter of Robt ffaulkner and Anne his wife was
baptised ffeb: 25

A Baptism at Chadwell St Mary, Colchester, Essex

Daniel Defoe's Oath of Loyalty to the Crown

Sep
22 Benjamin Doffoo of Stoke howington in the county of middlesex Singleman and Hannah Coales of St Georgas of Colgate in the city of howwich Singlewoman were married the twenty Second of September.

Benjamin Defoe's Marriage Record

June 6 Benjamin Son of Mr Benjamin D Foe Gent & Hannah his Wife in St George of Colgate Baptized by me — r T Finch

Baptism of Benjamin's First Child

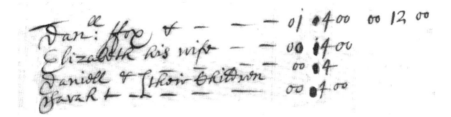

Setting up Home with Elizabeth Sammen 1695/6

Sophia daughter of Daniel de foe by Mary his wife was born the 24 of December 1701

Sophia De Foe, Record of Birth at St John's Parish Church, Hackney

The Will of John White, weaver and Citizen of London

dissenters so that it was a significant but minority readership. The indications are that Daniel began to be alienated from this readership early in his writing practice. In *An Appeal to Honour and Justice*, Daniel reveals that he disappointed many dissenters who wanted to support James II's proposed abolition of religious discrimination against dissenters. This position rests on Daniel's resistance to the toleration of ideals which lay outside the 'true path' of religious belief; he never extended his arguments for religious toleration to include Roman Catholics, even when his own religious commitment to dissent had weakened.

As life continued to secularise, writers began to attach their fanatical adhesion to religious communities to political 'factions' and 'parties' (from the 1680s to Whigs and Tories) and to the patrons who represented them in affairs of state. The transfer carried an emotional charge; opinions expressed in the newspapers of the time were bitingly partisan, and those who claimed to be part of a 'true faith' were reviled in the crudest of terms for any step away from the path.

From around the first decade of the eighteenth century the professional author began to appear. It became possible for an author to make a generous living from the sale of his own texts. If the need for money was acute, whether or not it was fed by greed or avarice, the necessary funds could be obtained from writing.

Any writer must have an acute sense of his audience. Between 1704 and 1713, Daniel was seen to be writing and editing the *Review* for a dissenting audience. However, the *Review* reached, for most of its nine-year life, a circulation of only 400 readers, and to be really useful to his paymasters, Daniel had to reach a much larger audience. The Tory newspapers, whether moderate or extreme, such as *Mists Weekly Journal*, had circulations twenty-five times higher than the *Review* at 10,000 copies.

Daniel started his own Tory newspaper, the *Mercurious Politicus* and contributed to others. When political patronage suggested it, and times had changed, he founded the Whig paper, the *Whitehall Evening Post*, and, for the remainder of his life, Daniel thought nothing of contributing to or editing rival papers while denying that he was doing so. Daniel's prodigious journalistic activity took business away from his 'true Tory' or 'true Whig' competitors. No wonder that they were outraged by this fraudster with his opportunistic, lying and unscrupulous competition. And then there was snobbery. Daniel, as non-Oxbridge, was derided as an illiterate ignoramus and not a gentleman.

There were other reasons for dislike of Daniel. In England, to be described as 'too clever by half' is not to be complimented. Daniel was very clever and resourceful, vainglorious and presuming. It was all too much. While he might have been respected for what he had achieved, he was not liked. The biographer looks in vain for evidence of friendship and enduring love. There are no extant records which show that Daniel moved hearts or performed good deeds: he is not to be found preserved in correspondence passed down to posterity because of its importance to others.

There may have been something more than this: his sexuality. The way he displayed himself and his sexual conduct may have prompted feelings of aggression which gave the edge to other objections to his character and behaviour.

For all these many reasons, the most distinguished of his competitors and commercial rivals were scornful of Daniel. They observed his efforts to present himself as sensible, balanced and unemotional and were envious of his knowledgeable writing on agriculture, trade and commerce. They knew him to be busying himself in political intrigue, despairing over the prospects of success, and amusing himself by taunting political opponents into furious outbursts, while in the columns of a moderate *Review* he was chiding them for their bad temper. To Swift, Daniel was a 'stupid, illiterate, fanatic', while Addison described him as 'a false, prevaricating rogue'. What neither could afford to do was to ignore him.

It was an announced objective of the *Review* to provide a commentary on public affairs, 'Purg'd from the Errors and partiality of News-Writers and Petty-Statesmen of all Sides.' Daniel went further than this in stating that 'the avoidance of party extremism was to be one of [his] lifelong ambitions'. These objectives were not to be achieved but it can be fairly observed that, together with others, Daniel did much to lift periodical journalism out of rabid politics. In the *Review* he offered consistently good and intelligent discussion of current affairs in a way that would be recognisable as such today. What was remarkable about Daniel's contribution to the journalism of his day was his effortless ability to write knowledgeably on a wide range of subjects, from those of major public significance to the trivial and amusing.

The balanced viewpoint, until his fall from power and influence in 1708, and then on his return in 1710, was Harley's; the most successful and talented of political propagandists over a period of twenty years. Daniel was not Harley's only mouthpiece. Others, such as Davenant, Swift and Toland were highly influential and talented writers and pamphleteers. Daniel was one voice among many and directed by Harley to the specific audience he could reach.

It might be argued that Daniel's was not one voice but many, for he cultivated a wide variety of tones: sarcastic, hilarious, mock humble and indignant. When Mr Review was moderate, honest, candid and plain dealing, readers knew that it was but an act and dissimilar from the real Daniel Defoe.

John McVeagh[151] points out what is obvious to any reader: that no matter how infuriating the editor of the *Review* might be and how annoying his instability and waywardness, his was the voice of genius. McVeagh quotes the most amazing of Daniel's metaphors. Daniel wrote:

Multitudes of mushrooms have obtained upon the World whose Birth was the Produce of meer Vapour and Exhalation; who, as they sprung up in the dark Midnight Moments of Trade, when her eyes were shut, and when she doz'd with Dreams, and hagrid with wandring Ghosts of Trade Whymsies; so they were born to evaporate by Time, and dye in the handling, that by the Nature of them were destin'd to dissolve like a Cloud, and spin out their own Bowels like the Spider; that had nothing material in them, but being merely imaginary in their Substance, must of course be lost in the handing up and down, and leave nothing but Cobweb, and a tangl'd Husk of emptiness in the Fingers of those Fools, that were deceiv'd with the Appearance.

Such writing is a presage of fictions to come and for it the reader might forgive Daniel everything. But what does it mean? Today, a journalist might write the passage as follows: today many trade projects and schemes are promoted which are so lacking in substance that no one but a fool would give them the light of day.

In the period 1698–1703 Daniel had established a reputation as a revisionist writer of singular intelligence. Whatever the reservations about his character, and no matter how specious and self-seeking his motives, there is no denying the contribution he made. In *The Poor Mans Plea* (1698), Daniel argued for equality before the law, in *The True Born Englishman* (1701), for equality regardless of origin, in *The Original Power of the Collective Body of the People of England* (1702), for the right of the people of England to govern themselves, and in *A Hymn to the Pillory* (1703), for a writer's freedom of expression against the tyrannies of the State.

In the longer period 1704–14 there was no comparable contribution. No doubt the terrible punishments of the pillory, prison and bankruptcy stilled his willingness to speak his own mind. It was more prudent to speak in disguised voices and in the interest of those able to protect and pay him.

In this ten-year period there are now ninety-three pamphlets and articles placed in various periodicals attributed to Daniel Defoe, of which fifty are thought 'probably' to be by him.[152] Of the ninety-three, twenty-two are written on Scotland, two are panegyrics and nineteen, directly or indirectly, are written on religious themes, leaving some fifty others on diverse subjects.

If Daniel's reputation was to depend on an appreciation of his output in these years he would have been virtually unknown to posterity even as a footnote. His writings, however, are interesting for a number of reasons. The anticipation and expectation of reading the latest copy of the *Review* in a favourite coffee bar must have been an experience for many. Letting a quarrelsome and argumentative fellow into one's club would have raised tempers, but then, annoyed and irritated though men might be, in the end one could not do without him and his views. It is a human necessity to know not only what you believe but most emphatically what you do not.

The style of Mr Review was to pre-empt disagreement by assuming the readers' objections in advance, so denying them the right to form their own opinion. The adoption of this mode of debate as a conversational gambit would lead to few dinner invitations.

In a developed article or pamphlet, it is difficult for the reader to know Daniel's perspective: his 'real opinion' is hidden or disguised, which is either what he intended or could not avoid. In *The Shortest Way* his use of satire had led him to the pillory. In 1713–14, it led to his arrest and imprisonment.

Daniel's instability and alarm was always felt most at dramatic times of transition: a change of monarch, the defeat of an administration, a religious upheaval. The transition from Harley to Godolphin in 1708[153] had been smooth, since they were of similar mind, but the return of Harley in 1710 and the parliamentary election of that year, which resulted in a Tory administration, were more difficult for Daniel. Queen Anne was ageing and the transition to a new monarch was problematic.

Between July and September 1710, Daniel threw in his lot in with Harley and got back on to his 'payroll'. Parliamentary elections in 1710 and 1712 had produced majorities for the Tories but the initial administrations formed would be best described as coalitions. The over-riding public issue of the day was to bring the ruinous war with France to an honourable conclusion. Painfully, negotiations were conducted for such a peace while the war continued.

The Whigs had supported the war to secure trade advantages and out of fear of the return of the Jacobite Pretender. When the commercial part of the Utrecht Treaty came before Parliament, the Whigs organised to defeat it. The Whigs argued that reciprocity of trade relations with France would be ruinous to English traders and merchants. Harley clung to a moderate policy of peace with honour while the Tory party split between moderates and right wingers, hungry for power by whatever means, and organised through the October Club.

As the Tory party drifted to the right, Jacobite hopes rose that they might benefit from division. The Jacobite Court and its agents in Paris were active and Harley was undoubtedly in touch with them. He asked for their assistance for the administration's chosen list in the elections of 1712. On a mission to Scotland to report on elections there, and to conduct business of his own at the expense of the English taxpayer, Daniel became aware of a secret list of peers to represent Scottish interests in the new English parliament which included at least four Jacobites. Money was distributed to Scottish Jacobites to keep them sweet. Daniel may have been the agent for these payments.

It would not have been at all clear to Daniel how long Harley could be expected to stay in power, for he lacked the support of the Court, and it seemed obvious that peace could only come with the ousting of the Duke of Marlborough, the nation's hero. This being so, the possibility exists that Daniel was playing a double game: that he was writing in a disguised manner for Jacobite right-wing Tories such as St John, for prudence and moderation for Harley, and for his own personal safety, and a little principle, for leading Whigs.

The question remains unanswered as to the extent to which Harley might have moved to retain his own power and influence by a deal of some kind with the Pretender. The evidence is conflicting. Undoubtedly, Harley needed to take account of the possibility, if only to carry English Jacobites along with him. But would he have countenanced supporting an invasion? Feiling is judicious in balancing the probabilities. He writes, 'Harley with all his moderation and commonsense, had never ranged himself with the Hanover Tories... [But] he never ceased to have some hopes on both sides. He talked about beginning secret official negotiations with James but he never did it.' At the very end, Harley needed to draw back to his old Whig friends and allies.[154]

Daniel walked the same tightrope. He seemed to write something for Harley and then something different to appease the Whigs. Daniel pleased no one. What he succeeded in doing was to increase the number of his enemies. The Whigs never forgave Daniel for supporting a government that insisted on a peace treaty with France on terms, as it seemed to them, which would favour the French, for supporting the establishment of the South Sea company in competition with Whig alternatives, and in writing in support of a commercial treaty with France which would have permitted cheap French wines to enter the country. There was much more besides in his behaviour and views which they found odious.

According to Daniel Defoe, but not substantiated by any extant record, at some time in 1705–6 Daniel's wife Mary and her children moved into a house in Kingsland, Hackney. Their move may have been caused by the death of Joan Tuffley who had been cheated by Daniel in business dealings in the 1690s, and who was providing lodgings for his family. In 1706 (H 68) Daniel wrote to Harley stating that his family had been re-housed and that he was dealing and speaking with his wife for the first time in fourteen years (since the date of his bankruptcy in 1692). Daniel was not living with Mary but he may have borne the expense of their move.

In 1706 there might have been a new understanding. In return for Samuel Tuffley re-housing his grandchildren in a house of their own, Daniel may have agreed to make a regular financial contribution to Mary and to provide for the children's education. The Tuffleys may have specified a method of payment to ensure that regular funds reached Mary. When Daniel writes to Harley (H 96) asking for payments to be made directly to Mary, and assuring him of Mary's diligence and honesty in handling it, this method of payment may have been stipulated by the Tuffleys as a condition of their help. The Tuffleys would have been anxious to ensure that money was received by those in most need of it and that it did not disappear into the deep well of Daniel's needs. Of course, there is another possible explanation:

Daniel may already have arranged for the interception of the money and it was appearance that counted.

Daniel spent very little time in Hackney. He had a number of abodes. At this time, when in the City he lodged either with the Sammens, with his brother-in-law Robert Davis, or in Chambers in the Temple, and when in Scotland he occupied what lodgings he could afford. This pattern was now well-established. Like the proverbial sailor, he visited many parts and had a 'wife' in every port. He returned home from his various voyages, sometimes battered and penniless, on occasions with booty in his knapsack, and sometimes not; there were always distant sounds from the front, and sometimes presents of money in the post.

It is said that you may measure a man by the quality of his enemies. Throughout 1713 Daniel must have been reassured of his worth. On 23 March a past creditor from Great Yarmouth began an action against Daniel for the recovery of a £1,500 debt. When Daniel was evasive he was arrested and imprisoned. It was believed at the time that Daniel's enemies had put up this creditor to punish Daniel, and, if so, it was a shrewd move for his carelessness about his past debts had always been his Achilles' heel. The creditor had been shrewdly selected for the sum at issue was very large and the creditor was unwilling to compromise. Daniel spent eleven days in prison before the debt was paid. Rumour had it that Harley had paid the sum in full.

Undeterred, a few days later his journalistic rivals, backed by their own paymasters, contrived to have him arrested for three pamphlets which they alleged were written in favour of the Pretender. Their titles did not help Daniel: *Reasons against the Succession of the House of Hanover, And What if the Pretender Should Come?* and *An Answer to a Question That No Body Thinks of, viz. But What if The Queen Should Die?*

A minor Whig, William Benson, Thomas Burnet and George Ridpath, of the *Flying Post*, all of them under prosecution for seditious libel, persuaded Lord Chief Justice Parker to proceed with a case against Daniel, and, with great skill and determination, they pursued it until November, 1713.[155] Harley must have thought enough was enough. He was drinking heavily and had not recovered from an assassination attempt by the French spy Guiscard. In the end, Daniel had to petition the queen for a royal pardon she must have been unwilling to give and to rely on St John (Bolingbroke) to get it signed.

Daniel pleaded the pamphlets to be ironical and that subject to the usual stylistic rules it was clear to the reader that he had been mocking the claims of the Pretender. But was it clear, and was it his intention? Daniel's opponents had shrewdly taken passages from all his pamphlets and built a convincing case that he was arguing for the Pretender. As with *The Shortest Way* all attempts by Daniel to explain his intentions made the situation worse.

In his later defence of the most problematic pamphlet, *And What if the Pretender Should Come?* Daniel writes that it, 'being written ironically, all the first Part, if taken asunder from the last Part, will read, as in all Ironical speaking must be, just contrary...But taken whole, and of a Piece, can leave no doubt that they are written to Ridicule and expose the very Notions of bringing in the Pretender'.

What is missing for the reader is the writer's perspective and level of commitment. Clearly, the objective of the piece is to cause offence but to do so at a distance. In this piece, as in others, Daniel's generalisations in one field of argument clash with another, causing the reader to be confused. The truth of it is that the offended reader is left to sort it out. The critical perspective is provided by the reader and not the text.

The reader might reasonably suppose that this writer, Defoe, is arguing for both sides or for causes which he could not possibly have supported in full. Queen Anne might well have thought that the writer saw good reason to support the Pretender, while the Pretender might think that the case for him had been thoughtfully conveyed and that the rest was dressing or obvious camouflage.

Daniel may well have written about what was really going on. In the *Minutes of the Negotiations of Mons. Mesnager* (1717), a brilliantly successful secret agent tells the reader of the credulity of the British public and how they love to read numerous pamphlets, some of which are placed by foreigners. A certain person wrote a piece in our cause, he says, for which a fee was paid but afterwards he realised that the man was a secret agent. The reader might assume, but who can say, for certain, that the man was Daniel.

How to accommodate oneself to uniformity in religious and political matters, without surrendering to the devil, is the problem Daniel sets out in *Robinson Crusoe*. There is an answer provided in cultural terms. It can be argued that Daniel's desire to accommodate variety belongs to an emerging spirit of realism. However, such a reasoning does not help the biographer, for it does not enable him to distinguish between two men of the same time, similar background and upbringing, where one man is impeccably honest and straight-dealing and the other the opposite, between one man who, being hungry, steals for his supper and another who goes to bed without food.

It is fashionable today, and it is thought to be moral, for the wrongdoer to admit to making mistakes; but there are other standards of morality. Daniel was capable of the most dreadful duplicity. In early August 1714 on a routine visit to the printer of the 'new *Flying Post*', William Hurt, Daniel discovered that Hurt had been arrested and that later his own printer, John Baker, had been arraigned. A tip-off from the Sheriff's office gave Daniel reason to believe that he would be arrested too. He went into hiding.

In April of that year George Ridpath, the editor of the *Flying Post*, had become a fugitive from justice. He dismissed Hurt and replaced him with a printer named William Hookey. Hurt being a doughty man tried to continue to publish the paper himself. He could not do it alone. Daniel decided to help him by writing a new *Flying Post* in competition with the old. Daniel's motive was to ruin Ridpath who was a prominent Whig critic of the Harley administration and an enemy.

On 19 August Hurt's *Flying Post* published a letter critical of Arthur Annesley, fifth Earl of Anglesey, and one of King George's regents, which could be read as alleging him to be a Jacobite (which he might have been but which was not provable on the date of publication of the letter).

The Secretary of State, William Bromley, concluded that the letter had been written by Defoe. The letter was recovered and despite Daniel's denials it was demonstrated to be in his writing. Bromley was a loyal supporter of Harley and protective of his interests but he had no hesitation in ordering Daniel's arrest on a charge of seditious libel. All Daniel's appeals to Harley were in vain. Even if Harley had wished to help, his powers were waning. On 27 July he had resigned as Chancellor and was expecting his impeachment. He could hardly help himself, let alone others.

The citation accused Daniel of 'being a seditious and malicious man and plotting and intending evil to the Queen…and to scandalise and vilify the memory of…the Queen and cause to be believe that [she]intended…that wicked and dishonest reports and reputation be created of the Officers in the Irish army'.[156] The matter could be read in this way. The three men were found guilty and Lord Chief Justice Parker deferred sentencing, 21 November was announced as the date for sentencing. Daniel took cover and disappeared.

Daniel used this time to make his peace with Lord Townshend, the new Whig Secretary of State. He was not in a strong position. In exchange for his freedom he was to continue as a government spy at a remuneration of a mere £100 per annum, to open a new Tory periodical, *Mecurious Politicus*, infiltrate as many Tory periodicals as possible to reduce their influence on the government, and to inform on the Tory presses. Daniel was asked to pretend that he had not mended his fences with the Whigs. Daniel had sold out completely. It was possible to argue that Daniel had been appointed as a 'Governor General' of the Press.

In Daniel's defence it might be argued that under Harley he had supported 'moderation', if in an intemperate manner, and that now he was to do the same again. The ends were to justify the means. After 1718, when public knowledge of what he was doing became general, there were few left standing who would have condoned his behaviour. Daniel was to suggest that he had written to Lord Chief Justice Parker and influenced him in his favour. Characteristically, Daniel could not produce a copy of the letter.

Subsequently, biographers have had great difficulty in 'justifying' or explaining Daniel's activities over the period of his practice as a 'mole'. Why did he do it? Of course, for the money, then for access to the men of power, with the receding hope of public office, for sheer excitement and intrigue, and then for continued involvement by proxy in the issues of the day, which in his imagination he could influence from a life lived at the edge and thus become a player of importance. Daniel could busy himself with the affairs of others while keeping secret about his own. What more could a budding novelist of genius wish for himself?

Chapter 14

The Loss Of Harley

'tho they joined like loving Friends.
Yet each had his peculiar Ends.

Anonymous pamphlet, 1708

OF ALL HARLEY'S DOMESTIC propagandists, it is likely that Daniel Defoe received the most money, an indication of their mutual importance and regard. Few people would have been capable of playing 'dirty tricks' such as penetrating and sabotaging an opponent's newspaper or compromising its editor.

From 1713 Harley's political position had been in decline and after the attempt on his life, which produced for him the title of the Earl of Oxford and temporary popularity, it became irrecoverable. George I, on his accession to the throne in August 1714, treated Harley with contempt. George, as the Elector of Hanover, had always been transparent in his politics. He believed that the interests of Hanover lay in the waging of a relentless war with France. He allied himself to the war party in the English parliament and steadfastly opposed the administration's endeavours to secure a peace.

The principal issue in the British politics which preceded him had been the ending of a ruinous war. Against the opposition of the Dutch and the imperial alliance, of which Hanover was a part, Harley's administration had worked with France to secure the unpopular peace which eventually came with the Treaty of Utrecht in 1713.

In the later stages of these negotiations the issue of peace had been inextricably mixed with the succession to the throne of England, for Queen Anne was in poor health. Steps had been taken to secure the protestant succession through George but there was the possibility that personal ambition and religious persuasion might yet result in victory for the Jacobite cause and the succession of Edward, the son of James II.

The Tory ministers responsible for the Treaty of Utrecht, which brought a peace which lasted fifty years, knew that on the accession of George I they would in all probability be impeached. These ministers had little choice in the matter. To the end of Queen Anne's rule in August 1714 both Bolingbroke and Harley felt it necessary to keep open lines of communication to the Jacobite Court in Paris. Their parliamentary majority, in which Jacobite members were numerically significant and thus had power to influence events, depended on it.

The queen had turned to Shrewsbury on Harley's dismissal on the eve of her death. Following it, Bolingbroke fled to France and eventually to the

Jacobite Court in Paris, so confirming the worst fears of friends and foes. Harley waited for the inevitable: impeachment by due parliamentary process and a spell in the Tower of London.

The parliamentary controversies during the period of Tory administration under Harley had produced some surprising and unpredictable alliances. At the beginning of Queen Anne's reign, Tory control appeared to be unassailable. The natural course of preferment would have appeared to the ambitious to be alignment with the causes of the 'country' party and the Church of England, but by 1713 the prospects for the administration seemed hopeless.

Earlier, Daniel, with an eye on the main chance, but in secret, wrote a memorandum to Harley which although undated is thought to have been written around 1704[157] in which he sought to trim his sails to catch new winds of possible patronage. How far was he willing to go from the principles and religious beliefs he was constantly urging? A long, long way, it would appear.

Daniel wrote that the new administration need do nothing for the dissenters. He argued that 'tis not necessary in the present juncture to restore the dissenters to offices and preferment's... [That he was persuaded to the view that] freedom and favour to the Dissenters is the directest method to lessen their numbers and bring them at last into the Church...some small management among the Dissenters by useful agents might be useful to settle the general temper'.

These thoughts of Daniel come under the general title of 'Methods of Managing the Dissenters'. In December 1713, nine years later, similar views of Daniel's became public when he wrote a pamphlet entitled, *A Letter to the Dissenters*. In this pamphlet, Daniel criticised both dissenters and Whigs. He pointed out that dissenters having their own schools was strictly against the law. As for the Whigs, they should not be trusted, for it was the Whigs who had betrayed the dissenters in abolishing occasional conformity in 1711. He asserted that the Whig insistence on the Hanoverian succession was making the Hanoverian prince a figure of alarm as if on accession his first pre-occupation would be to punish dissenters by removing their religious toleration.

This later pamphlet of Daniel's caused deep offence, as it was meant to do, for it was read generally as being accepting of the Schism bill which would abolish dissenting schools. Once again, Daniel threw doubts on the sincerity of the Whigs.

Daniel wrote the pamphlet in order to assist Harley's complicated manoeuvres which, as it turned out, could not prevent the passing of the Schism Act, 1713. Even at this late stage of the administration's life, when it was clear that its days were numbered, Daniel was writing at the behest and pay of either Bolingbroke or Harley against the causes he had himself advanced when entering the public arena. Both his natural allies and his enemies wondered about him in various states of irritation and annoyance. Did he really not care about the principles involved in his arguments? Would he do anything for money?

Daniel's problem was that he was Harley's man to the tune of not less than £700 a year and the protection against prosecution that went with it. Harley was never a 'party' man in an age which created 'parties' as a necessary part of the English constitution. David Mallet, an earlier biographer writing in 1750, wrote of Harley, 'it is rather wonderful that he sustained himself so long than that he sunk at last. In a nation agitated by Faction, he who will not be of a Faction must be crushed between them'. In the end Harley was crushed by the factions and Daniel's great fear was that he would be crushed too.

Some time around 1714 Daniel was able to move his family into a large house in Stoke Newington in London which it was said had four acres of land around it. He began to turn it into a fortress. A fortress was needed, for Daniel was subject to constant arrest and harassment over the duration of his stay.

One of Daniel's most noteworthy biographers, John Robert Moore, imagined Daniel leading a life distant from the struggles of the world: back in the bosom of his family, busy in the design and cultivation of a large garden, and diligently at work in his study, despite ill-health, on fiction of lasting fame.

Far more likely, he was as Robinson Crusoe, busily constructing a refuge from which he would continue to sally forth, restless for adventure, and which would enable him to keep his secrets behind bolted doors and shuttered windows. In Daniel's imagination, the refuge of the house was a kind of providential haven following a risky and dangerous voyage in a world in which he had come to grief on numerous occasions. It left open to him that he might still be recognised as a person of worth and a gentleman of distinction with properties in town and in the country, like many a successful London merchant.

One abode had never been an end in itself for Daniel, for like Robinson Crusoe he needed a 'forward base' in the form of a country estate. He had sought to root himself many times in country establishments and as he began to fortify himself in Stoke Newington he was planning the expansion of his estate in Tilbury.

To maintain his continued employment by a Whig administration Daniel was required to seek a peace. He needed it for other reasons. Throughout 1714 Daniel had been under the most intense pressure: imprisonment and the threat of unpleasant punishment, the loss of his political patron and the largesse he earned from the connection, the difficulty of selling out politically to the 'devil', and virulent daily attacks from friends and foes. Daniel had incredible resilience and self-belief but no one could have been proof against such mental assault.

Daniel had lost most of the daily disguises he could be proud of: there was no more Mr Review, and no easy passages, albeit through back entrances, in Whitehall. Daniel had pared away the many selves which enabled his survival; dissenters denounced him as a hypocrite and continued to deny him church membership, Whigs reviled him, while the Tories, who had never had any time for him, continued to despise him. Daniel was left with the dark, sordid and secret byways of life and with the inner core of a being which had since infancy been hidden from the light of a direct assault.

At night, when in a strange place and without company, his dreams would have been uneasy and he would have rehearsed the justifications of his behaviour until daybreak. One day in 1715 he could not prevent himself from writing them down as was his usual fashion and giving them to that part of his world that might be expected to read his words. To this end he published in February 1715 his apologia entitled *An Appeal for Honour and Justice*.

Daniel sought to defend himself against the many slanders he had received. It cannot be said that his defence is sober, grave and true. The reader of it would know to be lies such statements that he had received no money for his writing, that he wrote nothing except for the *Review* for a period of a year, and that he was not the publisher of the Mercator. As discussed earlier, Daniel did not fight in the Monmouth Rebellion, was not the personal friend of William III and had no special relationship with Queen Anne. There is no statement made in the entire pamphlet that can be accepted without qualification.

The terms of Daniel's apologia are emotional; he casts himself in the robes of Jeremiah as a victim of persecution and relates himself to the prophets, pleads sympathy for his wife and children and asserts that a 'steady adhering to Personal Vertue and to Public Peace will AT LAST restore [him] to the Opinion of Sober and impartial Men'.

And then in the true tradition of the stage he throws himself to the floor. The publisher informs the reader that before completing his pamphlet Daniel suffered a severe apoplectic fit. His friends, fearing for his life, thought that they should publish the work in the absence of its final approval by the author, and in the hope that he might recover. The whole show was prefaced by Daniel himself in that he begins his tract with the words that he felt 'Hints of Mortality'.

Of course, Daniel was sick at that time. There is evidence of breakdowns both in 1713 and 1714. The assaults of his enemies had struck home. Daniel was exposed to the threats of his enemies and to prosecution for his sexual behaviour.

Was the show a success? And had Daniel brought the house down? We might imagine a Defoe-like conversation in a coffee bar.

Mr Whig: Have you seen this? The latest Defoe. (Thrusting a pamphlet across the table).

Mr Dependable: No. Should I read it?

Mr Whig: Don't bother. He maintains that no one paid him for anything he wrote over the years and that he never wrote a word at anyone's instruction. Lying dog. All the world knows that to be untrue. Wrote against an unjust peace! The rogue thinks that none of us have any memory at all.

Mr Dependable: You're too harsh. Don't you remember him standing in the pillory for the right to speak his mind, for our right to speak out, to speak our minds, to stretch a point?

Mr Whig: Well, yes, I'll give him that. We were all in favour of freedom of speech, so why him, why him in the pillory? There was more to that than meets the eye. Anyway, that's history.

Mr Dependable: What else?

Mr Whig: He says he was the personal friend of William III and Queen Anne. In his dreams. They wouldn't have touched him with a barge pole. He should be employed to re-write the history books.

Mr Dependable: Well, he's exaggerating there, I grant you. History's very important. We should try to get it right. I agree the man's a rogue. Still, we need rogues, don't you think? To get things changed. But we mustn't be too serious about it. Nothing like a good public spectacle.

They laughed. What did it matter anyway? There were more interesting matters to consider.

To the biographer, what is most important is Daniel's state of mind. He needed, and believed in, his fantasies; he treated those two impostors, fact and fiction, as the same. He had always needed them and they had always played a part in keeping him sane. When in Essex, as described in *A Tour Through the Whole Island of Great Britain*[158] he writes as follows:

> all along this county it was very frequent to meet with men that had from five to six wives…[the reason being that when young lasses coming from the upland came out of their native uplands to live at lower altitudes they] 'got an ague or two, and seldom held it above half a year or so… in Candy Island, there was a farmer, who was living with the five and twentieth wife, and his son who was but about thirty-five years old, had already had about fourteen…]

Also in the *Tour* he writes of Southwold in Suffolk.[159] He writes:

> 'There is but one church …an extraordinary large church capable of receiving five or six thousand people, and but twenty seven people in it besides the parson and the clerk; but at the same time the meeting-house for the Dissenters was full to the doors having as I guessed from 6 to 800 people in it.'

The church he describes is St Edmundsbury, which could not hold more that a few hundred people. Southwold was not, in the early eighteenth century, a centre for dissenters and there is no local record of any single large gathering of dissenters in the town.

These two accounts are typical of Daniel's writings. Taken literally they are incorrect and absurd. However, in the second he is telling his readers that once there is no compulsion for parishioners to attend worship in an Anglican church and freedom for others to worship as they please, a majority of people would choose a Dissenting Meeting House. It happens that even this assertion has turned out to be untrue, for in England today it is the Roman Catholic church that has most adherents. But it might have become true.

The 'truth' in the first statement is that it is probable that women who married and chose, in the early eighteenth century, to live in the flatlands of Essex might well have been more prone to sickness and to a shorter life than an indigenous male. A statement which is wholly believable.

What can be said is that Daniel's prose is infinitely more enjoyable, pervasive and powerful than my pale insistence on truthful propositions. However, to take Daniel's assertions as 'truthful' is a good deal more absurd than an insistence on meaning.

This digression is necessary because it was a 'true' statement of Daniel's in the *Appeal* that his loyal defending of Harley had brought him 'bitter reproaches'. But it is true also that he was, at the time he made this statement, denying the authorship of the pamphlets published in Harley's defence: pamphlets that it is now supposed he wrote.

Between October 1714 and July 1715, Daniel wrote five pamphlets which might be supposed to be in support of Harley: *The Secret History of the White Staff*, in three episodes, the *Secret History of the Secret History of the White Staff*, and *An Account of the Conduct of Robert Earl of Oxford*, which followed them. Later, in June 1717, he wrote the remarkable *Minutes of the Negotiations of Monsr. Mesnager at the Court of England*. These works are highly unusual. They tell the reader far more about their author than Harley or the subjects discussed and could only have been written by a person of rare talent: a person with the ability to write in the best tabloid tradition, and the erudition and self-confidence to write a *Times* leader. A reader who decided he disliked the author would, nevertheless, find himself lost in admiration of him.

To establish what Daniel was really up to in writing these pamphlets, it is necessary to appreciate the background events. Harley had paid off his team of writers in July 1714 and the last payment to Daniel was made in this month. At this time, Harley cut off relations with Daniel, and never renewed them. Daniel had changed sides by December 1714 and was at work for the new Whig ministry. Harley was impeached in June 1715 and was imprisoned for two years in the Tower of London from the following month. The

Jacobite disturbances in Scotland, and the threat of an invasion of French troops under the command of the Duke of Ormond (who, like Bolingbroke, had fled to France), took place in July 1715. Severe reprisals against the rebels followed their defeat.

Harley had urged his team of writers not to write in his support and strongly disapproved of Daniel's pamphlets, which he believed made matters worse for him. In July 1715 he published a disclaimer in the *London Gazette*. Following this disclaimer, the *Flying Post* wrote that it was 'very hard on the Mercenary who wrote these pieces, to be accus'd of such Ingratitude, as to write Things on purpose to injure his bountiful Patron'.

An Account of the Conduct of the Conduct of Robert Earl of Oxford was published at or about the time of Harley's disclaimer. It is a well-constructed and clever refutation of the grounds for the impeachment and, therefore, stands out from both the earlier *Secret Histories* and from the later *Minutes of Mons. Mesnager*, published on or about the date of Harley's release from the Tower.

Daniel could not resist thrusting himself forward into the maelstrom. Although he was a minor figure on the periphery of events, he was compelled to present himself as at the centre. He was excited by the happenings of the moment, he was scared, and then, there was the opportunity to make money.

Part 1 of the *Secret Histories* is written in the third person. The narrator is omniscient, except that he admits that on occasions he relies on reports from others. He appears as an observer reporting speeches made by Harley to his ministerial colleagues. There is a struggle between good, as represented by Harley, and his enemies within the ministry who are evil. The observer describes the opponents 'as the blackest of treacherous Jacobite devils'.

Harley is cast as a self-sacrificing patriot. His quiet dignified defence of his policies is presented as being in the queen's interest. However, the queen is influenced by the arguments of his enemies who claim that Harley is as Jacobite in his sympathies as they are. The queen is deeply moved by Harley's defence, but the situation is not retrievable. She resolves to do without Harley's enemies and in a short time to restore the White Staff of office to him.

No one asks of a fairy story whether it is true or not, but for the record it was almost entirely 'untrue'. My paraphrase of the pamphlet might be thought unkind to Daniel in that it reads as a kind of pantomime, with Harley as the Principal Boy and the queen as the Good Fairy. It is possible that the story, which has been interrupted, might have a happy ending. Even in adversity good, in the form of Harley and Daniel, might triumph over evil.

In Part 2, Daniel concentrates on 'Harley's brilliant out-manoeuvring of the leading Scottish Jacobite nobles by having them sent up to Parliament as representative peers'. (This may or may not be true but it is a sentiment with which Daniel can associate himself.) The pamphlet ends with attacks on anonymous individuals (it is thought Mrs Masham, Atterbury and Harcourt). If there are heroes, must there not also be villains? There was still no happy ending.

In Part III the reasoning is troublesome. The central argument of the pamphlet is that Harley's greatest mistake was to force the repayment of the debt to the South Sea Company and so annoy the Whigs. Consequently, Harley had to rely on the High Flyers in the Tory party, although he kept his distance. This being so, the High Flyers formed their own alliance with the queen and acted against him. If this unholy alliance had succeeded they would have reasserted the privileges of the Crown.

The latter assertion depends on the assumption of the existence of a real danger of a change to the succession. Although the succession of the Crown and the nature of the administration might have seemed problematic to many at the time, with the benefit of hindsight it can be seen that it was not. Queen Anne, although sick and dying, held firm to her protestant convictions; the accession of George assured the continuation of a protestant monarchy, and George favoured a balanced parliament.

The charge against prominent members of the ministry of flirting with the Pretender for parliamentary advantage could be levelled as much at Harley as anyone except Bolingbroke. In contrast, the queen's commitment to a protestant succession was unwavering. In the end, she had the last laugh, for on the day before her death she appointed the Duke of Shrewsbury to the White Staff, and not Bolingbroke.

It might be objected that I have made out these pamphlets to be something of a pantomime act. They are a highly entertaining mix of fact and fiction, absurdity and truth. No one other than Daniel could have written them. They are to be admired. Millions of people attend pantomimes and hugely enjoy them: they are therapeutic and warming on cold days. The importance of these writings to this tale is that they show Daniel at his most creative, as a spinner of tales; it was a talent that would astonish and amuse later in his life.

The Secret History of the Secret History was written at a dangerous time for Daniel. With new change jingling in his pockets he had to back off from Harley. If it was impossible to abate the flood of abuse from commentators convinced that he was the author of *The Secret Histories* then he must hide or excuse himself. In *The Secret History of the Secret History*, he provides the smokescreen to his retreat.

Daniel imagines a conversation in a coffee shop between a Quaker and another person. The pamphlets are discussed. The latter argues that these tracts were written by Robert Harley, or that he provided the information to 'Daniel Defoe, or some such Scribbler, as for Money he might get'. The truth was, says the citizen, that it was all the fault of rascally booksellers keen to make money. The Quaker takes a different view (and, of course the verisimilitude of a Quaker is undeniable) by saying that a friend of his had spoken to Defoe and that he was at the time 'in a very Dangerous Condition, having had a Fit of Apoplexy'. Defoe, the Quaker's friend had reported, had revised some of the sheets at the printer's request. Thus the two versions amount to the same in the end. Defoe was not at fault. The explanation is given credence by the honest Quaker and Daniel's explanation is given strength by assuming it has some of the gravitas of a 'Dying Declaration', and anyway, he was too weak to resist 'rascally booksellers'.

What Daniel achieves by this pamphlet is to thoroughly confuse the perspective for the reader. The author of the *Secret Histories* is an omniscient observer providing a believable narrative explaining Harley's fall, and now, like Alice in *Alice Through The Looking Glass*, he is rapidly disappearing from view.

In *Minutes of the Negotiations of Mons. Mesnager at the Court of England*, which was published in 1717, Daniel as the narrator has virtually disappeared while leaving his stamp upon the work. This pamphlet creates the fictitious memoirs of Nicholas Mesnager, Louis XIV's envoy to London in 1711, and subsequently at the Utrecht peace conference. While Mesnager is presented as a loyal servant of Louis XIV, he is displayed by Daniel, as are the occasions witnessed, in a grandiose manner which the reader supposes is a self-projection of the author. Through Mesnager, Daniel presents a satirical view of the English: they are 'as easily made slaves as other nations…betray their own liberties and rights…for money…sell their votes…talk high…[but are] publicly managed'.

The main purpose of the pamphlet is to exculpate Harley for a faulty peace treaty and to place the blame on an unnamed minister (who might be supposed to be Bolingbroke). To this end, Daniel invents both situation and dialogue. Daniel gives his readers a complicated joke. Furbank and Owens quote as follows:[160]

> I [Mesnager] attempted once or twice to furnish my self with another, [a scribbler who would be willing to write in the French cause for money] but could never get one like him, a certain Person, who the Swedish Resident, Monsieur Lyencroon, recommended, wrote an excellent Tract in our Interest entitled Reasons why this Nation [meaning England] ought to put an End to this expensive War … but afterwards we understood that the Man was in the Service of the State and that he had let the Queen know of the hundred Pistols he had received.

In 1711 Daniel had probably been the author of a pamphlet of the same name and Lyencroon was a sworn enemy of Daniel's. What then does Daniel ask the reader 'in the know', the reader who matters most to him, to understand by his 'joke'?

Daniel wants the reader to know that he was at the heart of the whole affair, and that he had deceived the French in the service of Queen Anne. Despite the deception he was highly regarded by the French, even by Louis XIV's own representative who was so close to the French monarch. He wishes the reader to aceptthat even his sworn enemies recognised his excellence and knowledge as a writer of tracts. While denying his authorship in public, Daniel could not resist leaving the reader with his imprimatur.

A biography of an eighteenth-century person is rendered difficult by the absence of the material open to the writer of a contemporary subject: there are no photographs, no sound records of the subject's voice, no record of the way he walked, and no friends or acquaintances willing to give the writer their views. In his writings Daniel set out to offend. The pamphlets discussed above are full of jibes and innuendoes. When he was operating undercover, Daniel's self-centredness and vanity would have caused offence. If he were spying on someone, and let them know of it by spoken asides and omissions, it would be deeply offensive.

Not every recipient would take offence lightly. It is not at all likely that Nathaniel Mist, the proprietor of *Mist's Weekly Journal*, would have turned the other cheek. Daniel claimed to his Whig masters[161] that during 1715–16 he had started *Mercurious Politicus*, a moderate Tory newspaper, gained control of *Dormers Weekly* and was in charge of the management of *Mist's Weekly*. In January 1718 he began a Whig version of *Mercurious Politicus* with the title *Mercurious Britanicus* and then, in September 1718, he re-started the long-established *White-Hall Evening Post*.

Secret though he maintained his influence to be, he would have been quite unable not to have revealed his activities. *Reeds Journal* could not resist the temptation to publish details of his involvements. In the doggerel of the time:

He wrote for all cause[s] that did yield him most,
Mists Weekly Journal, White-Hall Evening Post,
Two Mercury's each month one for the Whigs,
The t'other fraim'd to pleas the Tory Priggs.[162]

If it were known to the world, it was known to Nathaniel Mist. He was an unusual man. A former seaman, Tory and Jacobite sympathiser, he had sufficient erudition and competence to build a successful newspaper. Nevertheless, he must have welcomed Daniel's contributions.

From time to time Mist got into trouble with the authorities for offensive and seditious articles and the finger of suspicion always pointed at Daniel. Mist paid Defoe 20 shillings a week to begin with, which he raised to 40 shillings in September 1718. Anecdotally, it was suggested that to hide himself Daniel arranged for these sums to be paid to his gardener.[163]

On two occasions Mist was arrested and imprisoned and on one he was pilloried. Daniel had to work hard with the ministry to absolve himself from blame, for no one believed him and it was often difficult to explain his role without lying. At these times of Mist's imprisonments, Daniel played a greater part in the output of the paper.

William Lee, a hagiographer of Daniel's with a vivid imagination, suggested that some time after 24 October 1718 there was a violent argument between Daniel and Mist. The basis for this is Lee's supposition that Mist found out that Daniel had been paid by successive ministries over six years to spy on him, and to Daniel's reference to a man who had been rescued by him from prison on three occasions and yet drew a sword on him. Daniel's imagination was at least the equal of Lee's, so his version of a quarrel is suspect also. It seems far-fetched to imagine that the whole world knew the nature of Daniel's involvement with Mist's newspaper but not its working editor and proprietor. The discovery by Lee of Defoe's payment by the ministry for his role in the newspaper came as a great shock to him. Lee supposed that Mist must have suffered a similar reaction.

For all these reasons, recent biographers have tended to discount the story. However, perhaps Lee's intuition had served him well. In seeking to control Mist, Daniel would have needled him. Daniel would have been justifiably concerned not to be dragged into prosecution by an intemperate editor who altered his copy and encouraged other contributors in seditious comment which he, Daniel, would have avoided. He pressed Mist too hard.

And then Mist would have had his own causes of complaint. Whatever Daniel might say about saving Mist from himself, he had exploited the cover of ministry employment. Daniel felt that the cover was perfect for publishing whatever he felt compelled to write while putting the blame on Mist.

What the two men had in common, and which kept them together, was the need to be controversial to make money; they were bonded by mutual intemperance and a willingness to take risks by writing whatever they saw the need for and whenever they were inclined to do so. Perhaps in 1724 it was once too many times for Mist and he resorted to physical violence, including the threat of fighting a duel.

In the midst of these excitements and alarms, Daniel's mind was turning to other things. There was no profit to be made in pamphlets and he had difficulty in placing his work.[164] His health was not good and he felt too old for the games he was playing. Reading habits were changing and there was an appetite for tales of adventure and for fictional accounts. Religious dissent had weakened and he had lost an audience. He knew he would never make a fortune from what he was doing: at any moment the political game of musical chairs could find him without a seat at the tables that mattered. He did not think that he should abandon his life-long dreams of wealth, position and ease. He needed to take stock of himself. There was life in the old dog yet.

FICTIONS

1719 to 1723

Chapter 15

Origins And Beginnings

...but the within, all that inner space one never sees, the brain and heart and other caverns where thought and feeling dance their Sabbath.

Molloy
Samuel Beckett

DANIEL DEFOE HAD ALWAYS been a writer, if not by birth. Writing was the compulsion of his early life: he wrote in order to explain himself, to retain control, to defend himself against others and to demonstrate his superiority. At first, he hid himself in anonymity for the shame that what he wrote would be disapproved of by the puritan community from which he came. Later he did so to avoid persecution by a vengeful state. In the end, he was motivated by psychological necessity, habit and preference to present his work in a cacophony of voices and perspectives.

A creative writer can only offer the world himself. His act of doing so is painful and the process arduous. The writer seeks protection in character, situation and plot. The veil may be drawn closely and yet the reader finds the writer at his desk before a bobbing candle in all-consuming self-absorption. Reluctant though he may be, the writer must find his audience.

There came a point in Daniel's life when he could let go, cease to hide, and present himself, although remaining in disguise: when he could commune with his past and come to terms with an 'ill-spent' life.

Of course, he wrote about the moment:

I had here a most happy and comfortable retreat, though it was a kind of exile... Here I enjoyed everything...except going home...Here I enjoyed the moments which I had never before known how to employ – I mean that here I learned to look back upon a long ill-spent life, blessed with infinite advantage, which I had no heart given me till now to make use of – and here I found just reflections were the utmost felicity of human life... Here I wrote these Memoirs...Perhaps when I wrote these things down I did not forsee that the writings of our own stories would be so much the fashion in England, or so agreeable for others to read, as I find custom and the humour of the times has caused it to be.[165]

Over the five-year period from 1719 to 1724, Daniel wrote three fictions of the highest quality and four others of interest. After 1724 there was one other work, *A Tour Through the Whole Island of Great Britain*, of enduring value. His reputation rests on this output. This judgement is not to belittle his earlier written work or to exclude other writings but to argue that little or no attention would have been give to them but for this five-year purple patch.

Earlier, I have argued that had Daniel died in 1703, the year he was imprisoned and pilloried, posterity would not have remembered him at all. This judgement might be thought severe, but James Sutherland, the most civilised and pleasant of Daniel's biographers, was almost as harsh. He wrote that in 1718, had Defoe died, 'he would not have been quite forgotten, but it [was] unlikely that any one would have considered it worth while to write his biography'.[166]

Sutherland wrote that, 'Hitherto he was given up to *party* [italics and quotation marks are mine] and that party writings ...rarely survive the occasion that gave rise to them...but that then Defoe did something for mankind.' He wrote *Robinson Crusoe*.

If the biographer were to follow Sutherland's judgement he would give little consideration to the vast number of works that came to be ascribed to Daniel or any detailed consideration of his journalistic output, but it is easy to understand the reasons why so many disagree.

I have expressed the conviction that throughout the 1680s Daniel was writing, but that this work is not extant. It is a pity to have lost this output because the missing works would have told the biographer a great deal, but I see no reason to invent an output.

This book does not set out to provide a literary evaluation of Daniel Defoe's works but it is important to consider their unique quality for it is an essential part of understanding him. Literary criticism convinces in the achievement of completeness, in its tidiness, in a drawing together into satisfying and illuminating patterns. In contrast, the biographer is all too aware of untidiness and confusion, of the intertwining of human lives, its chanciness, and the difficulty and inevitability of making choices.

Daniel developed a distinctive narrative voice. He wrote in what he proclaimed to be plain English, as opposed to the classical prose of Oxbridge writing conventions. It was the language of the streets, of the new mercantile class which in his lifetime became an essential part of the reading public. Daniel was of the street. In that part of his life that is denied to us, his movement, diction and vocabulary, he may well have been a rough and even unpleasant customer in the hurly-burly of everyday life.

This distinctiveness has confused many biographers involved in the ascription of works to Daniel Defoe. In the end they mostly agreed with Novak when he wrote, 'all [named biographers] believed that they were capable of recognising Defoe's style and ideas. I have published my reasons for believing these works were by Defoe and I have not changed my mind about them'.[167]

If literary judgements are to be made on the basis of pamphlets and articles in news-sheets, they may not take full account of what is obvious to most readers: journalists write in house-styles for a known readership. Daniel could and did write for a wide range of news-sheets and periodicals. In the end, he would write anything in any style or narrative voice for anyone who paid him.

Daniel's journalistic enemies thought him an illiterate windbag with a high-flown, hyperbolic and repetitious style that picked him out as the author of works which he had written anonymously. Sometimes they were right, but then he could and did write in a highly organised and economical style with considerable forensic ability. This was a style and a method which pleased the purist.

Contemporary critics disliked Daniel's dogmatism: his belief that when he had declaimed something to be true that it was so. John Richetti wrote about Daniel's style as follows, 'Relentless insistence, iterated and reiterated, illustrated inventively and exhaustively, may be Defoe's signature as a polemicist.' Writing about two of Daniel's many pamphlets on occasional conformity, he continues:

> Defoe's mode is a hammering, defiantly uncompromising and unforgiving literal-mindedness… the polemical edge grows very rough and unsparing as Defoe proceeds to accuse occasional conformers of becoming 'Pimps to their Secular Interest…'. Defoe projects a distinctly oratorical force and gravity that shares the stage with his demotic vigor and almost comic single and literal-mindedness [which] may be said to shift away from [the] oratorical.

Logically, if Daniel Defoe did not write all the pamphlets and articles that Novak and others ascribe to him on the basis of distinctive style, then there must have been others writing in a similar style and with similar ideas. Of course, there were many. If the considerations are religious, political or, in a wider sense, cultural, Daniel Defoe dipped into the common pool with others. It is extremely difficult, although not entirely impossible, to assert that he added anything to the sum of human knowledge or insight.

Why then does Daniel survive as an enduring subject of enquiry? The short answer is that he wrote *Robinson Crusoe* and then, encouraged by the public response, wrote other fiction of enduring interest to readers. The longer answer is more complex and interesting. Victorians and twentieth-century humanists and academics came to believe in the Whig version of history: in the idea of progress and the inevitability of an historical transition to universal rights, equality, social justice and the liberty of the subject under the law. Such a viewpoint requires heroes, and Daniel Defoe fitted the bill.

American academics often see themselves in an optimistic New World. The best and most common endings in American fiction and film are happy: right tends to triumph and evil is defeated. For them, Daniel is a precursor to such liberal optimism and on the side of the angels.

In contrast to this iconic and heroic view, it is clear that Daniel Defoe was a talented rogue of poor character. As I have argued in previous chapters, he had a difficult childhood and emerged from it with a desire for wealth and amorality in the ways he chose to pursue it. The defects of character from which he suffered led him into numerous scrapes and difficulties and frequent imprisonments and bankruptcies. He was severely punished. There was something peculiar in Daniel's puritan legacy: he needed to be punished.

Daniel had strong drives and inclinations that he could not control. He did not wish to control them, although in his quieter moments he persuaded himself that it would be preferable to do so.

Daniel was a busybody: a restless and hyperactive fellow, into everything and anything from which he could obtain an advantage, especially if it were financial.

Vainglorious and proud, the most expensive of human emotions, he was envious of the success of others. He believed that their success was gained at the expense of his own. Long past the point when it was credible to others, he wished to be the Lord Mayor of London or any other dignitary of the City. He agitated for public office and social recognition as a gentleman.

Daniel had the most remarkable appetite for life. It is obvious that he was a voracious reader and had a prodigious written output. He was highly competent and reliable in a master-servant relationship when he was well and promptly paid.

In everyday life, Daniel had a poor grip on reality. When he was free from real fears and anxieties, he invented them. He was thin-skinned and chose to assume insults and raillery against him when there were none. And if none, he was quick to give offence to correct the position. Probably he preferred low life to high and, if not, he did not wish to avoid it. As fast as he made money, he speculated and lost it, and when he owed it he arranged his affairs so that his debts were not paid.

Daniel was remarkably resilient and able to believe in himself and worked prodigiously hard in the most dangerous and difficult of circumstances. While he would not profess it, this resilience was based on a Calvinistic belief that his salvation was pre-destined as one of the Select Few. This path required acts of repentance. Sins were necessary and inevitable, even desirable, and the Devil was believed to be active and unavoidable, but he had the assurance of the conviction that God would not desert him. It would have been better to remove God from his heaven completely but to do so would have threatened his salvation. Rejected by his fellow dissenters, by 1720 Daniel had lost any real religious belief and had drifted into the attractions of deism: the sin which was beginning to say its name.

In short, by 1719 he had all the attributes required of a novelist. Needing money he looked around for better ways than journalism and speculation for acquiring it.

Around 1717 Daniel drifted into a religious crisis. He did not wish to abandon the dreams of riches and social position that continued to seem possible in a secular world, but he was fearful that what remained for him as religious belief would become unsustainable. For Daniel, the two aspirations of religious certainty and social ambition had always been inextricably linked: dissenting beliefs would triumph as a majority conviction and all the barriers to his social advancement would disappear.

Daniel had never supported attempts to recreate a national church; he did not champion the achievement of a national religious unity based on a comprehension of all truths and never wrote in support of it. In this it might be argued that his views were fully in line with revolutionary principles. Locke, in his first *Letter on Toleration*, defined a church as follows, 'A church, then, I take to be a voluntary society of men joining together of their own accord, in order to the public worship of God in such a manner as they judge acceptable to him and effectual to the salvation of their souls.' These beliefs of Locke, which were at the heart of the Glorious Revolution, had come to be accepted as true, even though institutional rigidities seemed to deny it. Religion was becoming a private matter. It was to become a general belief that there was no spiritual authority in society.

The Anglican Church has never been immune from ideological changes within the society it serves. The evidence of change, of the tolerance within Anglicanism of a wide variety of views and practices, became obvious to all. Benjamin Hoadly, the Bishop of Bangor (a See he never visited) epitomised the changes which discomfited Daniel. When Hoadly's views became a matter of public controversy, Daniel unwisely took issue with him and in a remarkable manner.

Hoadly was the son of an Anglican clergyman and a graduate of Catherine Hall, Cambridge. He was a firm believer in Whig principles and an advocate of political and religious freedom. In 1715 the Whig administration persuaded George I to make him a bishop. In this they were following a policy initiated under William III to weaken the influence of the High Flying Anglicans by the appointment of low churchmen to the bishopric. However, the High Flyers in the convocation of the Anglican Church, encouraged by Anne's commitment to reverse the trends set in motion by the Glorious Revolution, remained in the majority.

In the five-year period 1715–20, Bishop Hoadly became a zealous partisan of what is called religious liberty. In this he was part of the thrust of Lutheranism and Anglicanism in the seventeenth century into which he was born. Across Europe the subjection of Church to national governments was rejected. In a sense, the emergence of Calvinism and other dissident nonconformists was a reaction; religious dissidents of all persuasions struggled to reverse the movement to a wider liberty by an insistence on sectarianism and everywhere they were defeated.

Hoadly created controversy in a pamphlet entitled *Preservative against the Principles and Practices of Non-Jurors* (1716) and by a strongly argued Erastian sermon, preached in the presence of King George at the end of March 1717, and published shortly afterwards, on the theme of 'the Nature of the

Kingdom or Church of Christ'. Essentially, Hoadly argued that religion was a private matter and a man's conscience his own. He denied that 'the church possessed authority to oblige anyone to external communion or to pass any sentence which should determine the condition of men with respect to the favour or displeasure of God'.

The Lower House of Convocation sought to take proceedings against Hoadly, but King George stood firm. Convocation was dismissed. A furious and ill-tempered pamphlet war broke out to which Daniel contributed his mite. According to an earlier bibliographer, J.R. Moore,[168] there are fourteen pamphlets written on the controversy by Daniel over two years, from various and contradictory points of view, whereas Furbank and Owens attribute only two. Not unreasonably, Furbank and Owens are reluctant to assume, given the lack of internal evidence, that he could have written them all. They offer a number of reasons why he might have done so, but dismiss them all as having an extreme or 'ultimate' quality, 'making out Defoe to be some kind of monster or unique phenomenon'.[169] If it is to be maintained that he did write many more pamphlets on the subject than ascribed by Furbank and Owens then some sort of credible explanation is required.

Earlier in this book it has been argued that Daniel became schizoid as a result of a difficult childhood and that he was unable to rest long in any one identity without taking refuge from it in another. It has been argued also that he suffered from a kind of multi-personality disorder that could be triggered whenever a threat to the centrality of his personality was experienced. Daniel reacted to such a triggering with fear, excitement and a volume of words. To deal with the threat, he assumed other identities for short periods of time, the function of which were to protect his core self from overwhelming anxiety but which, in their nature, could only be temporary resting places, and which required their own disguises and special voices. Such a condition as Daniel's is more common than is often recognised. It is a serious and disabling personality disorder but it does not make the sufferer a 'monster'.

The fourteen pamphlets ascribed by J.R. Moore have characteristics that can be associated with Daniel. Three use Quaker or pseudo-Quaker voices common to other writings of Daniel's. One uses that of an Armenian merchant to the Grand Mufti, which is also a voice used by him. The narrative voice is often amusing, jocular or teasing, as is common in Daniel's writings. Sometimes the narration is punchy or sarcastic; in other instances it is sober, severe and without irony. Daniel wrote in all these styles and voices.

The issues raised by the debate were important to Daniel, but it cannot be said that he had anything coherent to say about them. To nonconformists, Hoadly's views could be claimed as a vindication of their historic claims to the right of religious self-government. They could tease Hoadly about that. Perhaps it could be argued, they suggested, that he should resign as a bishop and join them, for he was coming round to their point of view. But then it dawned on them that if toleration was spreading within the Church of

England, if doctrinal issues were of lesser importance, then they might be better off, more comfortable and protected, within Anglicanism.

Schism is a characteristic of the radical left and was rife among nonconformists at this time. What, after all, did Quakers, Independents, Presbyterians, Baptists and Congregationalists have in common? They debated these distinguishing features up and down the country. In London, meeting at Salters Hall, dissenting ministers had sought valiantly to achieve unity. Persecution had bound them all together. But if they were to be tolerated by the established Church, what then did they all stand for?

In 1719 James Pierce, a nonconformist minister in Exeter, was removed from his congregation for his doubts on the Trinity. Daniel had corresponded with Pierce and also knew Martin Tomkins, a minister in Stoke Newington who became involved in the debate about Pierce's removal. This issue was raised at Salters Hall where, unwisely, a minority sought to test opinion by the production of a document reaffirming the Trinity. The majority refused to sign and kept their consciences to themselves.

What was really at stake was the authority of the various denominations these ministers represented. Ministers were united in believing that there were doctrinal disputes which might justify the removal of a minister but divided on the tests that should be applied. Disputes about the Trinity were peculiarly difficult to determine. Most representatives continued to follow the catechism of the Anglican Church which required commitment to three persons in one: the Father, the Son and the Holy Ghost. However, those who thought that Biblical scriptures should be the test naturally took the view that the three parts of the Godhead were not equal and looked to Jesus for the basis of their beliefs. Others who, in the end, were in a minority wanted confessions of faith and not the Bible alone to be used. The majority remaining in this general meeting became known as 'non-subscribers' (to the catechism definition of the Trinity), which was a crude way of distinguishing them, and those who withdrew became known as 'subscribers'.

Daniel was not a minister, or even a member of a dissenting church, and his presence at Salters Hall would not have been permitted.[170] It is not known what he thought about the debate. Daniel might have thought that the debate added to the grist as something to write about, but there was no money in it and he had none to lose by self-publishing.

However, when the storm of public debate had died down, and he could ruminate on it in the safety of his own dwelling, he must have been a sadder man. If he was to hold on to the conviction which had propelled his life so far, if he was to dwell on what had happened to him without melancholy, and if God's influence for good could no longer be relied upon, then he was abandoned to his own devices and on his own without any certainty of redemption.

The loss of God's providence would be unbearable and he could not suffer the doubt. Daniel Defoe needed to write about it. He wrote *Robinson Crusoe*.

Chapter 16

Robinson Crusoe

I, Robinson Crusoe...hereby declare...that the story, although allegorical, is also historical...Farther, that there is a man alive and well known too, the actions of whose life are the just subject of these volumes and to whom all or most parts of the story most directly allude.

Serious Reflections of Robinson Crusoe
Daniel Defoe

ROBINSON CRUSOE WAS FIRST published in 1719 and was immediately successful, re-published several times in its first year, and rapidly followed by two sequels.[171] At the outset it was attacked by several critics of whom Charles Gildon was the most prominent.[172] Gildon attacked the book as being fictional and a work 'design'd against the public good', a criticism which today would be regarded as absurd. At this time fiction was held in poor regard and the limited number of works in this category was held in contempt by an educated elite. The criticism reflected also the poor public regard in which Daniel was held and the belief that through the life of Robinson he was giving a deceptive version of his own life.

In defending himself Daniel was unwittingly defending literature itself. He wrote, 'All these reflections are just history in a state of forced confinement which in my real history is represented by a confined retreat in an island; and it is as reasonable to represent one kind of imprisonment by another as it is to represent anything that really exists by that which exists not.' Just so, might have said his critics, that is the whole and entire point: he sets out to deceive us and makes a virtue of it.

An unresolved issue is whether Daniel actually deceived us. Later in the century, it was alleged that Daniel had stolen the idea of *Robinson Crusoe*, or even a manuscript, from Alexander Selkirk who had voluntarily spent four years on his own on an island in the Pacific. On Selkirk's return in 1711 he was given a hero's welcome and was much written about.[173]

Daniel might have met Selkirk in London where he lived from time to time over the next few years. He might also have collaborated in the writing up of the two journals of Woodes Rogers and Edward Cooke whose expedition rescued Selkirk and brought him back to London. Neither of these two men had writing skills and they required the assistance of others to tell their stories. Both their accounts included brief mentions of Selkirk 'living alone four years and four months on an Island'. Later in the century, the *Encyclopaedia Britannica* added credence to the story of plagiarism by spreading the rumour of Daniel's bad faith in the matter.

Richard Steele, who wrote about Selkirk at the time,[174] alleged later that Daniel had stolen a manuscript from Selkirk. Novak writes, 'Defoe was supposed to have encountered Selkirk in Bristol and either absconded with the manuscript or pretended to take it away to make improvements.' It is possible that Daniel did just that. There is good evidence that he met Selkirk at Nailsea Court, the home of Nathaniel Wade, who played a distinguished role on the side of the rebels in the Monmouth Rebellion.[175]

In the quotation above the 'man alive and well known too, the actions of whose life are the just subject of these volumes', has been thought of as Daniel talking about himself, for it is a common device of his to place himself in the third person. However, in the context of admitting his writings to be allegorical and not historical, it is not the most obvious and logical interpretation. Might not Daniel be referring to Alexander Selkirk?

In general, biographers are inclined to dismiss these rumours of theft and plagiarism on general grounds. At the time Daniel would have been familiar with the many foreign adventure stories of public interest;[176] and there was a general philosophical interest, much debated, on whether a man could live in a state of isolation. Selkirk's story is different in many ways from Daniel's. And then, of course, Daniel would have borrowed in some sense from Selkirk; writers of fiction are hungry creatures, there is a limited number and variety of plots and necessity obliges them to become great 'thieves'.

Whether or not Daniel had a base document of Alexander Selkirk's, it cannot be denied that he spun the material into a story that only he could have written. In *Robinson Crusoe* the narration is in the past tense and told from a distance. The story starts in a literal manner with recognisable particulars, some of which can be recognised by the reader of his fiction and of the early chapters of this book to be Defoe's. The reader becomes aware of other messages that need to be decoded but probably does not have the information to do so.

Robinson was born in the year 1632 in the City of York, which was about the date of Daniel Defoe's putative grandfather Daniel Foe, of a merchant from Bremen living in York (his 'father' James Foe was a merchant), and with two brothers, one a Lieutenant Colonel serving in Flanders under the famous Colonel Lockhardt, who was killed in action at Dunkirk, and another who had disappeared without trace. His mother's family name was Robinson and the name by which the family was known became Robinson Kreutznaer (Crusoe). Thus Robinson came from a family of good reputation on his mother's side, with a good estate on his father's, which had been gained by trade. These origins placed his family in the 'middle station in life' between the two extremes of poverty and riches, from whence came happiness. Robinson was given a 'competent share of learning, as far as house education and a free school generally goes', as was Daniel.

There is a political message signified in this opening and particulars of a personal kind. Robinson's first brother had a rank directly under the Cromwellian Colonel Lockhardt, which gives Robinson an important revolutionary link with the Roundheads and the 'Good Old Cause'; a cause that would be defeated in the Restoration of 1660. He also, as with the disappearance of the second brother, was gone from him and no more. As I have shown elsewhere, Daniel had an elder brother who served as an officer in Marlborough's armies and a younger brother who died or disappeared.

Daniel did not visit York in the *Tour*. He mentions it once in disparaging terms as being lesser than Sheffield. Its significance would appear to be that its bishop ranks in second place behind Canterbury in the hierarchy of the Church of England. Thus, the advice given to Robinson by his father to keep to his station in life, which is 'wise and grave', is identified with the Anglican Church whereas by dissent a man was free to gain riches and social position.

Yorkshire does, however, have a previously unknown significance for Daniel. On his way to Scotland, and at other times, Daniel visited Halifax and Leeds. He spent time in Halifax in 1705, 1712 and 1718. Rumour has it that he wrote *Jure Divino* and *Robinson Crusoe* there.[177]

Robinson dissents from his father's advice to gain a profession and decides as soon as he is able to seek riches on the high seas. The reader can assume immediately that Robinson is going to be punished and even cast out for disobedience to his father's wishes. Sure enough, he was punished when the ship he was on capsized off the Yarmouth coast. If he had returned home at this time he might have been greeted as the prodigal son. 'But...ill fate pushed [him] on.'

His companion's father said to him, 'Young man will you go to sea any more...I would not set my foot in the same ship with thee...depend upon it, if you do not go back, wherever you go, you will meet with nothing but disasters and disappointments.' In this he was saying what had been said to Daniel early in his trading life: 'not only will you bring yourself to ruin but we shall be capsized by you too'.

This man seems to have taken a dim view of Robinson's character. He may have thought that although Robinson/Daniel had come from a solid bourgeois family he did not value its advantages. He was unable to pursue a steady course in a profession in which his father would support him; he was reckless and did not profess prudence, and he had avarice for riches and position at any cost which seemed ridiculous and threatening to others.

Robinson did not go back home but made his way to London. He joined in a venture with others and began to earn money by trading, having raised the starting capital of £40 from his relatives. He then set himself up for a difficult trading trip to Guinea.

Something very like this had happened to Daniel. As a very young man he became a trader, not as the master of a ship but as a merchant adventurer who would eventually become the part owner of a ship. He had chosen the path of Mammon and was about to make real money, and the greater the risk the greater the reward. Merchant adventuring was highly dangerous and put you at the mercy of pirates. Daniel came to the conclusion that the difference between a pirate and a trader was not great and that business at its most reputable was amoral and, at its worst, immoral and dangerous.

Robinson's ship was attacked by a pirate ship and he was taken into slavery. In real life, Daniel got into debt and became enslaved by his creditors and could not easily escape their clutches. Eventually, Robinson manages to escape the pirates by flight to Brazil where he became a planter and prospered. Daniel became bankrupt but succeeded in making his way to Tilbury where he prospered with the aid of a corrupt government appointment and the help of patrons.

In Brazil, by hard work and diligence, Robinson became after four years a successful planter. He bought land and acquired a slave and was 'coming into the very middle station, or upper degree of life which my father advised me to'. Then the Captain of the vessel on which he had travelled to Brazil reached a deal with Robinson that on his return to England he would salvage Robinson's goods and merchandise left in London for the payment of £100. This £100 came from the wife of a merchant in London and the Captain invested the money in 'all sorts of tools, iron-work, and utensils necessary for [his] plantation'. It may be that it cost Daniel £100 of someone else's money to get goods, and other items, out of hock in London to a creditor, to assist him to trade on in Tilbury. And then 'increasing in business and in wealth [Robinson's] head began to be full of projects and undertakings beyond [his] reach; such as are indeed often the ruin of the best heads in business'.

Three merchants came to him with a proposition involving a trading trip to Guinea where they were to obtain and trade slaves. Robinson was to have an equal share of the slaves without providing any of the stock. Robinson thought 'such a voyage was the most preposterous thing that ever man in such circumstances could be guilty of. But I that was born to be my own destroyer could no more resist the offer [than I could] my father's good counsel'.

This period of Daniel's life was 1695–9 and then by extension into 1703–4 and his second bankruptcy, when he became accountant to the Glass Commissioners and bought (or cultivated land already bought) at Tilbury. His starting salary as an accountant was £100 and rose to £150. He occupied a handsome house and lived like a gentleman.

At this time, Daniel was rooting around for investment projects in which he could involve himself even though he had no money. He published these ideas in *An Essay on Projects*. As has been commented on earlier, on the back of a single order for pantiles initiated by Thomas Dalby, one of the Glass Commissioners, and with inadequate capital, he invested in a factory producing bricks in Tilbury. This proved to be the route, although not the only cause, of his second bankruptcy. As for the woman who was so generous to him, we can but guess that there was one, but her name and role is unknown.

Robinson set sail for Guinea in September 1659 when he was twenty-seven years of age. Daniel might well have made his first significant sea voyage at the age of eighteen in 1679. As every reader of *Robinson Crusoe* knows, this voyage had the dreadful outcome of the ship capsizing in a great storm. Of the eleven men who took to the waters in a lifeboat only Robinson survived. He was washed ashore on a desert island.

For most readers of *Robinson Crusoe* anything that happened to him before the shipwreck and anything after his rescue is of little or no interest. For them, the drama lies in Robinson's struggle to survive on the island. From the outset the reader is aware that the account he is going to read is not just about the economics of survival but about the religious, social and political consequences of Robinson's stay on the island.

From the beginning Daniel has trouble with time. Describing Robinson's struggle to reach the shore, Daniel has difficulty with sequence. At the start of the passage which describes this, Robinson seems to have reached the shore. He is 'upon the land almost dry, but half-dead'. However, as the passage proceeds he is swamped by another wave, and twenty or thirty feet beneath the surface, still swimming towards the shore. Then he says, 'I strook forward against the return of the waves and carried forward'. He takes to his heels and runs toward shore, but does not make it. He struggles again. Finally, he holds on to a rock and attempts another run onto the shore which finally brings him to the cliff and safety.

This description is emblematic of the struggles and anxieties of Daniel's spiritual life. There is no escape from his danger except from the medium of life itself (the sea of time) and by holding on to a rock. On the island there is no normal meaning to time. There is only God's time. This gives Robinson's story a pristine simplicity free from all the constraints of time or the usual spatial continuities. Robinson remains restless but the story itself is simple in outline and exists in the imagination as myth, even when allowing for Robinson's obsessive and realistic activity in recording his sojourn on the island. The narrative is spoken in the past tense and looking back. However, as the point of reference chosen by Daniel is outside him to a power outside normal reference (that is, to God), the recollective powers of his memory are distorted and attenuated. This frame of reference produces instability and, as with his other fiction, an atmosphere of constant anxiety. While Robinson/Daniel attempts sequential narration, it is always an unsure guide and fails to produce verisimilitude. As Robinson says in his poem, *Eternity*:

What we have been, and what we are,
The present and the Time that's past
We can resolve into nothing here,
But what we are to thee, at last.

Daniel/Robinson needs assistance. The reader knows that Robinson was on the island for some twenty-eight years: exactly the time between the restoration of the monarchy under Charles II and the Glorious Revolution of 1688. Thus it can be assumed that this period of time is significant to Robinson/Daniel, as we know already it is, and that Daniel is about to give the reader an allegorical account of his life during this period. It is exactly what he does.

Safe on shore he was elated in the contemplation of his deliverance as a sole survivor. Early in his life he was certain that God had selected him for deliverance as one of the Select Few. This belief had sustained him through many setbacks and hardships. But later he thought his prospects of survival on this desolate island to be dismal. He thought that, 'I had great reason to consider it [deliverance] as a determination of Heaven, that in this desolate place and in this desolate manner I should end my life...why Providence should thus completely ruin its creatures and render them so absolutely miserable...that it could hardly be rational to be thankful for such a life.'

He had felt himself to be alone in Brazil but now he was utterly castaway and without hope. He would not have survived if the ship and its contents had not been available to him. In all his vicissitudes Daniel had always preserved, put to one side and hidden, what he needed to survive, to the condemnation of creditors who knew that he could pay them, for the assets to do so were available.

Now he set out 'like debtor and creditor' the position he was in as the first capitalist on the island. Among the evils, he wrote that he had been singled out and separated from the world to be miserable and divided from human society without any soul to speak to or relieve him, among the blessings was that God had singled him out to be spared from death, that he would not starve, that there were no animals to hurt him and that God had sent the ship 'in near enough to the shore, that [he had] gotten out so many things as [would] supply [his] wants, or enable [him] to supply [himself] for as long as [he] would live'.

Robinson resorted to enclosure and barricade for protection; he decided to record his progress in written form with the use of a journal, and to physically record the passing of each day. Daniel had done the same. His house at Stoke Newington was described as a kind of fortress with heavily constructed doors and many locks. From the fortress he had created and furnished, Robinson was to sally out. He constructed a kind of pale under the side of a rock and brought all his goods into a cave. Caves had fascinated Daniel from the days of his youth as a kind of refuge from the world, and he refs to them elsewhere in his fiction. He camouflaged his habitation so 'if any people were to come ashore they would not perceive anything like a habitation'. All his life Daniel had to hide from people in the certain knowledge that many of them were wanting to do him damage.

Gradually, Robinson explored his island as Daniel had explored *The Whole Island of Great Britain*. He discovered that much of the island was more pleasant than that part in which he had built his 'fortress' and though he wished to avoid discovery at any cost he 'resolved [to] build me a bower and surrounded it with a strong fence, being a double hedge as high as [I] could reach...so that I fancied now [I] had my country house...and began to enjoy [myself]'.

This is what Daniel had done all his adult life. Although based in London, he had at various times established country homes and farms. It was what successful gentlemen did: they made money in the City and established fine homes for themselves in the country. And from this country vantage point eventually Robinson moved about the whole island. Restlessness drove him away from his fortress, wherever he had established it. In Chapter 12 of this book, I suggested that the north of the island (which was by far the most pleasant) depicts Daniel's recollection of Scotland.

It has been suggested that on this island Robinson had a conversion to belief in a Christian God. Daniel writes:

> I had this terrible dream. I thought that I was sitting on the ground when the storm blew after the earthquake, and that I saw a man descend from a great black cloud, in a bright flame of fire, and light upon the ground...I could just bear to look towards him...He was no sooner landed upon the earth but he moved towards me with a long spear or weapon in his hand to kill me...I heard a voice so terrible that it is impossible to express the terror of it; all that I can say I understood was this: 'Seeing all these things have not brought thee to repentance, now thou shalt die.' At which words, I thought he lifted up the spear that was in his hands to kill me.

Robinson was so frightened by this experience that he turned to the Bible, which he had not read for many a year, and resolved to put his trust in God's Providence. Robinson confesses to himself that 'a certain stupidity of soul, without desire of good, or conscience of evil, had entirely overwhelmed [him], and [he] was the most hardened, unthinking, wicked creature among our common sailors'. I have suggested that when Daniel writes about pirates or sailors, we might substitute in their place the word merchant. If so, he is referring back to his days as a merchant and to the reprehensible behaviour he was charged with in his earlier days.

This conversion is to a threatening Old Testament God and the cynical among readers might think that it would not last long. After discovering the footprint in the sand Robinson says to himself, 'Thus my fear banished all my religious hope, all that former confidence in God, which was founded upon such wonderful experience…of His goodness.' Thus to Daniel/Robinson, God could be believed in only if his Providence was exercised in his favour.

This terrifying and disturbing dream is interesting in other ways. Freud argues that the theory of anxiety-dreams belongs to the psychology of neuroses and that neurotic anxiety arises from sexual sources.[178] Robinson's dream is of a highly threatening 'father figure' committed to the punishment of misdemeanours and sins, even unto death. The spear which is thrust aggressively towards him is an obvious, and highly threatening, phallic symbol. For a long time Daniel/Robinson had repressed the neurotic memory of such threats and now, liberated by isolation, the earthquake, lightning and a great storm, the repression is lifted and punishment for transgressions is accepted.

Robinson's reaction to the dream is interesting in another way in that he confesses that he has not been a practising Christian for a long time. It has been argued here that Daniel had been expelled from his membership of a church since his bankruptcy in 1692, although he sought to maintain a reputation as a religious and pious man.

In discussing Daniel's/Robinson's fears it is necessary to take a wider view than individual psychology. There were conceptual difficulties for many people in understanding how an increased population, particularly in London, could be fed, clothed, sheltered and buried. Carol Houlihan has written of, '[t]he urban bind of the age, the confinement of too many bodies into crowded, diseased cities'. Flynn believes that these factors created a fear of engulfment and desperation to seize what you could, and led to a breakdown of the moral order and a weakening of the belief in the just use of God's providence. In such a world, the mediation of differences and conflicts is highly problematic. In Daniel Defoe it can readily be seen as an agonising and unresolved experience of life which he explores in his fiction.

When Robinson is obsessively counting his possessions and food stuffs, when he ruminates that he need only grow a crop sufficient for his immediate needs, when he is calculating just how much seed he needs to put aside for future years, we can see him anxiously looking forward towards self-sufficiency. Thus Novak can suggest that Daniel was obliged to develop the 'problem of necessity' to explain his secular mediation. The anxiety to provide for necessities may also explain Daniel's constant movement away from the City to the countryside, to farming, and the provision of his own food. Robinson finds that where he travels on the island, and where he establishes his 'second home', is a source of new fruit, meat, fish and vegetables.

On the other hand, the reader can rely on psychology to explain Daniel's/Robinson's fears. If we follow Freud and his disciples in a consideration of Daniel's early life it can be argued that fictional hoarding and constant counting of physical objects might be regarded as anal retention. Simon Lesser has suggested that there is a quality in *Robinson Crusoe* for which the only accurate term is anal eroticism: the sublimation of early feelings of retention into a love of money, power and worldly success, all of which dominated Daniel's adult life. Homer Brown, in a fascinating paper, has argued from an analysis of Swift's poetry that Swift had anticipated Freud's assertion of anal eroticism.

However, there are other modern ways of explaining a literal obsession with physical objects. For example, that it is an attempt to obtain verisimilitude in a state of danger and instability when God's providential intervention, once implicitly recognised as certain, could no longer be relied upon to mediate.

It might be argued that all these influences and factors are at work in this incident in *Robinson Crusoe*. Daniel writes:

at low water I went aboard [on the shipwreck and for the twelfth time] I discovered a locker with drawers in it, in one of which I found two or three razors and one pair of large scissors, and ten or a dozen of good knives and forks; in another I found about thirty-six pounds value in money, some European coin, some Brazil, some pieces of eight, some gold, some silver. I smiled to myself at the sight of this money... [and said aloud] what art thou good for? Thou art not worth to me, no, not the taking off the ground; one of those knives is worth all this heap...However, upon second thoughts, I took it away.

Although isolated, Robinson only invites the society of others once his mastery over them is recognised and accepted. When the incident that every reader remembers occurs and Robinson sees the imprint of a man's foot upon the sand, he is 'terrified to the last degree'. He rushes home and fortifies himself within his fortress, which he calls his castle [as he says] 'for so I think I called it ever after this and slept none that night'. He had dreamt about the possible incursion of others and had imagined that by it he would obtain a servant and subject. When he meets Friday for the first time, Robinson achieves his mastery over him by demonstrating an ability to kill creatures with his gun and by insisting that he be called master. Even then he barricades Friday in at night in case Friday should attack him. In the perfect world that Robinson seeks to create on his island, he is the master; there are subjects, all of whom love him and recognise his authority, and once this state has been achieved men can be free in their consciences.

To achieve this unity, Friday is presented as a European with 'all the sweetness and softness of a European in his countenance': his hair was 'long and black, not curled like wool', the colour of his skin was 'not quite black', his face was 'round and plump', and his nose 'small not flat like the Negroes'. That is, he was presented as a man fit to be a subject.

Friday responds as a loyal subject would be expected to behave: when taught the scriptures in the right manner, he becomes a better Christian than Robinson (who, presumably, has been exposed to false teaching). When

Friday's father is rescued from the savages, Friday shows great love and consideration to him. Daniel writes, for Robinson, 'It is not easy for me to express how it moved me to see what ecstasy and filial affection had worked in this poor savage, at the sight of his father...nor can I describe half the extravagances of his affection after this.' Why, the reader might well ask, was it so difficult and emotional for Robinson to witness a loving son and accept filial affection?

Robinson came to realise from exploring other parts of the island that it was endangered by the possibility of invasion by savages and that they might eat him. The fears of engulfment, the consequences of the body being the source of food for others, put him into a fright. His first true appreciation of the dangers was historical; he discovered the remains of the 'skulls, hands, feet, and other bones of human bodies; and particularly, I observed a place where there had been a fire made, and a circle dug in the earth, like a cockpit, where it is supposed the savage wretches had sat down to their inhuman feastings upon the bodies of their fellow creatures'. He vomited, sped away and thanked God 'that had cast my first lot in a part of the world where [I] was distinguishable from such creatures as these'.

In Daniel's imagination, the country where God had chosen to place him (Daniel/Robinson) was, of course, England; the creatures that God had distinguished him from were the High Flyers in the Anglican Church. They were no danger unless assisted by invasion from abroad. And the evidence of their bad faith was historical, for men had suffered incarceration, burnings and horrible deaths.

When a large party of savages reach the island with the intention of eating their captives on the beach, Robinson marches out in a rage to do battle with them, accompanied by Friday. It is a major confrontation. Twenty-one savages are killed and two prisoners, Friday's father and a Spaniard, are released. Events then move very quickly. Robinson's two new subjects, heavily armed, paddle away in a canoe to rescue Spaniards and Portuguese imprisoned by the savages, while Robinson assists a Captain to quell a mutiny on his ship anchored in the bay of the island. They then sail away in it, arriving home in June 1687.

These events read as a struggle against French influence with the Spanish and Portuguese as allies and sea power triumphing in the end. In Lisbon, Robinson finds the old sea captain who tells him that in his absence his interests have prospered and that he holds profits for him. It takes time for Robinson to sort out his affairs but when he did so he was left with a fortune of £5,000. In real life, this brings to mind the position after Daniel's imprisonment in 1703–4. As research for this book shows, Daniel received back-pay from the Glass Commissioners for thirteen years after the duties came to an end.

In 1694, his wife having died, Robinson revisits his island now colonised by the Spanish and the Portuguese. Robinson divides the island into parts with them, while reserving the ownership of the whole to himself. He then sought to populate the island with English people.

If the reader had reservations about how Daniel would mediate his story to a conclusion, all doubt is now removed. In his new colony Robinson's rhetoric has been one of absolutism in which the subject must submit. Daniel does not speak the language of the social contract; for Robinson, an understanding between monarch and subject follows an anterior condition that presupposes in an act of time that they have entered into a mutual compact, tacit or explicit. It is an understanding upheld by force of arms, 'with a naked Sword by my Side, two pistols in my belt and a Gun upon each shoulder'. Not for Daniel or Robinson the Lockean view that, 'no man in the state of nature, hath a right to more land [...] than he can well manure himself and his Family'. Robinson demands the whole island.

At the end of Robinson's story, and conveniently, his wife dies. At the beginning of the sequel, *The Farther Adventures of Robinson Crusoe*, she dies again and during this account (which I do not intend to discuss here) he re-marries, to a woman that none of his companions would have chosen. This woman, being plain and ordinary, turns out to be quite the best of the selection.

In reality, his wife Mary Tuffley did not die. But in the language common to Daniel, he might have become 'dead' to her, although not to others. After his first bankruptcy there was a long-standing rupture from Mary which has been considered earlier in this book. Following the publication of *Robinson Crusoe*, as I will argue, there was just such another.

Chapter 17

Colonel Jack And Captain Singleton

I believe my case is the case of the most of the wicked part of the world, viz., that to be reduced to necessity is not only a temptation, but is such a temptation as human nature is not empowered to resist.

Colonel Jack
Daniel Defoe, 1722

COLONEL JACK AND CAPTAIN BOB belong to a group of fiction which can be categorised as stories of travel and adventure. However, it would also be possible to categorise them as 'dressed up tales of crime'. Daniel Defoe presents his tales without Victorian 'pathetic sentiment'. He depicts men and women who are the 'most matter-of-fact creatures in the world: they rob and cheat, fornicate and have children…with no trace of emotional stress and no romantic sentiment'.

John Richetti has written that he had approached Daniel's fictional characters with great expectations only to find them shadowy and disappointing. What is arresting and absorbing is Daniel, the narrator, for it is his self-absorption with his own tale in all its many twists and contrivances which grips the imagination.[179]

Daniel's early life and its relation to these two books have been commented upon in an earlier chapter. Taken together, and with *Robinson Crusoe*, they tell the same tale: a respectable family, with pretensions to gentility, but one which rejects the protagonist and casts him out into the care of others with no regard for him. They tell the story of a life lived on the edge and a falling into depravity through deception and petty crime. In *Colonel Jack* the reader is told, '(my nurse) had a good piece of money given her to take me off their hands, and deliver him (my father) and my mother from the importunities that usually attend the misfortune of having a child to keep that should not be seen or heard of'.

Daniel gives us a bastard as his central character, with a bastard brother known as Captain Jack, who is one year older than him, and a younger boy called Major Jack. Daniel/Colonel Jack narrates the story and bosses the stage. Jack's sibling experience is similar to Robinson Crusoe's, for he had one brother killed and the other disappeared without trace.

These three brothers are devices for telling one story. They have very different characters. The displacement of the worst characteristics on to two brothers enables Daniel/Colonel Jack to establish a distance between the crimes committed and his conscience and desire to repent.

Daniel tells the reader that these boys, 'were hopeful boys all three of us [but that] promised we would all be rogues. Captain Jack was squat, big and strong-made... sly, sullen, reserved, malicious, revengeful... brutish, bloody, and cruel in his disposition...was an original rogue...for he would do the foulest and most villainous things'. This description is of Daniel's elder brother Daniel, the Lieutenant-Captain in a cavalry regiment. Daniel writes that Captain Jack in this time fell into bad company and was punished for it. If Daniel senior had signed up to serve as a soldier and had misbehaved, this might well have been what happened to him.

Major Jack was 'merry, facetious. Pleasant...had something of the gentleman in him...was full of jests...had true manly courage...was the most generous and most compassionate of creature alive...[and] wanted nothing but honesty to have made him an excellent man'. This Jack is probably the 'John' identified earlier who is the son of the 'nurse' or some other variant of domestic carer, in James Foe's household. Meanwhile Will, the companion to the boys, and in particular to Colonel Jack, is Daniel's cousin Will.

And Colonel Jack himself?

He was poor, unhappy, [and a] tractable Dog [willing and capable and able to learn anything and] ...set out into the world so early, that when he began to do evil he understood nothing of the wickedness of it...[he] had a natural talent for talking [and] passed for a bold resolute boy...but shunned fighting...was wary and dextrous in [his] trade [of thieving]. Although dirty from sleeping rough, he was thought a handsome boy. The composite picture is of a boy who could do almost anything: a rogue who could lend himself to any wrong-doing but whose respectable looks and ability to speak well could get him out of scrapes.

When the nurse of these three boys dies, they are thrown onto the streets and left to make their living by occasional jobs, begging and stealing. At night they got into the ash holes and nealing arches in the glass house near Rosemary Lane, or at another in Ratcliff Highway, which kept them warm but dirty.

It is not commonly thought that these descriptions of boys in the nealing arches could be anything other than fictional accounts, since a young and intelligent lad from a respectable Presbyterian home could not possibly be found there. However, the three Jacks find themselves there because their nurse had died. The domestic arrangements in the Foe household might have broken down with James Foe away on business and the boys left to roam.

The boys might also be there by inclination and as an easy way to make money. These ash holes were pick-up points for male prostitutes. If the young Daniel had been abused as a boy, it might not be strange for him to think of selling his body to make money, for making money on the street was what Daniel did. Did Daniel give the truth away by telling the story of a gentleman who invested money for him after an encounter and who he visited more than once? Might he have been a client who tried nevertheless to help the young Daniel and who was good for fair treatment and a worthwhile payment?[180]

These young boys seem to have started out on the streets when Colonel Jack was twelve and they retreated into the 'country' when he was eighteen. From a modest beginning they drifted into more serious street crime and into a gang: pickpocketing, snatching, assaulting and burglary. Colonel Jack keeps himself at a distance but is gradually drawn in. Captain Jack, his actual brother, gets caught and is flogged three times, Will is condemned to the gallows and hanged. His fictional killing sets a boundary to crime and acts as a warning to the boys of the dangers they are running.

All this might have been observed by Daniel on the streets of London and he may have gained the knowledge of the tricks he describes from both his own imprisonments and the boasting tales and demonstrations of fellow prisoners. But when Daniel writes of bills of exchange, their theft, conversion, and the fraudulent game of 'finding them' for a reward, the reader knows this is closer to home for Daniel. The accounts given in *Colonel Jack* do not ring true. When confronted with their loss, the owners put stops on the bills. Apart from the loss of interest the owners would incur until they were replaced, they would have had little incentive to pay money to get them back. In the games the boys play they are too 'clever by half' and the victims far too complicit.

In real life, bills of exchange were of interest to Daniel because they were a method of creating money when needed and they could be fraudulently converted. Sutherland describes two cases taken out against Daniel involving a misuse of bills of exchange.[181] In 1692 Daniel was charged with wrongfully converting a bill of exchange for his own use. He was accused of conspiring with a clerk, William Marsh, to defraud a York merchant of £100. 'According to the plaintiff, the clerk had picked up a bill of exchange in his master's chambers while his master lay dead in another room, and had handed it on to Defoe, who gave him £60 for it.' Daniel had a plausible defence but the case went against him and then, almost immediately, he faced a similar charge. Daniel was involved in the formation of a company to exploit an invention of a Cornish inventor, Joseph Williams, who procured a patent for 'a certain new engine for diving of great use and benefit'. Daniel became the secretary to a company formed to exploit the invention. Joseph Williams contributed by paying his share in bills of exchange. Williams charged Defoe with having done him out of a considerable sum of money in concert with a Thomas Williams (who was also involved in the first case). Once again Daniel offered a plausible defence. The case ended inconclusively.

Colonel Jack describes two occasions when he was arrested and brought to court. In each case he outwits the Justice. On the second occasion, when acquitted he asks the Justice to order the Constables to return to the place where he was arrested and 'to declare publicly there that he was honourably acquitted' in order to protect his reputation. As Colonel Jack was a young rascal living on the streets, the reader might suppose that there was no reputation to protect and that Daniel was referring to a real-life incident of his own.

In the Preface to *Colonel Jack,* Daniel writes that every vicious reader will be encouraged to a change, and it will appear that the best and only good end of an impious misspent life is repentance. Sure enough, the 'appearance' of repentance is created. Colonel Jack becomes terrified that his life of crime might end in the gallows. He repays money he has stolen from a poor old nurse and her maid, for he was truly sorry for them and they had done nothing to deserve the crime against them.

This repentance is very short-lived, for when Captain Jack and he decide to flee London and make their way to Scotland where they would be safe from the law, they steal a horse. They set out on foot (it was a long way to Scotland). At an inn, the ostler asks the Captain to hold a horse while he assists another customer. The Captain says to the Colonel, 'turn up the lane, I'll overtake you'. 'So I went up the lane, and in a few minutes he was got up upon the horse and at my heels. 'Come, get up,' says he, 'we will have a lift if we don't get the horse by the bargain.' I made no difficulty.'

It was rumoured that Daniel stole a horse on the way to Scotland and the allegation was used by his enemies to damage his reputation.

At eighteen, Daniel was embarking on a life of trade, the practices of which he considered no different in morality from crime on the streets. Colonel Jack embarks on journeys and events which lead him to Virginia. It is not likely that Daniel ever went to Virginia but he did go abroad to many other places, for he started to become a merchant.

When he reaches Scotland, Colonel Jack enlists in the army, deserts, and is bamboozled into travelling as a captive to Virginia and then sold to the owner of a plantation. Here he is put in charge of Negro slaves and argues for their humane treatment. After some years of hard work, Colonel Jack becomes a merchant and planter in his own right and a man of middling prosperity. However, all Daniel's protagonists share his restlessness. As with Robinson Crusoe, Colonel Jack is off on his adventures again. He returns to Europe and serves with the French army in Italy and with the Old Pretender.

As I have suggested in the chapter on *Robinson Crusoe*, mentions of slavery refer imaginatively to being in bondage to creditors. Thus, Colonel Jack has a period of bondage to creditors followed by a return to trading and the ownership of land. The escape to service with the army is for Daniel a common release both in life and in his fiction.[182]

Colonel Jack then experiences a number of marital adventures. Daniel writes of multiple marriages in *Moll Flanders* and *Roxana* and the tantalising consideration is the extent to which he is writing about his own life in these three books.

Colonel Jack's first wife (according to Jack) ran up debts and was loose with men: having one child with him, she then has another with someone else. When he shut up his home and deserted her, she sent a bully to demand money from him. It is tempting to suggest a neat inversion to real life: it was Jack/Daniel who ran up debts, spent her money, fobbed her off with a worthless bill of exchange, and got roughed up for his misdeeds.

Jack had made it clear to his wife that he had disliked women but she had been cunning and had ensnared him. The outcome of the marriage confirmed his worst fears, but there was a hope of reconciliation when his wife apologises to him and he makes money available to her.

Following Daniel's first bankruptcy, as has been argued earlier, there was a breakdown in Daniel's relationship with his wife Mary and some sort of reconciliation late in their lives. So, when the first wife returns at the end of Jack's marital adventures, there is congruence in the happening.

Wife number two was encountered in Trent: 'in an unusual height of good humour' he 'consents to be married to the daughter of a burgher with whom he had lodged and who had been 'too cunning for me'. In France he suspects his wife of adultery (falsely, the reader thinks), kills her supposed lover in a duel and then abandons her as a whore. There is up to this point, Jack argues, no legality in the arrangements in that he was not divorced from the first wife (although Jack has already told the reader that he had obtained a decree of divorce from the Ecclesiastical Court).

This contradiction, as Daniel might have told readers, is 'a contradiction and no contradiction'. The choice of Trent is the clue, for it is a signifier: it was there, at The Council of Trent, that Roman Catholicism confirmed its objections against sodomy and put Michelangelo at risk. It is likely that this 'wife number two' is a same-sex union. Somehow Jack/Daniel got involved in a matter of honour which resulted in a duel and the need to leave France and return to London. Jack argues elsewhere that he obtained a legal divorce, so the position is somewhat obscure. Nevertheless, Jack abandons 'wife number two' on a false pretence. All this is played out over a period of six years.

If these happenings occurred in real life, it is likely that it is more than one event and over different passages of time. The duel may have pre-dated Daniel's first marriage when he was travelling on the continent. Or perhaps it did not happen to him but to his elder brother. The relationship occurred in London. It could have been with Thomas Neale. There is other evidence that Daniel was involved with Neale, and if so it would have been between 1693 and 1699, a period of six years, and was ended by Neale's death.

The third 'wife' was a melancholy widow met on a stage-coach from Canterbury to London, at Rochester. She gives Colonel Jack three children but then takes to drink, becomes a whore and dies. When Daniel is seeking to dismiss a woman it is often on the excuse that she drinks too much and is unfaithful. Daniel's account is a gross distortion of his 'marriage' to Elizabeth Sammen, who bore him three children.

The reader can warm to 'wife' number four. This woman has a name, Margaret, and a nick name, Moggie. The daughter of a business associate and living a mile away, she was in the habit of dropping in and looking after the children. Jack resolved to love her, 'as [he] married two gentlewomen and one citizen, and they proved all three whores, [he wanted now] an innocent country wench'.

Sequentially, this third wife was Mary Norton who was a simple country girl. Daniel trivialises this relationship in *Colonel Jack*. The evidence suggests that Mary Norton was a devoted woman who looked after his children well and stayed a good friend to Daniel. But Daniel signifies his attachment to Mary Norton with a crude joke. The marriage to Moggie, which was a private wedding, was arranged by a man who professed to be a doctor of physic, but who was really a Romish priest in orders, in 'his own study, that is to say, in his oratory or chapel, a little room within his study'.

If the enquirer did not know better, he would conclude that this was not a real wedding with a real woman, for there are dubious elements to the story. There seems to be no good reason for involving a Romish priest who 'usually passes for a doctor of physic' in a ceremony, for if a private wedding were required the couple could affirm their marriage bonds to each other in the presence of others. Daniel professed to be firmly anti-Catholic, so why, it might reasonably be asked, would he wish to involve a Catholic priest in a ceremony?

What Daniel describes is not a wedding at all. In the early seventeen hundreds some priests within Catholic and High Anglican churches condoned homosexual behaviour although their church officially condemned it. Priests in highly decorative and coloured robes staged elaborate masses and their decorative attraction and the practice of chastity attracted homosexuals to and into the church. When Daniel writes that 'we were married in the doctor's study that is to say, in his oratory or chapel', he is referring to a drag party in a Molly house or private home.

The ritual for homosexual men attending a Molly house or a private gathering in a house for sex is that they would engage themselves in activities which enabled them to choose a partner before retiring to a room called a 'chapel' where they would become 'married' and then have sex. Transvestism and cross-dressing was usual and the host, often dressed in colourful church robes, undertook the ceremony.

Daniel did enter into a 'marriage' with his country wench but he could not help wishing to denigrate it. He needed to signify it as a sham: 'Hey guys, you know what it is really'. This private wedding would have counted for something but, of course, Colonel Jack was already married. His bad luck with women continued for, after having borne him a daughter, Daniel the writer of fictions arranged for her death. Moggie left him a daughter and died from a fall while pregnant with another. A date, 1715, can be put on this 'marriage' because the Jacobite rebellion and the invasion of the Scots occurred during it. In 1713–15 Daniel was to abandon Mary Norton, taking his daughter Sophia with him, so in a sense it would be true that she 'was dead to him', as was his son Benjamin Norton.

In the end, and it was a long time in coming, Colonel Jack, Mammon satisfied, was reunited with his first wife and he was able to repent in perfect pleasure and ease. For twenty-four years, he had lived a life of levity and profligate wickedness. Now he had leisure to reflect and repent. Jack is aware that he repents 'with advantage', although how far 'it had pleased God to give the grace of repentance when he gives the opportunity [he recognised] was not for [him] to say'.

In *Captain Singleton,* Daniel gives his readers a beginning which will now be very familiar to them. Captain Bob, as he becomes known in the story, was abducted by child stealers when two years old. There is a suggestion of a genteel background, as with Robinson Crusoe and Colonel Jack. He is passed on as an item for sale to a beggar and then a gypsy woman before going into the care of various parishes. He acquires a master who takes him to sea. Losing one master, he acquires another. Again, the reader is given a difficult boy and a reckless and immoral young man. Daniel gives us a warning about Bob early in the narrative. He writes, 'I was reputed to be as a mighty diligent servant to my master. I was diligent indeed, but I was very far from honest, which by the way, was their very great mistake.'

There was a mutiny and Bob, with other supposed mutineers, was put ashore. Although young, Bob became a leader. His advice was bold and reckless but the situation for the castaways was perilous. No one else came up with any good ideas so he became a leader by default. Bob has a dismal view of the humanity he was sharing: 'Thieving, lying, swearing, forswearing, joined to the most abominable lewdness, was the stated practice of the ship's crew…[and] they were, generally speaking, the most complete cowards that [he] ever met with.'

Nevertheless, he was seen as no different. A fellow mutineer says to him, 'My lad' says he, 'thou art born to do a world of mischief; thou hast commenced pirate very young; but have a care of the gallows, young man; have a care, I say, for thou wilt be an eminent thief'. All of which echoes the views of his companion's father who commented upon Robinson Crusoe's behaviour on his first voyage.

These men, having failed in various attempts to escape their plight by sea, reach the shore of Africa and embark on a perilous journey across the continent to the Gold Coast. On this imaginary journey these men experience many adventures and succeed in acquiring gold, ivory and other valuable merchandise. It is a voyage of pillage and aggrandisement, which has been admired and likened to Robert Drury's *Captivity in Madagascar* which was

206

published in 1729. Daniel seems to have pieced together this account from contemporary geographical records and travellers' tales.[183]

In the course of their journey across Africa from Madagascar to the Gold Coast the mutineers encounter many different tribes of natives; some are friendly and hospitable but others are highly aggressive and must be fought and killed. These accounts cannot be taken literally. Imaginatively, these Africans represent obstacles to the ultimate achievement of gold and riches. They can be bribed with trinkets and the most loyal can share in the proceeds.

Captain Bob returns to England, but not for long. He squanders his wealth and most of it was gone in two years 'of folly and wickedness'. There was no alternative to doing it all again. This experience suggests Daniel's first bankruptcy. For a time he had prospered and then recklessness and poor judgement caused his financial ruin.

Second time around was going to be different. Bob shipped himself on a voyage to Cadiz. His ship was obliged to put in to shore and, once there, Captain Bob joined in a successful mutiny and embarked on a career as a pirate. Daniel writes, 'as I have hinted [I was] an original thief and a pirate even by inclination before, was now in my element and never undertook anything in my life with more particular satisfaction'.

A mutiny, which seizes a ship, enables the mutineers to get their starting capital: the ship, its men, armaments and provisions. Now they are free to accumulate capital by plunder; capital which would never come their way by honest means. As Bob says on his first venture 'We must be pirates or anything to take the first ship…to get our liberty [to accumulate wealth].'

Daniel introduces the reader to a complicated game of geo-politics where companies, such as the East India Company, operate as independent states, ruling the waves with sixty gun ships, and where deals and bloody battles determine booty, which is as likely to be the trading of slaves as gold and merchandise. The name of this game is to accumulate capital by conquest and to avoid battles that might be lost; the penalties for failure are the gallows or rotting in a foul prison cell.

In the course of this aggrandisement Bob acquires as an ally a grave and senior Quaker, William Walter, who gives him sage advice. William teaches Bob that if his object is the making of money, which Bob agrees it is, there were means other than naked force to achieve it. Bloodshed should be avoided whenever there were other and better means to achieve one's objectives. William proves to be a masterly diplomat and negotiator: he wins round men who might be enemies by addressing their needs and not their principles and he negotiates alliances.

William demonstrates to Bob that there is little difference between pirates and merchants; for booty to be real, he teaches, it requires to be traded, while the activities of merchants need to be protected by the sword. When a slave ship was captured, William prevented the punishment of the black slaves who had overthrown and killed the slave-masters. He argues that they had been very badly treated and that it was natural for them to rebel. However, William had no wish for them to be released. He arranged for them to be sold at a handsome profit.

The icon to be admired was Captain Avery, the master pirate. When things go badly for Captain Avery his position and fortune is protected by the swelling force of Bob's band of pirates who between them have several ships and over a thousand men under their command. But even at their most powerful, the forces and wealth under Captain Bob and his allies do not match the power commanded by Captain Avery in his prime.

What can you do with such wealth when it is clear to all that it has been gained from doing ill? Where in the world can you enjoy it without fear? Daniel writes, 'As to the wealth I had, which was immensely great, it was like dirt under my feet; I had no value for it, no peace in the possession of it, no great concern about me for the leaving of it.'

Could they reform, repent, and enjoy this wealth as well? William gives the right answer:

> To quit what we have, and do it here, is to throw away to those who have no claim to it, and divest ourselves of it, but to do no right with it; whereas we ought to keep it carefully together, with a resolution to do what right with it we are able; and who knows what opportunity Providence may put into our hands to do justice, at least, to some of those we have injured?

Once more, Daniel mediates his conclusion with proper deference to Mammon and worldly riches. This time he goes further. There could for him be no more favourable outcome than legitimate royal approbation. William Walter and Captain Bob have many doubts but decide to return to England. There they would pass for brothers. Thus Bob could marry William's sister, Mary, and Daniel's imagination could create a legitimate and incontestable protestant succession: William and Mary, of course, but also 'Walter' (Lucy Walter, the mother of the illegitimate Duke of Monmouth, the rightful protestant heir to the throne). And then there were Daniel's real-life wives: the two Marys.

Chapter 18

Moll Flanders

The life of MOLL FLANDERS has been so notorious, that a Man can never go into Company, but they are talking of her; Some [say] there never was such Person in the world…others affirm there was such a Woman, [and that] they knew her personally…

Anonymous pamphlet, Dublin, 1730

IT MIGHT BE THOUGHT a feasible proposition to seek autobiographical information on Daniel Defoe from fictional first person narratives where the narrator is unarguably masculine. The search is far more problematic when the narrator, as in *Moll Flanders* and *Roxana*, is a woman and, moreover, when the women written about are first a common prostitute and thief and secondly a courtesan.

I am not alone in thinking that this autobiographical information exists. Ian Watt writes, 'Moll Flanders is suspiciously like her author, even in matters where we would expect striking and obvious differences. The facts show that she is a woman and a criminal, for example, but neither of these two roles determines her personality as Defoe has drawn it.'[184]

Seemingly, it is not necessary to argue that Daniel reinvented his life through a woman. It is persuasively argued that the character of Moll Flanders was drawn from several female criminals known to Daniel: in particular, Moll King who survived several sentences of transportation, when she might have been hanged, and Calico Sarah. Flanders has a double meaning: it is, of course associated with a kind of cloth but also, at the time, with prostitution. If the two meanings are merged in a name the result could be Moll Flanders.

Moll Flanders was born in Newgate and almost lost her life there. Daniel spent a considerable time in Newgate and he certainly met female thieves there, including mothers who had given birth to children in the prison, and he would have heard their astonishing tales with sympathy. A long stay with fellow criminals creates an empathy with them and it is easy to suppose that Daniel would have thought himself into their imagination and circumstances. Daniel may even have met Moll King there.[185]

But Moll Flanders is not either of these women: it is Daniel Defoe. His/her story is not a picaresque tale of roguery of the kind that Daniel acting as a crime reporter had written as a young man; it is, like *Robinson Crusoe*, a kind of autobiography told with a degree of psychological understanding.

If it is accepted that Daniel put himself into the guise of a woman, that he invented a new genre to tell a 'woman's' story, the obvious question is why he felt compelled to do it. The success of *Robinson Crusoe*, and the ease with which he was able to tell his life stories through other fiction must have given Daniel great self-confidence. Daniel felt able to write of a real self: of his life as a homosexual and a woman. His real life stretched to cross-dressing and disguising himself as a woman, and it excited him to pretend. Assuming the identity of a woman was a necessary and enjoyable part of Daniel's life. He longed to be able to be a woman. Fiction offered him a paid opportunity for being one without the danger of detection. But he longed to be detected, to be spotted, and so he leaves the reader with clues.

Daniel knew that to reveal himself as a woman in real life was dangerous; he enjoyed the danger but could not afford for his sexuality to be generally commented upon. He had public personas to protect, no matter how damaged; identities which would have been undermined by exposure of his sexual activities. However, by 1722, Daniel might well have gained sufficient self-belief to conclude that he could continue to appear as a woman so long as he remained in literary disguise.

Moll Flanders falls into two parts. The first and major part concentrates on Moll's activities as a wife, on five occasions, and as the mother of numerous children; the second part relates her life of crime. This structure is strikingly similar to *Colonel Jack* where the first hundred pages are devoted to petty crime, and the balance to his five marriages and consequent children. Both books are episodic with the loosest and most improbable of linkages. Their central characters proceed from a state of innocence to petty and then more serious offences, both are threatened and narrowly escape execution for their misdeeds. In both books the characters claim some distinction on the grounds of gentility; their aspiration is to better themselves socially and their problem is to find a way not only to survive but to climb the social ladder.

Moll's mother was 'transported to the Plantations' and some relation of her mother, acting in the role of a nurse, took her away. She has a recollection of wandering among Gypsies. This description is very close to that of Bob in *Captain Singleton*. Like Bob, Moll was taken into parish care. Moll's parish was in Colchester, a town which features large in Daniel's history and where he might well have had relatives. Like Jack and Bob, Moll received the rudiments of an education. It was proposed by the parish that she be put into domestic service as being the only viable economic future for her other than prostitution.

Moll succeeded in avoiding domestic service until she was fourteen, for she wished to be a gentlewoman, by which she meant to be able to work and pay her own way. By working hard at her nurse's profession of lacemaking, it seemed that she had proved the adult world to be wrong: she had demonstrated her ability to find her own way. Unfortunately, her nurse and guardian died. The nurse's daughter robbed Moll of money by which she might have maintained her independence and now she had no other choice but domestic service. She became part of the household of the Mayor where she was well treated. Moll deceived herself that she was a young lady in a respectable family. She knew herself to be pretty and that she 'had the Character too of a very sober, modest, and virtuous young lady'. To the sons of the family she was no more than a pretty chambermaid and, as such, she was regarded as fair game.

The story from this point is known by millions of sympathetic readers. The elder brother, under the pretence of undying love and one hundred guineas, succeeds in obtaining her as a mistress and getting her pregnant. Meanwhile, the younger brother, or so we are told, genuinely falls in love with her to the notice of his family who then treat her coldly. Moll tells the elder brother that 'he had Engaged himself to marry [her], and that he had all along told [her] she was his Wife, and [that she] looked upon [herself] as effectually so, as if the Ceremony had passed'.[186] Thinking better of it, for she would bring him no dowry, he succeeded in fobbing her off with his younger brother. She married him despite loving the elder brother and had two children before he died five years later. Having been recompensed by the family and with the grandparents caring for the children, she was loosed upon the world.

This account rings true. Female domestic servants were all too prone to sexual exploitation but the most adroit and pretty of them made something of their natural attributes. However, it is a disagreeable fact that abuse within the family is most commonly centred on the female in control, however she is described. Let it be supposed, for the moment, that the male head of the family is absent on business for long periods of time, and that a young and impressionable boy is left with a doting but aggressive female carer and sisters: might not the boy be the victim of a snare and find himself set loose on the world?

Might this have happened to Daniel in any of the households of which he was a part? If it had happened it would have scarred him and dramatically shaped his sexual orientation and behaviour for life. If he had been one of the two brothers engaged in a like deception, he would have recalled the emotions of all the participants.

If this account in *Moll Flanders* is chronological, it is an episode at the youthful stage of Daniel's life. However, Moll's second marriage is easily referenced as being Daniel's first known marriage to Mary Tuffley. Moll found, 'this amphibious Creature, this Land-water-thing call'd a Gentleman Tradesman – a Draper!' He spent a great deal of her money very quickly. They had a coach and horses and several servants and 'liv'd like Quality', with the consequence that he soon became bankrupt and fled to France. He advised Moll to recover what she could from the house and flee while he disappeared. The creditors scrambled for what they could and Moll fled to a safe place in the Mint.[187] When Daniel, who traded as a hosier, became bankrupt in 1692, his wife found a 'safe place' with the Tuffley family while

Daniel 'got out of town'. At the time he 'broke', it was said that he was living very grandly with a coach and horses and five servants.

Moll took up with a widow who invited her to go home with her. Mary Tuffley, after 1692, lived with her aunt Joan Tuffley, who was a widow. Moll seeks another husband of means with the aid of a friend. She has very limited means and thus her chances of finding an honest man of substance, given a marriage market with a surplus of marriageable women, were not great.

Daniel rehearses all the stratagems open to Moll and it is clear that he has practised them. In the course of doing so, he gives an example of a courtship which appears to be his with Mary[188], in which he reveals a marriage portion of £1,400 given by the woman to the man. This may well be Daniel's marriage portion.[189] If so, Mary's family was successful in hiding part of her wealth. Daniel writes, 'for she like a prudent Woman … plac'd part of her Fortune so in Trustees without letting him know any thing of it, that it was quite out of his reach, and made him very well content with the rest'.

Moll/Daniel gives an example of a young lady courted by a Captain who took exception to her enquiries as to the true state of his finances and estate. Moll/Daniel advises her friend to spread bad rumours about him, that he was not 'the Man as to Estate he pretended to be'. Moll added the information 'that he was under a Necessity of a Fortune to support his Interest with the Owners of the Ship he Commanded: that his own Part was not paid for, and if it was not paid quickly his Owners would put him out of the Ship and his Chief Mate was likely to command it, who offer'd to buy that Part which the Captain had promised to take'.

At this point the reader is thoroughly confused. There is nothing in Moll's recounted history at this point which would make her so very knowledgeable about male strategies and women's defences in the negotiation of a dowry and a marriage portion; nor is there information about how she is so knowledgeable about the affairs of a man she has never met.

For good measure, Moll/Daniel continues, 'I added, for I confess I was heartily piqued at the Rogue, as I call'd him, that I had heard a Rumour too, that he had a Wife alive at Plymouth and another in the West Indies, a thing which they all knew was not very uncommon for such kind of Gentlemen'. This gentleman, when pressed to come clean, turned up 'undeniable Evidence of his having paid for his part of the Ship; he brought her Certificates from his Owners' as evidence that the reports of their intending to remove him was untrue.

The reader might conclude that the knowledge of all this was the author's self-knowledge. In the period 1688–92 Daniel was involved in a dispute over a ship he owned named Desire.[190] In the summer of 1688 he sold the ship but agreed to continue to hold a quarter-share and to pay his contribution to fit her for sea. The new owner, Robert Harrison, put sail in her but came to grief. The vessel proved un-seaworthy and as a consequence was lost to a French man-of-war. Harrison sued Daniel for his losses. Daniel argued that he had sold the ship outright to Harrison but not being paid he agreed reluctantly to continue with a quarter-share. He also argued that Harrison had not produced a suitable contract for the sale, and then had ignored him entirely. In effect, having confused all the issues, Daniel was not a partner at all. Well, was he an owner, or part owner, or not? The outcome of this Chancery suit, if there was one, for they tended to drag on, is not known. But at a later date, and after his bankruptcy, it appears that Daniel did after all have an interest in the ship, so perhaps Harrison was right.

Moll let it be known that she had a fortune of £1,500 and this, together with the stratagems she had discussed with her friend, was sufficient to catch her third husband. She confessed that she had deceived this man and that her fortune was much smaller, but she succeeded in codging him into acceptance. However, when they went to Virginia, providence punished her for it, for after a while she discovered that his mother was her own (transported from Newgate) and that she had married her own brother.

At this point the cynical reader begins to suspect that the narrator is unreliable. Is all this complicated tale no more than Daniel writing about himself? Perhaps disappointed by the first marriage, bankrupt and needing the money, he was on the trail of another dowry from a 'wife' acquired by private treaty or arrangement and regardless of its legitimacy? Needs must, he might have argued, but surely it would be a sin.

When Moll confesses the sin of incest to her husband, he forgives her, but of course there could be no future together. Generously, he accommodates her wish to return to England. However, the goods he gave her, and which were on board ship, were ruined in a storm on the way back, forcing Moll to rely on the good will of others. And this too must have been a punishment for sin.

At this point in the narrative, Moll recounts the tale of a relationship with a gentleman which amounted to a private marriage. In the course of this account, Daniel gives his readers an interesting diversion, for Moll meets this gentleman near Bath. He courts her in an ambiguous manner. In the end Moll succumbs. They live together amicably in the country for two years without consummating their union. When later she produced a boy, this gentleman arranged for her to be accommodated in a fine apartment in Hammersmith, London. He claimed to have 'a wife but no wife': that is, his wife 'was distemper'd in her Head, and was under the Conduct of her own Relations'. [191]

Moll lived for six years 'in this happy but unhappy Condition, in which time [she] brought him three children but only the first of them liv'd; and tho' twice in those six years she moved home, yet [she] came back the sixth year to [her] first lodgings'. The gentleman became severely ill and, not hearing from him, Moll seeks him out in London. She disguises herself as a servant maid and discovers what relations were in the house, that his wife might recover from her maladies, but there was little hope of his survival.

But when he does recover, Moll receives a letter from him announcing that he could not continue the relationship. He thought his recovery to be miraculous and that it behoved him to repent his sins and reform by breaking with her. They reached a financial settlement, favourable to Moll, and a release favourable to him, together with a promise that he would look after the child.

This phase in Moll/Daniel's life has puzzled biographers In interpreting it, the usual caveats apply: it is not one episode in Daniel's life but several. The dates are confusing because Daniel's imagination concentrates on events and incidents and not on the passage of time; he needs to be obscure, to hide incidents in his own life; and, most importantly, the reader must gender-reverse the characters to ascertain the truth.

Working backwards from the gentleman's/Daniel's illness takes time from 1714 when Daniel was ill and thought himself to be dying. Eight years earlier, the duration of the gentleman's relationship with Moll/Daniel would take us to 1706, the date of Daniel's arrival in Scotland.

Moll had been out of the country for eight years and came back into England. Daniel came into England from Scotland in 1707, but revisited from time to time until 1712. Daniel was in Edinburgh in the winter season of 1709 until December. Being elsewhere and in the country refers to Tilbury.

At the date of writing *Moll Flanders*, Daniel had come into the country on two occasions between 1695 and 1704, a period of nine years, and from 1705–6 to 1714, similarly a period of eight to nine years. He was planning to do so for a third time. Daniel/Moll had two phases of living with the mother: in the first, she had two children but only the boy survived and in the second, three children, of whom only one survived, whose gender not being stated can be assumed to be lesser, that is, a girl. In real life, as I have argued elsewhere, the mother is Mary Norton and the children are Benjamin Norton and Sophia. The gentleman in this part of the account is Daniel.

If so, who is the gentleman who came to Bath? In this story Bath is chosen by Moll as a 'diversion' and by Daniel for its sexual associations. The town is notable for its hot springs which were regarded from Roman times as having medicinal value. In the *Tour*, Daniel writes that 'the town is taken up in raffing, gaming, visiting, and in a word, all sorts of gallantry and levity'.[192]

Did Daniel/Moll invite a gentleman to Bath? The elements of Moll/Daniel's account of the gentleman's visit are as follows: the gentleman had singled her/him out in the previous winter season; he came down again in the spring season with another gentleman and two servants, and he was a 'Man of Honour and of Virtue as well of a great Estate'. Before anything happened between them he paid Moll/Daniel money; he was then cajoled into giving her/him £200 pounds; the gentleman was ill but she/him looked after him; they had sex together and the gentleman paid another £50. He stayed in this state for five weeks, fifteen miles from Bath; during this time Daniel went by coach to Bristol, the gentleman then went to London.

In the previous winter season of 1709, Daniel was in Edinburgh. In July 1710 Sir John Clerk decided to go from his home in Edinburgh to Bath, for health reasons. The essential elements from this story, taken from his journal, are as follows: he 'fell ill of a great cold' in April 1710, he resolved 'to take a journey into England the length of Bath' against the advice of his physicians. On that journey the cold abated a little. He had left his new wife, who had recently given birth to a son, in a state of anguish and was doubtful 'if ever I should see her again'. He travelled with two agreeable gentlemen friends, and he was driven to travel by 'some secret and irresistible impulse'. He stayed in Bath for about six weeks and during his stay made an excursion to Bristol where he visited [his] good friend and Brother, Mr Baron Scroop. While in Bath he became ill again and had to take to his bed. He then went to London.[193]

The congruence of these two accounts, which contain a large number of elements, is remarkable. It has to be conjectural, but I maintain it to be highly probable, that a sexual encounter took place between Daniel Defoe and Sir John Clerk on his 'visit to Bath'. Furthermore, I believe that it was an event in a much longer relationship which lasted three years, from the date of Daniel's stay in Edinburgh in 1706/7.

John Clerk's use of the word 'Brother' in this context suggests that Baron Scroop might have been a Mason, for this term is used to describe a fellow Mason. Daniel, in using the description of 'being singled out' by his gentleman, might be referring to an invitation to join a Masonic lodge when he was in Edinburgh. If so, Clerk and the two gentlemen who accompanied him, Robert Clerk and Major Leblanc, might have been responding to an invitation to have a good time in Bath from a fellow mason. There is something disagreeable about the account. However, it is wrapped up and sanitised, Daniel was asking money for sex at the rate of £50 a time.

It might be thought that despite the plausible case I have made for Daniel being an active and perhaps predatory homosexual the evidence presented to this point in Daniel's story is no more than conjectural. However, the case for Daniel having had a sexual relationship with John Clerk is as near to conclusive as is possible and beyond any serious doubt. The unresolved issue from this point on is not whether Daniel is homosexual but the nature of his sexual behaviour.

If it is assumed that the gentleman in London is Daniel, how would that fit with what is known of the particulars of his life? Around 1714 Daniel had moved across the road in Church Street, Newington to a new and larger house, an event which supposes some sort of rapprochement with Mary Tuffley and his Newington family. He had been ill in 1713 and at the time of his authorship of *An Appeal* in 1715. This pamphlet had been difficult for him to write and was emotional in tone. Ostensibly the pamphlet is an apologia for his life and an explanation of his conduct since 1704 but it is memorable for his contrition at the effect of his behaviour upon his family. He writes:[194]

> I think I have long enough been made a Fabula Vulgi, and born the Weight of general Slander; and I should be wanting to Truth, to my Family, and to my Self, if I did not give a fair and true State of my Conduct By the hint of Mortality, and by the Infirmities of a Life of Sorrow and Fatigue, I have reason to think that I am not a great way off from, if not very near to the great Ocean of Eternity…Wherefore, I think, I should even Accounts with this World before I go that no actions (Slanders) may lay on my Heirs Executors, Administrators, and Assigns, to disturb them in the peaceable Possession of their Father's (Character) Inheritance.

The Tuffleys would have been highly concerned at Daniel's illness, for in the event of his death who would look after Mary and the children? The Tuffley family had borne the brunt of looking after them from 1694. Of course, there were other considerations. The children in Mary Tuffley's care included Hannah and Benjamin who were Daniel's children, but also the children of other father(s). Daniel had been caring for his children by Elizabeth Sammen and Mary Norton and contributing some financial help to the Tuffleys. How was a fair balance to be struck? Modern parents struggling to do the right thing by children from multiple marriages know all too well the difficulty of the decisions they take. Now the Tuffleys would have descended upon the stricken Daniel demanding that he sort things out before it was too late.

For Daniel there were related issues. How, as he weakened, was he to conduct the rest of his life? One thing was certain, he was being pressed hard. He would have to move back to London permanently. He would have to cut himself off from Mary Norton or at least to declare to others that he was doing so.

There were issues for Daniel which could not be frankly stated unless the Tuffley family were much tougher and more worldly-wise than is known: with Harley's power weakening, or even gone, for the exact date of this family conference is not known, he had no protection. It might no longer be safe for Daniel to be removed from sources of help in London. And without money from Harley, Daniel would have to work much harder in London to make ends meet: he simply could not afford to maintain an expensive establishment in Tilbury.

At the heart of Daniel's difficulties was the state of his mind. There was at the core of his being his psycho-sexual demands. How could he meet their imperatives in a world turned cold against him with the loss of protection from Harley? He was ageing. He could no longer be someone's 'princess'. It was time to be more of a 'father'.

*   *   *

Moll found herself in funds again and after losing some money when a goldsmith with whom she had left money went bankrupt, she looked around for someone who could help her preserve it. She went to a bank where she found that there was someone willing to pass her on to a friend who might help her, to discover that he was more willing to possess her than her money. He too had a wife and she 'had been Distemper'd or Lunatick, or some such thing'. In his case, this meant that she had cuckolded him. He asked Moll to marry him once his divorce had come through.

While she waited, Moll permitted herself to marry another on the false pretence on her part that she had a fortune, and a deception by him both of a fortune and a large estate in Ireland. Moll found herself pregnant by husband number three and returned to London to have the child while her husband halted short of London, which he dare not enter. She lodged in Clerkenwell, an area of poor reputation, and had her baby in a lodging of ill repute.

She was persuaded to give up the child to marry husband number four, her banker's friend, who had obtained a divorce and remained passionate in his resolve to marry her. At the inn at which they stayed, and where they were married, there was a sequence of strange events: husband number two, a legitimate husband, who had given her his blessing to marry again, appeared as a traveller at the inn. Next, there was a hue and cry because highway robbers were thought to be in the vicinity, on the Dunstable Road, and constables searched the inn.

It is my conviction that when Daniel is describing Moll's relationships not involving children (or where they are promptly got rid of) they are always based on real life same-sex arrangements involving money or some other pecuniary advantage. I believe it is possible to establish the identity of these people but I have not had the time to do so here. I offer it as a challenge to biographers who follow me, to do so. After all, there are some interesting possibilities: a gentleman believing he has prospects of a substantial estate in Ireland, but who appears to be mistaken; a husband from the north (Halifax?), a gentleman, dealing in gold and precious stones, whose business fails, a London banker.

There is terror involved in these events which must have sprung from Daniel's own experiences: being caught up in a web of false pretences involving the same and the other sex, the fear of entering London, the possibility of discovery, and the need to buy off the constables searching the premises. If these events are sequential from Daniel's repentance and rapprochement with the Tuffleys, it would be obvious that when feeling better he recovered his habitual proclivities.

217

And then there was a death, without which there could not be a new beginning; husband number four was first bankrupted and then, from the resulting depression, died.

I realise that a work of art is over-determined: that it is capable of being interpreted in many ways and that no one explanation is exclusive of others. The reader will recognise that I am single minded. I am looking in Daniel's fiction for evidence of his real life, but I am not seeking to assert that the passages and events which command my attention are not capable of other analyses and meanings for I recognise that they have that quality.

From this point in Moll's story, when she commences her life of crime, I maintain that the episode mostly covers Daniel's life between 1714 and 1722, with flashbacks to earlier happenings in his life. I accept that the story is also based on Daniel's understanding of how a person like Moll lives her life at a certain age. However, Daniel uses this street knowledge biographically to understand the life he led.

It is easy for the reader to have sympathy with Moll's plight. Daniel was writing from common observation. Early in a woman's life she could live on her wits, obtain a husband, inherit estates, and move on if the circumstances did not suit her. However, once the childbearing days were at an end and her good looks gone, making her way could involve desperate acts of management.

Daniel would have been conscious also that the passage of time had not been kind to him. For some years now he had been writing on any side on the questions of the day, publishing pamphlets anonymously, living corruptly, and resting in many a refuge in dread of a knock on the door. In a real sense, and he must have felt it, he was prostituting himself to the highest payer.

Moll's life of crime starts with petty thefts which appal and excite her. Readers are familiar with an early crime:[195]

> there was a pretty little Child ... going home, all alone, and my Prompter, like a true Devil, set me upon this innocent Creature; I talk'd to it, [the child] and it prattl'd to me again, ... I led it [into an alley] that goes into Bartholomew Close...the Child said that was not its way home...I said, I'll show you...the Child had a little Necklace on of Gold Beads, and I had my eye on it...and took off her Necklace and the Child never felt it...Here the Devil put me upon killing the child in the dark Alley, that it might not Cry...but I turn'd round to another Passage and bade it go back [and then passed through in a maze of named streets] mixing with the Crowd of People usually passing there, it was not possible to have been found out...[The fault was] the Vanity of the Mother to have her Child look fine...a Maid set to take care of it taken up ...with some Fellow...I did the Child no harm.

Moll thinks that, 'the Devil put things into [her] head'. However, no loss would result from the Devil's prompting but for people's carelessness, for which they were to blame. The child was distanced from the reader by the use of the third person: the use of 'it'. It might have been necessary to kill the 'it' to hide the crime. But she often thought of the child with kindness.

This passage shows Daniel at his best as an observer of incident and event: the geographic particulars give conviction that the event was actually observed; the child is captured in innocent enjoyment of dressing up for a dancing lesson; Moll's deception is believable, and the stand-off and distancing of the writer is masterly. But what sort of morality is this?

Moll gets drawn into 'the trade'. She becomes well off and could have lived comfortably on her ill-gotten gains but she 'had still a cast for an easie life... Reason dictated for perswading me to lay down, Avarice stept in and said, go on, go on'. Moll/Daniel tells us that the virtuous and hardworking life can be very boring. As Moll tells the reader when choosing a second husband, 'I was not averse to a tradesman...on the other hand those who came with the best proposals were the Dullest and most disagreeable Part of the World.'

On occasions Moll is caught up in court appearances. She conducts herself adroitly and avoids punishment. But each time she appears her credibility is reduced and her name gets known to the Justices.

Now in her fifties (as Daniel was in real time), she finds her age is against her yet there are still moments when she can sell her body, and she is still able to pretend that what she/he is doing is something more reputable than prostitution. When in her/his fifties she/he is able to give sex to a gentleman who regards her as a fine woman and who pays her. These events become exceptional.

Then to the astonishment of the reader, Moll steals a horse. Daniel writes, 'I was standing near a Tavern Door, there comes a Gentleman with Horse back...he stay'd pretty long in the Tavern...the Drawer call'd to me...hold this horse a while, till I go in...yes, says I and take the Horse and walks off with him very soberly.' Not knowing what to do with the horse Moll decides to leave it at an inn with a note. This was, 'Robbery and No Robbery', and quite pointless in the context of Moll's story. The account is very similar to Daniel's account of a theft of a horse in *Colonel Jack* and to the real-life allegation that Daniel had stolen and returned a horse on his way north.

It is necessary for Moll to use many disguises as she becomes known in the City as a thief. Sometimes she dresses as a fine lady, on occasions as a widow-woman, and on some occasions as a beggar woman. And then Moll contrived another disguise: this was to 'Dress...up in Mens Cloths, and to put herself into a new kind of Practise'.

The technique I am using, and which has proved so fruitful, is one of gender reversal. Daniel is telling us that for reasons of his own, and they are of a particular kind, he dressed up as a woman. It proved difficult to be, 'so Nimble, so Ready, so Dextrous at these things in a Dress so contrary to

Nature', so he stopped the practice. Actually, one might well think it easier in a man's clothing and more difficult the other way around. Daniel is telling the reader of times when he appeared as a transvestite: it was just one of the things he did. And when Moll/Daniel gets taken to bed in these clothes she/he is fearful (thrilled) that she might be found out.

Eventually, Moll gets caught and sentenced to death for robbery. Perhaps this was not a crime she had committed. She had acquired a bad reputation and the Judge thought it time to get rid of her. Sent to Newgate, she was in a desperate plight awaiting execution when a minister of religion intervenes on her behalf. In the belief that she was truly repentant, the sentence was commuted to that of transportation to Virginia.

This incident is revealing. Moll resists the approach of the Ordinary at Newgate. The Ordinary was the minister appointed to the prison for the spiritual reclamation of prisoners. It was known that Ordinaries specialised in obtaining confessions from prisoners which they wrote up in pamphlet form for profitable sale on the streets. The outside ministers who gained access to the prison may have had a similar interest but without the same influence. In an earlier chapter it is argued that Daniel did this work when a young man and may have done it again in the 1720s.

The minister tells Moll that 'a Reprieve was not a Pardon'. Nor was it as certain as it seemed, for a fortnight later Moll was still dreading that she would be included in the next dead warrant in the ensuing sessions. In the prison, Moll meets her legitimate husband who was also threatened with the death penalty but not, as yet, tried. The minister obtains a Transportation Order for him as well, but only as a result of the intervention of 'some great person'.

These exchanges in the prison have the hall-mark of actual events which, perhaps, involved Daniel. It is entirely possible that Daniel made money by using his influence with powerful persons to get people released from gaol, or their sentences made more lenient. At various times in his life it is probable that he earned money in this way.

There is a happy ending. Back in Virginia with her husband, Moll finds that her dead mother has left her a plantation. She and her husband have the remains of ill-gotten gains and they are soon making money again. They work hard on their plantation and become prosperous. Her brother (husband) dies, conveniently. She is reunited with her son and all 'liv'd together with the greatest Kindness and Comfort imaginable'.

They return to England, Moll being seventy years of age and her husband sixty-eight, having perform'd more than the limited period of transportation...[and]...resolve 'to spend the Remainder of [their] years in sincere Penitence, for the wicked Lives [they] have lived'.

When he wrote these lines in 1722, Daniel was planning his retirement to the 'country' in Tilbury. There he could be reunited with Mary Norton and his Quaker friends. Daniel may well have thought that such a tidy and much to be hoped for resolution would be desirable for him, but I doubt that he believed that he would be able to bring it about.

Chapter 19

Escape From The City

I began my travels, where I purpose to end them, viz, at the city of London...
A Tour Through the Whole Island of Great Britain
Daniel Defoe, 1724–27

AROUND 1720 DANIEL MADE approaches to the Borough of Colchester about taking out a lease on forty acres of heath land in Kingsland, near Tilbury in Essex. Kingsland was poor agricultural land but rich in sources of timber, which he wanted to exploit. While estimates vary on the amount of money Daniel earned from sales of *Robinson Crusoe* and on other books he published around this time, he made enough to pay the thousand pounds needed for the lease. On the 27 August 1722 he was present to sign it at a meeting of the council.

His daughter Hannah was a co-signatory. Daniel had several purposes in involving his daughter. No doubt he genuinely wished to provide for her financial future.[196] Since 1706, as promised to the wider family, he had assisted with Benjamin's education; later, he had helped both Benjamin and his son Daniel study for the law at the Middle Temple. Involving Hannah in the paperwork for the lease and any changes to it had the advantage to Daniel of complicating any legal action that might be taken by a creditor or any other person demanding money from him.[197]

Daniel hoped to make money. There was a business purpose to his actions. The land contained various buildings and it was Daniel's intention to restart in these buildings the manufacture of bricks and tiles, which he had attempted successfully at Tilbury in the 1690s, and to develop a farm. He could trade more successfully by selling both bricks of various types and farm produce.

On such a farm, he could find a refuge from any who might seek him out in the City. In Tilbury there were good people who could care for him. There was Mary Norton, her relatives and their Quaker friends, they might look after him, if it transpired that he needed their help. He wanted to involve his son Daniel. These good people would be the kind of influence that Daniel junior needed. His son enjoyed being in Tilbury and maybe he could make his fortune there when his father was gone.[198]

There is no fool like an old fool. In his sixties Daniel began to trade again, using his network of factors and merchants, and dealing in a wide variety of goods. He sold timber from his land; corn, cheese, butter and veal from his farm, and oysters, anchovies honey, leather and cloth from his merchant trading. Daniel had always underestimated the capital requirements of financing the start up of a business and providing for its work in progress. Tilbury was no exception. Daniel was not willing or able to devote the detailed and steady attention to his enlarged estate to make a success of it.

Daniel entered into an agreement with John Ward, a fellow dissenter, for the establishment of a brickworks and the farm. When these plans did not work out he sought to diddle Ward who, being an obdurate fellow, sued Daniel. In 1724 Daniel could not pay the rent and Mary came up with two hundred pounds as a mortgage. It seems unlikely that Mary had that money; far more likely was that he owed it to her father. When Daniel could not pay the debt, it was secured as a mortgage on the land in Mary's name, with interest. It took Daniel four years to repay the loan.[199] Daniel disappointed the corporation. Twice, the Chamberlain's office records trips to Stoke Newington in pursuit of arrears and it was noted that Daniel was a delinquent payer.[200]

It is highly puzzling to the biographer to explain Daniel's shortage of funds. He was beginning to be able to dictate terms to publishers of his fiction and to obtain advances; he was working prodigiously hard in the production of a stream of profitable works, and old creditors had been paid and were fewer in number. Why then was Daniel in dire financial straits in the last decade of his life?

While Mary Tuffley would have been indifferent to what Daniel did for his own children or what in the future he might do for his daughter Sophia, now living in her home at Stoke Newington, she must have been concerned for the future well-being of her daughters Maria and Henrietta. But then, as in the past, she knew that she could look to her family for assistance, and that is what had been arranged. Meanwhile, Daniel had to care for Daniel and Sarah as best he could. Not only their mother, Elizabeth, was involved in their parental care, for Elizabeth had other children to look after, but Mary Norton who would have helped Daniel out.

Daniel knew that he would not be able to exist in old age without a source of money other than that earned from journalism or from the self-financing of pamphlets. In his lifetime, it is not likely that he made much money from pamphlets and as time passed he became less fashionable or relevant. Daniel was to find it hard to reach an audience when he could not do his own thing, as with the *Review*.

The hopes of political patronage finally passed with the demise of Harley in 1714. What was left to him now was trade. But involvement in trade had one serious disadvantage: unless entirely centred on Tilbury it put him back in London, where he no longer felt safe. He began to believe that he was being spied on and was vulnerable to arrest and humiliation at any time.

The commercial success of *Robinson Crusoe* surprised and encouraged Daniel. If Crusoe could be a success then other fictions would bridge his income deficit. He needed the cash. The great burst of literary activity in the period 1719 to 1722 was designed to fill Daniel's income shortfall. For a time it did, but as the receipts declined, and more was expected of him from numerous family members and from others, he was in trouble again. There was a brief moment when he could use his new-found money to build capital for the future, he tried his best to use it intelligently and well.

But in reaching out for his trading past, Daniel had not reckoned on one thing – old age. While the spirit was willing, the flesh was weak. Constant journeys to and from Tilbury were difficult and tiring for him now. Undaunted, and yet again, he set out to write into the record his past: his journeys around England, ostensibly written from activity in the period from 1722–26, but drawing heavily upon his days on the road as a merchant as far back as the 1680s.

A Tour Through the Whole Island of Great Britain is widely admired as providing a comprehensive view of Britain at work in the early eighteenth century. Social historians have tended to see it as by 'far the best authority for early eighteenth century England'.[201] In a way they are right, but in important respects they are wrong. The opinion is mistaken in the sense that it would be wrong to regard *The Journal of the Plague Year* as history. The *Tour* is an account of what Daniel Defoe observed and thought about as he travelled through Britain in his capacities as merchant, intelligence agent, gentleman farmer and fugitive, or rather what Daniel had experienced and felt able to tell the reader about.

The *Tour*'s great merits are often recounted. The narrator embarks on his task with relish: his voice is fresh and uninhibited, his vision remarkably sharp, and each part of his journey is as brightly and freshly observed as if it were today and the account was being given in the reader's living room. Each place is given life as he observed it, and there is often a telling and amusing anecdote to underline his understanding. In Dunwich, rapidly disappearing beneath the sea, fifty churches had been reduced to one. Daniel writes with an acute feeling for the mutability of things: 'By numerous examples we may see, /That towns and cities die as we'. Daniel's eye for process occasionally inspires as literature, but the mutability he mostly dwells on is the rise and fall of great families and the pretence of things for which he claims he has little regard.

As in *Robinson Crusoe*, Daniel busily assesses importance by a head count. In the *Tour*, numbers are wildly exaggerated for effect. In Lowestoft, the fish landed, cured and shipped to London are counted, although the reader cannot be expected to recognise the significance of the number, and sometimes evocatively, 'when Norfolk turkeys obligingly come on foot in droves of three hundred to a thousand to supply the London market'. At Wey-Hill the reader is told by a grazier answering boldly that, 'there were five hundred thousand sheep sold there in one fair'.

Daniel draws innumerable historical pictures. In Newbury:

the first line of the Prince of Orange's army were posted...where the Irish dragoons had threatened [in Reading] to burn and plunder the town, and cut all the peoples throats'. In Towton, 'the most cruel and bloody battle was fought between the two houses of Lancaster and York...there fathers killed their sons, and sons their fathers [and] 'tis certain no such numbers were ever slain in one battle.

The narrative perspective is that of a merchant at a time when manufacture, although in its infancy, was of great significance. There is little sense of colour or shape. There is hardly any revelation of person or relationships, although his travels must have resulted in fascinating and revealing human contacts. Harwich is revealed as 'far from being famed for good usage to strangers, but on the contrary is blamed for being extravagant in the public houses'. The reader will recall that in *Roxana*, Harwich people taunted 'Amy' 'with having in her terror [of a storm] confessed to all the men she had previously slept with'. Only Daniel knew the meaning of this, for these were the jolly jack tars he had slept with in these Harwich inns

When in Colchester, Daniel tells the reader that, 'On this shore are taken the best and nicest, though not the largest oysters in England,' we wish him to continue and tell us about his very own oyster seller safely snug at home a short distance away.

But the *Tour* succeeds in the way that an inspired tourist guide attracts today: it provokes the reader to visit or return to a place, to observe it afresh and to challenge, if he dares, the vision that Daniel has given.

Daniel Defoe lived his life in the City of London but as often as not he was not in it. When a young boy he had fled the City with his family for fear of the plague and then, twenty to thirty years later, for fear of his creditors or persecution for his sexuality.

He must have asked his parents, 'Why has the plague visited the City of London?' One question would have begot another, and he would not have liked the answers. These questions, which he asked repeatedly in *The Journal of the Plague Year* and in *Due Preparations for the Plague*, constitute a literary paradigm which seems to embrace the whole of Daniel's world; both of his imagination and of a busy, compelling and chaotic City of London under threat.

In this life, Daniel seemed unable to avoid behaviour which he thought of as being sinful and immoral. He cheated, fornicated and plotted the downfall of others; he disguised these acts from the authorities, civil and religious, but God would not be deceived, for even the fall of a sparrow was known to him. Would not he, a sinner, and others like him, be punished for their sins and in their lifetime?

In *Due Preparations*, punishment is predicted. The mother tells her son that 'a plague might reduce the nation to a state of barbarity... all will be filled with horror and desolation, everyone mourning for himself... and a messenger sent from God to scourge us from our crying sins'.

In 1722 Daniel is looking back allegorically in the disguise of history. At first, Daniel persuades his readers that he is telling a story of historical fact. It is known that during Daniel's life he obtained the weekly bills of mortality which counted deaths by City parish during the plague and which show the deadly and remorseless spread of it. He may have obtained the bills and had access to a journal kept during the plague from his Uncle Henry, the narrator HF of his story.

In Daniel's writing, and often in conflict with the concrete detail of the text, there is always a providential point of reference, but, unlike the mother, Daniel's narrator is robust and secular. For HF, it is always the responsibility of government to provide for a just and ordered society, and then for the individual to make his own moral choices. If society was not ordered and just, then the individual was bound to look to himself and, if so, men would fall into erroneous ways and society as a whole would experience the judgement of God's providence.

It was regrettable that it would follow from this argument that virtue, in itself, would not necessarily be rewarded in this life. Surely, it was part of the Christian message that virtue would be smiled upon by God? HF ponders the issue, virtue must have a value, individual sins must be punished, and virtuous men rewarded? If not, why should any man bother with it? HF does not find an answer to his question, for he says, 'I did believe that many good people would, and did, fall in the common calamity and that it [virtue] was no certain rule to judge of the eternal state of any one.' What HF observed was that there was terror in these uncertainties, and it was no accident that the plague occurred in London with its rapidly growing population, disease and crime. The City could not clothe and feed itself and the rich and avaricious grew fat at the expense of the poor.

HF says to himself that if this were the case, and he certainly seems to have thought it was, no one was really safe. A man might be in the very last stages of dying of the plague but not know it; he lay with his wife, ate with his household, worked in his business and walked in the street unknowingly, and then he was gone and others were infected.

The way out of this distress could only be by the route that would have saved people in the beginning. If the City of London was allowed to take charge of social affairs absolutely then good order could be established. The Court and its hangers-on had deserted the City, the pulpits in Anglican churches were empty, and now could be the time when good Presbyterians would occupy the churches. This in itself might not save the population, but it would be a beginning.

It was difficult to comprehend in the best of times, given the burgeoning growth of the City, how to dispose of the dead. But now, at night-time, the dead were to be found in almost every street. Yet in the morning, all the festering dead had been swept up in the death-carts and dumped in the churchyards. Somehow the City succeeded in burying its dead. In the two parishes of Aldgate and Whitechapel where the plague had raged violently, pits were dug:

> Into these pits they [the City authorities] had put perhaps fifty or sixty bodies each [then] larger holes were dug [soon they could not dig them larger and soon] they ordered this dreadful gulf to be dug – for such it was, rather than a pit. In some pits 'people that were infected and near their end, and delirious also, would run to those pits, wrapt in blankets or rugs and throw themselves in...and bury themselves.

The regulations for dealing with infection required the shutting up of houses and the prevention of anyone leaving them. In this way the spread of the infection could be limited at the cost of condemning all those within the house to certain death. It was a difficult policy to accept and many did not do so: they broke out of their dwellings and escaped across the rooftops, as soon as they could. And who could blame them? Some fought the watchmen to get out, while others bribed them. Time and again Daniel returns to the issue of private sacrifice for the public good; time and again, he was unable, to his own satisfaction, to resolve this conflict.

Daniel really needed to satisfy himself that there were means of escape as of right: not because you were strong and could overwhelm the watchman, rich and willing to bribe him, or agile and able to slip out of a window. In Daniel's many imprisonments, food and blankets had to be brought in and warders bribed so that prisoners could slip away. What statistics survive show that the majority of prisoners bribed their way out of prison and did their best to hide. However, the experience of the plague was worse than this, for people might escape from the building, evade the watchman in the street but still be unable to get out of the City.

With the breakdown in law and order came a vast increase in robberies and murders, even though the thieves could take little advantage from the goods and chattels they acquired. HF went to the post office where two men were talking at a window. Daniel writes, 'In the middle of the yard lay a small leather purse with two keys hanging at it, with money in it, but no one would meddle with it because they did not know but the person who dropped it might come back to look for it. I had no such need of money, nor was the sum so big that I had any inclination to meddle with it.'

The man in the post office decided to take it. Elaborately, with the assistance of gunpowder and a pair of tongs, he singed the purse and retrieved the coins, shook the money out into a pail of water and carried it away. In these dreadful times even the poor were careful of themselves.

For Daniel there was no absolute imperative in a decision to take money. Daniel did not recognise the commandments not to steal or covet other men's goods. The decision HF had to make was carefully weighed: the amount was trifling, he was not in need at the moment, others would see him, the owner might return at any time, and the purse and coins might be infected. This was an acquisitive society and a world of relative values. If it had been more money, perhaps not so very much more, then the purse would have been his: 'finder's keepers' and 'fortune favours the brave'. If he had really needed the money, HF would have had no difficulty in justifying taking the purse.

HF ruminates that in the face of a common danger the issues that divided people, such as religious practice and dissent, were of no consequence and tolerance was practiced, but alas, once the danger had past the people would split apart. Such a policy of toleration had never been Daniel's.

Some men believed they 'saw apparitions in the streets and heard voices that never spake'. They looked at the clouds and saw strange shapes and figures. They told others that they 'had seen a flaming sword in the sky with a point hanging directly over the City'. Once HF joined a crowd that had gathered 'to see what a woman told them appeared plain to her, which was an angel clothed in white, with a fiery sword in his hand, waving or brandishing it over his head. HF could not see this angel and, moreover, did not think it was there to be seen. Similarly, he did not put his faith in astrologers, although the trade flourished. It became common to see signs set up at doors: 'Here lives a fortune-teller,' 'Here lives an astrologer.' Nor did HF put his hopes in the wearing of charms, philtres, exorcisms, amulets or the signs of the zodiac.

On the other hand, what else did people have to rely upon? It was the physics and the apothecaries who had led the dash to safety away from the City. 'How many poor people found the insufficiency of those things, and how many of them afterwards carried away in the dead-carts and thrown into the common graves of every parish with these hellish charms and trumpery hanging about their necks.' In all these things HF is a thoroughly modern man: while he might touch wood or carry a rabbit's paw for good luck, he did not rely on either. He believed it was far better to depend on his own wits and those of others.

As a truly modern man Daniel looked for a scientific explanation of the infection. First, the infection was not home-grown: it was carried into the country on boats from Holland. No one caught it 'but who received it in the ordinary way of infection from somebody that was infected before'. Physicians believed that the infection 'may lie dormant in the spirits or in the blood vessels a very considerable time: that is it was incubated and thus a period of quarantine was helpful', but they were divided on how long this period should be. These views and the measures taken to deal with the infection were sensible: isolation, the burning of clothes, the imposition of quarantine were all helpful until such time as rats could be controlled, public hygiene improved and antibiotics developed.

When winter was coming on and frosty mornings seemed to purify the air, the plague abated. Gradually, life seeped back into the City. The bad old ways could be resumed. Indeed, life was worse than ever. It was difficult to understand the reasons for God bothering to impose his punishments if, when the going was really tough, he just gave up on his creation.

DESCENT TO
DARKNESS

1724 to 1731

Chapter 20

Roxana:
The Fortunate Mistress

That unhappy Girl...Broke in upon all our measures...she brought me to the Brink of Destruction...have trac'd me out at last...if Amy had not by the violence of her Passion...put a Stop to her...

Roxana
Daniel Defoe, 1724

AS WITH MOLL FLANDERS, it is easy to imagine that the character of Roxana, a woman of modest beginnings who becomes a high-class courtesan, is culturally derived. She is a composite of the excesses of the Court of Charles II, with its French mistresses, George I's German mistresses, and popular actresses of the day. The book has a very long title.[202] It offered the prospect of a salacious secret history and a mix of biography and sexual scandal. But whatever the social construct, what Daniel Defoe provides is, as ever in his fiction, a reading of his life and social and material aspirations and a critical moral commentary.

Roxana came over from Poitou in France in 1683. This was the year before Daniel's marriage to Mary Tuffley and two years before the persecution of French protestants came to an end. Here, the reader must be aware of Defoe's use of time, since chronologically the book ends at the same time as it begins.

Roxana's father was a wealthy merchant who could do well in London, unlike the other poor religious refugees who thronged at his door in pursuit of financial help. Daniel writes disparagingly of them as, 'miserable Objects of the poor starving Creatures, who at that time fled hither for Shelter, on account of Conscience, or something else'.[203] This opinion seems to fit oddly with the views expressed by Daniel in *The True Born Englishman* and elsewhere which are encouraging of immigrants and immigration.

These views may reflect attitudes to his own family who arguably might have suffered from such opinions and now wanted the door to be shut firmly behind them. While Daniel clearly recognised the value of trade and the importance of population growth in maintaining Britain's power in the world, there is something physiocratic in his economics; he seems to believe that at any one time wealth is finite and that if it is possessed by one person another will be deprived of it.[204]

Roxana grew up to be a comely and accomplished young woman possessed of 'Wit, Beauty and Wealth'. At fifteen years of age her father married her off to an 'Eminent Brewer' in the City for a marriage portion of two thousand pounds, and then, as with all Daniel's fictional fathers, he disappeared from the scene. He died. Here, the story is developing along familiar biographical lines. Daniel's marriage to Mary Tuffley was clearly a financial arrangement with the family of an eminent cooper for a marriage portion of some £1,500.

And so it proceeds. Like Daniel, the brewer is financially and socially feckless. He keeps servants and a coach and horses. He had an old father who helped manage the business but then, of course, he died. Roxana's father left her money, but in the care of her brother who, being a reckless merchant, lost all his own money and her inheritance as well.

Thus all she was left with was a perfect fool of a husband who lost his way as well as his money. He bankrupted himself, absconded and she never saw him again.

Daniel, when bankrupted in 1692, left his family by Mary Tuffley in the hands of her family. Probably, part of Mary's wealth was safely tucked away out of Daniel's reach and it might have been drawn upon to help them. As for the rest of Mary's potential resources, her father's will sought to keep Daniel well away from Mary's legacy. It must have been a series of events that angered and frustrated Daniel.

In *Roxana* the narrator's perspective shifts between characters with considerable adroitness. Despite the unreliability of the narrator, however, it can be seen that the similarities between the facts of Daniel's life and Roxana's story are strong.

Roxana states, 'My Husband had two Sisters, who were married and liv'd very well, and some other near Relations that I knew of, and I hop'd would do something for me.' But they did not do so. Daniel had two married sisters, Mary and Elizabeth, in similar comfortable circumstances, but so far as is known they did not help Mary Tuffley either. Roxana sends for the help 'of a poor Woman that had been a kind of Dependant to the Family' who arrives with an ancient aunt. Their advice was that as four of the five children were born in the same parish as a relative in a position to help, they should be sent there, but that if they were to be rejected by her they could be taken into the care of the parish.

This Roxana resolved to do. Her maid Amy contrives to get all the children into the house and 'marches off' as quickly as she can. There is some confusion about numbers. There was an odd child born out of the relatives' parish who 'was already taken Care of by the Parish there' [where it was born]. When the relatives discuss the situation, the number of children has been reduced from five to four. The uncle-in-law is kindness itself. He is a religious man and in a true spirit of charity brings the children up as his own, against the prudent opposition of his wife.[205]

Arguably, at this time, Mary had two living children by Daniel: Benjamin and Hannah, the first-born girl, Mary, having died.[206] Daniel was born out of their parish to Elizabeth Sammen and may have been included by Daniel/Roxana in her account.

Daniel introduces the reader to his maid by writing, 'AMY, (for that was her Name) put it into my Thoughts'. Amy's function in relation to Roxana appears to be as a guide to her innermost thoughts and an agent acting out her wishes, even when she has not received an explicit instruction to do so. This being so, it has been suggested, and I shall follow it, that Amy is not truly an independent person but an aspect of Roxana's psyche: the agent of her desires and needs.

It is part of my thesis that often Daniel is Roxana and that a gender reversal is needed to make sense of what is going on. The landlord has an eye for the main chance. In compassion for her distress, he gives her one year's rent-free tenure and with the children out of the way he can gradually ease his way into her affections. The landlord explains that, ' tho' he was under such engagements that he could not Marry [her for his] Wife and he had been parted for some Reasons, which make too long a Story to intermix with [her] own yet that he would be every thing else that a Woman could ask in a husband'. This approach is best understood by a gender reversal: it is Daniel who is seeking to help out with the rent.

As a reality check, it is helpful to ask whether Daniel was a landlord in the 1690s and, if so, might he have lived close-by, perhaps in a property of his own, to a deserted wife and children? Bastian writes that:

> there are records of an abortive attempt by Defoe to become a property developer on his own account. Some time before 1696 he drew up a project to pull down two old timber-built houses adjoining Woolstaple Market in Westminster and replace them by twelve brick built houses divided by a passage leading from the market to the river-side, but the scheme came to nothing.[207]

However, Backscheider claims that Defoe had bought the two houses and that he was told by Christ's Hospital that he could proceed with the development if he bought, and included in his scheme, a neighbouring property. Daniel became the sole owner of the additional lease, 'in March 1700…[and] appears to have lived there at least part of the time until he fell four years in arrears on his rent. He lost the lease in 1705'.[208] It is possible, therefore, that if Daniel lived there off and on between 1695 and 1705 he is the landlord in *Roxana* and that he is referring to actual events in his life.

If so, Roxana/Daniel was delivered of an illegitimate son whom Daniel/the landlord took legal steps to take care of. At this time he was described as a 'charming Child who did very well', but later the reader is told that although she did what had been promised to support the child at a distance, she had never cared for it.

In the course of this tale, Roxana encourages 'Amy' to have sex with him/the landlord, and for a while she was shared between them. If the perspective is changed there would be two men knowingly sharing the same woman. When children were born of both men they would have been pushed out into the care of others. Daniel is suggesting here that he made arrangements to support an illegitimate son. Roxana had a premonition that her landlord husband would be killed and sure enough when they went to Paris together on business he was killed. Later, Roxana is accused of arranging his death.

As it stands, the autobiographical account of these arrangements is unsatisfactory. I am inclined to think that the real story is of two men who find themselves sharing the same woman and having two children by her during this time. If so, this is a description of Daniel sharing with the Sammens, and Daniel junior is the illegitimate son. As a lodger, Daniel might have helped out with the rent.

Daniel is repeating here the story of Moll Flanders with the two brothers. A repetition of this kind suggests that Daniel might well have been part of a sexual triangle early in his life in one or other of the numerous household arrangements he experienced.

Roxana/Daniel then embarked on a style of life that needs some explanation. As has been argued earlier, it seemed obvious to the young Daniel that the road he must follow to glory and riches was one which led to royal patronage. Merchant adventures could lead to riches but not necessarily to elevation to the highest positions in society. Under Charles II common people could obtain the highest positions in the land by 'selling themselves' to kings and courtiers: Nell Gwynne could achieve as much socially as the most opulent and aristocratic of royal mistresses. A man such as the Duke of Marlborough could become, as Wolsey before him, mightier and wealthy than the king himself, although starting from a relatively humble beginning, but once favoured, such a man could prosper only with royal approval. The Stuart courts did not distinguish between female and male favours: sexual favours were enjoyed regardless of gender and rewarded by similar patronage.

Late in the book Roxana decides to marry her Dutch merchant. Their combined wealth was considerable. Then she hears a rumour that the Prince she had met and who is discussed below was still alive and seeking her.[209] Daniel writes:

> But in an evil Hour…the fine things she (Amy) had said about the Prince, began to make strange Work with me; the Notion of being a Princess, and going over to live where all that had happen'd her, would have been quite sunk out of Knowledge as well as out of Memory, (Conscience excepted) was mighty taking; the Thoughts of being surrounded with Domesticks; honour'd with titles; be called HER HIGHNESS and live in all the Splendor of a Court; and which was still more, in the Arms of a Man of

Such Rank, and who I knew lov'd and valued me; all this, in a word, dazzl'd my Eyes; turn'd my Head; and I was truly craz'd and distracted for about a Fortnight, as most of the People in Bedlam, tho' perhaps, not quite so far gone.

This is ecstasy. The Dutch merchant could, and did, buy a Baronetcy, and he would inherit the right to be called Count in his own country; she could become a Lady in England and a Countess abroad, which would be gratifying in the extreme: but, oh, to be a Princess!

There are explanations for such ecstasy other than a desire for worldly possessions and position. In London in 1727, there were show trials following arrests at Molly houses and private homes. The people arrested were ordinary people with homes, wives and children to support. Nevertheless, they were dubbed sodomites, paraded through the streets in carts and sometimes executed. A prurient public was regaled with accounts of what went on at these gatherings. It appeared there was competition to be 'the hostess with the mostest'. The very best dubbed themselves 'Princess'. London society was agog with the story of Princess Seraphina.

In the paragraphs that follow, I interpret Roxana's story with this in mind: that to Daniel Defoe it was necessary, of course, to accumulate wealth. The crowning purpose of his life was royal patronage which demonstrably led to wealth. But as important was protection against arrest on a charge of sodomy. Only the patronage of a class system and the protection of powerful men could save him from the worst and most horrible of punishments. The laws against sodomy were savage and arbitrarily enforced but it was the poor and ordinary that were attacked by the law. Those of higher station were immune from the threat of arrest and their power could reach out and save people. In his every day life Daniel did his best to protect himself but at any time an enemy could inform on him. The law was difficult to enforce because people needed to be caught in the act. However, in these show trials it was clear that there were agents at work and people might be caught. What was needed was a powerful patron who could get you released from custody before too much damage to your reputation was done.

Daniel was willing to do anything to achieve this purpose of aggregating wealth and buying social position, including the use of his sexuality. He achieved office under the Crown only when William III came to the throne. William was a practising homosexual. He surrounded himself with young men at all times in his life and gave himself unreservedly in his friendship with men such as Romney, Shrewsbury, Vaudemont and Keppel. When in Holland, Huygens noted 'the frequent private and lengthy visits to William's rooms of a handsome captain of the cavalry, Dorp'. In England, William's lifestyle was not considered abnormal. The Duchess of Orleans wrote, 'that nothing is more ordinary in England than this unnatural vice'.

William was generous to his friends and highly discreet. William's Dutch biographers, Henri and Barbara van der Zee quote Burnet, speaking of a king he admired but never liked. Burnet said 'He had no vice but one sort, in which he was cautious and secret.' They then continued by quoting Swift (a friend of Betty Villiers who had a close emotional attachment to William): 'it [the emotional attachment] was of two sorts – male and female – in the former he was neither cautious nor secret'. As for Daniel Defoe, his attachment to William was public knowledge. It is not suggested here that Daniel had anything other than a sexual fantasy about William.

After the death of her husband in France, Roxana was approached by a 'Gentleman' of a Prince sympathetic to her loss. The Prince was not a French subject. When the Prince first saw her he took her in his arms. The Prince rewarded Roxana with a small pension, other sums of money, and a grant of two thousand pounds a year. When the Prince visited her by arrangement in the evening, she fell to her knees and did not rise until given permission to do so. The Prince said, 'give me leave to put aside my Character…my Quality sets me at a Distance from you…[but I] resolve to make you happy, and to be happy with you…he took [her] in his Arms…[and she] lay with him all Night'.

The Prince came secretly on many other occasions and Roxana became pregnant. He advised her to go to a country house for the confinement. Daniel, when employed in his Crown office as accountant to the Glass Commissioners, set up a house and establishment in Tilbury.

The Prince had other mistresses but for the time Roxana was his favourite and he showered her with gifts. Roxana for her part wished the Prince to know that he could rely on her. She says, 'How my Lord…Have you kiss'd me so often, and don't you know whether I am painted, or not? Pray let your Highness satisfie yourself, that you have no Cheats put upon you: for once let me be vain enough to say, I have not deceiv'd you with false colours.' In the literal sense the statement was untrue. This is a woman getting on in years and almost certainly wearing make-up. It is far more likely to be Daniel protesting his loyalty when his sincerity has been impugned.

At this point, Daniel/Roxana seems to make a mistake. Roxana tells of a good figure although she has had six children by her true husband and two by the landlord, whereas previously she had talked of five children by the former. Mistakes as to the number of children will continue to be made by Roxana and by Daniel in real life.

It is not all plain sailing for Roxana/Daniel, she/he slips into depression, despairs at the folly of men of quality buying sexual favours, and is overwhelmed with the guilt of her/his abandonment of her/his children and the contempt of her/his relatives: 'I that was despis'd by all my relations, and my Husbands [Wives] too; I that was left so entirely desolate, friendless, and helpless, that I knew not how to get the least Help to keep me from starving; that I should be caress'd by a Prince for the Honour of having the scandalous use of my Prostitute Body, common before to his Inferiours; and perhaps would not have denied one of his Footman but a little before, if I could have got my bread by it.' It is a little difficult to share this emotion, for Roxana appears to be leading a very soft and enjoyable life and to be truly loved by an interesting and engaging man, which she freely admits on other occasions.

The language becomes more extreme. The reader is invited, 'to draw the just Picture of a Man enslav'd to the Rage of the vicious Appetite; how he defaces the Image of God in his Soul; dethrones his Reason; causes Conscience to abdicate the Possession, and exalts Sence into the vacant Throne; how he deposes the Man and exalts the Brute'. Is this not Daniel speaking of himself? He continues: 'had he himself [the Prince] known the dirty History of my Actings upon the Stage of Life, that little time I had been in the World, how much more would those Reproaches have been upon himself'. Is this not, and taken in its context, the language of the crudest form of homosexual exchange?

A method of communication opened up by the Prince is the use of a particular gentleman for whom 'Amy' developed affection. Later 'Amy' admits that she had met this man over 'a hundred times'.[210] 'Amy' confessed to Roxana 'that she lov'd the fellow so much'. While a relationship with William seems far-fetched, it is much more probable that Daniel/Amy had established a friendship with a person favoured by the Palace. The most obvious candidate is Thomas Neale, who had access to the Palace and was instrumental in securing Daniel's place as accountant to the Glass Commissioners.

Loyalty to the Prince involved a foreign trip with him. On this trip, Roxana thinks about the Prince's wife. She describes the Princess as the 'Best Lady in the World'. This kind and gentle lady knew that her husband had had affairs with others but she tolerated them. The Princess had been pregnant three times but had not produced a child. William's wife Mary was supposed to have been pregnant three times without producing a child, one pregnancy was certainly aborted, but there are doubts about the others, although not doubts shared with the general public.[211]

In Paris, the first husband, the brewer, is found, enlisted as a kind of Horse-Guard. He turns out to be a scoundrel and an unscrupulous beggar. He would put it about that he had a wife and five children to support in England whereas, of course, he had not supported them. It must have hurt Daniel to write these words. Being a danger to Roxana's new position in society, the husband has to be avoided and spied on.[212] All good things come to an end. William III died and Daniel/Roxana, wealthier because of him, returns to London from her 'country residence', resolved to continue her pursuit of both position and riches.

The next phase of Roxana's/Daniel's story is chronologically a period between 1703 and 1715 but with events that stretched to 1724, the year of publication. The period is divided into a prelude and two unequal phases. A first phase when she/he felt free to pursue fantasies of political influence, riches and social position, and a second and shorter period, when Roxana recognises that she would not realise all her fantasies and seeks a reconciliation with her past.

It is entirely possible to argue, and some have done so, that Roxana's mental health was in steady deterioration throughout her life and its contradictions finally led to mental breakdown.[213] I have argued that the contradictions of Daniel's complex personality were the result of an extremely difficult childhood. A breakdown of some kind was inevitable. It needs to be added that, if Daniel's story is to be properly understood, he may have come to suffer from a sexually transmitted disease and the 'medicines' used to treat it.

The first episode begins with Roxana's escape from France. There is a plot to indict her with the crime of killing her second husband, the landlord, and stealing his property. There is some logic in the accusation of theft since her landlord is legally married to someone else and she has no valid claim to his possessions. This prelude evokes Daniel's imprisonment for seditious libel in 1703. In both cases there was a logic which permitted incarceration, a 'deal' on the table which would enable release, supposing the accuser got an advantage, and death, if things went wrong. In both cases the good offices of someone else were required to affect an escape from the jeopardy.

Roxana was helped to escape from France by an honest Dutch merchant who could have kept her well and seemed to love her dearly. In rejecting his advances Roxana is turning her back on the boredom of trade to fulfil her fantasies of power and privilege. Roxana says to herself, 'that the Measure of Wickedness was not yet full. I continued obstinate against Matrimony'.[214]

Apart from London, Paris and Amsterdam were the two main centres for openly expressed homosexuality in Europe. They all became dangerous for homosexuals from the beginning of the eighteenth century. Penal action was taken on a large scale in Paris in 1715 and in Holland in 1717.

Back in London, Roxana is catapulted back to the reign of Charles II. There are two main reasons for the time change. Daniel is anxious to distance his story from the actual to protect himself from retaliation by people who would recognise themselves, and although debauchery and corruption was as prevalent under George I as the Stuarts, it was easier and more credible to write back in time to the Stuart period.

Daniel completes his disguise by the use of a number of techniques. He identifies people by name, but in a coded manner. He speaks approvingly of some: Sir Robert Clayton, for example, a Stuart financier of dubious fame who assists Roxana to grow her capital and income but who was in actual life criticised publicly by Daniel on many occasions.[215]

Daniel then gives his readers a literary spoof, one without parallel in English literature (and perhaps a spoof within a spoof), which has been passed down over nearly three hundred years without any public comment.

The reader becomes aware that he is reading a sexual fantasy. It is for Daniel a gay fantasy. It reads when interpreted in this way as part of the gay sub-culture of his times, redeemed by the quality of the writing.

Roxana, as Daniel presents her, is a woman in her late forties who has had ten children. Roxana tells herself:

> I was rich, beautiful and agreeable, and not yet old; I had known something of the Influence I had had upon the Fancies of Men, even of the highest Rank; I never forgot that the Prince de-- had said with an Extasie, that I was the finest woman in France; I knew I coul'd make a Figure at London, and how well I coul'd grace that Figure; I was not at a Loss how to behave, and nothing less than of being Mistress to the King himself.[216]

London at this time was full of cultivated and socially well-positioned young women. It would seem, to almost any reader, that Roxana's confidence in her sexual attraction must be over-blown.

Nevertheless, Roxana establishes herself in an apartment in Pall Mall, off St James, in the centre of London's thriving and sophisticated gay culture, with its Molly bars and clubs. Her lodgings were 'handsome… and very richly furnished [she had] a Coach, a Coachman, a Footman and a Gentlewoman [and]… 'walk'd sometimes in the Mall'. Roxana tells the reader that 'seeing Liberty seem'd to be the Men's Property … [she] would be a Man-Woman'.[217]

Then Roxana began to act in a new sphere. She observes that the 'Courtiers…were as wicked as any-body in reason could desire them…and that a Woman who had any-thing agreeable in her appearance coul'd never want Followers'. Roxana began to organise Balls at which 'fine Gentlemen came masked as in Masquerade, […] and played cards and danced with Ladies'. She believed that the king came, the Duke of York and the Duke of Monmouth. On these occasions, she dressed in her Turkish Dress and danced in a fantastic manner.

What Daniel is describing is what would now be called a 'drag party', at which men could dress up in women's clothes and other men, masked so that they could not be identified, for sodomy was still a crime, could dance, flirt and have sex with them. The Duke of Monmouth was known to favour indiscriminate sex, while the Duke of York was notorious throughout London society as being a transvestite.

Is this gay fantasy of Daniel's rooted in real life happenings? When Roxana/Daniel describes absenting himself from the scene for three years and a month with a person whose identity she could not reveal, it is known now that she/he is describing a homosexual affair. This period of time coincides with Daniel's visits to Scotland which took place in 1707–10. Daniel is describing his homosexual relationship with Sir John Clerk which was demonstrated in the chapter on Moll Flanders. It is interesting that Daniel could calculate the exact duration of this affair.[218]

How much else is taken from the actual events of Daniel's life? Roxana/Daniel encounters a Lord who wants to make a private arrangement and who turned to her and talked of love. Roxana responds that this is, 'a point so ridiculous to me, without the main thing, I mean the Money, that I had no patience to hear him make so long a Story of it'. This Lord was obliged to consider a financial arrangement worth five hundred pounds a year and occasional other payments.

Roxana/Daniel decided to be less accessible to others and her Lord gave her a new lodging where he could come at any time. Roxana/Daniel did well out of this relationship, 'for tho he did not contract for five hundred pounds a year…yet he gave me Money so often, and in such large Parcels, that I had seldom so little as seven to eight Hundred Pounds a Year of him, one Year with another'.

Roxana/Daniel became tired of her Lord who, nevertheless, persisted with her. His star was not in the ascendant, however, and although Roxana was grateful for his money, she had had enough of him. If pressed, she tells the reader, she could explain that she had good cause. (Might it be a cause of blackmail?)

The only person to support Daniel over the years from 1704–14 was Lord Robert Harley. He paid Daniel an annual annuity of four hundred pounds and numerous other sums for services rendered; sometimes he paid much larger amounts to keep him out of prison. Daniel never doubted that Harley would get him out of trouble; whatever the circumstances, he invariably came up with the cash required.

Harley lost power in 1708, regained it in 1710, and finally fell in 1714, at the end of the period discussed here. At the end, Harley was not in a position to help Daniel even if he had wished to do so. When Harley resigned in February 1708, Daniel wrote him a letter in which he said that he had visited Harley at his home in London and 'would be back the next night, as by your Ordr'.[219]

But for the growing evidence of Daniel's homosexual activity, the reader might think that Roxana's fantastic account, if Daniel is the subject of these events, is allegorical: not historical as a statement of fact. After all, it is clear biographically that over this period Daniel was prostituting his talents with very little discrimination and he may well have felt his wayward experiences as a form of prostitution.

There is little doubt, however, that Harley was involved sexually with Daniel. For Harley's money, Daniel did more than write: he gave sex and he procured it. Up until 1714 Daniel knew that he was safe from almost any type of prosecution because Robert Harley would not risk what Daniel might say if he was under arrest. Robert Harley would not dare to seek excitement in a club or a tavern, but Daniel could; Daniel did Harley's 'dirty work' for him. If this is seriously doubted, how then does any biographer explain Harley's overwhelmingly generous financial support of Daniel over so long a period of time, and his willingness to finance Daniel's public office with the Glass Commissioners for thirteen years past its due-by-date and at risk to himself?

Robert Harley was a remarkable man with many gifts and activities. He was a writer of distinction and, more importantly to this tale, a founding member of the Scriblerus Club with Arbuthnot, John Gay, the writer of the Beggar's Opera, Thomas Parnell, an Irish poet, Alexander Pope and Jonathan Swift. This group were committed to the ideal of mutual support and love for each other. During 1711–12 the Club met weekly, often at Harley's London home.

Outwardly, the group eschewed erotic homosexuality and described themselves as homosocial. Robert Harley in 'offering love' to Daniel/Roxana was acting in the spirit of the club. This obfuscation was necessary because of the danger of the times. There was agitation in London against homosexual behaviour and several arrests and trials had been staged. Harley was a powerful guarantor to members against conviction, but nevertheless the group maintained outwardly the idea, rooted in the concept of the 'English Gentleman', that they stood for epicene all-male friendship. However, it is known that Addison and Steele were a couple for some time and that there was other homosexual behaviour within the group. It may well be that their occasional public attacks on sodomy were really an attempt to defuse criticism.

In the spirit of the Scriblerus Club, it is entirely possible that Harley might have talked to Daniel of his undying love and of a bond between them resting on eternal friendship. What else they talked about at this time is a matter of speculation.

On her return to England, Roxana was anxious to discover what had happened to the five children she had left with relatives. 'Amy' was charged with the task of contacting them and offering financial assistance, while not revealing Roxana's identity. Of the five, two were dead and one son and two daughters had survived.

Earlier I have argued that while it is widely supposed that Daniel and Mary Tuffley had produced eight children, two of whom had died, that I believed that Daniel was not the father of them all. Daniel had fathered two of the surviving children, Benjamin and Hannah, three children by Elizabeth Sammen and two by Mary Norton. Further, I have argued that Mary Tuffley had children by other men. How many, it is not known, but they included Maria and Henrietta. Thus, when Daniel writes about his children, the numbers he quotes are entirely dependent on the context.

Roxana's son was amenable to offers of help and she assisted with his education. Daniel, of course, assisted Benjamin to attend Edinburgh University.[220] However, the description of this son as being employed as an apprentice in a humble trade does not suggest that this son is Benjamin who Daniel assisted to study law. The reader needs more information. There was one daughter amenable to Amy's questions, who could be assisted, and knew where her mother could be found, but there was another daughter who was challenging. The challenge to Roxana is confusing for Daniel's readers because it comes from this hidden and unexplained 'daughter'. The heartrending and chilling story of this girl's attempt to be recognised by her mother, which appears to end with her murder, takes up a significant part of the last thirty per cent of Roxana's story.

J.M. Coetzee, in his fictional account of Susan Barton's attempt to persuade a fictional Daniel Foe to write her account of being cast away on a desert island with Crusoe and Man Friday, introduces a child seeking her mother. The child says that her name is also Susan Barton. Once the girl comes to the door accompanied by a woman pleading her case. Susan Barton endeavours to persuade the girl that she is mistaken. She says to her:[221] 'The world is full of stories of mothers searching for sons and daughters they gave away once, long ago. But there are no stories of daughters searching for mothers.' It is true, of course: girls seek their fathers.

Daniel is challenging his readers to detect him but he does not wish to be caught out. It is time for a gathering of the suspects. Alas, there is no Hercules Poirot to assist. Readers of this story at this point in the narrative might well be willing to admit that Daniel entered into private marriages with Elizabeth Sammen and Mary Norton and that in total Daniel/Roxana appear to admit to ten children. But it is all very confusing. Who is the 'son' working at a humble trade and content with his lot? And where does this strange 'daughter' at Roxana's door come from and what does she want?

Readers might shrug their shoulders in confusion. But there is a serious issue here because as the story develops it seems to be the case that 'Amy' has murdered this 'daughter'. But was there the death of a child at all? And if there was, did Daniel/Roxana commit the crime? No body was found, at least to our knowledge.

'Amy', acting on her own initiative but in the spirit of the assassins of Thomas à Beckett in her willingness to do anything to protect Roxana from the threat of discovery, enticed the girl away and sought to bribe her to stay away. In Daniel's/Roxana's experience a large sum of money was usually sufficient to deal with most problems. But 'Amy' was unsuccessful. The girl wanted something more than the usual sum of money. The girl had taken to following Roxana around with a determination to confront her and to broadcast to the entire world that she knew Roxana as a courtesan, and that Roxana's attempt to disguise herself as a Quaker widow and then as the wife of a reputable Dutch merchant was fraudulent.

On the face of it, the situation is incredible. This Dutch merchant does not seem to be greatly concerned about Roxana's past. He was a man of the world and could have had few illusions about Roxana. Anyway, he was infatuated with Roxana and love is blind. It is difficult to believe that he would be concerned about anything this girl had to say about her 'mother', or that this newly married merchant would choose to abandon Roxana if he learned of her past escapades.

Daniel/Roxana writes, 'It was in this time that Amy gave me the History of her Greenwich Voyage, when she spoke of drowning and killing the Girl, in so serious a manner, and with such an apparent Resolution of doing it, that as I said, put me in a Rage with her, so that I effectually turn'd her away from me…and she was gone.'

The context for this chilling episode is important. Roxana had taken refuge in a Quaker's house. This is almost certainly the house of Mary Norton and the exchanges between Roxana and the Quaker woman read as real exchanges. There is an intimacy and discretion between the two people. It becomes clear that Mary knows nothing of what happens when Daniel goes elsewhere, or what he is up to. She covers for Daniel and the less she knows the better.

From the story it is clear that the child knows a good deal about Roxana/Daniel and where she/he lived, the places they visited and personal information about her/him. Daniel writes, 'I (Roxana) was now under a new Perplexity; for this young Slut gave so compleat an Account of everything in the Dress, that my friend the Quaker colour'd at it.' If this girl is Roxana's daughter this unpleasant and impersonal manner of talking about her is strange. The girl is certainly well-informed about Roxana's goings-on. The 'young slut' had been present at the house in Pall Mall where Roxana had worn the dress and had danced. The dance has been described by me as a 'drag party'. What was this 'young slut' really doing there?

In *Roxana*, *Moll Flanders* and *Colonel Jack,* Daniel uses signifiers: words and terms which would indicate to contemporary readers other hidden or less explicitly expressed meanings. When 'Amy' was seeking to persuade this girl to take the money and go away, she met her in Greenwich Park. Daniel's contemporary readers would know the park to be a notorious pick-up point for prostitution. When 'Amy' fails, she puts the young woman into lodgings there.

Roxana, who had agitated so long about whether to go to France or Holland, eventually leaves for Holland with her spouse and his son, leaving the management of her affairs with the Quaker wife/Mary, with whom she had lodged. Daniel/Roxana writes, 'Here, after some years of flourishing, and outwardly happy Circumstance, I fell into a dreadful Course of Calamities, and Amy also [so somehow, without explanation, they were a pair again, she and Amy] …I was brought so low again, that my Repentance seem'd to be only the Consequence of my Misery, as my Misery was of my crime.' What was the crime?

In all of this the Quaker widow played a major part. She was supportive, loyal and accommodating to Daniel/Roxana. She was a simple widow but showed remarkable poise and good sense. Even to the end, and in the knowledge of what he got up to in London, she stood by him and continued to play a part in his affairs. She hung in the wind.

Well, did Daniel/Amy kill this troublesome child? It is not at all clear that he/she did because Daniel might mean that he 'put her out of his way'. There is form. Three times in his fictions, Daniel writes of the temptation to kill the little girl in the alleyway from whom he wishes to steal a necklace, in order not to be caught out in the act of doing so. But he did not do so, did he? And then there is the disappearance of his own younger brother, as fictionalised in *Robinson Crusoe*, and the abduction of Bob in *Captain Singleton*. But, how could he be accused of a crime when it is not at all clear that there was one, or, if there was, whether he had been involved. In *Moll Flanders*, the Justice who sentenced Moll to hang had had enough. Moll was known, she had form too, and though her story was plausible, as Daniel's often were, he found her guilty nevertheless. And then the Justices might well have had information about other crimes which Daniel has not confirmed for his readers but only hinted at. The language used by Daniel in describing dreadful events needs to be read carefully. The circumstances are troubling and the mood is dark. But there is no corpse and the principals get on with their lives.

That, Ladies and Gentlemen, might be the summary of the case put before a jury by a Judge. As it stands, there is no alternative for the Court of Public Opinion other than to dismiss the case for lack of evidence. There is no case to answer. Or is there?

Roxana's story, unlike Daniel's other fictions, does not have a happy ending. It becomes a dark tale as does Daniel's own. Out of this confusion there is no repentance. All that can be said is that for a moment there is grief and a foreboding that all is not well.

Chapter 21

Crime

I remember I had occasion to wait upon Mr Jonathan...I came again and again [but] it being only a silver-hilted sword...there was no coming at it.

The Life and Actions of Jonathan Wild
Daniel Defoe, 1725

IT WAS AN AGE of crime and Daniel was a person of criminal mentality who committed crimes. Of course, one man's criminal offence is another man's peccadillo but by any reasonable measure defrauding your business partners, fellow investors and creditors would be regarded as criminal. Stealing a horse is more than a misdemeanour and robbing your relatives, except in a divorce court, is surely more than a frowning matter.

Some crimes evoke sympathy. Daniel's ordeal on the pillory arouses immediate indignation because he was the victim of an unjust use of power. There is a basic principle at stake: the individual right to speak one's mind and the liberty of the press to make it possible to do so. An individual with criminal intent may claim this right, however, and he is entitled to do so.

An unjust criminal law evokes protest. When William Brown was charged with sodomy in 1726, a crime recorded in graphic detail at his trial as a 'put up job', he pleaded guilty and offered a simple defence. He stated that he believed 'there is no Crime in making what use I please with my own Body'. Of course, today it is accepted that he has such a right, but we regard it as wrong to profit from the sale of our neighbour's body or to traduce his children.

There will always be controversy about the causes of crime. It is difficult not to accept that a propensity to commit crime can be developed in some people at a very early age and that it would be encouraged by poor methods of detecting and deterring offences, but statistically, wherever there is great wealth conspicuously on display, and vast inequality in its distribution, crime flourishes. It did so in London in the early eighteenth century. Primitive criminal justice and penal systems and inadequate policing were unable to deal with rising crime. Honest citizens were in an uproar and demanded severe sentences, the breaking up of criminal gangs and civic action to change matters for the better. In the 1720s London was at the centre of rising crime and public uproar; those like Daniel, who lived at the edge, were in great danger.

The cynic might think, 'well nothing has changed then', but he would be wrong. In the eighteenth century it was far, far worse: a poor, female or disadvantaged person could be hanged publicly for over two hundred crimes as petty as stealing a necklace or committing a wrongful sex act. They could be left to rot in a diseased and dank prison cell until all debts were paid, but if you were rich you had little to fear unless you were excessively ambitious for political power or incredibly stupid.

Ultimate power over policing in the City lay with the Privy Council working through a Recorder in the City and the High Burgess in Westminster. London was loosely defined. The Lord Mayor of London, whose power diminished beyond the City Walls, had little to do with the High Burgess. Death Warrants were confirmed by the Privy Council and so at the highest level they could be put aside and some other penalty, such as transportation, substituted for them. Justices of the Peace were the practical instruments of the state in administering the law. They were assisted in their tasks by a motley crew: sometimes by a High Constable but most commonly by beadles, the watch, city marshals and various bodies of men under the sheriffs.[222] Constables were unpaid and selected by rota but the best of them could become regular, although unofficial, paid policemen. There were others: the Privy Council had its own police, the King's Messengers; the Press Messengers operated against authors and the press; the Sheriffs were assisted by their Sergeants, Javelin Men, bailiffs, prison officers and men recruited to deal with emergencies, also the court of Aldermen in the City had its own small police force. The powers of these forces of law and order overlapped, so creating rich opportunities for villains to work the system. But what helped the professional villain most was that the system was corrupt.

There was little public money to support the system. At the highest level, offices were bought and those who had purchased them expected, in the absence of a fat gratuity from the state, to earn their money corruptly: mostly, but unpredictably, those brought before them could buy their freedom from the justices themselves or by bribing or intimidating the witnesses – but not always.

Paradoxically, those who were most successful in filling public offices were most likely to administer justice fairly. Sir William Thomson, the City Recorder from 1713–39, who found the courage when a Recorder to do his duty and take on Jonathan Wild, was also Solicitor General and Baron of the Exchequer and a Member of Parliament for Ipswich.

Those who feared publicity most, such as Daniel, needed to be able to buy themselves out of trouble immediately and without publicity. When Daniel commented in the *Review* about prosecutions for sodomy in 1707, his article was concerned only with the unprecedented publicity given to the trials. He argued that publicity was a 'Bad Thing' and that the trials of sodomites should be carried out in secret.[223]

The evasion of publicity and the corrupt system itself was threatened by a kind of democracy from the street supported by the Crown. In 1690, the Society for the Reformation of Manners was established in Tower Hamlets in London. The declared purpose of the society was the suppression of bawdy and Molly houses, street prostitution, profanity, and the improvement of general manners. The societies spread throughout London and across the country.

The societies had a systematic and inventive way of working. They networked, passing information between themselves and the authorities. Each society established an organisation of four stewards per ward, two for each parish, and a general committee. These representatives gathered the names and addresses of offenders and informed the local Justice of the Peace. If prosecution was not initiated they took their own or paid others to do so. In the thirty-six year period to 1726 it has been estimated that the societies were responsible for over ninety thousand prosecutions.

Corrupt systems are tenacious in their own interests. In August 1729 the Reverend William Rowland accused two Justices of the Peace in the Middlesex Sessions of letting several persons accused of sodomite practices escape when they had been brought before them. The Justices took offence, arrested Rowland and condemned him to stand in the pillory at the end of Chancery Lane, to the indignation and concern of the local population.

By 1724 Daniel was no longer working with Nathaniel Mist, the proprietor of *Mists Weekly Journal*. Twice, in 1718 and 1720, Mist was gaoled for seditious articles for which he blamed Daniel. It was a difficult relationship, for Daniel was being paid by both the government and Mist. The truth of this must have become known by Mist but as he needed Daniel's talents as a contributor he tolerated what he knew and disliked. At any time violence might occur between them. It was no secret that Mist had Jacobite leanings and that Daniel owed it to the government to restrain him, but Daniel may have been responsible for getting him gaoled or released or both. The rights and wrongs are difficult to assess but the practical result of their falling out was that Daniel lost his last journalistic assignment. He could claim to be a professional writer and earning good money but this was never enough for him.

By 1722 it seems probable that Daniel began to work for *Applebee's Weekly Journal* which specialised in the reporting of crime. Applebee had access to Newgate Prison and its Ordinary. Applebee's reporters took down prisoners' confessions, wrote them up and published them. These confessions fell into the literary genre of criminal confessions which had been popular in some form or other for over a hundred years. There is no doubt that crime reporting was of immense fascination to Daniel and that he had involved himself in it for most of his adult life.

William Lee claimed that Daniel was busy reporting on crime for Applebee, that he was Applebee's man, whereas earlier he had been Mist's. There was a great public curiosity about convictions under the new criminal laws and in crime stories. Applebee's were keen to exploit the market and Daniel's skills might well have been in demand. If Lee is right, Daniel had moved away from political reporting into fiction at this time and was evolving into a professional writer.

In addition, and spoiling the neatness of 'career' choice, Lee claimed Daniel's authorship of numerous other articles for Applebee including those in support of the Anglican Church. The evidence for all these attributions is virtually non-existent: they rely on Lee's feelings that Daniel's was the guiding hand behind a diverse range of contributions and styles. Furbank and Owens de-attribute all the Applebee articles and fiction and their logic is sound. However, William Lee is not always wrong. If there was money in it, Daniel would have been alert to earning it and he was entirely capable and willing to write in any guise so long as he could do so secretly. His fictions between 1719 and 1724 were all written anonymously.

Richard Holmes, who has considered the evidence recently[224], concludes that Daniel was the author of at least two of the five biographies on the lives of John Sheppard and Jonathan Wild. I agree with Richard Holmes's judgement. I think Daniel wrote *The True and Genuine Account of the Life and Actions of the Late Jonathan Wild*, published by Applebee in 1725. Logically, as I accept this, but without the same certainty, I must accept that there is some likelihood that he did other work for Applebee and this may have included biographies of John Sheppard.

Richard Holmes believes that *The True and Genuine Account* is much better written than the others he considers, and in the style of Defoe, which it is, but my reasoning for authenticating it is different. Daniel has a habit of introducing himself in a work, usually by a change in tense, as a sign of his authorship. He does this in *The True and Genuine Account*. The reader of this biography becomes aware of similarities with other Defoe fiction. A great deal of the first half of the book is devoted to the ingenious ways in which Wild organised his fencing of stolen property. Wild has thought through every angle of these deceptions. The reader knows from *Colonel Jack* and *Moll Flanders* that Daniel is as knowledgeable as Wild.

Daniel shows himself extremely well informed about changes in the law which made it a felony to receive any reward for the recovery of property and about the effects of this law on Wild's activities. Wild was forced to turn to other crimes: burglary, blackmail and the exploitation of children.

Wild was a short and brutal man with surprisingly astute powers of organisation. Clearly, Daniel admires his versatility and cunning, the way Wild stood back and used others, and the ease and skill of his deceptions. The Defoe reader realises that he has seen this roguery before. In *Colonel Jack* the three Jacks are busy with all these crimes even including scams with bills of exchange.

That is not all that is familiar. In both *Colonel Jack* and *Moll Flanders* the principals learn to change the nature of their crimes as the legal framework changes. When Daniel tells of Wild, late in his regime of crime, exploiting, 'the young generation of thieves' and corrupting the poor children of

London, his accusation is sexual. Daniel writes, 'many a boy he has picked up in the street…to breed them up to thieving, and to ripen them for the devil'.

From other sources we know how Wild used these boys: they were bait to entrap sodomites who were then pounced upon, arrested for sodomy or, if they preferred, obliged to pay hefty fines. This villainy was certainly a way around the new anti-racketing laws and the victims were hardly likely to complain.

In *Colonel Jack,* Daniel writes of poor boys on the street who 'all made a shift though were so little to keep from starving', who 'slept under the nealing houses' and 'failed not to fall among a gang of naked, ragged rogues…wicked as the devil could desire to have them be at so early an age, and ripe for all the other parts of mischief that suited them as they advanced in years'.[225] These are not the observations of Daniel's childhood but of his youth: they are the reflections of a young male on the streets.

And then, suddenly, Daniel gives the game away. He writes, 'I had occasion to… wait upon Mr Jonathan with a crown in my hand.' It was a down payment to begin the task of recovering a lost article, which improbably turns out to be 'only a silver-hilted sword'.[226]

The cynical reader would conclude that no one as street-wise as Mr Defoe would seek the assistance of the notorious Jonathan Wild and that there must be another cause. Impetuous and incautious, Daniel immediately reveals to the reader the nature of his involvement. He introduces a 'Lady' who is 'seeking the recovery of a gold watch with trinkets and some diamonds about the watch'. She offers the enormous sum of twenty guineas for its recovery and in the end pays much more. Every reader knows what is coming. Who on earth, they might ask, was responsible for exposing a 'Lady' to the charms and stratagems of Wild? It is just too absurd.

Richard Holmes suggests that 'in his smoothly bamboozling a respectable lady client' Wild shows us his power over women. Wild does show what a smooth operator he is with the ladies, but readers of earlier chapters of this book will recognise that the 'Lady' in question, the one he is bamboozling, is a man pretending to be a woman. Wild is equally adept at being smooth with them. On the occasion that Daniel describes, Wild is being given a pay off by Daniel and enjoying the confrontation with him.

This ominous connection will be seen to have dreadful consequences for Daniel, but in the immediate, it gave him the strongest motive to write on Wild and no little excitement and gratification at his demise.

A reader will pose an obvious question. Was Daniel a real criminal and, if so, did he commit crimes that would concern us today? There is no doubt that Daniel was always attracted to crime and criminals and that he wrote criminal confessions and, later, biographies, but if this made someone a criminal, we would have the deepest suspicions about Agatha Christie.

It has been argued that criminal biographies are best understood 'as a kind of cultural practice, as socially determined and socially sanctioned discourses which in one way or another, 'glossed over' or made tolerable sense of criminals, their crimes, and the punishments they have to suffer'.[227] From this it can be argued that the criminal in written texts is essentially mythic and that in raising this myth the writer offers readers 'an opportunity to explain puzzling aspects of their world surrounding questions of agency'. In real life this statement might be regarded as a slur on honest men exposed to the same or similar cultural or personal environments as the villains discussed.

When Daniel creates criminal characters, is it safe to assume that they are entirely fictional and to be understood as cultural and social constructs? I have argued that Daniel's 'criminal fictions' are largely autobiographical and that the reader can draw from them information about real events and relationships that were experienced by him. Of course, Daniel uses myth and other fictional writing techniques to gloss over these events and incidents (as he did in real life), but the reader gains the impression that the writing, which is almost always in first person narrative, reveals Daniel the author.

The question remains. Was he (did he) actually do some of the things he writes about, or is he drawing only upon street observations and the chat he heard when in prison? It is best in addressing the questions to start at the beginning. Was Daniel as a young man involved in street or other crime for which he might have been punished? His appearance might offer a clue. All his life Daniel was reluctant to have his likeness portrayed. The rare exceptions are intended to portray him in a statesmanlike fashion for particularly portentous publications. Nottingham, when seeking his arrest, had no compunction in stating that he had 'a large mole near his mouth' and his enemies did not draw back in describing him as having, 'Warts, Wrinkles, Wens and other Flaws'.[228] However, 'official' or formal paintings show him without defect.

There is a simple explanation. Daniel was vain and the painter obliged by brushing out the principal defect – the wart, mole, or wen – and by taking the portrait from his good side. But the deformity may have another explanation. At some time, he may have been branded and later sought to disguise or remove the disfigurement.

In England, branding was common until the reign of Queen Anne. A prisoner found guilty of a capital crime was asked whether he had anything to say before sentence of death. At which point, he could plead Benefit of Clergy. The prisoner would be asked to read verse 1 of Psalm 51 of the Bible in Latin. If he succeeded (sometimes with the assistance of a court chaplain) his sentence would be a whipping or a fine. The practice was then to brand the prisoner so that the plea could not be repeated were the prisoner to be before the court again. This was usually done on the palm of the hand but sometimes, well into the reign of William III, on the cheek. Branding was also a punishment in its own right when for some reason it was thought useful to keep the prisoner alive.

If Daniel had offended when abroad, branding would have been more likely than in England. During Daniel's overseas journeys, when he was in his teens, he may well have fallen foul of offences that were avoidable in England. Branding might have been a penalty he incurred for killing a man in a duel.

In the numerous attacks on Daniel's reputation in the press, it is tempting to read that behind some of them is a secret agenda. When Daniel is forced to declare himself innocent of charges arising from the reformation agenda, of 'drinking, whoring and swearing', it is tempting to conclude that he is handling the easier part of a wider accusation, for the prelude to lewd behaviour was a street invitation from a stranger to drink beer in a tavern. Similarly, when such a critic mocks him for his Latin, there might well be an assumption that he learnt what Latin he knew from a court chaplain.

As I have suggested, the evidence from Daniel's fiction comes closer than mere conjecture. The possibility is that Daniel not only knew but at some time associated with Jonathan Wild, the master criminal who was hanged for his crimes. In 1715 Wild took lodgings at Mrs Seagoe's in Little Old Bailey and, later, in a house in Great Old Bailey. Daniel, off and on, had lodgings of some sort in the Old Bailey from 1706 until his dying days in 1730.

Daniel's biographical account of Wild in *A True and Genuine Account* is highly controlled and focuses on Jonathan alone. Missing is any mention of Charles Hitchen, the Under City Marshall, who put Jonathan into business when he appointed him his deputy in 1713. Their partnership lasted a year. In 1718 Hitchen, fighting a turf-war, tried to discredit Wild by attacking him in pamphlets of astonishing frankness. He set out to describe every stage of Wild's career and activities. Wild retaliated with a pamphlet of his own. Both men misunderstood the effect of their pamphlet war on public opinion. It hastened the day when both of them would come to grief.

Hitchen was a notorious homosexual and so were his 'boys'. He had bought his public position for £700 and was determined to get a return on his money. Hitchen is often described as 'a large, ungainly and... comic figure', but he was effective in many ways. Daniel must have known Hitchen and his lieutenants, William Field and Christopher Plummer. Unfortunately, it is not known which of these two master thieves, Wild or Hitchen, Daniel admires most; because of Wild's capture of John Sheppard, it might be supposed that Daniel's admiration was restricted to Wild but as he dare not write about Hitchen, it is impossible to know.

Daniel must have known John Sheppard the thief and escapologist because it is impossible to write including all the detail seen in the works credited to Daniel without the benefit of intimate discussions with him. If Daniel can be attributed with two biographical works on John Sheppard, *The*

History of the Remarkable Life of John Sheppard and *A Narrative of all the Robberies and Escapes of John Sheppard*, both of which were published anonymously by Applebee in 1724, it would be a remarkable achievement. They are very different works. The *History* is in many ways too crude to be wholly attributed to Daniel, but there are passages of brilliance. It is this inconsistency that suggests that in this biography, as in others, Daniel is editing other people's work. It can be imagined that an editor had thrown it to him across a desk with an invitation to soup it up, or the opposite, Daniel perusing it and exclaiming, 'Is this the best you can do?' – and then offering to spin it into something much better.

A Narrative is brilliantly written in the first person. The text is ambiguous, as is Daniel's narrative perspective, and our admiration for Sheppard, which is instinctive, is always qualified by another judgement – the narrator's – that he may be a brutish and ultimately stupid and dangerous thief and best put out of the way for ever.

There is no doubt that Daniel was capable of writing both these works. It is an easy judgement to make that, when taken together with his biography of Jonathan Wild, Daniel had become a master of criminal biography. Like all great achievements, it could not possibly have been the outcome of a contemporary curiosity on his part but the result of practice over thirty years or more. The other side of the de-attribution controversy of so many Defoe works, is the probability – as has been argued earlier – of missing works. These would include many 'confessions' Daniel had written up as a young man which are sadly no longer extant or acknowledged. A dominant impression of at least two of these works on Wild and Sheppard is that Daniel wrote with very great control, particularly when handling a first person narrative. It is tempting to suggest that he was painfully conscious of the need not to cause unnecessary offence or to reveal himself where that could be avoided.

Daniel cannot be condemned by an accusation of guilt by association. Much stronger evidence than is presented here would be needed to establish criminal acts other than those that are known and admitted by Daniel.

While it cannot be known which of the many articles in Applebee's Journal, as attributed by William Lee, were really written by Daniel, what can be asserted is that those he did write were anodyne and prosaic – as were the pamphlets it is known he published under the pseudonym of Andrew Moreton. There were three: *Every-body's Business is No- Body's Business*, 1725, *Augusta Triumphans*, which contained a section entitled 'An Effectual Method to Prevent Street Robberies', 1728, and *Second Thoughts are Best*, on street robberies, 1729. Daniel makes many practical suggestions: regulation of the hours of public houses, the closure of 'Night Houses', the end of price-fixing, better street lighting, and regulating the functions of domestic workers (!)

None of these worthy causes would set the blood coursing through many veins.

The executions of both Wild and Hitchen removed enemies but there were many imitators waiting in the wings who were only too eager to take their places. In their little black books was the name of Daniel Defoe in the column entitled Sure Touch.

Chapter 22

Later Writings

The Glory of a young Man is his Strength says Solomon Proverbs xx.29 and one of first Advices after that Expression, is give not that Strength unto Women.

Conjugal Lewdness
Daniel Defoe, 1727

SOME TIME IN 1726 Daniel stopped writing for Applebee's and his journalistic career, which had served him so well, came to an end. In *The Protestant Monastery*, a pamphlet Daniel published in 1727, he used the pseudonym of Andrew Moreton[229] whom he describes as a crotchety old man living with his sister. Perhaps this was the problem: he was a crotchety old man and no one wanted to listen to his grumbles. But I do not think it to be his problem.

Up to and beyond this point his writing had continued to be admirable and he used his experience to produce serious fiction with an increasing control of his narration. In the later period he was to produce in 1727 two works of outstanding merit, *A Tour Through the Whole Island of Great Britain* and *The Compleat English Tradesman*. As an old man he was looking back, as far back as his days as a hosier and general merchant. Daniel admits to thirty years back, but in reality it was nearer forty.

In looking back he displays nothing of self-doubt. He does not maunder on about his actions and their consequences, characteristics which might be expected of an old man. On the contrary, he writes with relish of the past, his mastery of detail is impressive, and he recaptures the worst moments of a trading career with the emotions he experienced at the time.

Daniel does not always have answers to the dilemmas of his life and leaves the reader as puzzled as he is. It would be wrong to argue that Daniel, in looking back, never experienced the self-doubt of old age: the creeping anxiety that one had got things wrong; the inability to distinguish between small errors of judgement in actions taken out of good will and major misjudgements arising from unworthy motives. However, it is entirely clear that Daniel's self-belief was intact. Daniel retained an amazing resilience: he could pass on, with a steely resolve to undertake the next task before him.

In this book, I have made little mention of Daniel's conduct books. Perhaps this has been a mistake because they do tell the reader something about Daniel. But my reasoning has been that these books tend to confuse judgements about Daniel's character and actions. Daniel wrote them for two main reasons: they were fashionable and he could make money from their publication, and, secondly, that he could establish, admittedly in his own unique fashion, an ideal standard of behaviour. Thus, it is always possible to say of Daniel that these ideal values were his own. Sometimes they may be and sometimes not. Usually he was nodding in the direction of other people's values, which is no more than the acknowledgement that vice gives to virtue.

The question that mainly concerned Daniel at this time was how best to explain himself: to himself, and to others. The questions involved were not capable of answers and, therefore, best approached with a sense of humour and with the use of satire. Daniel had long since ceased to be a practising Christian, in the sense that this term would be used in his time, but he did believe in the spiritual presence in the world of God and the Devil, of good and evil. If he had been a Roman Catholic it would have been easier for him: he could have genuflected before an alter and made a regular confession. As a protestant, he was denied these luxuries.

As Daniel grew older he was mostly concerned about his own personal devils for which, he believed the Devil himself was responsible, and he set out to explain him in *The Political History of the Devil*, 1726 (later, 'political' was dropped from the title). The book is written in two parts. In the first part Daniel sets out to provide an account of the Devil's presence and the history of his affairs since his biblical expulsion from heaven to the creation of man. In the second part, he seeks to provide an account of the Devil's involvement in human affairs with advice on how to recognise his appearances, the various guises by which he works and his earthly agencies. Daniel avoids the obvious Manichaean error: he accepts that the Devil is not physically present on earth and that it is the Devil's spiritual being that is written about.

Daniel can make the usual claim that the work was thirty years in the writing. It is true that he wrote in the Introduction to the *Little Review* in June 1706 that his intentions were to study the Devil's skill in promulgating vice and to identify the machinations by which his agents are taught to conduct their crimes. In his words, 'to make due Inquisition after the Improvement the Devil makes in the manufacture of Vice, and to discover him as far as possible, in all his Agents, and their Meanders, Windings and Turnings in the Propagation of Crime'.

It is not the purpose of this commentary to assess the soundness of Daniel's religious convictions. Here he states that to believe in God as the essence of good is also to accept the presence of the Devil as the ultimate evil. As perspective is always a problem in interpreting Defoe, it is necessary to recognise that from a commonplace theology he occupies the middle ground. This enables him to satirise freethinkers, deists and Platonists while making fun of the superstitious.

The general tone of the work is jocular and humorous which is indicative that the work is not a serious attempt to present general truths but an opportunity to mock himself and others. Irving Rothman draws attention to Daniel's attention to tone at the end of the book. Daniel writes:

It is true, this is a very weighty Point, and might deserve to be handled in a more serious Way than I seem to be talking in all this Book; but give me leave to talk of Things my own way, and withal to tell you, that there is no part of this Work so seemingly ludicrous, but a grave and well weighed Mind may make a serious and solid Appreciation of it, in which a clear Sight and a good Sense may not see that the Authors Design is, that they should do so.

But this is not the judgement of posterity, for the work does not survive as a judicious treatment of the theology of the Devil, nor as anything more than an amusing account of the follies of men in believing what they do. What does survive is the puzzle of what the work tells us of Daniel at this point in his life.

The God of *The History of the Devil* belongs to the Old Testament. It is characteristic of all Daniel's religious views that they dwell on sin, repentance, punishment and retribution. Absent is the love and sacrifice of the New Testament. Daniel reproduces the old and theologically discredited theory that Eve was specially chosen by the Devil to lead mankind astray. He writes that the Devil took note that 'there was a throne ready prepared for [Eve] for the sin of pride…that she was of a constitution to be seduced…that …if he could delude her…make a Devil of her [he] could ruin her husband [and that suggestions to the contrary] leaves too much room to legitimate the supposition'.

By this route is justified a male treatment of women as inferior to men and the root cause of evil, for it is through women that the Devil exercises his designs. The judgement is without mercy or mitigation. Daniel writes:

I cannot but observe…with some regret, that the Devil was not mistaken when he made an early judgement of Mrs Eve…qualifying her to be snare to the poor weaker vessel MAN; to wheedle him…abuse him…delude him with her crocodile tears…and terrify him…[and] not all the noise of Vulcan's hammers could silence the clamours of that outrageous whore his wife.

All this is unpleasant enough. But then, in an extraordinary attack, and for the amusement of a lampoon, Daniel seeks to persuade the reader that the majority agrees with him that man's troubles begin and end with women. He compares Rochester with Milton:

Let this describe the Nation's Character,
One man reads Milton, forty Rochester,
This lost his Taste, they say, when h' lost his Sight,
Milton had Thought, but Rochester had Wit,
The case is plain, the temper of the Time,
One wrote the Lewd, and t'Other the Sublime.[230]

It would not matter that Rochester was just such an atheist as arraigned by him earlier. His sexual exploits or sins may have been regarded as the work of the Devil, but Daniel justifies them by his judgements of women, and

Rochester is redeemed by Daniel for being amusing about his proclivities and sexual preferences.

Laughing at the Devil is a theme found in *A System of Magic or, a History of the Black Art* (1726). This booklet is a companion piece to *The History of the Devil* and was advertised as being so on publication in 1726. No doubt Daniel recycled some of the information he had researched. While claiming to provide a system, it was no such thing. What Daniel provides is a lampoon of the development of magic from the early days of the Magi to the present day. He sets out to detail the new types of magic invented by the Devil following the flood. Daniel argues, much as he did in *The History*, against tales of apparitions and so-called miracles. But superstition does not appear to be his main target, for he occupies his space with an attack on the evils done by atheists and deists in his own time. He considers, jokingly, the possibility of using ancient methods of punishment on them but decided against it on the grounds that there were so many of them that it could not be practical, as 'a Persecution must necessarily at this time be so bloody, that I know not what City, or Town, Inns of Court, Palace, and College or University (our own excepted) which it would not almost lay waste, desolate and make void of Inhabitants'. In truth, atheism and deism cut the ground from beneath his feet for these beliefs isolated value judgements on good and evil to rational discussion. The morality of an action was being debated at the time of his writing in terms of its effects, shunting arguments based on religious dogma into the sidelines.

In 1727 Daniel published a remarkable work, *Conjugal Lewdness: or Matrimonial Whoredom*, which has puzzled and disturbed his readers. He writes of what he calls matrimonial offences which he alleges make a Hell of the sacred state of marriage. The litany of sins he describes reads oddly to a modern reader: marrying for money, position or sexual desire, premarital fornication, having sex with a pregnant woman, or when she is menstruating, masturbation, a woman demanding sexual intercourse when the man does not want it, and the infection of a spouse with venereal disease.

The treatise can be read as an attack upon men in their marital treatment of women and thus used to reinforce the message that Daniel believed in companionate marriage. Daniel writes that:

upon the solid foundation of real merit, personal Virtue, similitude of Tempers, mutual Delights; that see good sense, good humour Wit and agreeable Temper in one another, and know it when they see it, and how to judge of it...It would call for a Volume, not a Page, to describe the happiness of this Couple. Possession does not lessen, but heighten their Enjoyments; the Flame does not exhaust it self by burning, but encreases by its continuance; 'tis young in its remotest Age; Time makes no Abatement; they are never surfeited, never satiated.[231]

Daniel lays a trap for unworldly readers: this is a statement of the ideal. In practice, the ideal does not exist and adults must make what they can of reality, and for Daniel, marriage is a largely unpleasant affair. He argues that very few marriages are happy. Many take place with no consideration of the compatibility of the couple but for money on either side. For Daniel, the need for money compels a person into marriage when in all other respects he would be better off by remaining single.

In Daniel's family there seems to be a tradition of men remaining single. However, for Daniel, it was love of money and possessions that drove him into marriage, and what use was that to him, when in no time at all he had blown the money and was looking at a woman he did not like, and who did not like him, and moreover who told him so in no uncertain manner. Daniel argues for monogamy, for which he advances many cogent reasons; men should not be beguiled entrapped, snared and brought into a state of matrimony which they would regret as a living Hell.

Such an argument can only be advanced by a man who dislikes women and almost everything that goes with marriage. Daniel's own experience of family life was a long way distant from the ideal and his sexual preferences were elsewhere. The confusion of several 'marriages' and the responsibilities of providing for many children by several different partners must have been a daily nightmare.

As he grew older Daniel cared less for what other people might think of him, although it remained as important as ever not to rile the authorities in their various forms. In *Conjugal Lewdness* he was able to express, admittedly in a disguised form, a sexual preference never previously brought into the light. He embarks on a condemnation of the practice of marrying children.

Daniel recounts a story of an elderly lady who, seeking to prevent her nieces inheriting her money, asked a father she knew to let her marry his young son. This lady argued that there could be no real objection to her proposal. She would be in her grave long before him, he would inherit and everyone would be better off from the union (except her nieces who were anxious to inherit her estate). The father had his doubts but in the end he agreed. This is how Daniel described the outcome:

But even this unsuitable match did not prove as unsatisfactory as might have been expected; for it pleased God that this woman lived to such a prodigious age, that the little boy was seventy-two years of age when he followed her to the church to bury her, and she was one hundred and twenty years old. This story I had attested to me by a person of an unquestioned veracity, who told me he was himself at her funeral: she was sixty five when she married and lived sixty-two years with her husband; she indeed made amends for the disparity of years by this, that she was a most excellent person, of an inimitable disposition, preserved the youth of her temper, and the strength of her understanding, memory and eyesight to the last; and, which was particularly remarkable she bred a whole new set of teeth, as white as ivory, and as even as youth, after she was ninety years of age.

In writing in this way, Daniel was dipping into the medieval tradition of remarkable tales and legends. Examples have been given in an earlier chapter. Daniel rarely mentions anything in his writings which do not have an emotional significance to him. At one level in this account, Daniel is drawing upon the beliefs of the ancient Greeks: a man who has sex with children can draw strength from them and live longer, children regard the sexual experience as natural and are not harmed, and they in their turn will draw on these benefits by having sex with their own children. Daniel condemns various forms of sex with children arising out of desires to obtain money, such as abduction and dynastic arrangements, but he sees a difference in marriage to children, a distinction which is obscure to the reader.

Conjecture, in the absence of tangible proof, is easily dismissed. *Conjugal Lewdness* is full of anecdotes and old saws, most of which are given to amuse the reader and indicate the worldly wisdom of the author. They serve this function well. It can be argued that the issues of sex with children were within the cultural exchanges and practice of the time and Daniel's inclusion of the subject is natural.

Of course, all this is true. However, it must also be true that the notion of sex with children was in Daniel's head when he wrote *Conjugal Lewdness*. What this means in the context of his life depends in part on what the reader believes about Daniel's state of mind and personal beliefs. In many ways, Daniel's value systems are rooted in the seventeenth century and, in some respects it can be argued, in even earlier times. Arguably, the very concept of childhood did not take root until the seventeenth century. In earlier times, children were regarded as miniature adults and were dressed and treated as such.

Attempts to portray Daniel as a man in advance of the state of knowledge and of the feeling of his time invariably break down. In general, English people of the early eighteenth century did not share the modern sentiments of the personal importance of close family life within nuclear families. High infant mortality seems to have hardened attitudes to children; to care too much, when they might be swept away at any moment by unavoidable sickness, is not in human nature itself. In Daniel's fiction children are treated very harshly. They are abandoned callously at the convenience of their parents and cast into the care of others without any further thought as to their well-being.

Daniel was a man who expressed himself as a homosexual. It is more acceptable to regard his homosexuality as being in the Romantic tradition: he asserted his masculinity to demonstrate his power over others and in this way he broke through and made fun of a rigid class system. In Daniel's youth his strength and courage would have enabled him to be predatory at will. Later, as his physical strength could no longer be taken for granted, he needed to be accompanied by younger and stronger companions. As he aged and a repressive legal system closed around him, he could no longer pick up in the street with equanimity and blackmail became an ongoing problem for him.

I have suggested more; some happening which is almost beyond speculation: that when a child, Daniel suffered from what would now be described as child abuse. If this is so, then everything we know about abuse suggests that the crimes are visited upon the next generation and that Daniel sought out and replicated these earlier traumatic experiences.

When Daniel mentions a conversation taking place, usually through a third person, it often turns out to be a conversation of his own. Did Daniel seek and obtain, probably for money or some financial consideration, access to a child for sex? Did he attend a private drag party for sex 'where children were on the menu?' If so, and if an offence occurred in the 1720s, he was placing himself in great danger. Stoke Newington was a small community. It had its own Society for the Reformation of Manners and Daniel was well known. If something happened in Newington, it was extremely likely that he would be spied upon, informed about, blackmailed, and in danger of arrest. A life-long problem was becoming a present danger.

Daniel ends *Conjugal Lewdness* with a kind of threat. Daniel writes that he has not been able to find words to describe certain vile and perhaps unheard of practices. The crime he wishes to reprove cannot be exposed because special language is needed to understand it: 'The Dialect these people talk is a great part of the Crime; and as it is not [to be used to reprove them] I talk in the dark and reprove by Allegory and Metaphor.'

Daniel continues by writing that if these people do not heed his words then they could expect no mercy. 'If they cannot [mend their ways] let them expect no Quarter…My next Attack shall be personal…I may come to Black Lists, Histories of Facts, Registers of Time and Sirname …. ' How come?' enquires the curious reader, 'How would you know such things?'[232]

Daniel seems to be seeking to protect himself. The Black Lists may include the names of people participating in 'drag parties' or other homosexual engagements. He seems to be stating that if they (authorities/informers) come at him, he can defend himself: he will name 'names' in believable detail and they (his persecutors) had better think twice about it for a prosecution would get nowhere. Men would buy protection and they (his persecutors) would come badly out of the whole affair.

This need to protect himself might have been Daniel's main reason for writing *Conjugal Lewdness*. Daniel sounds as if he is pressed into a corner, and from it he bays his defiance and sets out his apologia in advance.

Chapter 23

Endings

Loose Thoughts at first…Burn inward, smothering with unchaste desires…Burn up the Bright, the Beauteous, the Sublime. And turn our lawful pleasures into Crime.

Conjugal Lewdness
Daniel Defoe, 1727

HE HAD AWAKENED EARLIER but had fought off the effort to remain conscious, drifting into a space somewhere between reason and nightmare, which he sought to command, as he had done throughout a long life. Soon she would come to his room, draw the shutters and revive him. He heard a murmur of voices and a clink of plates from the kitchen as she prepared early morning victuals. Although she said nothing of it, he knew that their daughter came in the morning to be fed at his expense. He did not mind. Not really, for she was poor and no one else provided for her. Anything in moderation, he said to himself, smiling at the absurdity of the proposition as it applied to him. But he was pleased that she was there and that she too could be relied upon.

It pleased him also to be in Ropemakers Walk. The street was shady and quiet, cut off from the City traffic. There was no real point in passing through so the waters that disturbed him still would lap elsewhere. He had been thrown up and beached beyond the tideline. In the first few months he had posted a guard at the City end of the road but gained nothing, for no stranger was ever detected and the presence of the watchman being noticed he had paid him off.

He hoped Elizabeth would be all right. He had provided for her and given her his jewellery, and he had left with her the name and address of a contact who was holding money. The money would be released assuming that nothing untoward had happened. Not that he expected it. He trusted her, which was more than he could say about many who had sought to profit from him. There was money in the house but only just enough. It had been a life-time practice of his to squirrel away money in various places where it would be safe. On the whole, people had been very good about keeping this money for him and for modest reward. He had trusted this woman for over thirty years and knew her to be good – at least to him.

Now was the time to be careful. When a man weakened, there should be no bad tempered shrews governing his well-being. You couldn't be too careful about that.

His working papers were in his library in Stoke Newington and there they were likely to remain. Sometimes he thought that they should be retrieved, for there was work to be done, but then he procrastinated, perhaps everything that needed to be written had been, and the world could go hang. He closed his eyes again until the sounds died away.

As the circumstances of Daniel Defoe's birth were mysterious, so were those of his death. Unlike his birth, there is significant evidence to consider but it is capable of many and surprising interpretations.

The logical starting point from which to consider events is Daniel's friendship with Henry Baker, a man forty years his junior, which started, according to Baker, in 1724 while Daniel was completing *Roxana*. Baker was to marry Daniel's daughter Sophia five years later. The source of the information about Baker's relationship with Daniel and his engagement to Sophia is Henry Baker himself and the Baker family.

On Baker's death a memorandum on his dealings with Daniel Defoe was found in his papers.[233] Additional evidence comes from letters written between Daniel, Sophia and Henry, some of which are in the public domain and some not. Henry Baker made copies of correspondence between Daniel, Sophia and himself and later these copies were made available by his descendants to the biographer Thomas Wright who published extracts from them.[234]

It was unwise of Thomas Wright not to use originals and to be completely frank with his readers since the suspicion exists that he did not see all the correspondence and neither can he assure the reader that what he has seen is wholly accurate. In particular, while much has been disclosed about Henry Baker's letters little is said or disclosed of Sophia's replies.

It is odd that Henry Baker and his heirs were so keen to get down on paper and into the public domain their account of what happened. The suspicion is created that it was important to Henry to be able to produce his own version of events should it be needed and that later family members acted to protect themselves when confronted with Thomas Wright's biographical interest in their ancestor.

Henry started his memorandum account by explaining that in 1724 his financial prospects were good. He had every reason to believe that he could find a wife with a generous dowry and that as he had already accumulated a thousand pounds in savings only an imprudent marriage could disturb his worldly progress. He explains that although he did not expect a generous dowry from Daniel, he saw no reason for anything other than a reasonable sum.

The saving of a thousand pounds for a young man who had endured a difficult childhood is remarkable. Henry Baker claimed expertise in the teaching of deaf and dumb children. It is worth noting the peculiar arrangements he negotiated for teaching them. His clientele included the very rich. The Earl of Buchan owed Baker £728 for Baker's work in the period 1727–34. Baker required a parent to enter into a seven-year agreement and there was an entry fee. Clients had to undertake by contract to keep his method of instruction secret for a period of seven years. It has been estimated that he earned £300 a year from his teaching.[235]

Henry is at pains to inform posterity that from the very first meeting with Daniel's daughter Sophia he had fallen in love with her. He describes her beauty and loveliness as a 'Bloom of Health that tinctur'd every Charm', and he maintains that after initial hesitation Sophia reciprocated these feelings. Thomas Wright is in no doubt that the correspondence is between two lovers.

Unfortunately for Henry there is something of Malvolio in his approaches to Sophia, which gives his story away, and something also of the painful honesty of observation of the naturalist recording natural phenomena, habits which oblige him to accurately recall Sophia's reactions to him and which are so revealing to the reader.

From the beginning of his account, Henry makes a mistake He states that Daniel had sought an acquaintanceship with him in Stoke Newington when he took up a teaching post instructing the deaf son of a man called John White. Baker, who, or so he says, lived with a solicitor named Forster in Enfield, where he assisted his children, was instructing John White's son at White's house on three days of the week between Wednesday and Friday. Being free in the afternoons he sought out in local cafes what he describes as 'People of Fashion'. He took tea and played cards.

But he didn't meet Daniel there or at that time. Almost certainly this account is not to be relied upon. John White's house in Stoke Newington was the house in which Daniel had lived until 1708 and which he then rented out to John White. Whether he still owned a head lease or the freehold in 1724 is not known but that he had let it to John White from 1709 is beyond doubt. John White still occupied the property when he died in 1731.[236]

The probability is that Daniel and Henry Baker had met elsewhere. Given that Henry Baker's guardian was a bookseller in Pall Mall, it is highly likely that Daniel met him there. It was in *Pall Mall* (my italics) that Roxana held her 'drag party'.

Daniel might have introduced Henry Baker to John White on the declared purpose of teaching assistance for a boy thought to be deaf. However, the source of this evidence is Henry Baker. It might well be the case that Henry was a lodger but there is no independent evidence that the boy was deaf, and every evidence, as is shown elsewhere, that he was not.

In 1727, when it is said that Daniel and Henry had known each other for three years, Baker received an invitation to meet Mary Tuffley, her two unmarried daughters, and Daniel's illegitimate daughter Sophia. Baker writes in his memorandum, written self-consciously in the third person, that:

> Mr. D...., [was] a Gentleman well known for his Writings, who had newly built there a very handsome House, as a Retirement from London, and amused his Time either in the cultivation of a large and pleasant Garden,

or in the Pursuit of his Studies, which he found means of making very profitable. He was now at least sixty years of Age, afflicted with the Gout and Stone, but retained all his mental faculties.[237]

At the time he wrote these words, but not when he first met Daniel, Baker knew that Daniel did not own this 'handsome house'. He may have known also that Daniel was not there all the time. Baker writes that on many occasions he was not able to visit him at the house.

In the garden Baker met Mary and the three girls (Daniel was in his study) but then suddenly he was on his own in the garden with Sophia and tentatively making an approach for her hand. According to Baker's own account he asked her, 'Oh! My dear Miss Sophy! Tell me. I beseech you tell me, is your heart yet engaged.' Sophia replied, 'Yes, Sir, it is engaged, to God and to my Father; but none beside.'

The immediate impressions of these effusive protestations of love are that they are hokum-pokum. The initial garden scene had been pre-cast. Daniel had set it all up. Henry Baker's advance is clumsy and Sophia seemed unwilling to co-operate. She tells him not to bring his hopes too high and then says, 'Don't pretend a Passion you do not feel.' If he knew her better, says Sophy, he would think less well of her. He perceived her mind uneasy. He tells her of a true love of his, Cynthia, who had died of consumption. Somewhere backstage the violins struggle to make themselves heard. And then desperately he plunges at Sophia, 'She struggling from his Arms, replied with some Emotion, I too have had my Lovers but never loved.'[238]

Henry Baker had not met Sophia before this discussion. Immediately upon introduction he wishes to marry her. From this point on, in all the troubled negotiations for a dowry for her hand, Sophia was to obey her father in whatever he decided for her. Baker displays in his correspondence the full range of expression of a poetic young man in the first stages of young love. These flowery expressions do not appear to have been reciprocated by Sophia, what we know of her is the stubborn way she supported her father in Byzantine negotiations.

Baker was an ingenious and intelligent young man whose system for instructing deaf children seems genuine, although to a modern reader it appears peculiar. Later, he was to become a member of the Royal Society on the strength of work he had done on microscopes. According to his own account, Henry Baker was, 'left by an unhappy father to a relentless world' and he knew 'poverty …, want …, contempt …, misery and ruin'. He was abandoned into care and then at the age of fourteen placed with John Parker, a bookseller in *Pall Mall* (my italics) where he stayed for seven years. In April 1720 he went to stay with a relative, John Forster, an attorney living in Enfield. It was there he developed a method of teaching the deaf by practising on Forster's eight-year-old daughter Jane, who had been born deaf and dumb.

Henry Baker's teaching method was to seek to gain the complete confidence of any child he was teaching by behaving as a surrogate father to it. The child was told to think of him as its 'Father'. As he had lacked a father in his upbringing, he seems to have needed to play the role of a father himself, but given that he had not really experienced the care of one, it might be asked what degree of awareness he had absorbed and what exactly he was seeking to convey to his young charges.

When Daniel tells Henry that he will agree to the engagement of his daughter, Henry drops to his knees and exclaims, 'Can I call you Father?'

The engagement to Sophia went nowhere while Daniel and Baker argued about the terms of a dowry or dowry equivalent. Novak writes there were signs of tension in the family at this time, and dark undercurrents. At first Daniel (H 240) argued that Baker must 'take her as I can give her'. He then offered something in his Will (he died intestate), then cash of an unknown amount, which was rejected, then cash secured on the house, which he could not do without the consent of another, which was accepted. All this took two years.

Baker had alleged that Daniel had no right to his lease, which was right, for as it has been indicated here the freehold was owned by a Mr Sutton, and the Tuffleys had made certain that the head lease was assigned to George Virgoe, a London merchant, in order to keep Daniel's hands off it.

There are conflicts between Henry Baker's memorandum and his letters. In the memorandum Baker writes: Mr D. would give no Security but his single Bond for the due Performance of the Articles, tho' he had an estate in Essex of £----- per annum and a new built house at Newington, either of which would have been a satisfactory security: but he pretended these were already settled for Family purposes, which he could not break through.

From his correspondence, however, it is clear that Baker's solicitor had told him that Daniel did not have true title to the house. Daniel had been telling the truth. The Essex estate was held in the interest of Hannah and the house for the benefit of Mary Tuffley's daughters. Securing a mortgage for the benefit of Henry Baker and his daughter Sophia must have required the consent of the Tuffleys. It was a serious matter for them because a mortgage would undermine their security. Ten years after Daniel's death, Baker bought the freehold from Mr Sutton.

The correspondence revealed by Thomas Wright became unpleasant and blame for it is placed on Daniel Defoe. Baker writes in letters to Sophy, 'Whatever disregard your father shows me can never destroy my love or shake my constancy; he may go on to slight me,' and 'Your father is greatly angry with me for no other reason but because he has misused me.' Then Daniel becomes an evil genius and 'He, like a curst infernal continually torments, betrays and over turns.' Baker maintains that Daniel is 'all deceit and baseness…his purposes are always dark and hideous… [and he is] under the necessity of being crafty, ungenerous and dishonest'. On 1 February 1729

Baker proposes that he and Sophy should take poison and die in each others' arms.

But suddenly the conflict is over and on 30 April 1729 the couple are married. Daniel had succeeded in renegotiating the lease with Virgoe and Baker had settled for a bond of £500 secured on the house. Soon after the wedding Daniel leaves the house in Newington and goes into hiding.

So what really happened? What follows is speculative but probable. Daniel had struck up a relationship with Henry Baker before 1724. It is probable that Daniel knew Henry's carer, John Parker. Nothing is known of John Parker's motives in taking into his care a fourteen-year-old boy from the parish; they may have been honourable or dishonourable. It is possible that Henry Baker had been fending for himself as best he could on the streets as Daniel may have done.

Daniel had been seeing John White's son, as revealed in disguised form in *Conjugal Lewdness*, and may even have taken him to a 'drag party' in Pall Mall and perhaps the party arranged by 'Roxana'. In the period 1719–24 this 'drag party', or another similar event attended by Daniel and Henry Baker, was penetrated by police or informers. Daniel and Henry Baker came under suspicion. To cover himself when prosecution drew nearer, Daniel needed a good cover story and persuaded Henry first to go and stay at Richard Forster's in Enfield and then at John White's house. It is not likely that Henry could teach White's son, even assuming he was deaf, because it would be unlikely that he could afford the tuition fees. The reward for White was money or deferred rent, and for Henry Baker the comparative safety of Newington, an introduction to Newington's gay life and the cover of a job.

In 1727 Daniel and Henry had been informed on again. Daniel might have suggested to Baker that suspicion would be averted if he became engaged to Sophia. What could be more normal than a father spending time with his prospective son-in-law? And anyway, there was much to be said for the cover of a marriage and a normal family life. Daniel might have come under pressure from the Tuffleys to get something done for Sophia and to get her out from under their feet. Daniel offered Sophia to Baker. In the end, Sophia thought it prudent and dutiful to carry out his command. But what did Sophia mean when she said, 'I too had my Lovers but never loved'. She might have been talking of admirers. If she knew the nature of the man she was talking too, she might have meant something else. Whatever was meant, Henry Baker thought it significant enough to record.

How real was the threat of prosecution? In 1726 the arrest and show trials of sodomites got very close to Daniel's home and would have scared him. At the time, and for some time before, he may have been paying protection money. Daniel may well have been shocked by an earlier notorious case in 1698, against naval officer Captain Rigby, in a case involving entrapment by a man called Bray, a member of the Society for Reformation of Manners. Rigby's defence was obscure. The case included allegations against Peter the Great in Debtford on his royal visit to London and ultimately caused the resignation from governmental office of William Bentinck.

In the 1720s the society was increasingly active in entrapping sexual offenders. There was a branch in Stoke Newington. Local clergymen and church members would have known Daniel.

Fortunately, Daniel came to the aid of posterity by piecing together the facts of his later life in *Conjugal Lewdness*. He could not help writing about his difficulties in a disguised form.[239] In Daniel's story recounting the marriage of a sixty-five-year-old woman to a ten-year-old boy, Daniel reveals the true story of what was happening to him and to Henry Baker, the boy, and the household ménage in Newington. The rules of interpretation are those I used to identify Moll's gentleman in Bath: gender reverse, remember, the story recounts events that are careless of precise time, and recognise that there is always more than one happening to describe.

The old woman approaching sixty is in fact Daniel who was approaching this age, and the two young 'nieces' who slight and neglect her/him, and who assume they are the beneficiaries of his estate, are Henrietta and Maria, Mary Tuffley's daughters by an unknown man. The girls can think that they might be beneficiaries of Daniel's estate, and in particular the house they are living in, because Benjamin, Daniel's legitimate son and heir, had either died, gone missing or departed for America.[240] Daniel sets himself the task of getting hold of the head lease for the Newington property against the opposition of the Tuffley family and sets the whole Newington household abuzz.

The old lady/Daniel decides to 'leave off housekeeping and retire into the country, [Daniel buys land in Tilbury], to end her Days, as she/he called it, in peace and do good with what she/he had'. The nieces/daughters 'employed other relatives to intercede with her'. She dwelt with one of her tenants, a religious and good man and took his advice. He urged her not to be too hard on the girls.

This tenant of Daniel's was John White of Church Street, Newington. Daniel was under pressure from John White because of an offence against his son. He met the White family at their home. John White's family consisted of a wife, a son called John, between nine and ten years old and a sister who was older.[241] She/Daniel told John White that he had resolved to give the two nieces £100 each (to keep them sweet), which left him free to come to an agreement. To the astonishment of John White, the old lady/Daniel told them that the best course was for him to marry the boy.

Daniel writes, 'The Tenant was distasted [and] was strangely surprised with the Proposal.' Daniel continues, 'I'll put him to school and afterwards put him to Prentice at London in a Good trade, and give one hundred pounds with him and to be sure, I shall be dead before he will be out of his

Time; and selling part of the Estate, he will have a good Stock to be set up with, and then when he is re-married will make a good jointure for a Wife.'

John White was embarrassed and the wife and daughter silent. Then Daniel makes a fatal error. He writes – in *Conjugal Lewdness* – that John White tells his wife that the proposal would 'take away all the Scandal which he was before concerned about [that is before the Proposal] on her account'.

However, John White was prudent: something more should be done for the 'nieces'. John White was aware that if a generous provision was made by Daniel for his son it might be put aside if challenged by Daniel's 'nieces' after his death. Daniel writes that he was 'unmoveable to that Part; and after some other Difficulties which the Old Tenant started, for he didn't come willingly into it, no not to the last, it was however agreed on, and she was married to the Boy'.

Of course, Daniel was not to 'marry' the boy. Daniel had warned his readers of *Conjugal Lewdness* that to write about certain vices required a special language with its own terms. In this context Daniel was to be a 'father' to the boy. He and Henry Baker would already have convinced the boy that they were 'fathers': the boy had been groomed.

Daniel's agreement with John White would have been incorporated in a legal document of some kind but it has not survived.

The Parish Records of St Giles, Cripplegate, where John White had his business and lived for a time, and where he first came to know Daniel, shows that John White had two children: one son by his present wife Elizabeth and an earlier daughter by a previous wife Susan. The prospective baptism dates are Elizabeth on March 19 1703 and John on 23 January 1708.

This daughter, Elizabeth, may have been told that she had in some sense had a new 'Father' too. She had listened, she may have watched, she may have attended, and she understood everything. *It is this young girl, Elizabeth White, who came looking for her 'Mother' in Roxana*: the young and persistent girl who threatened to reveal all; the girl that 'Amy', was unable to buy off, and had to' murder', if this is what she did.

The dates fit. Approaching sixty years would place Daniel around 1717–19. In 1719 following his success with *Robinson Crusoe*, Daniel was planning to buy land at Tilbury. John White junior, as the child in *Conjugal Lewdness*, was nine to ten years old and his sister five years older. Five years later when, in *Roxana*, Amy was looking for Roxana/Daniel's 'son' and 'daughter' is around 1722–24, the date at which Daniel was finishing *Roxana*. Amy went looking for these children five years later when the boy would have been fifteen to sixteen years old. She found the boy, his youngest 'son' now aged 17, working as an apprentice, (and presumably not deaf) as promised by Daniel/Roxana and as provided by him. Here the dates are proximate but feasible.

As for the 'daughter', Daniel told his readers no more of her. Henry Baker had a lucky escape and no wonder he was so careful to do all he could to cover his tracks. And thanks to Thomas Wright, who unwittingly had cooperated with the Baker family to conceal the truth, the world has bought Henry Baker's story.

In September 1729 Daniel wrote to his publisher to tell him that he had been very ill and then nothing more was known of him for some time (H 250).

What then survived was a letter he wrote to his new son-in-law, Henry Baker, dated 12 August 1730 (H 251). This letter is quoted at length by a number of biographers. In it Daniel speaks of being abandoned by every friend and by every relative except those who are unable to give him any assistance.

Self-pitying comments such as these are common with Daniel, and so in themselves they mean little, but then he goes on to say that he is sorry that he [Henry Baker] is debarred from seeing him. Again self-pityingly, he complains that he is under a 'Load of insupportable Sorrows'. Daniel complains that he has 'rec's from a wicked, perjur'd, and contemptible Enemy, that has broken in upon my Spirit'. Daniel complains, also, that it is the behaviour of his son Daniel that grieves him most, that he is depriving his mother and sisters of their daily bread.

Daniel states in this letter that he does not 'have a Lodging in London, nor have I been at that Place in the Old Bailey, since I wrote to you that I was removed from him and that there is no way for 'Son or Daughter, Wife or Child' to come to see him, that they dare not come by Water, and by Land there is no coach'. Daniel says that he is at a distance from London in Kent. The letter is signed by him as 'About two miles from Greenwich, Kent'.

Daniel distinguishes between a 'Lodging' and a place at the Old Bailey and it is assumed in the letter that Henry Baker knew of both these places. Jonathan Wild had his various places of abode near the Old Bailey and it was at the heart of an area of ill repute.

This letter was written eight months before Daniel's death. In an earlier letter dated 9 June 1729, he wrote about his anger arising from family disagreements (H 249). He says:

Had Deb, The Hasty, the Rash, and So Far Weak, Said Ten Times as much to me, it had Made no Impression at all: But From Sophi, Thee Sophi! Whose Image Sits close to my affections, and who I Love beyond the Power of Expressing: I acknowledge it Wounded my Very Soul; and my Weakness is So much the more, as that Affection is strong; So that I can as ill Express The Satisfaction I have from your Letter, as I could the grief of what I thot an Unkindness.

Who might be the ancient enemy he is avoiding (assuming it to be a person)? Recent biographers have argued that suspicion rests on Mary Brooke who began a Chancery suit in 1727 over the administration of her late husband's estate. Mrs Brooke's husband had taken over the administration of the estate. There was an unpaid debt arising from Daniel's settlement with his creditors in 1692 and 1706. Mrs Brooke pursued its recovery. Daniel, as usual, deployed the defensive tactic of holding his creditor at bay by filing bills in Chancery in 1728 and 1730.

Following Daniel's death, Mary Brooke won her case for a debt of £427 and subsequently letters of administration were granted to her over Daniel's estate. Daniel, who had earned so much money in a long life, died intestate. Like many others before her, Mary Brooke believed that Daniel always had more assets than he declared. It is not likely that the persistent Mary gained much from her pursuit.

Mrs Brooke's claim was a civil suit. On the face of it, Daniel, although he would be concerned, would not need to flee from home ahead of Mrs Brooke being successful, and even if she were triumphant, Daniel probably had the means to settle the debt. After all, during the time she was pressing her suit, he had succeeded in paying off mortgages of £1,400 on his Tilbury land. Of course, if it were assumed that Mary Brooke's claim would be successful, other creditors, also ignored by Daniel, might press their claims and there would be further problems, but that was all wrapped up in future uncertainties. Those problems could not possibly be the cause of Daniel going on the run.

There are other difficulties in working out what is going on. When Daniel writes that he has given into his own son's hands the care of 'two dear unprovided Children' (H 251) the reader knows that if it is assumed he is writing of Hannah and Henrietta, two unmarried girls, of whom one was his daughter, living in the house at Newington, that the statement could not possibly be true. Hannah had been given an interest in the Tilbury land by Daniel, which it is said was producing an income of £300 a year, and he had provided her with South Sea stock. She lived happily on the income from land and stock, so far as is known, for the rest of her life. Mary Tuffley's inheritance from her brother Samuel was very generous. After Daniel's death she would have been housed and provided for very well. On her death, her daughters fared well.

Why was Henry Baker debarred from seeing Daniel and what would they have been talking about anyway? If it is assumed that Mary Brooke was spying on Daniel night and day (which, as I have argued, she had no cause to do) she would have had to employ a large team. To spy on a house around the clock requires six people: two people on each of three shifts. If Mrs Brooke was watching three premises, the two houses in Stoke Newington and Baker's house in Enfield, she would need to employ eighteen people! If Daniel was being hunted by Mrs Brooke, why would he hide out two miles from Greenwich, a distance from Stoke Newington which could be walked in comfort by anyone within an hour or two?

To solve these uncertainties requires a change in the premises of the discussion. First, the family Daniel is alluding to is not Mary Tuffley's but his own. The key is in the wording of the correspondence. Daniel writes of his family as consisting of 'Son or daughter, Wife or child'. A child is a person of up to fourteen years of age in the nomenclature of the times. If he had been referring to Mary Tuffley and her daughters Hannah and Henrietta, he would have written 'Wife and daughters'. Daniel's family at this time was his wife Elizabeth and their three children, Daniel, Sarah and Deborah. The elder son who might betray the family is Daniel junior and the child is Deborah, or Debs, who is younger than Sophia and less worldly-wise.

Henry Baker dare not meet Daniel because if he did, and there was an arrest, he would be in some danger of being caught up in a public scandal that would scar his life. In his letter, Daniel sent Baker a message: 'about two miles from Greenwich' is not an indication of place. In the gay community 'Greenwich' was understood as a warning.

It was in Debtford, two miles from Greenwich, that Captain Rigby met his sad fate, despite the presence of the Tsar of Russia. The great sailing ships of the East India Company brought their splendid ocean-going sailing ships up the river to the company's warehouses and made their repairs in Debtford docks. Across the river in Greenwich and Blackheath, the owners and senior officials of the Company built their splendid houses. Somewhere down the hill the rough mixed with the smooth and the rich with the poor. To this day Greenwich and Blackheath have harboured the villainous and successful and until recent times sailors have provided the entertainment.

Daniel was telling Henry Baker that he was keeping away from the trouble spots in London and that no one, not even his own family, was in touch with him or knew where he was to be found.

There are many possible reasons why Daniel junior may not have wished to respond to his father's need for cash. The son may have wished to avoid the risk of involvement with his father given the nature of blackmail threats Secondly, Daniel might have been unwilling to continue the leak of scarce resources which would otherwise go to his family. Perhaps Daniel did behave well, but to his half-sister Hannah, and to Elizabeth, Sarah and Debs.

Daniel died of a lethargy and was buried in Bunhill Fields on 26 April 1731. It is not known whether there was a funeral ceremony and if so who, if anyone, attended.

Daniel's family had secured what they could from him in his lifetime. Now Henry Baker and Sophia were to have the house in Stoke Newington. His daughter Hannah had an annuity secured on the South Sea Stock he had given her. Mary Tuffley Defoe had been left comfortably off by her father Samuel Tuffley. When she died in 1732 the proceeds from her estate were divided equally between her legitimate daughters. Daniel junior had the capital and income from the land in Tilbury. Hannah had a claim on the income but whether she pressed for it is not known. Daniel may have sold out promptly, for there were many 'Mary Brookes'. It was rumoured that he emigrated to America. And Mrs Brooke got next to nothing.

At the two anchor points of his life, London and Tilbury, Daniel's two additional 'wives' followed him to the grave. Elizabeth Deffoes was buried in Bunhill Fields in the City of London in 1737 and Mary Norton Defoe in Colchester, Essex.

The fate of Daniel's other illegitimate children is unknown with the exception of Benjamin Norton Defoe. I have been able to trace Benjamin Norton beyond London. Benjamin Norton's life in London as a hack reporter had been desperate. How true it is that 'his wife had nineteen children and that only three survived' is a guess, but the burial records of St John's Parish Church, Hackney, do record a distressing procession of infant burials. But then in the early 1730s the tiny coffins stopped arriving and Benjamin Norton can be traced elsewhere. Perhaps his ill-chosen career as a journalist had been inspired by Daniel and now that his father was dead there was no further need to pretend. Daniel's library was promptly sold after family members secured what volumes were of interest to them.

William Lee speculated that Mary was buried with Daniel, although there is no evidence for this. It was William Lee who organised an appeal to provide Daniel with a grander and more fitting memorial stone. Daniel's body was disinterred in 1870. When the grave was opened it was found to contain two other unnamed coffins containing female remains. The reporters present wrote that the unmarked coffins were in a very poor condition and fell to pieces when they were raised; Daniel's coffin, which had a brass plaque with the name 'Foes' engraved on it, was in reasonable condition.

The ceremony at Bunhill Fields to commemorate the new monument to Daniel Defoe was well attended. There were a number of dignitaries, many reporters and three women descendants of Daniel's. Mr William Lee, Daniel's most enthusiastic biographer, who had organised the whole thing, said a few words about Daniel's importance. Mr Clark, the editor of Christian Weekly, being an honest man, said that although the children of England had given their pocket money to the cost of the monument, adults had topped up the fund.

Some seventeen hundred people had contributed towards the cost of a handsome Egyptian pillar of Sicilian marble, seventeen feet tall and on a plinth which measured eight feet by four. Every one noticed that it replaced a very mean grave. Mr Clark said that very few people had questioned the propriety of the monument. While it was true that Defoe had incurred substantial debt, he had suffered, and it should be remembered that he had left us incomparable works of the imagination. It was from this suffering that Defoe had been able to 'place our religious and political freedom upon a true and lasting basis...he had helped to make us the people that we are [and that he was] one of England's moral and intellectual nobles...and an illustrious Englishman'.

Mr Forster, MP, had wanted to be present but was unable to attend. A letter from him was read aloud. Mr Reed, MP, said that Daniel 'rode forth in 1688 and was a favourite at the Court of William III. It was true, and the evidence was strong, that Defoe was not always true to the principles of the party he professed to serve [the Whigs]… and that if all his writings were not as we could desire, that he [Mr Reed] intended to practice the homily, 'I study peace and live in charity to all men'. Mr Reed said that Daniel 'was never false to the party he professed. He said that it was noteworthy that although Defoe had incurred great debt 'he had struggled on until he had paid every penny of it'.

Unfortunately, something went wrong before the ceremony was over. As the coffins were lifted there was a rush, which included children, to secure bones as relics. The police were called in to control the crowd and to prevent further desecration. For a moment it seemed that the coffin, which had restrained Defoe for one hundred and forty years in death might no longer be sufficient to contain him and he might burst forth to confound an admiring world.

Chapter 24

Postscript

The end, I say of everything is in the beginning, and you must look to the end, or you will never begin right.

Review, VIII, 514 (for 614)
Daniel Defoe

HE WAS ALWAYS RELIEVED to reach the end of a London Sessions for whatever anyone said, being a Justice was not fun. As the flotsam and jetsam of the capital drifted from his court leaving behind the familiar stale aroma of petty crime, his relief was palpable. Sometimes he thought that the best case for the abolition of poverty – and the criminals swept before him were undoubtedly poor – was their smell. The rank odour of poverty was inescapable.

It was his habit to open a bottle of port in his robing room and to drink it slowly in his high-backed leather chair before retiring to his home. He did it now. But before the warmth and haze had fuddled him there was a timid knock on the door, and then another, and yet a third, until he called it in.

There before him, awkward and stumbling, was a Special Constable attached to the thieve-catchers. He had noticed him many a time in the well of his court. He had an annoying habit of imitating a small dog: with fair hair flopping over his forehead, nose forward and mouth gaping. Panting, he blurted out:

Constable   Excuse me your honour. Can I have a word?
The Justice paused and then decided to humour him.
Justice   Yes, if you must. Get it out man.
Constable   I want to report a crime.
Justice   What crime? Speak up man, I can't hear you.
Constable   A murder, sir. A young girl, sir. At least I think it's a murder.
Justice   Do we have a body and is it in our jurisdiction?
Constable   No sir, not really, it's in Greenwich.
Justice   Greenwich? Nothing that happens in Greenwich has anything to do with us. No body, no crime. Don't waste my time.
The Constable did not shift himself, rather he twisted his feet inwards and contorted his body in a most alarming fashion. He wanted to say something more but could not find the words.
Constable   Yes, sir. I know, sir. But my wife said I must speak out and I couldn't think of anyone better than your honour to speak out to.
The Justice responded to flattery which he recognised to be entirely genuine.

276

Justice   Well, you're right there, Constable. So tell me, what do you wish to report?

Constable My wife was speaking to a woman in the market, sir. They meet there often. This woman – and she's a decent body – takes in lodgers. She takes in this nice young girl who tells her that she is going to meet her father, who she has not met for some time. And then she goes out to meet him at the jetty 'cos he's promised to take her down river, and that's the last she saw of her. So excited and full of spirit she was and

then nothing. A really nice girl. Confused, but excited.

The words had tumbled out in the end. He stopped and looked at the Justice.

Constable Well, it's not right sir. It's foul play. She thinks it and so does my wife.

Justice   Come, come, man. Are you saying that a father would murder his own child?

Constable That's just it, sir. Is he really her father? If you know what I mean.

The Justice was angry now. He was a father. Every morning there were bodies washed up in the Thames, some no doubt cast into the water at Greenwich, who came down on the tide, but he doubted if any were grown girls tossed into the drink by their fathers – by their mothers, perhaps, but that was another story. He wanted to bring this conversation to a halt.

Justice   Well, constable, I hear what you say. It's very sad. Bring me a body and some evidence and we can think about it some more.

The Constable held his ground.

Justice   (weakly) All right. Do we have a suspect? Do we have a name?

The Constable drew out a piece of paper with a name on it and gave it to the Justice. He looked at it and then turned his eyes to the ceiling.

Justice   I think we know this man, Constable. Do we not? Nothing will come of it, you know, for this man would be as slippery as an eel. And then, as parsnips are parsnips, some big wig would intervene and the case would come to nothing.

The Constable held his ground.

Justice   All right, I will give you a written authority to make some enquiries. Don't waste time, mind you, but ask about.

On his way home the Justice looked into the Thames. The tide was running fast now. If there were bodies there they would soon be among us. But then they might be swept on out to sea and never be seen again. Of course, the Constable was right, really, to care about the fate of this girl, of course he was. But unworldly, he thought.

He didn't make the law but merely applied it. He tried to be fair-minded, as others before him and, no doubt, after he was gone, but if human creatures were wicked, foolish or poor, the causes of their misfortune had nothing to do with him.

He did look down into the river as he walked. Occasionally he stopped and stared. Sometimes he thought he saw bodies floating beneath the swelling grey ripples of the water, but he was mistaken. But he had looked. It was only right to look.

The Justice was quite right to have his doubts. No body, no crime, is a useful adage in most circumstances. The body of Elizabeth White was not to float down the Thames and out to sea in anything other than Daniel's imagination.

When John White died in May 1731 he left a will which showed him to have two surviving children, John and Elizabeth.[241]

John White was shown to be a man of substance with two freehold properties in Stoke Newington, including Daniel's original property in Church Street in which he had lived to his death, premises in King Street, London, where he conducted his business, and a small dwelling house in Cock Street, Norton Fellgate.

He was able to leave his son an 'accumulated sum' of £7,500. His executors were charged with spending this huge sum of money, in current values, and ten times the value of Daniel's large property across the road, with building a property or properties on land for which £300 had already been put aside by a separate deed dated 2 July 1729. Such a sum would buy a 'palace'.

John White had made it an express condition of his will that his son should not occupy his house in Stoke Newington, even though it had been bequeathed to him. The wording of the will is, 'But he is not to live in my dwelling house, as it will be too expensive for him.' The much humbler dwelling in Cock Street was suggested for him.

According to the 1729 deed the £300 to buy the freehold became payable on the marriage of John White junior. The will reads 'by the deed dated 2 July 1729 upon the marriage of my son, John White, to his now wife agreed with John Freeke, citizen and barber surgeon and George Vereney, citizen and weaver. Vereney and Freake were the executors.

There is a dreadful contradiction. If John White's dwelling in Church Street was too large and expensive for his son to live in, why is it insisted upon that the whole of the sum of £7,500 be spent on providing him with what would amount to a 'palace'?

The provision has the hallmark of a previous deal: Daniel had set aside money for the purpose of housing John White junior with the provision of a house and land on John White's death. If John White's will were to be challenged after his death by Daniel Defoe, should he survive John White, or the heirs to his estate, or so it might have been advised to him, he would need to explain that Daniel had left money for the express purpose of housing John White junior, assuming him to be married. If John junior was already living handsomely in his own house the provision would be challengeable and all the facts would come out.

John White left £100 only to his daughter Elizabeth White, now married to a William Smith, and £300 to their son because 'I have already advanced them and provided for them'. But he anticipated difficulties with his troublesome daughter. His will reads that if 'they[William and Elizabeth] shall not comply or acquiesce in the will but shall contravert or take any course att law or in Equity or otherwise or use any other meanes to avoid the same and shall seake or endeavour to get any other part of my personall Estate then I doe declare that the aforesaid devises of three hundred pounds to their sonn John Lewin Smith and one hundred pounds to my said sonn in law William Smith and his wife shall be void and shall goe and be paid to and amongst the children of my said sonn John White'.

Why would there be the risk of a challenge? At this time there was a presumption in law that the elder son inherited from the father. In a normal course of things, a daughter would have no legal chance of challenging a will that provided for a son. However, Elizabeth was in a position to continue to blackmail, or sully the name of, John White her father and her brother John junior. John White was doing his very best to deter her: he had set the cost of any further challenge by her at a loss of £400.

The will suggests that Daniel's deal with John White had been hard to negotiate and more far-reaching than he had indicated in his fiction – although he had hinted at it. Perhaps he had to surrender the freehold of the property he rented to John White, provide a dowry for Elizabeth White, and make periodic lump sum payments or bonds to the family. These lump sums might over eleven years have accumulated to £7,500.

It might be considered a high price for Daniel to pay, and no doubt it was, but paying it was infinitely preferable to being paraded through the streets of the City in a cart with a placard round his neck on the route to his public execution. John White had proved himself a tough man to mix with, but then he held all the aces.

If this blackmail started around 1717–19 and continued to 1729, a period of ten years or more, Daniel's cash crisis in his later years when he was earning good money can be explained. In the period from 1727–29 John White might have tightened the screw on Daniel so preventing him settling a decent dowry on Sophia.

Dates are important. The date of the deed with John White was 2 July 1729, two months after the wedding of Sophia to Henry Baker. Daniel had to buy off John White before he could reach an agreement with Henry Baker. When Daniel went into hiding in 1730 he complained of 'a wicked, perjur'd and contemptible enemy, that has broken in on my Spirit'. If John White had been blackmailing Daniel for over ten years, and he was the enemy referred to by Daniel in his letter to Henry Baker, he was a good deal more successful than Mrs Brooke could ever have hoped to be.

As Daniel told his readers, John White was a 'religious, good, man'. John White was to be buried according to his will in 'my vault in the church of

Stoke Newington'. At almost the same time, Daniel was interred in an unmarked grave in Bunhill Fields. What the two men had in common was that they had both been blackmailers at some time. In the end, Daniel was left with hardly anything. The business in Tilbury had failed and what was left was under the control of his son Daniel; Henry Baker was free to walk into his house in Church Street and his enemies triumphed everywhere. Many a glass was lifted to him. Thank you, Daniel, for all your efforts on our behalf over a long life.

At the end Daniel had become what he had always feared: he was his very own victim.

Arrangements

Daniel Defoe's Relations With Women

	Daniel Defoe		Colonel Jack		Moll Flanders		Roxana	
	type	children	type	children	type	children	type	children
1. Legal Marriage 1	*	3	*	1	*	2	*	5
2	-	-	-	-	*	-	*	1
2. Private Marriage 1	*	2	*	3	*	3	*	1
2	*	2	*	1	*	1	*	1
3. Ménage à trois	*	2(1)	*	-	*	2(1)	*	2 (1)
4. Rapprochment	*	-	-	-	*	2	*	-
5. Reunion	*	1	*	-	*	-	-	-
6. Happenings	6	8	5	5	6	8	6	8

Notes:

Not additive

Defoe's fictions cover different periods of his life. *Colonel Jack* is the shortest and *Roxana* the longest.

For this purpose a ménage à trois is defined as a relationship between two "men" and a "woman."

Children By Mother
And By Name

Daniel's Children	Mary Tuffley's Children	Elizabeth Sammens' Children
By Mary Tuffley	By Daniel	By Daniel
1687–1691	1687–1691	1685–1707
Benjamin	Benjamin	Daniel
Mary	Mary	Sarah
Hannah	Hannah	Deborah
By Elizabeth Sammen	By Unknown (s)	By Nathaniel Sammen
1695–1708 (?)	1693–1697	1691–1698
Daniel	Maria	Nathaniel

Sarah	Martha	Elizabeth
Deborah	Henrietta	Mary
By Mary Norton		
Benjamin Norton		
Sophia		

Important Same-Sex Relations

Person	Period
Thomas Neale, MP	1692–1699
Lord Robert Harley	1699–1712
Sir John Clerk	1706–1710
Henry Baker	1717(?)–1728

Note:

In Defoe's fictions all sexual relations which do not result in children and/ or which are of short duration are same-sex relationships

Notes

Introduction

[1] Paula Backscheider *Daniel Defoe* (Johns Hopkins University Press, 1989), 4. Paula Backscheider's biography provides a wealth of new particulars, some of which are yet to be fully explored

[2] Peter Earle, *The World of Defoe* (London, Weidenfeld and Nicholson, 1976), 4-5.

[3] William Minto, *Defoe* (London, MacMillan, 1879), 2

[4] Samuel Horner, *A Brief Account of the Interesting Ceremony of Unveiling the Monument Erected by the Boys and Girls of England to the Memory of Daniel Defoe* (Hampshire Independent Office, 1871).

[5] Manuel Schonhorn, *Defoe's Politics: Parliament, power, kingship* (Cambridge University Press, 1989), 82.

[6] John Richetti, *Defoe's Narratives, Situations and Structures* (Oxford, Clarendon Press, 1975), 4.

[7] Victoria Glendinning, *Johnathan Swift* (London, Hutchinson, 1998), ix.

Prologue

[8] Quoted in Theodore F.M. Newton, *William Pitts and Queen Anne's Journalism*, Modern Philology, xxxii (1936), 279-302.

[9] James Sutherland, *The Restoration Newspaper and its Development* (Cambridge University Press, 1986), 190-191.

[10] The description given of him in a letter from an enemy.

[11] The term used in the seventeenth century for a gay man flaunting himself in public.

Chapter 1 Beginnings

[12] Backscheider,4. Backscheider made this discovery. Thomas Wright's conclusion that a branch of the Foe family lived in Chadwell St Mary, earlier in the century, is mistaken. The 'Foes' he identified are, on a closer examination, 'Roes'.

[13] *English Army Lists and Commission Registers*, Vol. V1, 1707–1714 (London, Eyre and Spotiswoode, 1904), 268. The exact date of the raising of this regiment is not known but in the opinion of the editor, Charles Dalton, it pre-dates the period. In a letter to Lord Halifax dated 5 April 1705, Daniel tells of it being delivered by his brother. Biographers have assumed that this was his brother-in-law. However, when Daniel writes of his brother-in-law he says so and when of his brother, he means it. See (H 29) and (H 36). Lord Halifax was Daniel's contact with the Duchess of Marlborough. Daniel was

paid for writing in support of the Duke. It would be a typical Defoe touch to have the letter delivered by one of Marlborough's own officers and, perhaps, to complete the effect by ensuring that that he did so dressed in full regimental regalia.

[14] Frank Bastian, *Defoe's Early Life* (Barnes and Noble, 1981), 167. Broad Street Ward, Poll Tax, 25 Jan 1692/3.
This readable biography is the first to explore Defoe's early life.

[15] CRO. Marriage Tax Assessments, 1695/6 Parish of St Benet Fink.

[16] CRO. Marriage Tax Assessments, 1695/6 Parish of St Bartholomews.

[17] T.C. Dale, *The Inhabitants of London in 1638* (Society of Genealogists, 1931).

[18] A.J.C. Guimaraens, *Daniel Defoe and the Family of Foe* (N&Q, March 1912), 241.

[19] *Colonel Jack* (1722. Hamish Hamilton, 1947), 208.

[20] ERO. Parish Records.

[21] *Colonel Jack*, 5.

[22] *Moll Flanders* (1722. Penguin Classics, 1989), 41.

[23] Katherine Armstrong, *Defoe: Writer as Agent* (Victoria B.C. English Literary Studies, Univ. of Victoria, 1996).

[24] Pat Rogers, *Henry Fielding: A Biography* (Elek, London, 1979), 84.

[25] In *Roxana* Daniel writes that, 'my Father was in very good Circumstances at his coming over, so that he was far from applying to the rest of our Nation that were here, for Countenance and Relief; On the contrary, he had his Door continually thronged with miserable objects of the poor starving creatures, who at that Time fled hither for Shelter, on account of Conscience, or something else.' The something else is money. In the later stages of the religious persecution in France, Protestants were paid money to emigrate. The father's response is typical of a second or third generation immigrant at any time and in any place.

[26] Bastian, 9.

[27] Backscheider, 25. The Butchers' Company confirms these lengths of time for an apprenticeship.

[28] James Sutherland, *Defoe* (Methuen, London, 1937), 2. Sutherland is the most readable of twentieth century Defoe biographers.

[29] Thomas Wright, *The Life of Daniel Defoe* (C.J. Farncombe and Sons, Ltd), 4. Wright discusses many ideas about Defoe no longer of direct relevance but of great interest.

[30] Maximilian Novak, *Daniel Defoe Master of Fictions* (Oxford University Press, 2001), 23. Novak has been the doyen of modern Defoe scholars. His work has achieved high levels of scholarship and erudition

[31] *The Life of Captain Singleton* (1720. Everyman's Library, J.M. Dent, 1906), 1.

[32] H.J. Habakkuk, *Marriage Settlements in the Eighteenth Century* (London, 1950). Lawrence Stone, The Family, Sex and Marriage in England, 1550–1870 (London: Weidenfeld & Nicholson, 1977).

[33] Sigmund Freud, *Family Romances*, 1908 (The Standard Edition of the Complete Works, London, Hogarth Press, 1959).

Chapter 2 Childhood

[34] Paul Dottin, *The Life and Strange Adventures of Daniel Defoe* (Stanley Paul, London, 1928), 5.

[35] Backscheider, 21.

[36] Presbyterians had long preached obedience to the civil authority and from 1662 were careful to distance themselves from apocalyptic voices urging rebellion.

[37] *Due Preparations for the Plague* (London, 1722).

[38] *A Journal of the Plague Year* (London, 1722), 104.

[39] Bastian, 34-5.

[40] Defoe's belief that he was predestined to be saved despite sin falls just short of a Calvinistic belief in Predestination, but he seems to slip into antinomianism; that is, that he would be saved whatever he did.

[41] Bastian, 34-47.

[42] Bastian 48.

[43] Bastian, 45.

[44] Novak, 35.

[45] Bastian, 77-80.

[46] *Review*, VII, 451.

[47] Furbank and Owens do not list this work as being Defoe's.

[48] *Memoirs of a Cavalier* and *Colonel Jack*. These duels were fought in or near Paris. While Furbank and Owens ascribe the first work to Defoe, I have some reservations and have not drawn upon it

[49] William Lee, *Daniel Defoe: His Life and Hitherto Unknown Writings* (London: Hotten, 1869), vol.1, 393-395.

[50] *A Tour of the Whole Island of Great Britain, 1724–26* (Penguin English Library, 1971), 60-63.

[51] *Captain Singleton*, 1.

[52] *Colonel Jack*, 3.

[53] *Captain Singleton*, 5.

[54] *Colonel Jack*, 8.

[55] Leigh Gilmour, *The Limits of Autobiography* (Cornell University Press, 2001).

[56] Simon Lesser, *Fiction and the Unconscious* (Boston, Beacon Press, USA, 1957).

Chapter 3 Growing Up

[57] Backscheider believes that the record of this land transaction should read 1687 and not 1678 and that the clerk recording it made a mistake.

[58] Samuel Wesley, *A Letter from a Country Divine to his friend in London Concerning the Education of the Dissenters, in their Private Academies* (London, 1703).

[59] Edward Calamy, *An Account of the Ministers, Masters, and Fellows of Colleges Who Were Ejected or Silenced after the Revolution in 1660*, 2nd edn (London, 1713), II, 145.

[60] Wright, 35. Thomas Wright believes that Defoe settled in Tooting, Surrey in the 1680s and preached there in association with Dr. Joshua Oldfield. While it seems likely that Defoe had some connection, the actual dates are unknown.

Chapter 4 On The Loose

[61] Keith Feiling, *A History of the Tory Party, 1640–1714*, 2nd edn (Clarendon, Oxford University Press, 1924, 1965), 245.

[62] K.H.J. Habakkuk, *Marriage Settlements*.

[63] Novak, 63.

[64] Cephas Goldworthy, *The Satyr: An Account of the Life and Work, Death and Salvation of John Wilmot, Second Earl of Rochester* (Weidenfeld and Nicholson, 2001), 180.

[65] Goldworthy, 240-241.

[66] Wright, 33-36.

[67] Novak, 56-58.

[68] Samuel Macey, *Money and the Novel: Mercenary Motivation in Defoe and His Immediate Successors* (Sono Nis Press, 1983), 48-49. Macey points out that dowries are of importance not only to Defoe but generally in eighteenth-century literature.

Chapter 5 Romance And Realism

[69] *Journal of the Plague Year*, 142-163.

[70] Bastian, 113.

[71] *Historical Collections or Memoires of Passages and Stories Collected from Severall Authors*, (William Andrews Clark Memorial Library MSH 6735M3) Quoted in Novak, 38-40.

[72] *An Appeal to Honour and Justice*, 175.

[73] William Chadwick, *The Life and Times of Daniel Defoe* (London, John Russell Smith, 1859), 27.

[74] Chadwick, 119-120.

[75] William Minto, *Daniel Defoe* (London, MacMillan, 1879), 7.

[76] Sutherland, 31.

[77] W. McDonald Wigfield *Monmouth Rebellion* (Moonraker Press, 1980), 59.

[78] W. McDonald Wigfield, *The Monmouth Rebels* (Alan Sutton, 1985), 11, 83, 94, 155.

[79] *The Present State of the Parties* (London, 1712).

[80] BL. CSPD, Calendar of State Papers, Domestic, J2, (James II).

[81] Backscheider, 48.

[82] W. McDonald Wigfield, *The Monmouth Rebels*, xv.

[83] Novak, 99.

[84] The list which included Defoe also included Azariah Pinney, whose sister paid £65 to George Penne for her brother's ransom. Her brother lived in the West Indies as a freeman. The queen's secretary had been given 100 convicts and he sold them to Penne. Peter Earle, *The Monmouth Rebels* (Weidenfeld and Nicholson, 1977), 179-180. Defoe was capable of astounding acts of audacity and daring beyond the scope and imagination of others.

[85] Quoted in Bastian, 122.

[86] *The Succession to the Crown of England*, 1701.

[87] Keith Feiling, 245.

Chapter 6 Making It

[88] *The Compleat English Tradesman* (1726. Alan Sutton, 1987).

[89] Pat Rogers, *The Eighteenth Century* (ed. The Context of English Literature, Methuen, 1978), 17.

[90] Sutherland, 28-29.

[91] Anonymous. *A Satyr against the French* (London, Randall Taylor, 1691), 5.

[92] David Kutcha, *The Three-Piece Suit and Modern Masculinity, England 1550–1850* (University of California Press, 2002), 101-102.

Chapter 7 Bankruptcy

[93] W. Eden Hooper, *History of Newgate and the Old Bailey: and a survey of the Fleet and Other Old London Jails* (Underwood Press, 1935).

[94] Sutherland, 31-32.

[95] Backscheider, 33.

[96] George Chalmers, *The Life of Daniel Defoe* (London, 1790), 5.

[97] *Review*, iii (1706) 141.

[98] It was written of Defoe in 1704 that he 'broke for a considerable Sum. His creditors run him into…Bankruptcy, but to no purpose, he having fraudulently … concealed his Effects. So that his Reputation amongst … Dealers is very Foule. He is a profest Dissenter, tho reck'nd of no Morals.' Quoted in Novak 76. Note 10. BLMS 28094 fo. 165.

Chapter 8 Marriage And Family

[99] CRO Marriage Assessments 1695/6 St Botolphs, Bishopsgate, City of London.

[100] St Giles, Cripplegate, Parish Register.

[101] Descriptions of Defoe's ostentatious mode of dress are an amalgam of several antagonisms: objections to a pretence of grandeur above his station in life; display of wealth, when he owed money to others; and of sexual display, which was intended to invite responses.

[102] *The Diaries of Dudley Rider, 1715–1716* (ed. William Mathews, London, Methuen, 1939).

[103] Mrs Brooke's attempts to enforce her successful Chancery judgement will always cause puzzlement until it is accepted that Benjamin was Defoe's legitimate heir and Daniel junior an illegitimate son.

[104] *Colonel Jack*, 216-222.

[105] As quoted in Wright, 128.

[106] *Roxana: The Fortunate Mistress* (Penguin English Library, 1987), 51.

[107] *A Journal of the Plague Year*, 122-126.

[108] James Sutherland, *Defoe* (London, Methuen, 1937), note 43.

[109] Sutherland, 57.

[110] ERO. Quaker Register Digests for Essex. The marriage of Richard Simmons to Mary Norton. T/A 904/1.
The will of Richard Simmons junr. D/ABR 22/422

[111] ERO. These records have been lost by the Record Office. I am indebted to Paula Backscheider for searching her notes for the missing information.

[112] Sutherland provides a good account of the dispute between Ward and Defoe, 215-216. There are various Chancery papers and schedules, PRO. C11/2578/31. In the papers lodged by John Ward there is a schedule of debts which Ward claimed was owed to him by Defoe. I am indebted to Paula Backscheider for the information, she noted in her research that Richard Simmons, carp. was included in the schedule.

[113] Mary Norton was a Quaker and seemed to be a simple person of a sweet nature. Her character and role in Daniel's life is revealed in *Moll Flanders* and *Roxana*.

[114] Bastian, 190.

[115] Bastian, 221-222.

[116] Sutherland, 185.

Chapter 9 Recovery

[117] *An Appeal to Honour and Justice*, 1715.

[118] PRO. C220/9 *Chancery Oath Books*.

[119] *Tour*, 281-282.

[120] PRO.E 351/1460 Excise General Accounts (Duties on Glass, Whitfield and Other Commissioners).

[121] Backscheider, 61.

[122] E.D. Bebb, *Nonconformity and Social and Economic Life, 1660–1800* (London, The Epworth Press, 1935).

Chapter 10 A Rush Of Blood

[123] I accept that Defoe is probably the author of *A Letter to a Dissenter from his Friend at the Hague*, 1688 and *A New Discovery of an Old Intreague*, 1690.

[124] I accept that Daniel put his name to this pamphlet and that he wrote it; but this closely reasoned, balanced and circumspect pamphlet may owe something to another hand.

[125] *Army Commission Lists*. Defoe's brother was on half pay as late as 1722.

[126] Schonhorn, 43.

[127] Feiling, 201.

[128] Donald Davie points out that religious belief and religious observance are cultural phenomena and 'Puritanism' is not synonymous with 'nonconformity' or 'Dissent'. Donald Davie, *A Gathered Church: The Literature of the English Dissenting Interest*, 1700–1930 (The Clark Lectures, 1976. Routledge and Keegan Paul, 1978), 5-6.

[129] *The History of the Kentish Petition*, London, 1701.
   Legions Memorial, London, 1701.

[130] This anecdote is well sourced. George Chalmers obtained the story from David Polhill, the son of one of the arrested Kentish Petitioners, who had heard it directly from his father.

[131] *Robinson Crusoe*, 163-4.

[132] Defoe must have known that publication would put him in grave danger. He may have thought that his faction would come out on top in the power struggle and that Nottingham would not dare move against him. In the end, he could not stop himself.

Chapter 11 Beyond The City

[133] *Roxana*, 13.

[134] J.A. Downie, *Robert Harley and the Press: Propaganda and Public Opinion in the Age of Swift and Defoe* (Cambridge University Press, 1979), 60.
An anonymous writer, who made a vitriolic attack on Harley and Defoe, accused them of meeting at Rummers coffee bar as close friends in 1701, 'where a Set of Whiggish Furies daily met', to write *Legions Memorial*. *The Welsh Monster or The Rise and Downfall of that late upstart, the R-t H-ble Innuendo Scribble*, (London, undated but assumed 1708) 30. BL.11601 d.20.

[135] Hymn to Victory, *True Collection*, ii, 138.

[136] Before his bankruptcy Defoe used a coat of arms on the side of his coach for which he had no paid right. He corrected this in 1702 but it is not certain whether he acquired the right through the College of Heralds or a livery company.

[137] John Kenyon, *Revolution Principles: The Politics of Party, 1689–1720* (Cambridge University Press, 1977).

Kenyon argues that what are now regarded as the principles of the Revolution were not much discussed after 1688. In public debate there were few mentions of Locke. Life went on as before and progress was understood to be evolutionary.

Chapter 12 Scotland

[138] Bastian, 155.
[139] Backscheider, 208.
[140] Backscheider, 208.
[141] Sir John Clerk, *Memoirs of the Life of Sir John Clerk* (Ed. John Gray, Nichols and Sons. London, 1895), 21-34.
[142] Clerk, 39-42.
[143] Daniel Defoe, *History of the Union*, 239.
[144] *Appeal*, 16.
[145] P.W.J. Riley, *The Union of England and Scotland: A Study in Anglo-Scottish Politics of the Eighteenth Century* (Manchester University Press, 1978) 240.
[146] Backscheider uses Defoe's correspondence with John Russell to provide a helpful commentary. It gives valuable insights into Defoe's relationships with eminent people in Scotland and his continuing business relationships.

Chapter 13 A Way With Words

[147] PRO PROB 11/492/31/246.
[148] Novak would have known of Sarah from Marriage Assessments, 1695/6 while Backscheider relied on William Lee for information on Martha.
[149] Tutchin, a journalist rival of Defoe's, was once charged for seditious libel and escaped punishment on a technicality. On a separate occasion he was beaten up in the street.
[150] Puritans believed that punishment for a righteous cause was a cause of justifiable self-pity, a practice thought contemptible by others.
[151] *Review* (ed. John McVeagh, Pickering and Chatto, London 2004), vol.2, Introduction.
[152] Furbank and Owens, 156.
[153] Sidney, First Earl Godolphin, had a reputation for competence, particularly in his conduct of the nation's finances. He served Charles II but his appointment as Queen Anne's first Lord High Treasurer was widely welcomed. He was close to Harley and shared many of his political positions. The break with Harley in 1708 was a tactical one and the pair remained good friends and collaborators.
[154] Feiling maintains that Harley was bound to take account of the Jacobite cause; his parliamentary position depended on it, and negotiations for a peace made the subject unavoidable. Feiling may be too sanguine.
[155] Backscheider provides a good discussion of the case.

[156] Backscheider, 380.

Chapter 14 The Loss Of Harley

[157] Sutherland, 277-282.
[158] *Tour*, 56.
[159] *Tour*, 80.
[160] Furbank,P.N. and Owens W.R. *The Canonisation of Daniel Defoe*(Yale University & London,1988)169-170.
[161] In a letter to Charles de La Faye, Under-Secretary in the Office of Viscount Stanhope, Defoe set out the basis of the tasks he had been performing for Lord Townshend for the past four years. When William Lee realised that Defoe was playing both sides off against each other through the editorial influence he exerted in Whig and Tory newspapers he was hard-pressed to justify the duplicity.
[162] Quoted by Novak, 504.
[163] Perhaps, Defoe's gardener had not been paid!
[164] *The Protestant Monastery*, 1727.

Chapter 15 Origins And Beginnings

[165] *Colonel Jack*, 344.
[166] Sutherland, 227.
[167] Novak, 5.
[168] John Robert Moore, *A Checklist of the Writings of Daniel Defoe*, 2nd edn (Hamden, Conn.: Archon Books, 1971).
[169] Furbank and Owens, 179, 200.
[170] Some biographers, Trent and Novak among them, have suggested that contemporaries had noticed Defoe attending church, which I am sure he did. However, it was most unlikely that he was a member of one.

Chapter 16 Robinson Crusoe

[171] *The Farther Adventures of Robinson Crusoe*, 1719.
Serious Reflections during the Life and Surprising Adventures of Robinson Crusoe, 1720.
[172] Charles Gildon, who was no friend to Defoe, made a forceful attack on *Robinson Crusoe*. He maintained Defoe was deceptive in writing about his own life and in a misleading manner.
[173] When Selkirk returned to London in 1703, he dressed up in 'a swanskin waistcoat, blue linen shirt, new breeches and shoes with scarlet laces.' He had been away for eight years and was given a celebrity reception. Diana Souhami, *Selkirk's Island* (London, Orion Books, 2002), 160.
[174] There is always a willingness to denigrate the success of others. Richard Steele did not believe Defoe was capable of writing *Robinson Crusoe*. One thing

is certain: Alexander Selkirk was not capable of writing anything, and a host of scribblers sought to do it for him. To their chagrin along came Defoe with *Robinson Crusoe* and stole their thunder.

175 W. McDonald Wigfield, *Monmouth Rebellion* maintains that Defoe visited Nailsea Court, the home of Captain Wade who took part in the Monmouth Rebellion, and met Selkirk there. He would almost certainly have discussed the battle of Sedgemoor, which Wade was present at and fighting in and Defoe was not.

176 Defoe met William Dampier and was familiar with his *New Voyage Round the World* (1697) and *Voyages and Descriptions* (1699).

177 Defoe had a life-long attraction for the sea, ships and sailors, and was familiar with Yorkshire ports through which he would have traded.

178 Sigmund Freud, *Interpretation of Dreams* (Oxford University Press, 1999), 380-385.

Chapter 17 Colonel Jack And Captain Singleton

179 John Richetti, *Defoe's Narratives, Situations and Structures* (Clarendon Press: Oxford University Press, 1971).

180 The reader will find in Daniel's account of the life of Jonathan Wild a half-admiring respect and a sense of honour among thieves.

181 Sutherland, 37-38.

182 When in hiding in 1703, Defoe wrote to the Principal Secretary of State, Nottingham, offering to raise a troop of horse to fight in the Netherlands in return for his freedom. Daniel was aware that prison release had been secured in return for military service by others. Perhaps his elder brother came to serve in a troop of horse in the same way.

183 The ascription to Defoe of *Robert Drury's Journal* was comprehensively rebutted by Furbank and Owens, *The Canonisation of Daniel Defoe*, 109-113. However, some scholars continue to detect Defoe's hand in it: to lose the *Journal* is to put in doubt other ascribed works.

Chapter 18 Moll Flanders

184 Ian Watt, *The Rise of the Novel* (London, Random House, 2000).

185 Novak, 599.

186 Until the Marriage Act 1753 a promise freely given between a couple constituted a valid marriage. Such a marriage was short of the full inheritance and dowry rights of a marriage solemnised in a church.

187 The Mint was located in Southwark, London. A debtor could secure a refuge there from prosecution for debt.

[188] Defoe claimed that he had secured a dowry of £3,700 with Mary Tuffley. Proportionately, Mary's marriage portion could be expected to be of the magnitude of £1,400–£1,500.

[189] Similarly in *Colonel Jack*, when re-united with his first wife, who turns out to be a rather better woman than he had first thought, the wife informs the reader that her Marriage Portion is similar to Mary's.

[190] Sutherland, 35-36, discusses Defoe's ownership of the *Desire*.

[191] The gentleman's explanation of the state of mind of his wife is repeated elsewhere in Defoe's fictions in relation to a first wife. These descriptions reveal how Daniel felt about his first and only legal wife, not necessarily her true condition. Defoe gave Mary Tuffley a good deal to be distracted about. On the other hand, she might have had a difficult and wayward character.

[192] Defoe writes about bathing in Bath, 'In the morning (supposing you to be a young lady) you are fetched…stripped to the smock, to the Cross Bath…the ladies and the gentlemen pretend to keep some distance…but frequently mingle…they converse freely, and talk, rally, make vows and sometimes love…'
The first turnpike road was between London and Bath.

[193] *Memoirs of the Life of Sir John Clerk* (ed. John Gray, London, Nichols and Sons, 1895), 75-76.

[194i] *Appeal to Honour and Justice*, 1715. As quoted by Backscheider, 357.

[195] *Moll Flanders*, 256.

Chapter 19 Escape From The City

[196] Hannah was joined to the lease so that she could benefit from the land. This provision is part of Daniel's attempt to provide for all his legitimate children by Mary Tuffley.

[197] Daniel nevertheless wished to benefit from the land in his lifetime. Hannah could be easily hoodwinked, as in his dealings with Ward, his farm manager, or her signature forged.

[198] Daniel was to prove less compliant than Hannah – and perhaps more sensible.

[199] Mary Norton's assistance to Daniel in 1722 shows that she was willing to help him out after twenty-seven years of being a wife to him; after five births and, no doubt, frequent heartbreaks, hurts and slights.

[200] Daniel, and perhaps Sarah, would have spent part of their childhoods in Tilbury. Later in life, Daniel junior may have felt himself at home there.

[201] G.M. Trevelyan, *English Social History: Defoe's England*, Penguin Books, 1964 vol. 4. Trevelyan writes that Defoe, 'first perfected the art of the reporter… So then, the account that this man gives of the England of Anne's reign is for the historian a treasure indeed. For Defoe was one of the first who saw the old world through a pair of modern eyes. His report…occupies the central point of our thought and vision.

Chapter 20 Roxana: The Fortunate Mistress

[202] The full title was 'ROXANA THE FORTUNATE MISTRESS or, a History of the Life and Vast Variety of Fortunes of Mademoiselle de Beleau, Afterwards call'd The Countess de Wintselsheim, in Germany. Being the Person known by the Name of the Lady Roxana in the Time of King Charles II'.

[203] Early immigrants from the persecution of the Huguenots were expelled for their religious convictions but later they were paid to leave.

[204] Novak, 553. Novak writes that Defoe held the East India Company to be guilty of exporting gold bullion to the East without benefiting Great Britain. As with all capital investment abroad, the test of whether it is in the national interest lies in the return on the investment to the donor country in the form of cash, goods and services. England has had, for most of its modern economic history, a net outward flow of investment.

[205] Daniel, in his own name and through fictional characters, makes numerous mistakes in his claims for numbers of children. These mistakes arise from the context: that is, all his children: children by Mary Tuffley; by Mary Norton, and still living; by Elizabeth Sammen; by those convenient to count, and so on.

[206] There are only two children of Daniel Defoe whose births are recorded in an Anglican church: Sophia, his daughter by Mary Norton and Sarah, his daughter by Elizabeth Sammen. There are no recorded births for any of Mary Tuffley's children. It seems that the Tuffley family disapproved of baptism and other recording of births in the established church.

[207] Backscheider, 192.

[208] Backscheider, 68.

[209] *Roxana*, 278.

[210] To gain favour in William's Court it was necessary to find a modus operandi which would break through differences of class and nationality.

[211] *Roxana*, 110-111.

[212] *Roxana*, 119 and 170.

[213] *Roxana*, Introduction. David Blewett writes that Roxana's 'is the most complex character Defoe ever created. Her story is the autobiography of a woman in the throes of a psychological disturbance so severe that eventually she becomes temporarily insane... [and that] As the novel advances Roxana becomes more and more mentally ill.'

[214] *Roxana*, 199.

[215] Sir Robert Clayton became very rich, a well-known Whig, Member of Parliament, and Lord Mayor of London in 1679–80. His career was one that Defoe would have liked to emulate. Thus, perversely, it became an objective of Defoe to attack him.

[216] Roxana had many fine offers of 'marriage'. None were sufficient but then her Lord (Harley) gave her a hint, and another gentleman also, that the king was among the Masks at her door. Although she could not say for certain, she thought it possible that she might have danced with the king. She could have captured a king.

[217] Roxana narrates that her new Apartments 'were handsome Lodgings indeed, and very richly furnished.'

[218] Daniel's recall of the exact duration of his relationship with Sir John Clerk is an indication of how much it meant to him at the time and in recollection.

[219] The intimacy between Harley and Defoe is shown in the fact that this letter could be sent immediately upon Harley's resignation, which is a point brought out by Backscheider, 253. This is true, but for Daniel the issues of loss of money and protection fuelled his anxiety.

[220] Benjamin Defoe was enrolled as a student in Edinburgh University in the autumn of 1709. Defoe had ambitions to develop a considerable business in Scotland and thought that Benjamin might be able to assist him in it. Benjamin turned out to be a disappointment in this respect.

[221] J.M. Coetzee, *Foe* (Penguin Books, 1987), 77.

Chapter 21 Crime

[222] Gerald Howson, *The Thief Taker General* (Hutchinson, 1970), 24-25. I am indebted to Gerald Howson for his comprehensive attempt to understand the machinery of detection and the judicial system of justice in the early eighteenth century.

[223] *Review*, Nov. 1707, vol. iv, no.124, 495-496.

[224] *Defoe on Sheppard and Wild*, (ed. Richard Holmes, Harper Perennial, 2004) Preface.

[225] *Colonel Jack*, 10.

[226] Lincoln Faller, *Crime and Defoe: A New Kind of Writing* (Cambridge University Press, 1993), as quoted in John Richetti, *Daniel Defoe: A Critical Biography* (Blackwell, 2005), 382.

[227] Daniel used a number of pseudonyms in his writing life and like an actor playing many parts tends to write dialogues suitable for the characters he assumes. Writing as a grumpy old man living with his sister gave him the opportunity to moan and avoid criticism. After all, it would be bad form to attack the elderly.

[228] Novak, 678. Novak maintains that Daniel is attacking his own gender whereas in reality Daniel is showing a strong dislike for women.

Chapter 22 Later Writings

[229] As quoted by Wright, 370.

230 BL C69.C.D. *Conjugal Lewdness, or Matrimonial Whoredom* (T. Warner, London, 1727), 405.
231 George Potter, *Henry Baker, F.R.S. (1698–1774)*, Modern Philology, 29 (1932).
232 Wright, 373.

Chapter 23 Endings

233 Quoted in Backscheider, 505. Turner, 'Henry Baker', 58: Yale Osborne fc 109/1, items 28, 89, and 92.
234 Quoted in Wright, 154-155. HRO. Stoke Newington Court Rolls 24 May 1717. Current Repository Guildhall Library. Ms 14, 233/2-11
235 Potter, *Modern Philology*, 29.
236 Potter, *Modern Philology*, 29.
237 *Conjugal Lewdness*, 357-364.
238 PRO. C11/6792/2.
239 In 1733 at Great Tey, Essex, close to Defoe's Tilbury estate, a Benjamin Norton was granted a badger's licence (a badger was a dealer or hawker, or one who sold from a small shop or stall). It would be nice to conclude that this was Benjamin Norton Defoe who had returned from unfriendly London pastures as a journalist to where he began and might be happy.
ERO. Essex Licenses :Q/RL b 1 p.18 Recognizances of badgers and licenced tradesmen.
240 *Roxana*, 232. 'my youngest son was alive…he was put out Apprentice, by the kindness and Charity of his Uncle, but to a mean Trade…she [Amy] found him a good sensibly mannerly youth; that he knew little of the story of his Mother or Father…'
241 PCC. PROB 11/644 dated 18 May, 1731.

Works Cited

The Writings of Daniel Defoe

Books

Many of the books listed below are available through good bookshops and through the public library system. Rare books can be read in England at the British Library and in other national libraries in Britain, Ireland and elsewhere.

Captain Singleton, 1720. Everyman, 1990
Colonel Jack, 1722. Oxford University Press, 1965
The Compleat English Tradesman, 1726. Allan Sutton, 1987
Conjugal Lewdness, T. Warner, 1727. BL C69.C.D.
The Consolidator, London, 1705
Due Preparations for the Plague, London, 1722
An Essay Upon Projects, London, 1697
Historical Collections and Memoires of Passages and Stories Collected from Severall Authors, William Clark Memorial Library: Ms.H6735M3
The History of the Union of Great Britain, Edinburgh, 1709
A Journal of The Plague Year, 1722. Penguin English Library, 1966
Jure Divino, London, 1706
Moll Flanders, 1722. Penguin Popular Classics, 1994
The Political History of the Devil, AMS Press Inc., Brooklyn, NY 11205, USA.
Robinson Crusoe, 1719. Penguin Popular Classics, 1998
Romances and Narratives by Daniel Defoe, ed. George Aitken, London, 1895
Roxana, or The Fortunate Mistress, 1722. Everyman, 1998
Sheppard and Wild, Defoe on, ed. Richard Holmes, London, Harper Perennial, 2004
The Storm, The Lay-Man's Sermon upon the Late Storm, an *Essay on the Late Storm*, 1704. Penguin Books, 2005
A System of Magick, London, 1727
A Tour Through The Whole Island of Great Britain, 1724-1726. Penguin English Library, 1971

Pamphlets

Daniel Defoe's pamphlets are not generally available. In England they can be read at the British Library.

An Account of the Conduct of Robert Earl of Oxford, London, 1715.

And What if the Pretender should come? London, 1713.

An Answer to a Question that Nobody thinks of, London, 1713.

An Appeal to Honour and Justice, London, 1715.

An Argument Shewing , that a Standing Army, with Consent of Parliament, is not Inconsistent with a Free Government, London, 1698.

Augusta Triumphans, London, 1728.

A Brief Explanation of a Late Pamphlet, London, 1703.

The Danger of the Protestant Religion Consider'd, London, 1701.

A Declaration of Truth to Benjamin Hoadly, London, 1717.

An Enquiry into the Occasional Conformity of Dissenters, in Cases of Preferment, London, 1698.

An Essay at Removing National Prejudices against a Union with Scotland, Parts 1, 2 and 3, London, 1706.

Every-Body's Business, is No-Body's Business, London, 1725.

A Friendly Rebuke to one Parson Benjamin, London, 1719.

The History of the Kentish Petition, London, 1701.

Legion's Memorial, London, 1701.

Minutes of the Negotiations of Monsr. Mesnager, London, 1717.

The Mock Mourners, London, 1702.

More Reformation, London, 1703

The Original Power of the Collective Body of the People of England, London, 1702.

The Poor Man's Plea, London, 1698.

The Present State of Jacobitism Considered, London, 1701.

The Present State of the Parties, London, 1712.

The Protestant Monastery, London, 1727.

Reasons Against a War with France, London, 1701.

Reasons against the Succession of the House of Hanover, London, 1713.

Remarks on the Bill to Prevent Frauds Committed by Bankrupts, London, 1706.

Second Thoughts are Best, London, 1729.

The Secret History of the White Staff, London, 1714.

The Secret History of the White Staff, Part 2, London, 1714.

The Secret History of the White Staff, Part 3, London, 1715.

The Secret History of the Secret History of the White Staff, Purse and Mitre, London, 1715.

The Shortest Way With The Dissenters, London, 1702.

The Sincerity of the Dissenters Vindicated, London, 1703.

The Six Distinguishing Characters of a Parliament Man, London, 1701.

Some Reflections on a Pamphlet Entitled, An Argument Shewing that a Standing Army is Inconsistent with a Free Government, London, 1697.

The Succession to the Crown of England, Considered, London, 1701.

The True Born Englishman, London, 1701.

The Two Great Questions Considered, London, 1700.

Other Writers

Most of the books listed in the sections below are available through good bookshops and the public library system. Rare books can be read at the British Library.

Biography

Backscheider, Paula. *Daniel Defoe: His Life*, Johns Hopkins University Press, 1998.
Bastian, Frank. *Defoe's Early Life*, New Jersey, Barnes and Noble Books, 1981.
Chadwick, William. *The Life and Times of Daniel Defoe*, London, John Russell Smith, 1859.
Chalmers, George. *The Life of Defoe*, London, 1790.
Dottin, Paul. *Daniel Defoe: The Life and Surprising Adventures of Daniel Defoe*, London, Stanley Paul, 1928.
Earle, Peter. *The World of Defoe*, Weidenfeld and Nicholson,1976.
—— *Monmouths Rebels*, Weidenfeld and Nicholson, 1977.
Gray, John, ed., *Memoirs of the Life of Sir John Clerk*, Nichols and Sons, London, 1895.
Healey, George Harris. *The Letters of Daniel Defoe*, Clarendon, Oxford University Press, 1955.
Lee, William. *Daniel Defoe: His Life and Hitherto Unknown Writings*, 3 vols., London, Hotten, 1869.
Minto, William. *Daniel Defoe*, London, Macmillan, 1879.
Moore, John Robert. *Daniel Defoe: Citizen of the Modern World*, University of Chicago, 1958.
Novak, Maximillian E. *Daniel Defoe: Master of Fictions*, Oxford University Press, 2001.
Sutherland, James. *Defoe*, London, Methuen, 1937.
Trent, William Peterfield. *A Biographical and Bibliographical Study*. MS biography of Daniel Defoe. Trent Collection, Beinecke Library, New Haven. Conn., c.1900-1927.
Wilson, Walter. *Memoirs of the Life and Times of Daniel De Foe*, 3 vols., Hurst, Chance, London, 1830.

Other

Armstrong, Katherine. *Defoe: Writer as Agent*, Victoria B.C. English Literary Studies, Univ. of Victoria, 1996.
Calamy, Edward. *An Account of the Masters and Fellows of Colleges who were Ejected or Silenced after the Revolution in 1660*, 2nd edition, London, 1713.
Dale, T.C. *The Inhabitants of London in 1638*, Society of Genealogists, 1931.

Dampier, William. *A Voyage to New Holland*, ed. James Williamson, 1697. Argonaut Press, 1939. *Voyages and Descriptions*, London 1699.

English Army Lists, and Commission Registers, vol.VI, Eyre and Spotiswoode, London, 1904.

Ermath, Elizabeth. *Realism and Consensus in the English Novel*, Princeton University Press, 1983.

Flynn, Carol Houlihan. *The Body in Swift and Defoe*, Cambridge University Press, 1990.

Freud, Sigmund. *Family Romances*, 1908, The Standard Edition of the Complete Works, London, Hogarth Press, 1959.

―― *Interpretation of Dreams*, Oxford University Press, 1999.

Furbank, P.N. and W.R. Owens. *A Critical Bibliography of Daniel Defoe*, London, Pickering and Chatto, 1998.

―― *The Canonisation of Daniel Defoe*, London, Yale University Press, 1988.

Gilmore, Leigh. *The Limits of Autobiography*, Cornell University Press, 2001.

Glendinning, Victoria. *Jonathan Swift*, London, Hutchinson, 1998.

Guimaraens, A.J.C. *Daniel Defoe and the Family of Foe*, Notes and Queries, March 1912.

Habakkuk, H.J. *Marriage Settlements in the Eighteenth Century*, London, 1950.

Horner, Samuel. *Notices on the Ceremony at Bunhill Fields Cemetry*, A new graveside monument to Daniel Defoe was subscribed to by children.

Hunter, J. Paul. *The Reluctant Pilgrim: Defoe's Emblematic Method and Quest for Form in Robinson Crusoe*, Johns Hopkins Press, 1966.

Lesser, Simon. *Fiction and the Unconscious*, Boston, USA, Beacon Press, 1957.

Locke, John. *An Essay Concerning Human Understanding*, ed. Alexander Fraser, Clarendon, Oxford University Press, 1894.

Macey, Samuel. *Money and The Novel: Mercenary Motive in Defoe and his Immediate Successors*, Victoria B.C. Sino Nis Press, 1983.

Moore, John Robert. *A Checklist of the Writings of Daniel Defoe*, Indiana University Press, 1960.

Newton, Theodore F.M. *William Pitts and Queen Anne's Journalism*, Modern Philology 1936.

Richetti, John. *Defoe's Narratives, Situations and Structures*, Clarendon, Oxford, 1975.

Rogers, Pat. *Henry Fielding: A Biography*, London, Elek, 1979, 84.

Schonhorn, Manuel. *Defoe's Politics: Parliament, power, kingship, and Robinson Crusoe*, Cambridge Studies, Cambridge University Press, 1999.

Souhami, Diana. *Selkirk's Island*, Orion Books, London, 2002, 160.

Spacks, Patricia. *Imagining a Self:* Autobiography and the Novel in Eighteenth-Century England, Cambridge Mass., Harvard University Press, 1976.

Sutherland, James. *The Restoration Newspaper and its Development*, Cambridge University Press, 1986.

Starr, G.A. *Defoe and Casuistry*, Princeton University Press, 1971.

Trevelyan, G M. *English Social History*, Penguin Books, 1944.

Watt, Ian. *The Rise of the Novel,* University of California Press, 1957.

Wesley, Samuel. *A Letter to his Friend in London Concerning the Education of the Dissenters, in their Private Academies,* London, 1703.

Index

physical appearance of
  Defoe, 13, 33, 59, 252
  mode of dress, 94,
    288n101
relationships
  with Henry Baker, 264–72
  with John Clerk, 144–5,
    149, 215, 241, 295n218
  with John White, junior,
    268–71
  with John White, tenant,
    268–71, 278–80
  with Nathanial Sammen,
    92–4
  with Nathaniel Mist, 177–
    8, 249
  with Robert Harley, 106,
    124, 131–5, 173–7, 216,
    242–3, 289n134,
    295n219
  same-sex, 282
  sexual, 60, 99, 100, 101,
    236
  with Sir Thomas Neale,
    104, 204
  travels with young men,
    134
  with William III, 107–8,
    115–19, 151, 238–9
  with women outside
    marriages, 100
  see also homosexuality
    above
  in Scotland, 143–51, 162,
    214, 290n146
  in Tilbury, 100–1, 107, 109–
    11, 294n200
  in Yorkshire, 191
POLITICS:
  arrest and trial for seditious
    libel, 126–9, 166, 240
  campaigning, 82
  at Charles Morton Academy,
    51–2

electorate, the, 140–1
employment, 76–7, 191–2
  accountant to the Glass
    Commissioners, 104–7,
    238–9
  as a government agent,
    143–5, 148, 149, 166–7
  in the 'intelligence
    service', 108, 132–3
  in journalism, 48, 118–19,
    135, 156–63, 165, 223
  propagandist for William
    III, 107–8, 115–19, 151,
    238–9
  in the Whig
    administration, 170–1
  the Kentish Petitioners, 123–
    4
  Monmouth Rebellion, 67–75
  parliament, 124–5
    and the Crown, 74–5,
      116–17, 121
  political 'parties', 158–9, 160
    Tories, 116, 118, 136,
      162–3
    Whigs, 73, 77, 116, 118,
      121, 125, 128, 162–3,
      166, 170–1
  political philosopher, 139–42
  and public projects, 115–16
  in Scotland, 143–51, 162,
    214, 290n146
    role in the union, 147–9
  Turkish siege of Vienna, 77–
    8
  the war of the Spanish
    Succession, 120–2
  and writing, 25, 88, 120–2,
    123
RELIGION:
  beliefs, 13–14, 25, 49, 52,
    64–5, 133–4 193, 257–8
    antinomianism, 285n40
    and church, 196, 291n170